*Comparative
Politics*

Comparative Politics

An Institutional and Cross-National Approach

Gregory S. Mahler

University of Mississippi

Prentice Hall, Englewood Cliffs, New Jersey 07632

Library of Congress Cataloging-in-Publication Data

Mahler, Gregory S.
    Comparative politics : an institutional and cross-national
approach / Gregory S. Mahler.
        p.   cm.
    Includes bibliographical references and index.
    ISBN 0-13-155466-2
    1. Comparative government. I. Title.
JF51.M423 1992
320.3—dc20   91-7847
                                                CIP

Acquisition editor: Karen Horton
Copy editor: James Tully
Cover design: 20/20 Services Inc.
Interior art production: Karen Noferi
Prepress buyer: Debra Kesar
Manufacturing buyer: Mary Ann Gloriande
Editorial assistant: Dolores Mars

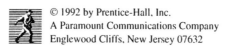 © 1992 by Prentice-Hall, Inc.
A Paramount Communications Company
Englewood Cliffs, New Jersey 07632

Printed in the United States of America
10 9 8 7 6 5 4

ISBN 0-13-155466-2

Prentice-Hall International (UK) Limited, *London*
Prentice-Hall of Australia Pty. Limited, *Sydney*
Prentice-Hall Canada Inc., *Toronto*
Prentice-Hall Hispanoamericana, S.A., *Mexico*
Prentice-Hall of India Private Limited, *New Delhi*
Prentice-Hall of Japan, Inc., *Tokyo*
Simon & Schuster Asia Pte. Ltd., *Singapore*
Editora Prentice-Hall do Brasil, Ltda., *Rio de Janeiro*

*For
Marjorie,
Alden,
and
Darcy*

Contents

Preface *xiii*

Part I: Comparative Political Analysis

1
Comparative Political Analysis: An Introduction *1*

Why Do We Study Politics?   1
How Do We Study Politics?   5
The Nature of Comparative Political Analysis 7
The Political System 14
Political Culture 18
The Concept of Political Development 20
The Institutional Approach 25
The Comparative Method in Perspective 26
Notes 27

2

Constitutions and Ideologies 30

Constitutions as Political Structures 30
Written and Unwritten Constitutions 31
What Do Constitutions Do? 33
Constitutionalism and Federal Government 36
The Separation of Powers 41
The Importance of Constitutions 42
Constitutions in Comparative Perspective 43
Ideologies 43
Constitutions and Ideologies 47
Notes 49

3

Political Development and Political Economics 51

Politics and Economics 51
Institutions and Economic Development 61
Political Economics and Political Development 68
The Future for Developing Nations 77
Notes 77

4

Legislatures and Legislative Structures 82

Introduction 82
One House or Two? 84
Relations Between Houses 89
Sizes of Legislatures 93
Political Parties in Legislatures 94
Legislative Committees 95
How Legislators Are Selected 97
Legislative Functions 103
Legislatures and Representation 106
Legislative Roles 107
The Legislative Process 110
Legislatures and Executives 112
Legislative Reform 113
Notes 114

5
The Executive 118

Introduction 118
The Executive Roles 118
The Presidential Executive 120
The Parliamentary Executive 124
Coalition Governments 138
The Executive Function: Public Administration
   and the Bureaucracy 141
Presidential and Parliamentary Systems:
   Some Comparisons 144
Notes 147

6
Judiciaries and the Legal Order 149

On the Comparative Study of Judiciaries 149
The Idea of Law 151
Legal Cultures 153
Sources of Law 156
Structures in Legal Systems 159
Judicial Functions 162
Judiciaries in the Political Arena 163
Courts in Comparative Perspective 167
Notes 168

7
Interest Groups, Political Parties, Elections, and Voting 170

Pluralism and Corporatism 170
Interest Groups 173
Political Parties 176
Electoral Systems 180
Political Participation and Voting Behavior 186
Groups, Parties, Elections, and Voting 187
Notes 188

8

The Individual and the Political Environment 191

The Political System Revisited 191
The Study of Political Socialization and Political Attitudes 193
The Study of Political Recruitment 201
The Role of the Political Elite 205
The Military 207
Political Participation and Political Violence 209
The Political Environment in Perspective 212
Notes 214

Part II: Area Studies

9

The British Political System 218

The British Constitution 219
The British Executive 223
The Civil Service 233
Local Government 234
The British Parliament 235
Political Parties and Voting 242
Summary 248
Notes 248

10

The French Political System 252

Constitutional History of France 252
The Constitutional System of the Fifth Republic 261
Unitary Government in France 263
The Executive Structure 264
The Legislature 272
The Constitutional Council 277
Party Politics and the Electoral Process 278
Summary 289
Notes 290

11

The German Political System 294

The German Constitutional Framework 294
Federalism in Germany 297
Executive Structures 300
The Legislative Structures 306
Political Parties and the Electoral Process 310
The German Political System 321
Notes 322

12

The Japanese Political System 326

The Japanese Political Heritage 326
The Executive Structures 329
The Diet 338
Political Parties and Elections 343
Summary 351
Notes 352

13

The Soviet Political System 356

The Union of Soviet Socialist Republics 357
Ideology 366
The Soviet Constitution 371
Structures of the Government 376
Structures of the Communist Party 389
Leadership and Succession 397
The "Interlocking Directorate" 399
The Soviet System in Perspective 400
Notes 401

14

The Mexican Political System 406

The Mexican Political Heritage 406
Political Stability 408
The Mexican Constitution 410
Mexican Federalism 411
The Presidency 412
The Congress 415
The Bureaucracy 418
Political Parties and Elections 419
Political Development and Economics 422
Revolution and Institutionalization 424
Notes 426

Index 431

Preface

This is a different type of introductory textbook in the subfield of political science that we refer to as "comparative politics." It exists primarily because of a perceived imbalance in other introductory texts found in the marketplace, and because of a belief that a different approach might, in fact, prove to be better.

To judge from texts and contemporary journals of political science, a "comparative approach" to the study of political science is both widely accepted and widely practiced today. There is, however, a debate over the exact nature of the "comparative" aspect of such an approach, dealing with whether this comparative approach is a general *perspective* of a certain subject matter, or rather a broad *method* of analysis.

We all know what comparison is; we begin comparing things early in life, and such behavior is basic to the learning process. It is quite clear that a great deal of the literature in print today that is called "comparative" does not *really* engage in comparison at all, but more accurately could be referred to simply as "area studies" material. In many cases, in fact, American political scientists have shown a tendency to label as "comparative politics" anything that is neither international relations, political philosophy, methodology, nor some subfield of American politics.

Most contemporary comparative politics textbooks use what might be referred to as a traditional "case study" approach to their subject matter. That is, they select a set of countries—usually Western European countries—and proceed to discuss each of these countries individually. In these texts there is virtually no real *comparison*; for example, asking the following: How does country A relate to Country B? Is the legislature in Country C more important in its political system than the legislature in Country D is in its political system? Instead of comparison, the books simply present multiple single-nation studies in one volume: politics in France, politics in Germany, politics in Great Britain, politics in the USSR, and so on.

This observation is not meant to suggest that this type of study is valueless—only that it doesn't do much in the way of teaching the student about comparison and political analysis. Students seeking cross-national comparisons and generalization are on their own with these books. This is more and more recognized today, and many contemporary comparativists have concluded that area studies volumes make it too difficult to undertake much comparison in the classroom. Students simply are given too little to deal with by way of cross-national analysis in their reading. It is expecting too much that from single chapters on Great Britain, France, Germany, and the USSR, a student will have any idea at all about the nature of cross-national political analysis.

An alternative approach is one that might be called a "pure cross-national approach." This type of study goes in the opposite direction from the "area studies" volumes. Rather than having chapters dealing with individual countries, these books are organized around political structures and political behavior, perhaps including chapters on legislatures, executives, political parties, leadership, and so on. Within each of these topical chapters, authors might discuss any number of nations to demonstrate all of the possible variations that might be found for the subject under consideration.

The "pure cross-national" studies have their own problems, though. Students using this type of text learn in a broad and comparative way about structures and behaviors that may be found around the political world, but have no specific, integrated illustrations of how the various components fit together in any single polity. The student may have learned, for example, about political parties in Britain in one chapter, about the British executive in another chapter, about the British parliament elsewhere, and so on. If this student wishes to integrate this exposure to Great Britain, more effort is required.

So we have come full circle. The problem with the area studies approach is that it is only case study, with virtually no cross-national perspective involved. The problem with the pure cross-national approach is that it is *too* cross-national, with virtually no integrated illustrations or case study material presented.

This book attempts to respond to the dilemma described above by balancing the two approaches. It begins with a cross-national analytic section, focusing on political institutions and political behavior that will appear again later in the text. The second part of the book presents a number of case studies, each of which is comparative in perspective.

There is a trade-off with this approach, of course. In one volume we cannot include all of the content of the area studies volumes as well as all of the content of the pure cross-national volumes. The trade-off, then, is one of breadth for depth. Rather than presenting four or five 100-page chapters, each detailing a different nation, this book presents a larger number of much shorter case studies; they might be referred to as "political portraits" of the nations examined.

Comparative Politics focuses primarily upon political structures and institutions, and especially upon the interaction of legislatures and executives. In doing so, it moves against the flow of many texts that put a great deal of emphasis—perhaps too much emphasis, in fact—on political culture, history, society, and individual leaders. This is not to suggest that these other approaches are wrong; rather, it suggests that for the *introductory* student a study of the more *concrete* structures of comparative *government* may be more useful than an introduction to the "softer" theories of comparative *politics*.

A number of reasons lie behind the selection of the executive-legislative theme. First, it is a good *vehicle for comparison*. That is, executives and legislatures are highly visible political structures, easy to identify, and the student studying comparative politics for the first time will feel more comfortable with these concrete structures than he or she would with softer concepts such as "leadership," "power," or "socialization," for example.

Moreover, executives and legislatures are relatively *easy to compare*, as political structures go, because they exist in virtually all political systems and because data are usually readily available dealing with them. Because legislatures and executives are generally among the most visible structures in political systems, the student will have a minimum of difficulty *identifying and classifying* them.

Finally, in terms of the discipline, comparative political analysis involves a "search for regularities," a search for similarities and differences in political structures and political behavior. The student will be more capable of identifying similarities and differences in a number of portraits focusing upon legislative-executive interaction than of identifying similarities and differences in much more complex political relationships, such as "power" or "political culture," especially where data for the latter are not readily available.

This does not mean, however, that *only* legislatures and executives are discussed in the chapters that follow. Political parties, judiciaries, constitutional frameworks, political economics, development and modernization, ideologies, electoral structures, political histories, and a number of other factors are also included in discussion where they are appropriate in developing our "political portraits." Following an initial section outlining the comparative framework that will be used as a basis for the rest of the book, a number of case studies—political portraits, to use the term we have already employed—are presented that will both introduce students to comparative political analysis and acquaint them with basic structural characteristics of a number of contemporary political regimes.

Acknowledgments

The idea for this project began, although it was not clear at the time, during my graduate school days at Duke University under the eye of R. Taylor Cole. We spent many hours discussing the various ways one might introduce undergraduates to the study of comparative politics, and I was then, and still am now, grateful for his instruction and advice.

This kind of book owes a great deal to all of the scholars

whose work is cited in the many notes in the text that follows. Comparative political inquiry is built on the work of those who have undertaken original field research in a variety of settings. Having undertaken such research myself, I know the challenges that can be experienced by those who seek to learn more about how other political systems operate. Without these efforts, we would not be able to engage in the kind of comparative discussion and analysis that is presented here.

I am happy to be able to acknowledge in a public way the role played by Karen Horton in this project. From her initial indications of interest in this endeavor throughout the publication process, she has been as supportive and encouraging as possible. Cecil Yarbrough at Prentice Hall saw the manuscript through the production process. James Tully undertook a careful reading of the manuscript, and his editing skills contributed to its quality.

I also want to thank the following reviewers contacted by Prentice Hall who made suggestions for improving the manuscript. I appreciated their sincere and constructive comments: M. Donald Hancock, Vanderbilt University; and Peter H. Merkl, University of California, Santa Barbara.

Finally, but by no means least, I want to acknowledge the role in the creation of this book of my students over the years. Their comments about and evaluations of other texts convinced me of the need for this one, and their comments on early versions of these chapters, and this book, helped me to revise and reformulate the chapters that are included here.

1

Comparative Political Analysis: An Introduction

Why Do We Study Politics?

"Politics." The word conjures up visions of campaigns, elections, and speeches. For the student who is a bit more politically experienced, the word may suggest other images, images such as legislatures, executives, courts, political parties, and interest groups. The more advanced student may also associate concepts such as policy making, power, or influence with the concept of politics.

One point that is clear to all students is that the term "politics" is an extremely broad one. It means all of the things indicated above, and more. Political science as a discipline can be traced back to the time of Plato (c. 427–c. 347 B.C.) and Aristotle (384–322 B.C.). Aristotle is often referred to as the first "real" political scientist—and we could add "first comparativist" to his credits as well—because of his study of the many political systems that he found in the political world of his time. His comparisons of constitutions and power structures contributed many words to our political vocabulary today, words such as "politics," "democracy," "oligarchy," and "aristocracy."[1]

The study of politics can be characterized as the study of patterns of systematic interactions between and among individuals and groups in a community or society. This study does not involve random interactions, but rather focuses upon those interactions that involve power, or authority. Aristotle saw many different types of relationships involved in the "political" association, but central to the concept was the idea of *rule*, or *authority*. In fact, one of the central criteria by which Aristotle classified constitutions in his study was by *where* power or authority to rule was located in the *polis*, the political system.[2] Much more recently, David Easton referred to politics as dealing with the "authoritative allocation of values for a society"[3]—the process by which social goals and standards are set, these standards being binding upon members of society. Harold Lasswell put the question succinctly in the title of his classic book, *Politics: Who Gets What, When, How?*[4] Thus, the study of politics may involve the study of legislatures, the study of voting, the study of political parties, the study of power, more generally the study of how public policy is made, or all of these, and more.

Why do we study politics at all? It could be argued that political scientists since the time of Aristotle have been studying the same things—constitutions, rulers, the ruled, and so on—and we have not yet managed to come up with anything that could be called a perfect society. Why do we continue to study politics, then? If we have not found what we are looking for by now, are we likely to? What *are* we looking for? These are all good questions, and they are hard questions to answer, too.

What are we looking for? Some political scientists are trying to learn about justice, what it is, and how to get it. Others are concerned with how social policy is made; they may study political structures that are involved in the policy-making process. Others seek to understand why one political party wins a given election rather than another political party. Others may seek to understand why people vote for anyone in an election. Still others study politics simply because political relationships seem to be important to our daily lives. In short, there are as many different reasons for studying political behavior as there are different aspects of political behavior to study. One thing, however, is clear: We cannot ascribe only to the discipline of political science the duty of finding the "good life"; political science is *one* of the social sciences concerned with helping us to understand the complex world around us. There are other social sciences, we should note, including economics, sociology, and anthropology, among others, which also study the same general types of social phenomena that we study.

The same type of question can also be asked in relation to comparative politics. Why should we study comparative politics? What can we hope to learn? Before we can answer these questions, we have to decide what "comparative politics" is, and how it can be said to differ from the more generic "politics." Many American political scientists tend to label as "comparative politics" anything that does not fit into one of the subdisciplines of international relations, methodology, political theory, or American politics. For them, the subdiscipline of comparative politics would include "politics in England," "politics in France," "politics in the USSR," "politics in Zimbabwe," and so on, with the general formula being "politics in X" where any nation other than the United States could be substituted for the "X."

It should be quickly added that American political scientists are not the only ones to do this. If one were to go to France, the study of American politics would be found within the subdiscipline of comparative politics; there, any area studies other than French politics would fall in the comparative basket. The same could be said for anything other than German politics in Germany or anything other than Canadian politics in Canada.

But comparative politics is more than that. Studying "politics in X" more properly can be referred to as "area studies." Area studies certainly is a legitimate kind of inquiry, but not one that necessarily involves any explicit *comparison*. In fact, Macridis and Brown many years ago criticized comparative politics at the time for not being *truly* comparative, for being concerned with single cases and area studies.[5] Comparative politics is—or should be—*more* than area studies.

When we speak of comparative politics in this book, we are talking about the actual method of *comparison*. We all know what comparison is; it involves terms of relativity, terms like "bigger," "stronger," "freer," "more stable," and so on. Comparative politics, then, involves no more and no less than *a comparative study of politics*, a search for similarities and differences between and among political phenomena, including political institutions (such as legislatures, political parties, or political interest groups), political behavior (such as voting, demonstrating, or reading political pamphlets), or political ideas (such as liberalism, conservatism, or Marxism). Everything that politics studies, comparative politics studies; it just undertakes the study with an explicitly comparative *methodology* in mind.

We could make the argument, in fact, that *all* of political science is comparative. The study of international relations compares diplomatic relations and strategies over time and between nations. The study of political behavior compares and contrasts types of activity in different political contexts. The study of political philosophy compares different perspectives of what ought to be and what is. Even the study of American politics is implicitly comparative, since we study the power of the president as compared to the power of the Supreme Court, for example, or why one interest group is more powerful than another, and so on.

To return to the question of why we should study comparative politics, then, an answer now may be suggested. Dogan and Pelassy observe:

> Nothing is more natural than to study people, ideas, or institutions in relation to other people, ideas, or institutions. We gain knowledge through reference. . . . We compare to evaluate more objectively our situation as individuals, a community, or a nation.[6]

The study of comparative politics is useful because it gives us a broader perspective of political phenomena and political behavior, and this broader perspective can contribute a great deal both to our understanding and our appreciation of the phenomena we are studying. We compare to escape from our ethnocentrism, our assumptions that everyone behaves the same way we do, to broaden our field of perspective. We compare to discover broader rules of behavior than we might find in more narrow studies.

For example, the simplicity and brevity of the Constitution of the United States is even more impressive when it is examined alongside the much longer (sixty-page) Constitution of the Soviet Union. We can better understand the significance of presidential government when we know about alternatives to presidential government. We can learn something about those factors contributing to political stability by studying a country that is regarded as being politically stable. We can learn even more by including a country *not* regarded as stable in our study, and looking for similarities and differences between the two countries.

How Do We Study Politics?

There are two broad paths on the road of inquiry; one is called the *normative* approach and the other is called the *empirical* approach. The normative approach focuses upon philosophies, norms, or "shoulds." The empirical approach relies on measurement and observation rather than theory or norm. Normativists might investigate exactly the same questions as empiricists, but they go about their investigations differently. Normativists might study justice, equality, the "good society," and so on, and so might empiricists. The difference between the two groups is simply in how these questions would be approached.

Let us take an example to highlight differences in approach. Let us suppose that we have two political scientists interested in studying the concept of "justice." The normative approach might focus on the concept of justice itself: What is justice? How do we decide what is just and what is unjust? Does the concept of justice ever change or vary? *Should* it do so? The empirical approach would not ask many of these questions. The job of the empiricist is not to ask what is better, or what *should* be, but simply to ask what *is*. The empirical approach might involve interviewing policymakers or justices and ascertaining what *they* feel justice is, and how they use that feeling in their work. It might involve studying capital punishment laws and their enforcement. It might involve examining economic distribution in a variety of settings in order to observe patterns of material distribution. In brief, although both approaches would study the same general subject, the approaches would be different.

In fact, the empirical approach does not utilize only one method of gathering information. Arend Lijphart has suggested that there are four basic methods of discovering and establishing general empirical propositions. One of these methods is experimental, while the other three are nonexperimental. The nonexperimental methods are the case study method, the statistical method, and the comparative method.[7]

The case study method[8] involves "the intensive study of individual cases. Case studies run the gamut from the most microcosmic to the most macrocosmic levels of political phenomena."[9] Micro-level work might focus on individuals; macro-level work might focus on political interest groups, regional groups, or institutional groups. An area study, as described above, *might* be a case study (such as voting behavior in Lesotho), but clearly not all case studies involve area studies. In this method, the investigator picks one case, whether that case be a single nation, a single voter, a single election, or a single political structure (such as a legislature), and studies it. Through the case study method one develops a certain amount of expertise in whatever one is studying, but the scope of one's study may be quite limited.

The statistical method involves more sophisticated forms of measurement and observation. Public opinion polls, survey research,[10] and various other forms of quantitative measurement are utilized to help make the measurement and observation that is characteristic of the empirical approach even more accurate.[11]

The comparative method may be likened to two or more case studies put together. We focus upon a particular political structure or behavior and examine it in a comparative perspective. We look for similarities and differences in different settings. We may do our comparison in one setting, but compare across time—diachronic comparison—for example, comparing a given legislature in 1989 with the same legislature in 1939 and 1889, in order to observe differences in the relative power and structures of that legislature. Moreover, we may compare institutions or behavior at one point in time—synchronic comparison—but compare across national borders, for example, examining the role of the legislature in Great Britain with the role of the legislature in Thailand or Jordan.[12]

These three nonexperimental methods are based exclusively upon observation and measurement. The experimental approach involves manipulation of variables. That is, whereas in the case study method one simply *observes* something, in the experimental method one *manipulates* one variable in order to observe its effect upon another variable. This is difficult to do in most aspects of political research, since we are asking questions of extremely broad scope and cannot absolutely control the environment within which we are operating. We cannot, for example, set up two identical presidential elections, one with two candidates, and one with three candidates, in order to see the relationship between the number of candidates and voting turnout. Society is too complex to enable us to manipulate and experiment with many political structures and institutions.

Each of the methods in the empirical approach has its own advantages and disadvantages for the researcher. The chief advantage of the comparative approach is the broad perspective that was mentioned earlier. For example, studying the British Parliament in 1990 may tell us a great deal about that institution. We will learn more about the *significance* of what we are observing, however, if we *compare* our observations—either compare our observations with observations of 1790 and 1890, or compare the observations with observations of the Indian Lok Sabha, the Japanese Diet, or the Israeli Knesset.

The study of comparative politics, or more properly, the comparative approach to the study of politics, is more and more common in the discipline today. We find comparative studies of legislatures,[13] political elites,[14] ideologies,[15] women in politics,[16] constitutions,[17] legal cultures,[18] revolutionary movements,[19] political executives,[20] and political parties.[21] We also find comparative studies of the role of the military in government,[22] of democracies,[23] of *new* democracies,[24] of political development,[25] of political culture,[26] and of political behavior.[27]

The Nature of Comparative Political Analysis

How do we go about using the comparative method? If we start indiscriminately comparing every object on the political landscape, in a very short time we will find ourselves inundated with similarities and differences, most of which will turn out to be trivial distinctions either in scope or in significance. Suppose, for example, that we examine the political institution of the legislature. One of the first things that we will note once we start our measurement and observation is that legislatures are *not physically* the same. One legislature may have 100 seats, another may have 75 seats, and a third may have 500 seats. One building may be five stories high, another only two. One legislature may have its seats arranged in straight rows, while another may have its seats arranged in semicircles; indeed, one legislature may give its members individual desks, while another may only have long benches upon which many legislators must crowd.[28]

So what? Before we get bogged down in inconsequential detail (and of course detail *need* not be inconsequential, but such may be the case if proper planning does not precede study), we need to plot a course of inquiry. We need to decide what questions we are interested in investigating, and why, and we need to understand the relationships between and among the objects of our scrutiny. In this book we are interested in presenting an introduction to the comparative study of politics. What does this mean? It means that we want to show *how* comparative analysis is undertaken, and *why* it is undertaken, and we want to provide examples of the types of things that one might look at while engaging in this kind of study.

In one very useful analysis of the values of comparative inquiry, Adam Przeworski and Henry Teune discussed two general approaches to the comparative method that they called the "most similar systems" design and the "most different systems" design. They argued that most comparativists use the "most similar systems" design: Investigators take two systems that are, for the most part, similar, and subsequently study differences that exist between the two basically similar systems. They may, then, observe the impact of these differences on some other social or political phenomenon. These studies are based on the belief that "systems as similar as possible with respect to as many features as possible constitute the optimal samples for comparative inquiry."[29] If some important differences are found among two essentially similar countries, "then the number of factors attributable to these differences will be sufficiently small to warrant explanation in terms of those differences alone."[30]

There is, however, a different approach to comparative inquiry that Przeworski and Teune call the "most different systems" approach. This approach allows us to select two or more systems to compare that may *not* be essentially similar. Instead of looking for differences between two or more essentially similar nations, focusing upon nation-states, for example, we look for similarities between two or more essentially different nations.[31]

The point of all of this is to indicate that a number of different approaches are possible within the broad framework that we call the "comparative method." The important consideration in all cases is a theoretical rationale: *Why* are we undertaking the comparison that we are undertaking? What kind of objects do we want to study? As we indicated earlier, the subjects of comparative political inquiry are as disparate and varied as one might imagine. Generally, it can be suggested that there are three broad *categories* of subjects of examination in the comparative study of politics: public policy, political behavior, and governmental institutions.

In studies of comparative public policy,[32] the focus of attention is upon *what governments do*. Comparisons may be made between governments of different nations, governments in various stages of development (e.g., "developed" nations vs. "underdeveloped" nations), or governments and policy over time (e.g., the government of Poland in 1970 and the government of Poland in 1990). Although the focus of attention is upon what governments *do,* these studies will invariably pay some attention to the related questions of how governments act, how it is that they do what they do, why governments act, and what the stimuli are that help the governments in question to decide to act in the direction that they do at the time that they do.

A second general thrust of study is oriented to *political behavior.* Studies of this type may focus upon voting behavior, political stability, political elites, leaders in politics, party behavior, and so on.[33] The central ideas of this approach involve the assumption that if one understands how people behave in a political system—and this includes all people, both the leaders and the led—then one will develop an understanding about the political systems within which that behavior takes place. This approach will include some discussion of comparative public policy, primarily as an example of the behavior that is the primary object of study, and may also include some study of the governmental institutions within which the behavior takes place.

The third general approach focuses upon the *governmental institutions* themselves. This type of study may focus upon legislatures, executives, courts, constitutions, legal systems, bureaucracies, and perhaps even political parties.[34] By studying the *institutions* of a regime, it is argued, we are in a better position to understand how the regime operates than we would be with either the behavioral approach alone or the policy approach alone. This approach, as with the others, may well include some secondary subjects of scrutiny. It is entirely possible that a study of governmental institutions might include a subject of policy output as an example of what it is that governmental institutions produce. In addition, a study of governmental institutions might include discussion of political behavior—both behavior of governmental officials and behavior of the public that may influence the government to act.

Often in comparative analysis we focus our attention on countries. Countries are important to study for a number of reasons, not the least of which is that they are the units into which the world is divided. That is to say, it would be difficult to engage in comparative research without touching upon the political structure that we call the *nation-state*. Beyond this, however, nation-states often are useful bases for analysis because of what they represent.

A "nation" and a "state" may not be the same thing. The concept of "nation" has been used in an anthropological way to denote a group of people with shared characteristics, perhaps a shared language, history, or culture. A "state," on the other hand, is a political entity, created by men and women, based upon accepted boundaries, and alterable by men and women. Political borders can (and do) change, either as a result of war, as a result of agreement between parties involved, or, perhaps, as a result of both. For example, the United States and Mexico have reached agreement over a method of having periodic meetings between the two countries to "correct" the mapping of their border because of the gradual movement of the Rio Grande!

It is possible to find self-proclaimed nations that are not "states" as the term was used above. For example, many Canadian citizens today who are living in the Province of Quebec argue that there is a French "nation" in Canada that should be recognized as a state and should be given independence. They are not content with being a self-perceived nation within a state, with an identifiably different language, culture, and heritage, and with the powers that the Canadian federal government gives to Quebec alone; many citizens of Quebec want to formalize their perceived differences with the rest of Canada and become an independent nation-state. Similarly, the notion of Zionism at the turn of the twentieth century was based on the idea that there was a "nation" of Jewish people that were "stateless" in a number of nation-states around the world, and a Jewish state was needed for them to call their home. This Zionist concept subsequently gave birth to the state of Israel. It is indeed ironic that in a very similar manner today Palestinians are claiming the need for a state of their own, independent of Israel, Jordan, and other Middle Eastern countries.

In any type of comparative political inquiry there are certain analytical problems that we should be aware of that might make our work more difficult than it otherwise might be. The first of these problems involves what we call the *levels of analysis* and relates to the types of observations and measurements we are using and the types of conclusions that we can draw from those observations and measurements.[35] Generally, we can speak of two levels of data, or observation: an *individual* level and an *aggregate*, or *ecological*, level. As its name suggests, the former focuses on individuals, the latter on groups.

We have all met what can be called problems of "overgeneralization" in our lives. This is the case when an individual takes an observation made at the general level, over a large population, and assumes that it can be validly applied to *every* individual within that population. For example, to take a nonpolitical case, let us suppose that an individual has had some negative experiences with fast-food restaurants in the past and has decided that she really does not like the food served in these establishments. One day she finds herself traveling and looking for a place to have lunch; the only places available are fast-food restaurants. She enters, expecting to hate the food, and finds to her surprise that the food in *this* establishment is much better than her past experiences would have led her to expect. What we have here is an instance in which she has made a general observation (i.e., food in a certain type of restaurant is not very good), and she has encountered an individual case for which her general rule simply is not valid, or correct.

In political science we refer to this type of error as an "ecological fallacy." That is, we take data, a measurement, or an observation from the broad "ecological" level and apply it to an individual case. The observation may be quite correct over a large population, on the general level as a generalization, but that does not mean that it will be correct in *every* individual case within that population.

More broadly, we have here a problem of two different levels of analysis—the individual level and the ecological, or aggregate, level. To take a political example, if we find on a national (aggregate) level that Republicans tend to vote more frequently than Democrats, that does not guarantee that every individual Republican that we might meet is going to vote and every individual Democrat that we might meet is not going to vote. It means that, on the whole, over the large population, Republicans as a group are more likely to vote than Democrats *as a group*.

To take another example, if we find in our cross-national research that the population of the Ivory Coast has an overall lower level of education than does the population of the United States (two aggregate-level observations), that does not mean that *every* citizen of the Ivory Coast is less educated than *every* citizen of the United States. It might in fact be the case that if we took a random sample from each nation we might select an American with a sixth-grade education and a citizen of the Ivory Coast with a Ph.D. from Oxford University. In short, then, an "ecological fallacy" involves (incorrectly) taking what may be a perfectly valid observation on the aggregate level and assuming that it will *always* apply to *every* case on the individual level. It may apply in *most* cases, which may be why it is a general observation, but we may be leaving ourselves in a vulnerable position if we assume that it will *always* apply in *every* case.

There is a reverse of the ecological fallacy, which is called the "individualistic fallacy." This occurs when we make an individual level observation and incorrectly generalize from it to the aggregate level. For example, to stay with the example we just introduced, it would clearly be incorrect to conclude from meeting one Oxford-educated Ph.D. from the Ivory Coast that all citizens of the Ivory Coast have Ph.D. degrees from Oxford, or that all Ph.D. recipients from Oxford come from the Ivory Coast. To be sure, there may be several, but we would be incorrect to generalize from this individual case to the entire population.

The importance of the "levels of analysis" problem can be summed up, then, by stating that observations made on one level of analysis, either the individual level or the aggregate (or ecological) level, are safely used only on that level. It does happen, of course, that we occasionally undertake study in a situation in which we are forced to use data from one level to learn about another level. We may not be able to afford to question every individual in the Ivory Coast about his or her level of education, and we may *have* to rely on ecological or aggregate data. If all we have available to us is aggregate-level data about education (e.g., average number of years of education), or health care (e.g., number of hospital beds per population unit), or some similar characteristic, then we have to do our best with the data that we have. We simply must keep reminding ourselves that conclusions we draw from one level of data must be used *carefully* on another level.

Another major pitfall in comparative analysis that we want to try to avoid involves making assumptions about the functions

performed by political structures. It is entirely possible that we will find in our research two institutions, or patterns of behavior, that look alike in two different settings, but which perform entirely different functions in their respective settings. We might study, for example, the House of Commons in Britain, and see that the legislature in that setting is most important in the process of selecting government leaders and in establishing governmental legitimacy. In another setting, however, a similarly structured legislature may not be at all significant in the creation of a government or in the establishment of legitimacy, and to assume that because the British House of Commons is significant in this regard that *all* legislatures are significant in this regard would be an example of an individualistic fallacy: generalizing from the individual (British) level to the aggregate (all legislatures) level.

Although the major role of the American legislature may be that of passing laws, the major function of legislatures such as those which existed in East Germany prior to German unification was *not* passing laws; in the East German case, the legislature met for only about two days a year, and simply "rubber stamped" everything suggested to it by the Communist party organization there. The primary function of the legislature in East Germany was that of being a showcase, to demonstrate that East Germany had a "democratically elected" legislature.

The converse of this is true, too. Whereas we might find one structure (e.g., a legislature) that performs two entirely different functions in two different nations, we might also find two entirely different structures in two different nations that perform similar or identical functions. To use the same general example we just used, although the Congress performs the legislative function in the United States, the real designing of legislation in East Germany was done by the Central Committee of the Communist Party, not the legislature (although the legislature did subsequently give its approval to the measure prior to its becoming "official").

This type of error of "overassuming" can be especially troubling when students from stable, established Western democracies turn their attentions to non-Western systems. The problem of *political ethnocentrism*—of assuming that because political institutions or relationships work one way in stable Western democracies they must work the same way in *all* political systems—is a real problem, and we must be continuously on guard against making these types of assumptions, or falling victim to cultural bias, especially when we turn our attention to political systems that are not stable, not "developed," or not Western. Indeed, this paragraph would represent a kind of Western ethnocentrism in its own right if we did not observe that in many settings the very institutions or patterns of behavior that we take for granted in the West—such as legislatures, or elections—may simply be alien, or irrelevant, to other political cultures. This is a subject to which we shall return in some detail later in this text.

When we undertake comparative political analysis, then, we need to keep our eyes open for errors that we can make by simply assuming too much. We must take the political environment into consideration before drawing conclusions or making broad generalizations; we must make sure to "scout out the landscape" to ensure that we have included in our analysis all of the factors that might be of significance *in that particular political system*. In some systems the list of significant factors might be very long; in others it might be very short.

The Political System

We have been discussing comparative political analysis, and problems that may ensue in the research process, but we have not as yet laid out any framework for establishing the ground upon which we will base our research. The central concept in discussions of political analysis is that of *the political system*. Generally speaking, not confining ourselves only to the political, there are two types of systems that we can discuss: "analytic" systems and "concrete" systems.

We are all familiar with the concept of a system. Such terms as "nervous system," "electrical system," "stereo system," or even "solar system" are all examples of instances in which we use the term "system" in our daily lives. When we speak of a system such as one of these, we are speaking of a *set of related objects*. With a "concrete" or "real" system we can actually see (or touch, or feel, or measure) the system itself. For example, we could actually touch the components of a skeletal system if we wanted to. In an electrical system we can touch wires involved and follow them along from one object to another. In the stereo system we can feel the parts of the system, the speakers, the amplifier, the turntable, the tape deck, and so on, and can follow the connecting link (wires) from one component to another. The solar system is a bit more difficult; although we cannot directly *touch* the force connecting the member units, we can measure it with sophisticated instruments and observations. These, then, are "concrete," or "real," systems.

Much more interesting for us as political scientists, however, are "analytic" systems. We can define analytic systems as groups of objects connected with one another in an *analytic* way. That is, it is our theories and perceptions that provide the links between the objects in question. The political system that we refer to as American government is not "real" or "concrete" in the same manner that the plumbing system of a house is. We cannot actually touch or feel the links between and among the House of Representatives and the Senate and the Supreme Court and the White House and the bureaucracy. (Literally, of course, we probably could make the argument that one could touch a telephone wire and trace it to a central switchboard where all Washington telephones are connected, and thereby claim that these institutions are, in fact, physically connected, but that would be stretching the point.) The important and meaningful connection among these institutions is *power*, and the power relationship that is to be found in the United States Constitution and in the American political tradition.

When we talk about "developing nations" or "the political left" or "legislatures" or "interest groups" or "the Middle East," we are using analytic concepts to bring together groups of objects—in many cases individuals, in other cases regions or institutions— that we perceive to have something in common. These are *political systems*, sets of political objects or political concepts that are theoretically related to each other in some analytic way. These systems of objects—analytic systems—are the basis of comparative political research.

We cannot stop simply at the level of the system, however. Systems can be broken down into *subsystems*. A subsystem is a component of a political system that is a system in its own right. "The American political system" has many subsystems, each of which could be studied on its own. To begin, of course, are fifty subsystems that we call states. If we wanted to, we could study the political system of one state on its own; if our *focus* is on the United States, however, the state would be perceived as a subsystem, not a system. Other subsystems of the American political system might be "the bureaucracy," "the legislature," "political parties," "men," "women," and so on. We can also talk about sub-subsystems, sub-sub-subsystems, and on and on.

Similarly, we can use the term "supersystem" to refer to that collection of objects of which our focus is only a part. If our focus is (still) on the American political system, then a supersystem might be "Western governments," or "democracies," or "presidential systems," all groups of objects of which our focus is simply an example. Table 1.1 provides an illustration of the way in which we can use these terms.

We can shift our point of focus, too. If our focus is the American political system, then the Congress is a subsystem, and the House of Representatives is a sub-subsystem, and the Foreign Affairs Committee of the House of Representatives is a sub-sub-subsystem, and Republicans on the Foreign Affairs Committee are a sub-sub-sub-subsystem. If our focus were the House of Representatives, the Congress would be a supersystem, the American political system would be a super-supersystem, and the Foreign Affairs Committee would be a subsystem. And so on.

Although these terms may seem confusing at first, they can be extremely valuable in our analysis of politics. Unlike chemists, or physicists, who may use sophisticated physical instruments to help them in their measurement and analysis, all that we have as political scientists to help us with our measurement, observation, and analysis are concepts and theoretical frameworks. Terminology, then, is important for us.

Just as with many of the other terms we have introduced in this chapter, the concept of a "system" is not as simple as it first appears. There have been a number of different approaches to

Table 1.1
Using Systems as Frames of Reference

Level	Set 1	Set 2
Super-supersystem	World governments	Constitutional systems
Supersystem	Democracies	Presidencies
System (focus)	*The American Political System*	
Subsystem	A state	The Congress
Sub-subsystem	A county	The Senate

political systems in the discipline over the years, each approach developing its own vocabulary and literature. Probably the two biggest contributions to "systems theories," in terms of their subsequent generation of literature in the discipline, have been made by David Easton and Gabriel Almond.

Easton's variation on the political system first introduced in the mid-1960s has been referred to as "input-output" analysis.[36] Although many political scientists today feel that Easton's variation never realized its potential as a theoretical framework capable of explaining the operation of the political system, it did give rise to a great deal of literature on "systems theory," and it can still be cited *as an example of one way* of looking at the political system, even if it does not provide all of the answers that earlier theorists had hoped it might.

Easton's analytic framework viewed the political system as a continuously operating mechanism, with "demands" and "supports" going in (inputs), and authoritative decisions and actions coming out (outputs). Demands are defined as "an expression of opinion that an authoritative allocation with regard to a particular subject matter should or should not be made by those responsible for doing so."[37] Supports are those inputs between the political system and its environment that remain after demands have been subtracted.[38] The framework includes very elaborate regulatory mechanisms for preventing demand overloads and for maintaining the smooth operation of the system.

The other major variation on systems theory was suggested by Gabriel Almond, and is referred to as "structural-functional" analysis.[39] This kind of analysis focuses upon what Almond refers to as political "structures," by which he means either political institutions or political behavior, and political "functions," by which he means the consequences of the institutions or the behavior, or needs or goals of the political system. This kind of analysis asks the basic question, "What structures perform what functions and under what conditions in a political system?" While "function" may be interpreted to mean "consequence," the framework introduces a new term as well, "dysfunction." Simply put, a function (or "eufunction") is a *good* consequence, and a dysfunction is a *bad* consequence.

Both of these approaches, it should be explicitly noted, are quite sophisticated and quite substantial—far beyond our ability to discuss them adequately in this context. In addition, they are not the *only* variations on what is referred to as systems theory. They are, however, the major variations, and the test of time has indicated their impact on the discipline of political science. The concept of the political system, whether we use Easton's input-output framework, or Almond's structure-function framework, or any of a number of other variations on the theme, is another tool we have at our disposal to help in our cross-national comparison.

It is important that we note that a political system need not be the same thing as a nation or a state. It may be convenient to use a nation or state as a point of departure in comparative analysis, but a "system" may be something else, as well. As we indicated above, we may want to study a "legislative system"; that is, a collection of objects that are in some analytic way related and whose relationship is based upon legislation or the legislature. We may want to study OECS—the Organization of Eastern Caribbean States. We may want to study electoral systems. We may want to focus our attention on the individual level and study the systems of political thought that give rise to political actions. In short, although nation-states are convenient to study because we can find them on a map and their borders are (relatively) clearly defined, many of the subjects of comparative political analysis do not lie clearly within one set of national borders.

Political Culture

The concept of *political culture* is terribly important in the study of comparative politics. As Gabriel Almond has noted, "Something like a notion of political culture has been around as long as men have spoken and written about politics,"[40] and related terms like "subculture," "elite political culture," "political socialization," and "cultural change" have also been used in a variety of settings since time immemorial. Indeed, Almond argues that the concept of political culture played a very important role in Plato's *Republic* when Plato observed:

> that governments vary as the dispositions of men vary, and that there must be as many of the one as there are of the other. For we cannot suppose that States are made of "oak and rock" and not out of the human natures which are in them.[41]

The concept of a political culture can be traced from Plato through Aristotle, Machiavelli, Montesquieu, Rousseau, Tocqueville, and up to modern times.[42]

Political culture, Almond tells us, "is not a theory; it refers to a set of variables which may be used in the construction of theories."[43] It consists of "the system of empirical beliefs, expressive symbols, and values which defines the situation in which political action takes place."[44] It "is concerned with 'psychological orientation toward social objects . . . the political system as internalized in the cognitions, feelings, and evaluations of citizens.' "[45] Among the major dimensions of political culture are included a sense of national identity, attitudes one holds toward oneself as a member of a policy, attitudes one holds toward one's fellow citizens, attitudes and expectations about governmental performance, and knowledge about and attitudes concerning the political decision-making processes.

In fact, scholars tell us, we can refer to three different directions in which political culture runs: a "system" culture, a "process" culture, and a "policy" culture.[46] The "system" dimension of political culture is made up of attitudes toward the nation, the regime, and the authorities who control power at any given time. This includes values related to national identity, regime legitimacy, institutional legitimacy, and the effectiveness of individuals who hold significant political positions. The "process" dimension of political culture is made up of attitudes toward the role that the individual plays in the political arena, and attitudes about other political actors. The "policy" dimension of political culture focuses upon the results of politics, the "outputs" of the political system.

As we suggested earlier, the importance of the political culture is that it refers to a number of political variables that we may use in our analysis of the political world and in our construction of political theories. Political culture has been argued to be significant in the process of political development, something to which we shall turn our attention in just a moment, in the development of regime legitimacy, in economic and industrial development, and in social integration and regime stability. It is a concept that we shall use on a number of occasions in this study, especially in the second half of this text when we turn our attention to some area studies to illustrate the importance of the political institutions and political behaviors that we shall examine in the first part of this book.

As we noted previously, however, when we consider political culture we must be aware of the danger of what can be called an *ethnocentric* approach to our study. We should not make the assumption that the way social relationships and institutions exist in our culture and society is necessarily the same way they exist in all other societies, or is the standard for institutions and behavior that other cultures strive to develop. There are *many* characteristics of what can be called "Western culture" that are definitely not sought by non-Western societies. Indeed, there are many characteristics of contemporary Western society that we do not like ourselves, such as contemporary crime rates, drug problems, the weakening of the nuclear family unit, and so on. We must keep in mind that Western capitalist democracies are *not always* the model chosen by others in the world, and whether we agree with this or not, we must be careful not to *assume* that our way is the only way.

The Concept of Political Development

At the same time that we state that one of the primary objects of comparative political inquiry is the nation-state, or the country, we should be sure to add a temporal dimension to our analysis. That is, we do not want to fall victim to the (often implicit) assumption that the political world always stays the same. Just as times change in relation to fashions and fads, so too do political eras change, and what may be acceptable behavior or thought in one era may not be acceptable in another. Throughout political history we can see the development, or popularization, of many different ideas over time: Tyrannicide (the killing of unjust kings) was argued to be "just" at one point in time; revolutions and democratic institutions flourished in the eighteenth century, and so on.

In addition to being able to trace the development of political ideas across time, it is possible to take a different temporal approach and look at the *development* across time of nation-states. Individual nation-states do not spring fully blossomed and mature into the contemporary political world. *Political develop-*

ment and *modernization* are processes, and sometimes these processes are effectuated speedily while at other times they take longer. Sometimes the evolution involved is gradual, other times it is abrupt, violent, and painful.

Often the terms "modernization" and "development" are used interchangeably to refer to the movement of a nation-state from one evolutionary stage to another. Some scholars, however, distinguish between the two terms:

> [Development is] an evolutionary process in which indigenous institutions adapt and control change and are not simply caught up in imitating and reacting to outside forces. Modernization is often contemporary, imported, and creates a dependency on the technologically advanced urban-industrial centers without helping local political and social institutions to grow and adapt. Development means that a system has some ability to be selective in the type and pace of changes, often imported, that occur in a country.[47]

In 1963 a long-term study of political modernization and political development was initiated by the Committee on Comparative Politics of the Social Science Research Center at the Center for Advanced Study in the Behavioral Studies at Palo Alto, California. This series of research projects yielded several studies that were published by the Princeton University Press in a series entitled Studies on Political Development.[48] Although a number of different subjects are covered in these studies, they all are based on the premise that political development—nation building—involves a number of "crises," and *all* nations, modern or not, go through these crises.[49] Each of these five "crises" will be briefly described here.

The Crisis of Identity

How do individuals in a political regime describe themselves politically? This crisis was faced in the United States in the late eighteenth century, when individuals had to learn to identify themselves first as Americans, rather than as Virginians, or New Yorkers, for example. Again in 1860, large numbers of Americans started to think of their primary political identities as something other than American (i.e., "Southerner").

In the contemporary political world, one of the major hurdles faced by new and developing nations is the need to help citizens develop a national identity. Failure to do so can result in national stress and possibly civil war: The situation in Lebanon in which citizens identified themselves not so much "Lebanese" as Christians, Moslems, or Palestinians led to a civil war there; Ibo tribesmen in Nigeria did not want to think of themselves as Nigerians, and attempted, unsuccessfully, to break away from Nigeria and form a new nation (Biafra). The problem, however, is not restricted to new or "underdeveloped" nations; many French Canadians today identify themselves as "Quebecois," not Canadians, and this places stress on the Canadian political system. The same can be said for the Sikh population in India's Punjab region, the Eritreans in Somalia, and the Tamil population in Sri Lanka, among others.

The Crisis of Legitimacy

The concept of "legitimacy" suggests a sense on the part of the public that the government in power has a right to exist, or is acting "appropriately." People may disagree with specific governmental decisions or actions without necessarily denying the legitimacy of the regime. In instances in which governments lose their appearance of legitimacy to a major proportion of the populace, they have great difficulty in staying in power and may do so usually only with the coercive support of the military. Recent regimes that were dissolved as a result of a crucial loss of perceived legitimacy were in Iran (with the downfall of the government of the Shah in 1979), the Philippines (with the downfall of the Marcos regime), and Nicaragua (with the downfall of the Somoza regime in 1979).

In other cases, regimes were not toppled but significant instances of social disruption occurred when groups in society ceased to recognize the legitimacy of government. The role of the Parti Quebecois in Canada, in advocating Quebec's secession from the Canadian federation, is a good case in point. Similarly, the behavior of the Sikhs in India's Punjab state resulted in many deaths and much social disruption. Perhaps most notably in recent years, many governments in Eastern Europe—including those of East Germany, Poland, and Czechoslovakia—fell when substantial segments of their populations concluded that the governments of these states no longer were legitimate.

To a large degree this refers to the same general phenomenon that is called "institutionalization" by Samuel Huntington in his classic work *Political Order in Changing Societies*. There he defines institutionalization as the "process by which organizations and procedures acquire value and stability. The level of institutionalization of any political system can be defined by the adaptability, complexity, autonomy, and coherence of its organizations and procedures."[50]

It is often difficult to define precisely the point at which a loss of legitimacy may become critical. Clearly, there will always be some people in any regime who do not feel that the regime is constructed in, or is acting in, a legitimate manner. Established regimes can tolerate some of this thought; newer regimes can tolerate less, since they have less of a "bank" of past legitimacy upon which to draw. At some point, that depends upon the regime and the political system involved; a loss of legitimacy may become critical and the system may suffer irreparable harm.

The Crisis of Penetration

Are laws enforced? Do the policy decisions of the government "trickle down" to all levels of society, or are there areas of the nation in which the laws and policy decisions of the regime simply do not apply? To the extent that a geographic district may exist in which the laws of the regime are simply ignored, or to the extent that certain specific laws or administrative guidelines from the government are ignored throughout the nation (e.g., legislation prohibiting the consumption of alcohol), we can speak about problems of penetration. Examples of this might include U.S. civil rights policies in the early 1960s when federal guidelines were not respected in southern states and, for example, the Mississippi National Guard had to be nationalized to enforce federal civil rights laws; recent policy in the Soviet Union related to *perestroika*; or government encouragement of birth control in some Latin American or African nations.

The crisis of penetration, then, refers to the government's ability to follow through on, and to enforce, its decisions. Governments that are not able to do this, that are not taken seriously by their publics, are less stable than others.

The Crisis of Participation

A system may suffer stress in both quantitative and qualitative dimensions of participation. Quantitatively, what some see as too little participation may result in a lack of legitimacy (e.g., an election in which only 15 percent of the population participated), and what some feel is too much participation—perhaps too many demands made—may put too great a burden on the structures of the regime that are designed to respond to such communications. Qualitatively, reasonably few demands that are in themselves extreme may put stress on the system. What should the role of the "mass" public be in relation to the "elite" of the regime? Examples of this type of question, which might create a dimension of crisis in a political regime, would be: (1) a racial majority demanding political opportunity in a regime that has been racially discriminatory, such as existed for many years in Rhodesia (now Zimbabwe) or such as exists today in South Africa; (2) a mass demonstration bringing hundreds of thousands of protesters together to criticize a regime, such as the types of demonstrations that were crucial in the downfall of Ferdinand Marcos in the Philippines in 1986 or the Shah of Iran in 1979; or (3) individuals refusing to pay their income taxes as an act of political protest.

The Crisis of Distribution

One of the most visible problems of developing nations today is a *material* one: food, medical supplies, housing, water, electricity, and so forth are either not being equitably distributed in a society, or, although equitably distributed, are not sufficient. (We should note, of course, that these problems are not *only* characteristic of "developing" nations. There are areas of the United States that are shocking examples of these same problems.) New nations have an incredible set of demands made upon them, and among the most visible of these demands are those related to distributive goods. Long food lines in Ethiopia, which led to food riots, resulted in the eventual overthrow of Emperor Haile Selassie in 1974. A lack of consumer goods in the Soviet Union has been credited with motivating Soviet President Mikhail Gorbachev to push for greater reforms in the economic sector in recent years. A society in which a group feels that it is not receiving its "fair share" of the material benefits of government is a society ready for revolution.

These five dimensions of crisis in relation to problems of political development start to tell the story of the concerns confronting many of the developing nations today, not to mention the older and more established industrial democracies. These crises are exacerbated in the developing world, though, by more readily apparent problems, such as low levels of literacy, poor general health care, high infant mortality, and an inability to control rapidly rising populations. To the extent that these and other problems remain and continue to become worse, new nations will continue to experience great instability and turmoil.

The study of political development and political modernization involves considerably more than has been presented in this section. We will devote a full chapter in this book to an examination of political development and political modernization and how they relate to a number of other subjects such as political economics.

The Institutional Approach

The approach to comparative politics that is used in this text is an institutional one. Although there is no doubt that either an emphasis on public policy or political behavior would be a vehicle that would "work" in an introduction to comparative politics, the institutional approach has been selected here for several reasons. First, it *lends itself to generalization* more readily than do the other approaches. When we learn how a "Westminster-model" parliamentary system works in Britain, and we subsequently learn that Grenada, Tuvalu, and India have essentially Westminster-model parliamentary systems, we can relatively easily, and relatively accurately, transfer a good deal of what we learned about one system to another. An emphasis on public policy (e.g., British housing policy) or political behavior (e.g., British voting patterns) would not permit this transferability.

Second, the institutional approach *is more enduring*. Although it is true that individual nation-states do change their basic political institutions on occasion, it is much more often the case that political institutions do not change either as radically or frequently as do individual policies or aggregate behavior. The French electoral system was changed in 1985, and subsequently changed again shortly thereafter, but this was a true deviation from the French norm and from the norm we shall see in other settings. On the other hand, housing policy, health policy, foreign policy, and environmental policy are subject to political change as the corresponding political climate changes.

Third, the institutional approach *lends itself to observation and measurement* more readily than do other approaches. Although polities such as Great Britain, France, or Germany have been the subject of a great deal of policy analysis and examination of political behavior, there are many polities in the world in which sophisticated policy analysis is simply not done, nor is analysis of political behavior undertaken. In those systems we *can*, on the other hand, undertake an examination of their political institutions.

To be sure, the institutional approach does not work *all* of the time; thus we will not restrict ourselves to only its use here. We shall discuss aspects of public policy and political behavior in our analysis here, but the *primary* vehicle for analysis will be that of political institutions. In the case of our study of the Soviet Union, for example, we shall observe that it is a polity in which an institutional approach has not worked very well, and *there* we shall focus our efforts in alternative directions. However, on balance, we believe that the institutional approach is the best vehicle for an introduction to comparative politics.

The Comparative Method in Perspective

Throughout the remainder of this book we shall endeavor to follow the guidelines that we have set down thus far as to the comparative method of inquiry. The value of the comparative method is in the broad perspective that it offers the student of political science; we will focus upon this broad perspective as we continue.

In the next several chapters we will develop a base for further inquiry. We will present a number of different political structures and behaviors comparatively, looking first at the existence of a structure in one setting and then at the same structure elsewhere.

We will also search for similarities and differences in the structures under examination, to try to understand how the political environments within which they exist have influenced them. Subsequently, we will turn our attention to a number of brief area studies "portraits," which will afford us the opportunity to better understand the political contexts within which the various political structures operate.

Notes

1. See Ernest Barker, ed. and trans., *The Politics of Aristotle* (New York: Oxford University Press, 1970), pp. xi–xix.
2. Ibid., p. 111.
3. David Easton, *A Framework for Political Analysis* (Englewood Cliffs, N.J.: Prentice Hall, 1965), p. 50.
4. Harold Lasswell, *Politics: Who Gets What, When, How?* (New York: McGraw-Hill, 1936).
5. See Roy C. Macridis and Bernard E. Brown, eds., *Comparative Politics: Notes and Readings* (Homewood, Il.: Dorsey Press, 1977), pp. 2–4.
6. Mattei Dogan and Dominique Pelassy, *How to Compare Nations: Strategies in Comparative Politics* (Chatham, N.J.: Chatham House, 1984), p. 3.
7. Arend Lijphart, "The Comparable Cases Strategy in Comparative Research," *Comparative Political Studies* 8 (1975): 159. See also Arend Lijphart, "Comparative Politics and the Comparative Method," *American Political Science Review* 65 (1971): 682–693; and Theodore Meckstroth, " 'Most Different Systems' and 'Most Similar Systems': A Study in the Logic of Comparative Inquiry," *Comparative Political Studies* 8 (1975): 132.
8. See James B. Christoph and Bernard F. Brown, *Cases in Comparative Politics* (Boston: Little, Brown, 1976) for a good example of this approach.
9. See Harry Eckstein, "Case Study and Theory in Political Science," in Fred Greenstein and Nelson Polsby, eds., *Handbook of Political Science: Strategies of Inquiry* (Reading, Mass.: Addison-Wesley, 1975), p. 79.
10. A very good essay on this can be found in the essay by Richard Boyd and Herbert Hyman, "Survey Research," in Greenstein and Polsby, eds., *Handbook of Political Science*, pp. 265–350.
11. For a good introductory level example of this approach, see Neil Agnew and Sandra Pyke, *The Science Game* (Englewood Cliffs, N.J.: Prentice Hall, 1978).
12. A good essay on the comparative method can be found in Michael Curtis, *Comparative Government and Politics: An Introductory Essay in Political Science* (New York: Harper & Row, 1978).
13. For example, Allan Kornberg, ed., *Legislatures in Comparative Perspective* (New York: David McKay, 1973); Jean Blondel, *Comparative Legislatures* (Englewood Cliffs, N.J.: Prentice Hall, 1973); or Gerhard Loewenberg and Samuel Patterson, *Comparing Legislatures* (Boston: Little, Brown, 1979).
14. For example, Robert Putnam, *The Comparative Study of Political Elites* (Englewood Cliffs, N.J.: Prentice Hall, 1976).

15. For example, Leon Baradat, *Political Ideologies* (Englewood Cliffs, N.J.: Prentice Hall, 1979).
16. For example, Lynne Iglitzin and Ruth Ross, eds., *Women in the World* (Santa Barbara, Calif.: Clio Press, 1976).
17. For example, Ivo Duchacek, *Power Maps: Comparative Politics of Constitutions* (Santa Barbara, Calif.: Clio Press, 1973).
18. For example, Henry Ehrmann, *Comparative Legal Cultures* (Englewood Cliffs, N.J.: Prentice Hall, 1976).
19. Thomas H. Greene, *Comparative Revolutionary Movements: Search for Theory and Justice* (Englewood Cliffs, N.J.: Prentice Hall, 1984).
20. For example, Richard Rose and Ezra Suleiman, eds., *Presidents and Prime Ministers* (Washington, D.C.: American Enterprise Institute, 1980).
21. For example, Kay Lawson, *The Comparative Study of Political Parties* (New York: St. Martin's Press, 1976).
22. For example, Eric Nordlinger, *Soldiers in Politics: Military Coups and Governments* (Englewood Cliffs, N.J.: Prentice Hall, 1977).
23. Arend Lijphart, *Democracies: Patterns of Majoritarian and Consensus Government in Twenty-One Countries* (New Haven: Yale University Press, 1984).
24. Enrique A. Baloyra, ed., *Comparing New Democracies: Transition and Consolidation in Mediterranean Europe and the Southern Cone* (Boulder, Col.: Westview Press, 1987).
25. For example, Monte Palmer, *Dilemmas of Political Development* (Itasca, Ill.: F.E. Peacock, 1973).
26. For example, Gabriel Almond and Sidney Verba, eds., *The Civic Culture Revisited* (Boston: Little, Brown, 1980).
27. For example, William Welsh, *Leaders and Elites* (New York: Holt, Rinehart & Winston, 1979).
28. For an incredible collection of comparative data dealing with legislatures, see Valerie Herman, ed., *Parliaments of the World* (London: Macmillan, 1976). There is an entire section of this 985-page book dealing with seating arrangements in legislatures, and make sure to note Table 21 on seating arrangements, which is itself seven pages long!
29. Adam Przeworski and Henry Teune, *The Logic of Comparative Social Inquiry* (New York: Wiley, 1970), p. 32.
30. Ibid. See also Dogan and Pelassy, *How to Compare Nations*, chap. 16, "Comparing Similar Countries," pp. 117–126.
31. See Dogan and Pelassy, *How to Compare Nations*, chap. 17, "Comparing Contrasting Nations," pp. 127–132.
32. For example, see T. Alexander Smith, *The Comparative Policy Process* (Santa Barbara, Calif.: Clio Press, 1976).
33. For example, Lewis Bowman and G. R. Boynton, eds., *Political Behavior and Public Opinion: Comparative Analysis* (Englewood Cliffs, N.J.: Prentice Hall, 1974).
34. There are few integrated and structural comparative studies. One is left to rely on more specific comparative studies, such as comparative studies of legislatures (see note 10), or comparative studies of executives (see note 16), for example.
35. Good discussions of problems of levels of analysis and other methodological difficulties can be found in Robert Bernstein and James Dyer, *An Introduction to Political Science Methods* (Englewood Cliffs, N.J.: Prentice Hall, 1979).
36. David Easton, *A Systems Analysis of Political Life* (New York: Wiley, 1965).
37. Ibid., p. 38.

38. Ibid., p. 159.
39. Gabriel Almond, "Introduction," in Gabriel Almond and James Coleman, eds., *The Politics of the Developing Areas* (Princeton, N.J.: Princeton University Press, 1960).
40. Gabriel Almond, "The Intellectual History of the Civic Culture Concept," in Gabriel Almond and Sidney Verba, *The Civic Culture Revisited* (Boston: Little, Brown, 1980), p. 1.
41. Ibid., p. 2.
42. Ibid.
43. Almond, "Intellectual History," p. 26.
44. Sidney Verba, "Comparative Political Culture," in Lucian Pye and Sidney Verba, eds., *Political Culture and Political Development* (Princeton, N.J.: Princeton University Press, 1965), p. 513.
45. Carole Pateman, "The Civic Culture: A Philosophic Critique," in Almond and Verba, *The Civic Culture Revisited*, p. 66.
46. This is a summation of much more detailed discussion in Almond, "Intellectual History," pp. 27–29.
47. Herbert Winter and Thomas Bellows, *People and Politics* (New York: Wiley, 1977), pp. 352–353.
48. Among the many volumes published in the series (Princeton, N.J.: Princeton University Press) were the following: Lucian Pye, ed., *Communications and Political Development* (1963); Joseph LaPalombara, ed., *Bureaucracy and Political Development* (1963); Robert E. Ward and Dankwart Rustow, eds., *Political Modernization in Japan and Turkey* (1964); James S. Coleman, ed., *Education and Political Development* (1965); Lucian Pye and Sidney Verba, eds., *Political Culture and Political Development* (1965); Joseph LaPalombara and Myron Weiner, eds., *Political Parties and Political Development* (1966); Leonard Binder et al., *Crises and Sequences in Political Development* (1971); and Charles Tilly, ed., *The Formation of National States in Western Europe* (1975).
49. See especially Leonard Binder et al., *Crises and Sequences in Political Development*.
50. Samuel P. Huntington, *Political Order in Changing Societies* (New Haven: Yale University Press, 1968), p. 12.

2

Constitutions and Ideologies

Constitutions as Political Structures

One of the first things that an interested student of comparative politics will find as he or she peruses the literature is the heavy emphasis that is placed on the *state* or the *nation* as the unit of analysis. This is not to say that all comparative research takes place on this level; certainly a good deal of research has focused upon individuals, or policy, or developing and developed societies, and so on, but the *nation-state* is a common subject of many studies.

Many characteristics of the state can be taken as the focus for a comparative study—we will examine a number of them in this book—including *structural* characteristics (such as constitutions, legislatures, executives, judiciaries, political parties, and interest groups) and *behavioral* characteristics (such as ideology, political participation, or political socialization and recruitment). The initial area of our study should logically focus upon the structures that describe the parameters of the system, the boundaries and definitions of the component structures found within the political system. In this way we turn our attention first to a brief examination of constitutions, and, subsequently, to a brief discussion of ideology and its place in political regimes.

It may be useful to think of constitutions as "power maps"[1] for political systems. That is, it is often the constitution of a nation that tells us the political "lay of the land," and that describes the manner in which power is distributed among the many actors in the political environment. We look to the constitution for an explanation of who has the power to do what, what the limitations on power are in a given political system, and what the relationships are between and among the many political actors we may find in a given nation. The idea of a constitution as a fundamental expression of the power relationships in a political regime dates back to the time of the Greek and Roman republics; constitutions were the focus for comparison in Aristotle's major studies of political systems.

Written and Unwritten Constitutions

Studies of constitutional governments often rely on the structure or form of those written documents that we call constitutions. Yet, government with a written constitution is not the same thing as a constitutional government. A *written constitution* is essentially a basic expression of the ideas and organization of a government that is formally presented in one document. Some constitutions are quite short—the U.S. Constitution, for example—while others are much longer, such as the constitution of the Soviet Union, or the even longer constitution of India. Some written constitutions are contained in one document, such as the Swiss Constitution, while others are found in several documents, such as the Canadian Constitution, which includes a "Constitution Act" as well as several other pieces of legislation and historical documents.

On the other hand, *constitutional government* can best be described as *limited government*. That is, there are certain things that the government may not do, whether it wants to or not; there are certain parameters beyond which the government may not go. The First Amendment to the U.S. Constitution is a clear example of this characteristic, stating in part that "Congress shall make *no law* . . . abridging the freedom of speech . . ." (italics added). This is an *explicit* limitation upon the powers of government to act in a specific field of interest.

The fact of the matter is that we can find governments without written constitutions that can properly be called constitutional regimes, and conversely we can find governments that do have written constitutions that do not properly fit within the behavioral parameters we have set for a regime to be called a constitutional government. Several examples may help to make this clear.

The British government does not possess a document called "The Royal Constitution," or some such name, which serves as the basic and central document for the political structures of the British political system. British political history points to a number of different documents that are part of the body of what is referred to as British constitutional law, including the Magna Carta (1215), the Bill of Rights (1689), the Act of Settlement (1701), and certain special acts of the British Parliament. On the other hand, scholars are agreed that Britain *does* possess a constitutional government. There *are* limits beyond which the British government may not go. Yet Britain does *not* have a single, written document that can be called a written constitution.

Although the Soviet Union has a relatively new (1977) constitution that is highly detailed and specific,[2] many would argue that the Soviet regime should not be called a constitutional government, because until very recently (and some might argue until the present time) there have been no effective limitations on governmental power there. Rights are conditional: Article 39 of the Soviet Constitution states that "the exercise of rights and liberties of citizens must not injure the interests of society and the state"[3]; Article 47 states that "USSR citizens, in accordance with the goals of communist construction, are guaranteed freedom of scientific, technical, and artistic creation . . ."[4]; Article 51 states that "in accordance with the goals of communist construction, USSR citizens have the right to unite in public organizations. . . ."[5] These few examples, which are typical of the document as a whole, show that expressions of rights do exist; however, they are always conditional, with the clear implication— which has been shown to be the case in practice—that if the government believes that the "goals of communist construction" are not being served, the rights in question may be lost.

There is one other distinction between these types of regimes, a bit more subtle, that should be made explicit here. One constitution *gives* rights, and the other *recognizes* rights. This is not merely a semantic difference. The Soviet Constitution, in stating that the government *gives* citizens certain rights, implies that the government also has the power to *take away* these rights. If rights come from the state, the state can certainly take them away. In the British (unwritten) Constitution, or the American (written) Constitution, rights are *not* given; they are *recognized*, by limiting what the government can do. The Constitution of the United States does *not* state that "citizens are given the right to free speech," although some people assume that it does. What is written in the U.S. Constitution is that "Congress shall make no law . . . abridging the freedom of speech, or of the press . . ."; these rights and freedoms appear to *already* exist, and belong to the people, and the Constitution recognizes this fact by forbidding the Congress to limit them. This is quite different from the Soviet case.

We can see that when we discuss constitutional governments, we are really not talking about whether there exists a single, specific document or not, but rather we are interested in a kind of political behavior, political culture, political tradition, or political history. The British Constitution is really a collection of documents and traditions, bound together in an abstract way. The American Constitution is a single document, with subsequent judicial interpretation and expansion. The forms may vary, but the behavioral results are the same: Limits are imposed upon what governments may do.

What Do Constitutions Do?

"Constitutions are codes of rules which aspire to regulate the allocation of functions, powers, and duties among the various agencies and officers of government, and define the relationship between these and the public."[6] Do constitutions make a difference? We have just argued that having a *written* constitution may not guarantee the behavior of a regime; does having *any* constitution matter? Today, more and more political scientists are putting *less* emphasis on a constitution as a significant structure in a political system. They argue that too often constitutions—

whether written or unwritten—are not true reflections of the manner in which a political system operates, and therefore the constitution is of little use or value.[7]

Furthermore, in many instances constitutions omit discussions of the political structures of the regime, which are crucial to the operation of that regime. For example, political parties are nowhere mentioned in the American (written) Constitution, yet it is difficult to conceive of government operating in the United States without political parties. To take another example, the Canadian (written) Constitution fails to mention the prime minister as a significant actor in the political system at all, yet there is no doubt that this is the single most important office in the Canadian political arena. The Soviet (written) Constitution guarantees certain rights, but practice indicates that these guarantees are hollow, indeed. Given all of this, why is it that constitutions seem to be universally accepted as necessary to a political system, whether they be written constitutions or unwritten constitutions? If a political structure is so pervasive, it must perform a very important function for the political systems in which it is found.

Several functions can be attributed to those political structures that we call constitutions, whether they are written or unwritten, whether they are "followed" or not, wherever they may be found. First, they serve as an expression of ideology and philosophy, a subject to which we shall return later in this chapter. Very often this kind of expression is found in a preamble to the constitution in question. For example, the preamble to Canada's Constitution Act of 1867 indicated that Canada would have a constitution "similar in principle" to that of Britain. This "similar in principle" clause was seen by scholars as incorporating—all by itself—all of the hundreds of years of British constitutional tradition into the Canadian political realm, and accordingly was regarded as being quite significant.[8]

Second, constitutions serve as an expression of the basic laws of the regime. These laws play a central role in the regime and are often so special that they can be modified or replaced only through extraordinary amendment procedures. Whereas an ordinary law can usually be passed with a "simple majority" approval of the national legislature—a majority of those present and voting at the time—basic laws of the regime expressed in the constitution usually require special majorities (two-thirds or three-quarters, for example) for approval. These special laws usually focus upon the rights of citizens; for instance, rights concerning language, speech, religion, assembly, the press, property, and so on.

Third, constitutions provide organizational frameworks for governments. Although they may not actually contain diagrams to explain how the various parts of the government interact with or relate to each other, these relationships are explained in the text of the document. It is common for constitutions to contain several sections, and to devote a section each to the legislative branch of government, the executive branch of government, the judicial branch of government, and so on. Constitutions will discuss power relationships among the actors in the political system, covering the legislative process, the role of the executive in policy formation, checks and balances among the actors, possibly including impeachment of the executive and dissolution of the legislature, and perhaps discussion of succession as well.

Fourth, constitutions usually say something about the levels of government of the political system. They discuss how many levels of government there will be, whether nations will be federal, confederal, or unitary. They often describe what powers fall within the jurisdiction of the national government, and what powers do not belong to the national government.

Finally, constitutions usually have an amendment clause. No matter how careful and insightful the authors of a constitution try to be, they simply cannot foretell the future with a sufficiently high degree of accuracy. Accordingly, constitutions may need to be amended or altered at some point down the road. A constitution must contain directions for its own modifications; failure to do so might mean that when change becomes necessary, the entire system could collapse for want of a mechanism of change.

Constitutions, then, whether written or unwritten, play an important role in the regimes in which they are found. Some constitutions will be more important in one of the functions described above than in others. For example, the Soviet Constitution may be more important as an expression of ideology than as a real organizational diagram of the government; until recent amendments, the Soviet Constitution only mentioned the Communist Party of the Soviet Union (CPSU) once, and then only in passing. Clearly, for most of the second half of the twentieth century the CPSU was more important than *that* to the regime. Similarly, the American Constitution is more important as an expression of governmental organization and as a guideline for the power relationships of the regime than as an expression of the philosophy of the regime; the latter is usually said to be better expressed in the Declaration of Independence and the Federalist Papers than in the Constitution.

Constitutionalism and Federal Government

An important dimension of our comparative study of politics involves how political systems are organized. In this respect we can identify several major options, including *unitary, confederal,* and *federal* political systems. It is important for us to understand the distinctions among these three organizational forms so as to appreciate fully some of the differences between governmental systems.

A *unitary system* is one that has only one level of government above the local level. In Great Britain, for example, although there are city governments, and indeed some county governments, true *sovereignty—the real power to make political decisions*—resides with Parliament, and Parliament has the right to control whatever powers the cities or counties might exercise. Parliament has the power to grant the cities and counties more influence, or to take away policy jurisdiction they may already control.

The chief advantage of this type of system lies in its simplicity—there is only one responsible government with which to deal. Unitary governments, however, have proven to be less effective over large nations than small nations, and they do not allow for ethnic and regional groups to exercise some degree of autonomy for themselves. Britain has a unitary government, and this style of government has been the subject of tension in the past because some citizens in Wales, Scotland, and Northern Ireland have argued that it does not give regional and ethnic groups as much power as they might like. France, Italy, and Japan are other contemporary examples of unitary nations.

A *confederal system*—sometimes called a confederation—is a union of sovereign states that retain their sovereignty and powers, but which coordinate their activities in certain respects. For example, a group of sovereign states may agree to coordinate their trade barriers, or their fishing activities in certain waters, or their oil production. The degree to which the units coordinate their behavior can vary greatly, as can the range of areas in which this coordination takes place. There are no true confederal states today; some have argued that the closest approximation to such an organization would be an international organization such as the European Economic Community.

The major advantage of confederations is their loose structure, which leaves a tremendous degree of flexibility and autonomy to member units. This allows these units to retain their individual characteristics and, to varying degrees, their own sovereignty to chart the directions in which they would most like to go. This same characteristic can be seen to be the main drawback of confederations as well: their inability to reconcile the varied interests of various member units. A confederation's citizens tend to identify most strongly with the member units, not the "national" unit, and priorities tend to be sectional, not broad. Often, action is taken only when all member units agree, which may mean that often no action is taken at all. Notable experiments in confederation that failed—the United States (1781–1787), Germany (1815–1866), and Switzerland (1815–1874)—were all reorganized as federations after it became clear that the confederal system would simply not further necessary common objectives.[9]

The European Economic Community (EEC)—often referred to today as simply "Europe"—began as an organization regulating tariffs among a small number of European nations; it has grown in power over the last several decades to the point at which it has become a real political entity in the region. European nations not only elect their own national legislators, but they also elect Members of the European Parliament (MEPs) to represent their region and nation in the European Parliament. The European Parliament has the ability to pass legislation regulating a wide range of economic issues in Europe.

In a *federal system* there are two levels of government above the local level, each enjoying sovereignty in certain specific areas. For example, the central government may have the sole authority to coin money, raise an army, or declare war; the intermediate level of government (e.g., states, provinces, cantons, Länder) may have sole authority to regulate education, criminal law, or civil law; citizens deal with both levels of government.

Federal governments have been shown to have numerous advantages over other types of governments.[10] Federalism allows for both the expression of regional goals and a coordinated expression of national goals. One of the advantages of a federal system for member states is that the national level of government can absorb, through economic redistribution among member units, some of the costs of new technology or programs that would have to be absorbed completely by member units in a unitary or confederal system.[11]

The concept of federalism can be seen to have its roots early in political history, as long ago as the historic Greek city-states, in fact. These early federations, for the most part, were not very stable or long-lived.[12] Modern federalism is usually dated from the American Constitutional Convention in Philadelphia in 1787.[13]

The number of federal states in the contemporary world is not great. Of the approximately 170 nation-states today, only twenty-one claim to be federal.[14] These twenty-one nations, however, cover more than half of the land surface of the globe, and include almost half of the world's population.[15] Federalism has proven to be a significant element "in situations in which sheer size, involving the separation and divergence of communities, has been the dominating feature."[16]

> Some authors argue that there is a direct correlation between large size and the advisability of federalism, and they quote Thomas Jefferson in support of their argument: "Our country is too large to have all its affairs directed by a single government."[17]

Of the six largest nations in the world, only China is unitary, and even China has some characteristics of federal government.[18] (The five other largest nations are the USSR, Canada, the United States, Brazil, and Australia.)

There are many smaller federations, as well, including Mexico, Venezuela, and Argentina in Latin America; Nigeria in Africa; Switzerland, Yugoslavia, and Czechoslovakia in Europe; and India in Asia. Many of these nations opted for federalism not because of their large land area, but because of regional, ethnic, or linguistic characteristics of component groups that made a federal type of organization necessary. In general, federalism allows countries involved to maximize economic growth and political strength, while at the same time allowing for the expression of regional characteristics.[19]

Switzerland, for example, chose the federal system because

it was best suited to the needs of that country's three language groups, German, French, and Italian. The Swiss Constitution, in fact, recognizes three official languages. Of the twenty-two Swiss cantons, there are eighteen unilingual cantons, three bilingual cantons, and one trilingual canton. The Swiss Constitution guarantees each citizen the right to communicate with the central government in any one of the three official languages.[20]

The federal system has also been adapted in Germany. Rather than establishing clear divisions between areas of jurisdiction of the Bund (the central parliament) and the Länder (the member units), the German Constitution allows for a broad area of concurrent jurisdiction. The upper house of the national legislature, the Bundesrat, is chosen by the Länder governments, and has an absolute veto over matters affecting the Länder, but only a "suspensory" veto over matters of "national" concern.[21]

There does not appear to be a universally accepted theory of federalism, nor, for that matter, a clear definition of precisely what behavioral attributes are characteristic of federal government. Ivo Duchacek has suggested that:

> the term itself is unclear and controversial. It is often used to describe a *process* of combining territorial communities that had previously not been directly joined. . . . In addition, federalism is also a term used to describe the result or the tools of the federalizing process—a constitutional federal system and its institutions.[22]

The most common characterization of a federal government is that it is organized on two levels above the local level, one national unit and a number of intermediate-member units. Both levels of government rule over the same constituents, and both levels of government have the power to make certain decisions independently of the other.[23]

William Riker has suggested a useful framework within which the many federal governments of the world may be measured. He has suggested that federations can be measured along a "centralized-decentralized" dimension. This dimension may be defined by the following minimum and maximum, illustrated in Figure 2.1:

> *Minimum*: The ruler(s) of the federation can make decisions in only one narrowly restricted category of action without obtaining the approval of the rulers of the constituent units. . . .

Maximum: The ruler(s) of the federation can make decisions without consulting the rulers of the member governments in all but one narrowly restricted category of action.[24]

The closer to the "minimum" end of the scale a federal government is, the more it can be described as a "peripheral federation." The closer to the "maximum" end of the scale a federal government is, the more it can be described as a "centralized federation."

Although most modern federations have proven to be more stable and long-lived than their Hellenic ancestors, not all experiments with federation since the late eighteenth century have been successes. The more "peripheral" a federation is, the weaker the center is as compared to the member units, the greater the centrifugal forces acting on a political system, and the greater the likelihood that the federation will not endure. Cases such as the United Arab Republic (1958–1961), the Federation of the West Indies, the Federation of Malaysia, and the Federation of Rhodesia and Nyasaland[25] are all illustrations of "premature federations"—unifications that took place before sufficient national integration and national development were attained—and are examples of unifications that did not last.

Federalism is significant as a political variable because the federal balance in a polity often influences the efficiency with which public policy is made.[26] To take one example, it is often difficult for the Canadian federal (national) government to set national policy because many substantial policy issues—such as health policy, education policy, much resource policy, and so on—fall within the policy jurisdiction of the provinces. Accordingly, if the federal government wants to enact a new health policy or a new job training program, it must frequently convene a meeting of the prime minister and the ten provincial premiers, or the country's education minister and the ten provincial education ministers, or comparable officials depending upon the policy area

Figure 2.1
A Scale of Federalisms

	"States" 1%		"States" 99%	
Centralized (maximum)	←			→ Decentralized (minimum)
	Center 99%		Center 1%	

involved, to "negotiate" a policy that will be acceptable to their respective governments. The provincial representatives will then return to their respective capitals and introduce the policy in their provincial legislatures.[27]

The Separation of Powers

The notion that centralized power is dangerous, that power must be a check on power, reached maturity in the eighteenth century, and its first real application was to be found in the Constitutional Convention held in Philadelphia in 1787. There, delegates to the federal convention continuously cited "the Celebrated Montesquieu," John Locke, Thomas Hobbes, and others,[28] in support of the idea that political power, in order to be safe, had to be divided. The legislature needed to have a check on the executive, the executive on the legislature, and so on. Many of the ideas of John Locke were adopted and found in *The Federalist* (especially Number 47), among other places, and expressed the philosophy that the executive force had to be kept separate from the legislative force.[29]

Constitutions express the power relationships among the many actors in political regimes. The American Constitution is explicit about the degree to which the president can take control of the work of the legislature (literally, he cannot), and the degree to which the Congress can take control of the work of the president (literally, it cannot). The situation, however, is one that *can* rapidly devolve into a stalemate: The president can veto work of the Congress, and Congress can refuse to pass legislative requests of the president, but neither can *force* the other to do anything. In other regimes the lines are much less clearly drawn. For example, in France the president can, under certain circumstances that we shall examine more closely later in this volume, simply issue decrees that have the force of legislation.

We will see in a number of instances throughout this book that the explicit lines that were drawn by the Founding Fathers to separate the executive and legislative branches of government were not, hindsight tells us, absolutely necessary to ensure democratic government. There are other power relationships, which we will discuss in later chapters, that are used elsewhere that have proven to be just as democratic and just as stable.

The Importance of Constitutions

Constitutions can be examined on two levels. On one hand, we can look at a constitution on a "piece" level, and examine it section by section to see what structures and behaviors it prescribes for a given political system. Further, we can speculate as to the implications of these structures and behaviors for political life in that system. On the other hand, we can look at a constitution from a different level, from the level of the political system, and ask the same question: What does the constitution do? The framework of analysis of David Easton is useful in examining this type of question.

In the last chapter we examined the concept of the political system, and we noted that Easton offered a variation of the general systems approach, which was referred to as "input-output analysis."[30] Demands and supports are fed into the political system as *inputs*. They are "processed" by the system itself; that is, the system is a giant conversion mechanism that is able to take demands and supports from the environment, digest them, and issue "authoritative allocations of values" in the forms of decisions and actions—*outputs*. These outputs filter through the environment as "feedback" and are subsequently reintroduced as new inputs, either demands or supports, and the cycle continues. The "digesting" and the "processing" phase of the system, what Easton labels "The Political System," is what government is all about: responding to demands and supports, making decisions, providing information, establishing legitimacy, and so on.

Instead of simply looking at a constitution from the perspective of what it says about the separation of powers, about the federal or unitary nature of the political system, about checks and balances, basic laws, amendments, and philosophy, we could ask the system-level question of how the constitution helps the political system to survive. To use the terms of Gabriel Almond that we introduced in the last chapter, what are the functions (consequences) of the structures that we refer to as "constitutions"?

Ivo Duchacek has performed just such an analysis, and his analysis offers some answers to the question "What does the Constitution do?" The answer that his study suggests is that a constitution helps a political system in the function of "system maintenance," survival of the system, by helping the system to respond to the various demands and supports that are directed to it in the form of inputs. The constitution and the corresponding constitutional framework of powers help to process demands and supports and help to convert them into outputs, which subsequently are reintroduced as inputs. According to the framework suggested by Duchacek, constitutions play a crucial role in the system maintenance function suggested by Easton. Demands and supports are processed more smoothly because of (1) commitment to responsiveness, (2) specific institutions for rule-making, enforcement, and adjudicating, and (3) commitment to goals, all of which are found in a constitution.[31]

Constitutions in a Comparative Perspective

The political structure that we call a constitution is a good place for us to begin our cross-national comparison, because it presents for us examples of some of the problems that we first discussed in the last chapter. We cannot be analytically rigid when we are examining constitutional frameworks in comparative perspective. Sometimes we will find a piece of paper entitled "Constitution," and sometimes we will not. The mere existence of a piece of paper or parchment is no guarantee that a political system is constitutional, as we defined the term at the beginning of this chapter. We have, then, the structures-and-functions problem that we mentioned in Chapter 1: The structure of a written constitution may perform different functions (have different consequences) in different political systems. Furthermore, different structures (in some places a written constitution, elsewhere tradition and custom) may perform the same function in different political systems. This is a scenario that we will see repeated in the next several chapters.

Ideologies

One of the functions that we ascribed to constitutions earlier in this chapter was that they sometimes serve as an expression of ideology and philosophy for a regime. The term "ideology" is one that is often emotionally charged, and "ideologue" is often used as a description for an individual no longer approaching a situation from a rational perspective. Originally, "ideologue" referred to a student of how ideas are formed, and ideology was "a study of the process of forming ideas, a 'science of ideas.'"[32] The purpose behind the introduction of the concept of ideology was "to provide the new secular educators with a systematic educational theory. The unashamed view of the ideologues . . . was that the minds of the young should be bent to new, more healthy purposes."[33]

Actually, the term "ideology" has a number of meanings and connotations:

1. One meaning is that of "deception," "distortion," or "falseness." It conveys the notion of *subjectivism* as opposed to objectivity.
2. Ideology also conveys the notion of a *dream*, an impossible or unrealizable quest.
3. Ideology means also what may be called the *consciousness* of a society at any given moment, the values and beliefs and attitudes that hold it together.
4. Ideologies often correspond to *social criticism*, confronting existing beliefs and attempting through argument and persuasion to challenge and change them.
5. Ideology also provides a *set of concepts* through which people view the world and learn about it.
6. Ideologies can be a call for *committed action*.
7. Ideologies often become, under certain circumstances, a powerful *instrument of manipulation*.[34]

Ideologies, then, in a more expressly political context, involve a set of ideas that relate to the social/political world, and which provide a general guideline for some action. One scholar has tersely indicated that "an ideology represents a practical attitude to the world"[35]; another has suggested that "ideologies are actually attempts to develop political accommodations to the economic and social conditions created by the Industrial Revolution."[36] Ideologies can serve many functions, as was indicated earlier. They can unite groups, serve as rallying cries, help to articulate philosophies, or serve as tools of political manipulation. In each of these areas, however, we can see the same two critical components: a relation to political ideas, and a relation to political behavior.

Ideologies give the regime its *raison d'être*, its sense of purpose, and serve as a philosophical point of reference for political behavior in the political system. Michael Curtis has suggested that all ideologies are amalgams of "facts, values, and mythology that provide some understanding of history and the supreme significance of or necessary leadership by a particular individual, group, class, or nation."[37]

Many different ideologies have existed in the modern political world. Some have come and gone in a brief period of time; others have been in existence for a long while. Some ideologies have had a great deal of influence on major world events; others have not. What we could call "classical liberalism" was a very significant ideology at about the time of the American Revolution, and continues to be significant today. Certainly Marxism is an example of an ideology that has had a very broad and profound influence in society, and an influence that has lasted for many years. Other "isms," including socialism, fascism, conservatism, and so on, have become part of our political vocabulary over the years.

Ideologies are often related to individually held attitudes toward political change, which are usually conceived as fitting along a "left-right" spectrum. The spectrum could be titled "degrees of change," as illustrated in Figure 2.2. The "left-right" metaphor dates back to 1798, at which time the French Council of 500 was arranged in a semicircular hall of representatives according to their self-determined place in the political spectrum.[38] Those generally supporting the monarch's policies sat on his right, while those who proposed changes in his policies sat on his left; hence, "leftists" today favor change and "rightists" prefer the status quo. It should be kept in mind that the positions in Figure 2.2 and the descriptions that follow relate to *classical* political values: Those who consider themselves conservative in the United States in the 1990s might not hold the same values as would a "classical" conservative in the 1790s.

The radical position is often associated with violence, although that need not be the case.[39] Generally, the radical position is that which is extremely dissatisfied with the way society (and politics) is organized and operating and is very impatient to undertake fundamental changes in society. Radicals favor drastic

Figure 2.2
The Liberal-Conservative Spectrum

and immediate change. Of course, not all radicals are alike, and we could certainly distinguish among more or less "radical" radicals, depending upon the intensity of their beliefs, the strategies they might wish to employ (including more or less violence), the immediacy with which they want changes undertaken, and so on.

The liberal position is obviously more content with society as it exists than is the radical, but the liberal still believes that reform is possible, and indeed necessary, in society. Among the many differences between liberals and radicals are their views toward the law.

> Since radicals are basically opposed to the political system that governs them, they are apt to see the law as one way in which those who control the society maintain their control. Hence, radicals find it hard to respect the law. Liberals, on the other hand, generally respect the concept of the law, and although they may want to change certain specifics of the law, they usually will not violate it. Instead they try to change the law through legal procedures.[40]

Liberalism includes a belief in human potential, a belief in the ability of individuals to change social institutions for the better, a belief in human rationality, and a fundamental belief in human equality.

The moderate position is one that is basically satisfied with the way society is operating, and one that insists that any changes that might be made in society should be made slowly, gradually, and in a way that will not be disruptive.

The classical conservative position is the position that can be described as being most satisfied with the way society is operating at the time, most satisfied with the status quo. The major difference between conservatives and liberals is that "conservatives support the status quo not so much because they like it but because they believe that it is the best that can be achieved at the moment."[41] Classical conservatives do not share the optimism of liberals that individuals have the capacity to improve society. They are more skeptical of human nature, and believe that human nature may be selfish. They place more emphasis on respecting institutions and traditions because they are not sure that they (or others) are capable of devising a better system. They believe in elitism.

Finally, the reactionary position corresponds to that of the radical, only on the right end of the spectrum. The reactionary position is one that proposes radical change backwards, that is, "retrogressive change," favoring "a policy that would return the society to a previous condition or even a former value system."[42]

It is important to note before we leave the left-right spectrum that it is *very much* a relative scale. Someone who is a "radical-liberal" may view a "moderate-liberal" as an "ultra-conservative." Description may be to a large degree a matter of perspective.

What is a radical policy today may tomorrow be a moderate policy; what is radical is one society may not be radical in another. To take but one example, it was not that long ago that talk of a Social Security system in the United States—in which the government became involved in a retirement pension scheme—was perceived as a radical socialist proposal, completely unthinkable. Yet, in 1990 no one in American society seriously advocates doing away with Social Security; individuals may propose ways of changing the way the system works, but not doing away with the system completely. Another example could be found in proposals for socialized medical care. Socialized medicine may be seen today as a radical policy proposal in the United States, but such may not always be the case; socialized medicine is not seen as radical in virtually all industrialized countries outside of the United States and has been incorporated as part of the public sector.

Constitutions and Ideologies

Care should be taken to avoid confusing ideologies—philosophies or values of political regimes—with the constitutional bases of regimes. The former concept asks the question "What does the regime stand for, and what does it want to accomplish?" The latter asks the question "Who governs, and how is power distributed in the political system?" As a general rule, "isms" refer to ideology, while "-cracy" refers to governance.[43]

Aristotle provided us with terms that are still used today to discuss both *good* government and *bad* government. The Aristotelian forms of *good* government are polity (rule by many in the general interest), aristocracy (rule by a few in the general interest), and kingship (rule by one in the general interest). The divisions of *bad* government are tyranny (self-interest rule by one), oligarchy (self-interest rule by a few), and democracy (self-interest rule by many).

Aristotle provided what has come to be regarded as the "classical" division of systems of government, based upon two dimensions: the number of rulers in a system, and in whose interest the rulers rule. The Aristotelian framework is summarized in Table 2.1.

Table 2.1
The Aristotelian Classification of Regimes

Number of Rulers	Rule in General Interest ("Right" Type)	Selfish Rule ("Wrong" Type)
One	Kingship	Tyranny
Few	Aristocracy	Oligarchy
Many	Polity	Democracy

Source: Based on *The Politics of Aristotle*, Ernest Barker, ed. and trans. (New York: Oxford University Press, 1970), pp. 113-115.

If a constitution, written or not, is perceived as a framework establishing the skeleton of a political system, the manner in which it is constructed, and the means by which it will operate, then an ideology should be perceived as the *goals* of that framework. To what end does the regime exist? What is its reason for being? What does it offer, distinct from other regimes, to justify its existence? These are all questions that are addressed by ideologies. *What* the regime wants to do, in a very general philosophical sense, is included in an ideology; *how* the regime will operate to achieve these ends is addressed through the constitutional structure of the regime.

Notes

1. Ivo Duchacek, *Power Maps: Comparative Politics of Constitutions* (Santa Barbara, Calif.: Clio Press, 1973).
2. See Robert Sharlet, *The New Soviet Constitution of 1977* (Brunswick, Ohio: King's Court Communications, 1978).
3. Ibid., p. 89.
4. Ibid., p. 92.
5. Ibid., p. 93.
6. S. E. Finer, ed., *Five Constitutions* (Sussex: Harvester Press, 1979), p. 15.
7. Ibid.
8. Richard Van Loon and Michael Whittington, *The Canadian Political System* (Toronto: McGraw-Hill Ryerson, 1976), pp. 169–170.
9. Thomas D. McGee, *Notes on Federal Governments: Past and Present* (Montreal: Dawson Brothers, 1865).
10. A very good recent study is that by Daniel Elazar, *Exploring Federalism* (Tuscaloosa: University of Alabama Press, 1987).
11. Frank Trager, "On Federalism," in Thomas Frank, *Why Federations Fail* (New York: New York University Press, 1968), pp. x–xi.
12. See S. Rufus Davis, *The Federal Principle* (Los Angeles: University of California Press, 1978), p. 11; and William Riker, *Federalism: Origin, Operation, Significance* (Boston: Little, Brown, 1964), p. 5.
13. See Sobei Mogi, *The Problem of Federalism* (London: Allen and Unwin, 1931).
14. Duchacek, *Power Maps*, p. 111.
15. Riker, *Federalism*, p. 1.
16. Arthur R. M. Lower, "Theories of Canadian Federalism—Yesterday and Today," in A.R.M. Lower, ed., *Evolving Canadian Federalism* (Durham, N.C.: Duke University Press, 1958), p. 3.
17. Ivo Duchacek, *Comparative Federalism: The Territorial Dimension of Politics* (New York: Holt, Rinehart & Winston, 1970), p. 198.
18. Ibid.
19. Ronald Watts, *New Federations: Experiments in the Commonwealth* (Oxford: Clarendon Press, 1966).
20. See Ursula K. Hicks, *Federalism: Failure and Success* (New York: Oxford University Press, 1978), pp. 144–171.
21. Ibid.
22. Duchacek, *Comparative Federalism*, p. 189.
23. Ibid., p. 191. See also Edward McWhinney, *Comparative Federalism* (Toronto: University of Toronto Press, 1962). A very good collection of articles on this subject matter can be found in the volume by Herman Bakvis and William Chandler, *Federalism and the Role of the State* (Toronto: University of Toronto Press, 1987).
24. Riker, *Federalism*, p. 6.
25. See Amitai Etzioni, *Political Unification* (New York: Holt, Rinehart & Winston, 1965), pp. 97–183, or William Livingston, ed., *Federalism in the Commonwealth* (London: Cassell, 1963).
26. A recent study of this problem is by Gregory Mahler, *New Dimensions of Canadian Federalism: Canada in a Comparative Perspective* (Rutherford, N.J.: Fairleigh Dickinson University Press, 1987).
27. A very good study of this method of policymaking is that by Richard Simeon, *Federal-Provincial Diplomacy: The Making of Recent Policy in Canada* (Toronto: University of Toronto Press, 1977). Simeon discusses

pensions, financial reform, and constitutional amendment as three case studies.

28. See especially Paul Spurlin, *Montesquieu in America: 1760–1801* (Baton Rouge: Louisiana State University Press, 1940); John Loy, *Montesquieu* (New York: Twayne, 1968); Arthur Prescott, *Drafting the Federal Constitution* (Baton Rouge: Louisiana State University Press, 1941); and Clinton Rossiter, *1787: The Grand Convention* (New York: Macmillan, 1966).

29. See John Locke, *Second Treatise on Civil Government* (especially chap. 13, "Of the Subordination of the Powers of the Commonwealth," pp. 87–94) in Ernest Barker, *Social Contract: Essays by Locke, Hume & Rousseau* (New York: Oxford University Press, 1970).

30. See David Easton, *A Systems Analysis of Political Life* (New York: Wiley, 1965), esp. p. 32.

31. Duchacek, *Power Maps*, p. 236.

32. Leon Baradat, *Political Ideologies: Their Origins and Impact* (Englewood Cliffs, N.J.: Prentice Hall, 1984), p. 6.

33. Howard Williams, *Concepts of Ideology* (New York: St. Martin's Press, 1987), p. xi.

34. Roy C. Macridis, *Contemporary Political Ideologies* (Cambridge: Winthrop, 1980), pp. 3–4.

35. Howard Williams, *Concepts of Ideology* (New York: St. Martin's Press, 1988), p. 122.

36. Baradat, *Political Ideologies*, p. 20.

37. Michael Curtis, *Comparative Government and Politics* (New York: Harper and Row, 1978), p. 41.

38. Curtis, *Comparative Government*, p. 158.

39. This discussion of the left-right spectrum and the five general attitudes to be found on it is based upon much more extensive discussion in Baradat, *Political Ideologies*, pp. 27–40.

40. Baradat, *Political Ideologies*, p. 30.

41. Ibid., p. 35.

42. Ibid., p. 39.

43. See William Ebenstein, *Today's Isms* (Englewood Cliffs, N.J.: Prentice Hall, 1973).

3

Political Development and Political Economics

Politics and Economics

A clear link exists between the political and the economic world. Economic status and power, on a national level, are often perceived as being associated with political status and power.[1] Nations with resources have the ability to influence nations without resources, and this is true whether the resources are oil, wheat, or chromium. Thus, it is important for us in this chapter to examine briefly the relationship between economic variables and political variables and to appreciate the very large differences in political and economic resources between the "developed" and the "developing" nations.

Developed and Developing Nations

In Chapter 1 we briefly discussed the concept of political development and the distinction between development and modernization, the latter having been described as "the process by which a society becomes 'modern.' "[2] One critic of the concept of modernization has suggested that modernization is not very helpful as an analytic tool because by definition the term "modernization" "is the equivalent of Westernization."[3] In a similar manner, one problem with the concept of "development" is, at least partially, that development implies a *normative* perspective.

> The starting-point is that we cannot avoid what the positivists disparagingly refer to as "value judgements." "Development" is inevitably a normative concept, almost a synonym for improvement. To pretend otherwise is just to hide one's value judgements.[4]

As a process, development is not only economic but is also "a multidimensional process involving the reorganization and reorientation of entire economic and social systems."[5]

Why is it that some countries are developed and others are not? That was the focus of much of the research in this field in the 1960s and 1970s. One of the classic works in the study of political development was by Walt Rostow, *The Stages of Economic Growth: A Non-Communist Manifesto* (1962).[6] Its emphasis was "on the psycho-cultural prerequisites of development,"[7] and it suggested that there were five stages of growth in the development process:

1. *Traditional society.* Prescientific, with a limit on how much economic development is possible.
2. *Preconditions for takeoff.* This involves the development of some science and expanded agricultural and industrial output, similar to that achieved in Western Europe by the eighteenth century.
3. *Takeoff.* This includes a rapid rise in the Gross Domestic Product, and expansion of economic and business institutions.
4. *The drive to technological maturity.* Here we include expansion of the investment base of the economy, and increased export markets with new products for the nation.
5. *High mass consumption.* This economy is based upon consumer goods and services, typical of those of the industrialized Western democracies today.[8]

Many criticized Rostow's framework because it assumed that all countries followed the same (predetermined) pathway to development, and because it was culturally (Western) biased. Although it is clearly the case that this framework should not be taken as an iron law that is universally applicable to all socie-ties—because all societies may not develop in the same stages, at the same time, and at the same speed—it is worth observing that there *are* some common patterns shared by many systems, as noted by Rostow. His work influenced many scholars but has not survived to the present day as a major influence in the discipline.

Another influence in thinking about development and mod-ernization was the work of Samuel Huntington, who in 1965 suggested that urbanization, literacy, modern communication, and mass participation could be seen as instruments of political *decay* rather than as instruments of progress.[9] Later Huntington expanded upon this idea:

> Modernization in practice always involves change in and usually the disintegration of a traditional political system, but it does not necessarily involve significant movement toward a modern politi-cal system. . . . Yet the tendency is to think that because social modernization is taking place, political modernization also must be taking place."[10]

Between the 1970s and the present time, the concept of "political development" as a discrete, identifiable process has been used less and less frequently as the basis for the analysis of Third World politics. Basically, it was concluded that the concept of development itself was ethnocentric; it was based on an (often unstated) assumption that the Western democracies were devel-oped and the countries of the Third World should aspire to become much the same as North America and Western Europe.

The distinction between the developed and the developing worlds sometimes is not as clear as we might like, although there is a general consensus of which nations belong to the two groups. Lists of developed nations include those that are members of the Organization for Economic Cooperation and Development (re-ferred to as the OECD). Excluding its three poorest members (Greece, Portugal, and Turkey), these nations had an average gross national product (GNP)* of over $11,000 in 1984, ranging

---

*The gross national product—the GNP—of a country is an estimation of the value of goods and services produced within a nation, and includes income sent into the country by citizens abroad, and excludes income that foreigners in the country send overseas. The gross domestic product—abbreviated GDP—is an estimation of the value of goods and services produced within a nation *not* including income sent into the country by citizens abroad, but including income that foreigners in the country send overseas.

from slightly more than $5,000 per capita in Ireland to over $17,000 per capita in Switzerland.

Frequently, the term "developing nations" is used interchangeably with "Third World"; strictly speaking, they are *not* the same thing. The term "Third World" refers to nations that are not in the Western, capitalistic, industrial, and (generally) democratic states, including the United States, Britain, France, Japan, and so on, and also *not* in what used to be called the East European Marxist-Leninist states, including the Soviet Union and its satellites.

It is usually not a good idea to define a term only by what it is *not*, because there may be tremendous variation left in the category one is examining; this is certainly true of the Third World. Some Third World nations have tremendous financial problems, such as Brazil, with a foreign debt of over $120 billion; others are extremely rich, such as Qatar with one of the highest per capita incomes in the world. To put Qatar and Brazil in the same category may make sense, but we have to be aware of what we are doing, and why.

There is a substantial literature devoted to the methodological question of how we should measure development. Often development is confused with economic growth; this can be a major problem in theory-building. If we believe that development is linked to poverty, unemployment, and inequality, for example, it is clear that a country's GNP can grow rapidly without our necessarily seeing any improvement in these three indicators of its "development."

One author has suggested that the term "Third World" implies a number of characteristics, including a colonial history; a relatively underdeveloped economy and level of technological development, especially when compared to the United States or Europe; a lack of interest and/or success in developing "modern" (that is, European) social, cultural, and economic institutions; and a commitment to work for greater world equality in the realm of economic and social policy.[11] Elsewhere, six common characteristics have been suggested as being typical of developing nations: (1) low levels of living standards; (2) low levels of productivity in work; (3) high rates of population growth; (4) high and rising levels of unemployment and underemployment; (5) dependence on agricultural production and "primary product exports"; and (6) dependence and vulnerability in international relations.[12]

The "third world" is one result of the process by which, since the late fifteenth century, the previously scattered peoples of the globe have been brought together into what is in many respects a single society, economy, and political system. . . . What distinguishes the third world is its peripherality. Economic peripherality has meant separation from, and subordination to, the dominant industrial economies which have developed especially in Europe and North America. . . .[13]

Developing nations include both low- and middle-income nation-states. The World Bank defines low income as it is used here as nations with less than a $410 per capita annual income. (For comparison, in 1988 Qatar had a per capita annual income of $27,000!) The average per capita GNP in these nations was less than $300 in 1984. Middle income nations were defined by the World Bank as those having more than $410 per capita annual income, and their average in 1984 was about $1,500 per capita.[14]

It is no coincidence, of course, that most members of what we call the Third World were the subjects of European colonialism, and most of the developed nations were the colonial powers themselves. Generally speaking, the significance of the system of colonialism can be found in "its lingering effects on the political and economic structures of Third World countries and on the psyche of colonized peoples, effects that have lingered because of the length and intensity of the experience."[15] European colonialism, among other things, created the "global political and economic order" which we know today.[16]

Although most of Latin America was independent by the middle of the nineteenth century, virtually the entire African continent was not independent until after World War II. We can find three interrelated sets of explanations for colonialism, socioeconomic, political, and romantic[17]; patterns of colonialism that existed around the world were often primarily economic in nature, where the colonial powers developed and exploited markets for their goods, as well as developing and exploiting sources of primary materials for their own industries. Thus the developing nations were sources of materials for industries in the colonial nations, and often did not develop any industries themselves.

Following the end of World War II most colonial empires began to be dismantled, and by the mid-1960s only a few colonial territories remained; by the 1980s there remained only a very few "microcolonies," as they were called, virtually all of them islands."[18] We can point to Bermuda, Martinique, the Falkland Islands, and so on, as examples of remnants of colonial empires; these few examples are dwarfed by the long lists of new nations that have emerged from colonial domination.

The Distribution of Economic Resources

A tremendous differentiation exists in how economic resources are distributed around the world. As described by one author, an "average nuclear family" household in North America would consist of a family of four with an annual income of about $25,000 to $30,000 who live in an apartment or a suburban house, with separate bedrooms for each of the children and the parents, with many consumer goods, adequate food, and with the members of the family receiving adequate health care. The children would be able to attend college, if they so desired, and would live to an average age of 72 to 75 years.

On the other hand, a "typical extended family" household in Asia would consist of ten or more people, including parents, five to seven children, grandparents, and some aunts and uncles. The combined annual income of the household, both in money and "in kind" (including the food they grow), would be between $150 and $200 per year, on the average. They would probably live in a single room, and the parents and the older children would be agricultural workers. Typically, there would not be enough food to eat, the children would not attend school beyond a few years of elementary school, and there would be inadequate health care.[19]

As many observers have noted, the process of development in recent years has given reasons for both optimism and pessimism. On one hand, a number of developing nations appear to have made real and substantial economic progress over the last two decades or so. According to the World Bank, the increase in the gross domestic product of the developing countries at large in the two decades between 1960 and 1980 averaged about 6 percent. Illustrations of this progress would include an increase in life expectancy (from 42 years in 1960 to 49 years in 1982), a decline in infant mortality (cut in half during this period), and an increase in primary school enrollment (rising from 50 percent to 94 percent).[20]

However, these figures are *averages*, and as such they indicate that although some groups of individuals and/or nations have enjoyed improvements in their lot in life, others have not enjoyed the same improvements. It is clear that most of the items that are measured by these figures—such as wealth, income, job opportunities, education, medical care, housing, and agricultural production—are not evenly distributed among nations. We can take as an example of this the per capita GNP of the United Arab Emirates of $11,900 annually in 1987—based upon oil production—with the GNP of Tanzania of $258—based upon not much of a developed economy at all.[21] Infant mortality rates per 1,000 live births vary dramatically: 205 for Sierra Leone, 129 for Bolivia, 8 for Denmark.[22]

According to one observer the "average per capita real incomes in the large majority of developing countries, especially in African and Asian low income ones, are no higher than they were in the late 1960s, and many seem to have retrogressed."[23] Among *non*-oil producing countries, their average per capita economic growth declined from about 3 percent annually in the 1960s and 1970s to almost zero in 1981, and negative figures in the two years thereafter.[24] Although some Third World nations have substantial oil or mineral resources, such as members of OPEC (Organization of Petroleum Exporting Countries); or Chile, Peru, Zaire, and Zambia, which control the world's copper supply; or Guinea, Guyana, Jamaica, and Sierra Leone, which control much of the planet's bauxite trade, "the vast majority of Third World countries are not so well endowed, being dependent on agricultural production."[25]

The "basic needs" approach to the study of development focuses on the question of the distribution of income and the distribution of "certain standards" of nutrition, health, and education services. It advocates "making the meeting of certain fundamental human needs a development priority," and is a widely shared approach to the study of the process of political development.[26]

Not only are there dramatic differences *among* nations in terms of many of the basic needs of life, but it is often the case that *within* nations in which there has been a net increase in the standard of living, this increase is not evenly shared. In fact, the national increase is usually a product of a significant rise for a minority of the population, while the majority of the population continue to exist with traditional standards of living. This phenomenon is illustrated in Table 3.1 by the cases of India and

Table 3.1
Distribution of Income in Six Nations, 1986

Country	GNP Ranking per Capita	Percent of Nat'l Income Received by Top 10% of Population	Percent of Nat'l Income Received by Bottom 40% of Population
United States	4	26.6	15.2
West Germany	10	30.3	16.8
South Africa	32	40.9	6.7
Poland	36	21.2	23.4
India	108	35.2	17.2
Tanzania	113	41.6	13.5

Source: Rankings from World Bank, *World Development Report, 1986* (New York: Oxford University Press, 1986), pp. 180–181; income data from George Kurian, *New Book of World Rankings* (New York: Facts on File, 1984), p. 101.

Tanzania. The case of South Africa is the most extreme. There the poorest 40 percent of the population receive only 6.7 percent of the national income, whereas the richest 10 percent of the population receive 40.9 percent of the national income!

International Financial Relations and Debt

The inequality between and among nations in their wealth and economic viability has led to a growing system of *international dependence,* in which the "have-not" nations have come to rely more and more upon the aid programs of the "have" nations in order to survive. In many respects "the history of the Third World is to a large extent the history of its incorporation into a global economy dominated by the 'core' industrialised countries of Western Europe and the United States."[27] The programs of these core nations include grants, loans, and in-kind assistance (e.g., wheat or tractors). The economic dependence of the developing nations upon the developed nations has grown into a major international problem in recent years as the international debts of some of the have-not nations have skyrocketed, and the likelihood that they will ever be able to repay their loans has decreased. The foreign-debt problem is especially troubling to some because it often carries with it the spectre of foreign intervention.[28] One recent study has suggested that over the next few years "Latin America will have to appropriate as much as about 30 percent of its export earnings for payment of interest on its external debt."[29]

Indeed, in July 1989 Brazil missed making a payment of $812 million owed to foreign governments, primarily because its trade surplus* with foreign countries had decreased in recent years, and Brazil's government was concerned that a payment of that size could adversely affect the national economy. Brazil's inability to keep up payments on its present debts in turn affects the ease with which it will receive future loans. Indeed, at the time that Brazil missed this payment, action had just been taken to freeze several loans, including $900 million in fund loans, $600 million in commercial bank loans, and about $1.5 billion in Japanese assistance. Recently the World Bank tabled plans for two loans to Brazil totaling $725 million.[30]

One scholar has argued that:

> it is high time for the foreign aid community to take a hard look at costs and benefits of its work in general systems terms. How much has been spent and how much has been gained in overall results? How much have taxpayers in advanced countries contributed, and to what benefit, to those who live in poverty. . . . Development organizations would be well advised to undertake self-evaluations to determine (1) to what extent they have helped the developing world; (2) to what extent they have caused or contributed to Third-World problems; and (3) who in the final analysis has benefited the most from the total amount of aid—the poor or the privileged of the Third World, Western commercial firms, or development bureaucrats, experts, and specialists?[31]

Many Third World nations are in the unfortunate position of having *single-product economies*, or nearly that, so that when their single crop or industrial product loses its value on the world market the economy of the nation is severely hurt. Among recent examples of this type of problem might be included the economy of the small Caribbean island of St. Vincent when the price of sugar fell sharply; the economy of Nigeria or Mexico when the world price of oil declined; or the economy of Chile when the price of copper plummeted. A virtually single-product economy can also leave a nation vulnerable if it sells most of its product to only one

---

*The trade surplus is the amount of the excess of value of sales of Brazilian goods over the value of imported goods.

other nation: One of the reasons that Brazil's economy took a downward turn had to do with its dependency upon world agricultural markets and the failure in the world market of some of its cash crops.[32]

Part of the problems faced by Third World countries can be attributed to a lack of economic independence that we suggested previously. It has generally been accepted that the economic success of Third World nations is very dependent upon the economic growth and expansion of the large industrialized nations.[33]

Economic development often in practice means *industrialization*, because economies entirely dependent upon agriculture do not have high GNPs. The world's poorest nations are primarily agricultural and rural, whereas the richest nations are industrial and urban. Associated with industrialization we can find higher literacy, higher GNPs, lower infant mortality, better health care, and a generally higher standard of living.

Economic Nationalism

There appears to be no clear-cut definition of exactly what economic nationalism is, or what set of domestic and international policies are mandated by economic nationalism. According to Peter J. Burnell, the term, however, "often carries, and is intended to carry, considerably normative weight, favourable or pejorative, depending on who is stating the claim."[34] The general idea implied by the term usually involves a strong feeling that the interests of the nation, as defined in a certain way (e.g., social, political, economic, cultural), should take priority in economic policy-making, regardless of past practices, long-term goals, or short-run economic hurdles.

Economic nationalism does not necessarily mean opposition to all foreign interests, for what is in the interests of one's own nation may also be in the interests of others. Similarly, the primary targets of economic nationalism may not be a specific country or group of countries, but could be a type of multinational corporation (e.g., mining companies), or all foreign multinational corporations for that matter.

Typically, the economic goals of nationalists involve developing industry in one's own country, broadening markets in international trade, decreasing economic dependence upon one or a few other countries, and regaining (or gaining for the first time, for that matter) domestic economic control of important sectors of the economy (e.g., regaining control of the copper mines from foreign multinationals in Chile; nationalizing the asbestos mines in Quebec; or developing a domestic soft-drink market in India). The overall goal, then, is "a desire for greater national economic independence."[35] Additionally, there have been regional variations on the theme of economic nationalism, such as "pan-Arabism," "pan-Islam," "pan-Africanism," "Asian cooperation," and "pan-Americanism," to name some of the more visible examples.[36]

Foreign investment is often a target of economic nationalism. This type of investment is often sought by developing nations, because it brings to a nation much-needed capital, thus helping to create industry and jobs, which in turn help to create other industries and jobs. Problems may develop, however, when specific foreign industries become too large and powerful, or when a government suddenly perceives that it is not able to control the direction of its own economy because substantial economic actors—often the multinational corporations—have their own goals and strategies. According to Burnell, "Experience has shown . . . that foreign direct investment . . . will not necessarily bring to an LDC [less developed country] many, let alone all, of the possible benefits" sought by the promotion of foreign investment.[37]

Institutions and Economic Development

Because our stress in this book is on political institutions, a word should be said about how the institutions on which we will be focusing our attention affect political development and economic policy. As one source notes: "Given the difficult task of creating political order in Third World countries, the processes of selecting and implementing constitutional processes are important. If constitutional processes fail to take hold, as is the case in many Third World countries, political development is greatly retarded."[38] Specifically, do institutions help shape the distribution process of economic values? Do institutions affect economic stability? Do some structures enhance economic development or detract from it, and why?

In recent years, more attention has been paid to "institutional" development in the Third World. This is for several reasons, primary among which is that "national economic management capacity is critically dependent on the efficient functioning of a few key national institutional processes such as budgeting and personnel management."[39] Moreover, as one author has noted:

> To shorten a long and complicated story, the failure of development efforts is assumed to be due basically to the weaknesses of the political systems of the LDCs [less developed countries]. Given the paramount importance of the political system in providing leadership and direction for all other systems—economic, social, and administrative—the political system's inability to fulfill its role adversely affects the performance of all other sectors.[40]

Economic development is dependent on the capacity of a number of institutions to respond to both project and policy initiatives.[41]

The purpose of economic policy in both developing and developed nations is the same: to guide or control the economy in such a way as to influence the size, growth, and distribution of its gross national product.[42] There is, obviously, an extremely wide range of policies that might be available to any government to use to influence the economy, including government expenditures, the level and composition of taxes, the role of local governments and other organizations in making and administering policy, monetary policy and institutions, trade policy, protectionism, and tariffs and exchange rates. These activities, and others, may be used in four broad areas of policy intervention including (1) altering the distribution of income through policies designed to change prices; (2) redistributing ownership of assets; (3) redistributing income through progressive income and wealth taxes; and (4) direct transfer payments and public provision of goods and services (e.g., public health programs, school lunch programs).[43]

Centralization and Decentralization

The concept of the political centralization of economic planning has been shown to have a direct relevance for the process of economic and political development.[44] During the years after 1970 many Third World governments tried new approaches to economic and social policy-making that included "decentralized authority for planning and administration to state, regional, district, and local agencies, field units of central ministries, local governments, and special-purpose organizations."[45]

been a fairly consistent movement to encourage local government and local administration.

> It seems that local government exists as a form of bureaucracy, but the constant revival of the concept of local elections reflects either a form of collective conscience that reminds leaders of the positive values in self-government, or a pragmatic approach that recognizes the value of local participation for achieving central goals.[48]

Pakistan, Thailand, Malaysia, and the Philippines are also among Asian nations that have undertaken experiments in decentralization in the last two decades.

Not only can government structures be slightly decentralized through a federal organization, but administration can be decentralized, too. In Thailand the government undertook between 1967 and 1981 to decentralize the administrative process to be both more flexible and more responsive to local needs. Actions undertaken by the government included decentralizing industrial management, basic economic services, and social services, so as to increase the number of people who could benefit from governmental services and increase production opportunities for business. This included giving local authorities power over how some development funds would be spent, seeking local input on how villages should be organized and planned.[49]

An African example of this movement toward decentralization can be found in the case of Kenya, where the government began to decentralize planning and administration responsibilities in the early 1970s. This move to decentralization was prompted by a dissatisfaction with the results of planning undertaken by the central government, and by a desire on the part of local leaders and administrators to play a more active role in the overall planning process.[50]

In Latin America the process of decentralization has met with great institutional opposition, primarily because "concentration of decision making within central government ministries, often referred to as overcentralization, is a fundamental characteristic of Latin American governments."[51] Much of the push toward decentralization in Latin America has resulted in the creation of "autonomous" government agencies; in a sense it is a curious form of decentralization because power still resides at the center, but it is placed with a different structure at the center.

As used here, the term "d₁
ring planning and administra₁
government in a political system
tions, local governments, or specia₁
tions.[46] Several good reasons exist ft
administration in the Third World. Sp₁

1. Allows planners and managers to be c₁
   are trying to solve;
2. Minimizes "red tape," which results from
   vices;
3. Helps to increase officials' awareness of local
4. Encourages penetration of policies into hinterl₁
   far removed from the nation's capital where gove₁
   may be viewed as irrelevant;
5. Allows for greater representation for ethnic, religi₁
   groups in society in the policy-making process;
6. Encourages the development of leadership and adi₁
   experience among people who might never have that o₁
   all decisions to be made at the center;
7. Increases the efficiency of government at the center by
   officials at the center from having to spend a great deal o₁
   making decisions that could be made by individuals at the fie₁
   local level;
8. Increases communication and coordination between the center an₁
   the more remote areas of the nation;
9. Encourages more citizen participation in planning and administration;
10. Decreases the domination of the policy-making process by "en-
    trenched local elites who are often unsympathetic to national
    development policies and insensitive to the needs of the poorer
    groups in rural communities";
11. Encourages greater flexibility and innovation;
12. Allows leaders to locate facilities and services in communities
    where they will be more useful than communities that might be
    selected by centralized leadership;
13. Increases stability and national unity by encouraging participa-
    tion; and
14. Increases the efficiency with which public goods and services are
    delivered to the people of a nation.[47]

In Asia many of the best examples of conflicts over decentralization can be found in India, where despite a centralized federal
system established by the British colonial government, there has

For example, there are over 500 decentralized organizations and what have been called "parastatal enterprises" that have been established by the Mexican government, including Petroleos Mexicanos (the state petroleum corporation, PEMEX) and the state coffee marketing board as illustrations of decentralized organizations, and numerous banks, hotels, sugar mills, and food industries as examples of parastatal enterprises. Additionally, over 800 independent commissions and councils, including the National Council on Agriculture and the Federal Commission on Electricity Rates, are significant public organizations involved in the creation and administration of public policy.

These parastatal enterprises operate legally, much as would private corporations, the greatest significant difference being that they have representatives of the government on their boards of directors, and their activities are generally subject to the oversight of the government. The centralized organizations are legally distinct, own their own property, and have their own governing boards, but they fall under provisions of administrative law rather than commercial law, as is the case with parastatal enterprises.[52]

Other attempts at decentralization in Latin America have resulted in regionalization, in the case of Venezuela seeking "to establish a new level of government between the center and the states and municipalities that can plan and coordinate the activities of all government units within each region."[53]

It is interesting to note that at the same time that we can identify movements toward decentralization of government in Third World countries around the world, the motivations for decentralizing planning and administration are not always the same. In some countries a desire for greater political legitimacy is the driving force; elsewhere the motivation comes from demands from regional, ethnic, tribal, or religious groups for greater participation in the policy-making process. In most instances, however, decentralization was seen as a way to make government more responsive, more efficient, and more effective.

Legislatures and Development

The link between elected assemblies and political development is a very significant one, because legislative institutions help to provide the legitimacy for the change and "dynamism" that are inherent in the term "development".[54] Very often the legislature as an institution is especially vulnerable to attack in a developing system because it is one of the few institutions specifically oriented to promote discussion, interest articulation, and thereby the legitimacy of the regime:

> The legislature is the political institution most likely to define political issues, and policies to resolve those issues, in sectional terms. The legislature is also perceived by executive decisionmakers as a body which lacks the expertise necessary to properly consider complex issues, and as a threat.[55]

As an institution, the legislature is especially concerned with the development of linkages between the political center of the nation and the nation's more peripheral regions. Legislators are often concerned with such issues as political representation, resource allocation, and public support for the legislature and, thereby, the regime.[56]

Bureaucracy and Development

One of the major problems faced by developing nations, to which we alluded above, is that they do not possess the number of individuals with a sufficient level of bureaucratic skill to keep their new governments running relatively smoothly. Some new nations, such as India, were left with a reasonably large pool of trained talent when their colonizing powers left; elsewhere, in Africa for example, colonial powers pulled out of nations without leaving behind an adequate cadre of trained and experienced administrative talent.

The implications of this shortfall are immediately clear. Although the term "bureaucracy" may have negative connotations in many parts of the world, all nations need a body of individuals to administer programs, oversee the development of policy, and participate in the day-to-day operation of the government. Developing nations are, in respect of this need, no different from developed nations; their problem usually lies in not having an adequate supply of bureaucratic talent. As one observer noted, "African administrators whose responsibilities until recently were characterized by routine are catapulted to the top of the hierarchy, where they are expected to advise ministers and politicians regarding major programs of economic and social development."[57]

We shall return to a discussion of the role of the bureaucracy in Chapter 5, which examines the political executive.

Political Parties and Development

Other political institutions, apart from those described in a constitution, may have an impact on political and economic development. Such development-related issues as political participation, political legitimacy, national integration, and the management of conflict can be affected by political parties as well as by constitutional structures such as legislatures, for example.

Political parties clearly have an impact on types and levels of political participation, especially movements and demands for political participation, which "are a characteristic feature of political development."[58] Although the existence of political parties "does not in itself guarantee that governing elites . . . will welcome expanded political participation,"[59] parties are associated with the kind of debate, discussion, and interest group activity conducive to expanded participation.

Political parties are a vehicle to mobilize the populace, and thus are an almost absolutely necessary structure for a system involved in political development. Even a one-party government can be democratic and mobilizing and thereby helpful in the developmental process.

Parties also can be significant in the process of legitimization of political authority, important in the development process. Parties assist in the processes of political recruitment and political socialization, and help to pass on the political culture of the regime from one generation to another.

Although parties are not absolutely essential to the process of national integration (because we can identify a number of nations that resolved their "crises of national integration" before the advent of political parties), they can be very important in this function for contemporary developing nations. According to one view: "In most new nations of Asia and Africa, governing political parties are concerned with two elements of national integration— the issue of control over the nation's territory and the issue of subjective loyalties."[60]

Finally, political parties can be important vehicles for the resolution of conflict in developing systems. Parties often serve as "brokerage" mechanisms helping to facilitate conflict between and among groups in societies, especially in societies in which democratic elections are the vehicle for the selection of leaders.

Other Influences on Development

These three structures, legislatures, bureaucracy, and political parties, by no means make up an exhaustive list of the political structures and institutions that can influence the process of political development. Rather, they are indicated here simply as *illustrations* of the types of linkages that can exist between political institutions and the development process. Indeed, substantial research has focused on the impact of communications on political development,[61] the impact of education on political development,[62] and the political culture on political development,[63] to name only a few of the behavior and institutional subjects of inquiry in this regard.

Political Economics and Political Development

The problems suggested by the interaction of political economics and political development are faced everywhere in the contemporary world. Economic development requires political leadership and "control, integration, and coordination of financial and personnel management at the national level with conventional development efforts."[64] One useful indicator of the importance of political control for economic policy "lies in the priority which economic development has as a political goal of government."[65] As one observer has noted:

> All societies (developed and developing, rich and poor, high, middle, or low income) are faced with decisions concerning production, consumption, resource allocation, distribution, and growth. How these decisions are made, as well as their outcomes, depends on the interplay of a variety of general and specific factors. The general factors are those over which countries have very little or no control, for example, natural resource endowments, economic size, and international economic forces. Specific factors include a given country's unique history, the sociocultural environment, and

the government's political ideology as is normally reflected in specific programs and policies it is willing to pursue.[66]

Theories of Development

The problem with much of what has been called "development theory" is that it has not adequately explained the phenomenon of development and evolution of political systems. "Dependency Theory" became popular in the 1960s, and suggested solutions to the problem of a lack of economic development. The most common explanation of the theory was that underdevelopment was not simply a temporary condition leading, eventually, to development, but rather that underdevelopment was directly related to—and some said caused by—the expansion of capitalism and industrialism elsewhere in the world.[67] "The tendency to use the formula of *dependencia* to explain everything that seems wrong in the Third World has been at once understandable and quite damaging. . . ."[68]

Dependency theory made some important contributions to an understanding of the political world, however.[69] It showed us that modern developing nations differ in significant ways from the industrializing Western nations of the past, that world economic conditions offer constraints to today's developing nations, and that there is an interaction between political, social, and economic factors in the process of development.[70]

Generally speaking, four broad schools of "development theory" can be said to exist, or to have existed,[71] although as we noted earlier they are no longer widely used. These are the liberal model, the historicist approach, the managerial approach, and the neo-Marxist approach.[72] We shall briefly describe each of these approaches here.

The *liberal model* of development suggested, most simply, that the process of development is a linear one, that stages or developmental phases are passed in the same order, and that all countries go through the development process. The "advanced" nations, the assumption went, started the process of development earlier, and the developing countries were simply at an earlier stage of the process, and would follow the evolution of the developed nations.

The *historicist approach* objected to the assumption of the liberal model that all countries would follow the same process.

These social scientists suggested that not all societies started their evolution at the same point, and they further suggested that because many Western characteristics were missing in a great number of developing societies, "many of the institutional configurations that characterized the transformation of Western societies were unlikely to be duplicated in subsequent modernization of other societies."[73] In other words, not all systems would follow the same pattern of political evolution, but rather would mature as a consequence of particular national characteristics.

The *managerial approach* focused, as its name suggests, less on the broader questions of how political structures and behavior evolved, and more on questions of how problems are solved in society and how policy is made and evaluated. One of the most influential voices in this school moved his emphasis from having the goal of development be democracy, to having the goal of development be stability and institutional order.[74]

Finally, the *neo-Marxist approach* focuses not on the stages of development, or on the specific factors that influence development, or on how problems are solved in the development process, but rather on the "pathology of development, namely underdevelopment."

> The central idea of the neo-Marxist is that far from being independent occurrences, the development of the industrial countries and the underdevelopment of poor countries are opposite phases of the same historical process. . . . The historical process of the expansion and development of capitalism throughout the world simultaneously generated and continues to generate both economic development and structural underdevelopment.[75]

Problems of Development

It has been concluded, generally speaking, that "the cumulative benefits of economic growth have not 'trickled down,' or have not otherwise been sufficiently 'diffused' to the masses of the population in the developing world."[76] Indeed, whatever scholars' differences in theoretical approaches to problems of development, there is some general consensus on practical problems: "those on the Left and on the Right as well as those in the middle tend to agree that the rate of growth achieved by most less-developed countries (LDCs) after four decades of foreign assistance is less than satisfactory, if not disappointing."[77] There are a vast number of general problem areas that are significant across these LDCs, a few of which we shall briefly discuss here.

Population. At the end of the 1980s the world's population was estimated to be nearly 5.5 billion people. United Nations projections predict a world population of over 6.1 billion by the year 2000, and over 8.3 billion by the year 2025.[78] Population is a significant issue in the study of development for two distinct, but interrelated, reasons. First among these, of course, is the argument suggested by Thomas Malthus in 1798 (*An Essay on the Principle of Population*) that the increase in population in a society will outstrip any increases in production or economic growth to be found in the economy, and that the only way for societies to avoid a "condition of chronic low levels of living" was for people to engage in "moral restraint" and limit the growth of their families.[79] Second, it has been argued that population increases often have favorable or unfavorable effects on the growth rates of economies.

At the beginning of the eighteenth century the world population doubling time was 240 years; at the beginning of the twentieth century it was 115 years, and in the 1930–1950 period it was 70 years. As illustrated in Table 3.2, the world's population has increased the *rate* at which it is increasing, and today the world's population doubles approximately every 35 to 40 years.[80] Furthermore, as shown in Table 3.3, the proportion of the world's population living in the "underdeveloped" world is increasing: In 1950 approximately 67 percent of the world's population lived in

Table 3.2
World Population Increase

Year	Population
1750	731,000,000
1800	890,000,000
1850	1,171,000,000
1900	1,668,000,000
1950	2,525,000,000
1980	4,432,000,000
2000	6,121,000,000 (predicted)

Table 3.3
Concentration of World Population (in millions)

	1950		1980		2000	
	Number	*Percent*	*Number*	*Percent*	*Number*	*Percent*
World, total	2,525		4,432		6,121	
Developed	832	33.0	1,131	25.5	1,271	20.8
Underdeveloped	1,693	67.0	3,301	74.5	4,849	79.2

Source: Based on data provided in J. Faaland and J.R. Parkinson, *The Political Economy of Development* (New York: St. Martin's Press, 1986), p. 169.

"underdeveloped" nations; by the year 2000 it is expected that this figure will rise to almost 80 percent.

Although the size of one's family may be a matter of personal concern, it also has national and societal implications: If a nation's population grows at a rate faster than the increase of its economy, to take a simple illustration, the increase in the amount of available food will not be adequate for the increase in mouths seeking that food. Conversely, of course, a population that is too *small* may limit the potential expansion of an economy; a nation cannot increase its factories if there are no people to work in those factories.

Not only is the *growth* of population a problem but so too is its *distribution*. Increasingly, populations are moving out of the rural areas of nations and into urban centers, often in search of jobs and a better life. Ironically, with this movement comes an increase in slums and overcrowded and unhealthy living environments. Beginning in 1975, Mexico City has had a growth rate of 160 percent; Calcutta grew at a rate of 114 percent; Bogota, Colombia, experienced a growth rate of 193 percent. Correspondingly, 60 percent of Bogota's population live in slums; 46 percent of Mexico City's population live in slums, and 67 percent of Calcutta's population are residents of slums.[81]

India was the first developing country in the world to officially adopt a family-planning program: In the 1970s it was hoped that the government would be able to reach 90 million couples and convince half of them to limit the size of their families. To do this the government set up over 5,000 family-welfare planning centers in rural settings across the country. The program was criticized for a number of reasons, one of which was that it overestimated the effectiveness of its "motivators," individuals who were charged with advocating smaller families.

> What . . . can you hope to accomplish in preaching family planning to a mass of starving illiterates living in dilapidated huts and unsanitary conditions, suffering from diseases and disabilities, and for whom life is an unending chain of misery, degradation and deprivation?[82]

One critical study estimated that in the period 1968 to 1969 less than twenty-one sterilizations and fewer than eight IUD insertions were done for every technical staff person in the program, not a very impressive rate of results.

In 1976 the Indian government started a new program that in effect included compulsory sterilization; over 7 million individuals were sterilized as part of this effort. This type of public policy raises some significant philosophical warning flags: How far do we want governments to regulate personal behavior? This program may have been more effective than its predecessors in terms of "results," but politically "the revulsion against this contributed to the downfall of Mrs. Gandhi's government in 1977."[83]

One study has suggested that there are six general policy options available to governments in their efforts to control population:

1. Through media and educational efforts to try to persuade people to have smaller families;
2. To establish family-planning programs to provide contraceptive services to encourage smaller families;
3. To provide economic incentives (and disincentives) to encourage smaller families;
4. To move families away from urban areas and toward rural areas to balance the distribution of the population (although this option does not limit growth);
5. To coerce people into having smaller families through laws and penalties;
6. To raise the social and economic status of women, thus encouraging delayed marriages and smaller families for professional women.[84]

There are clear reasons why a government might want to establish population-planning policies. The problem is that population policy runs squarely into questions of religious belief and issues affecting the most personal of family decisions, and governments have not been very effective in putting their policies into force. From an individual perspective, it may be a rational policy for a rural villager in Africa, for example, to have a large family: Without a social security system, this individual will be supported in his old age by his children. The best way to make sure that he has many children to help support him when he is old is to have many (more) children when he can, since he must allow for some level of infant mortality. From the national perspective, of course, this is *not* an optimal policy, since if a single family has, say, ten children, and each of those ten children marry and have ten children, and so on, the population growth will rapidly become an intolerable burden on society.

Quality of Life. Many people in Third World nations are constantly struggling against malnutrition and disease. Life expectancy in 1988 averaged about 49 years in the least-developed countries, as compared with 57 years in other Third World nations and 73 years in developed countries. In the mid-1970s, almost half of the population of the developing world (excluding China), over a *billion* people, lived on inadequate diets, and one-third of them were children under the age of two.[85]

Education. In many Third World countries, the "education industry" is the largest consumer of public revenues.[86] Literacy rates remain quite low in developing nations, averaging only 34 percent of the population in the least-developed countries, compared with 65 percent in other Third World nations and 99 percent in the developed world.[87] Overall, it has been argued that "educational systems largely reflect and reproduce, rather than alter, the economic and social structures of the societies in which they exist."[88]

Agriculture. It is clear that agriculture-based economies are not associated with rapid economic development. As industry expands, agriculture's share of the overall economy declines. Among the poorest countries in the world, only Benin has less than half of its population working in the agricultural sector; in many of the poorest countries more than 80 percent of the population is engaged in agriculture. In Bangladesh this figure exceeds 90 percent.[89] Although countries differ greatly in their agricultural resources (including the quality of the soil, irrigation, and so on), new varieties of grains and plants and technology can make a remarkable difference in the economic productivity of an agricultural economy.

The basic objective of international concern over agriculture, of course, is to guarantee that all people will have adequate food supplies. The goal of governmental policy-making in this area is not only to expand food supplies by increasing production, especially in low-income, food-deficit countries, but also to maximize the stability of supplies in the face of production fluctuations and to secure access to food supplies on the part of all, especially the poor people and poor nations.[90]

Industry and Employment. One of the most important questions that governments must face in this area has to do with the distinction between the public and private sectors of the economy. Often these questions are preempted by fundamental ideological positions of the policy. For example, Lenin would not have considered private enterprise as a tool of national economic policy; conversely, state-owned industries are not popular tools in systems based upon free enterprise. It is often the case that "the net effect of these various influences, except where there is a total commitment to public ownership, is that a mixed industrial sector emerges, partitioned (but not always neatly) between public and private operation."[91] In most developing countries, in fact, state-owned enterprises, such as utilities, transportation companies, or major industries, are common.[92]

Trade, Debt, and Foreign Economic Relations. The problem of international debt, and particularly debt owed by developing nations to developed nations, is one that is attracting more and more attention today. Debate focuses on who is to blame for the developing nations not being able to pay their obligations, how the problem should be resolved, and what structures should be developed to prevent these problems from recurring in the future.

Many argue that the current debt problem reflects a gross financial irresponsibility on the part of the debtor nations, suggesting that they continued borrowing money to "prop up" their societies without any regard for the future. Others suggest that this simply isn't true, that the developed nations actually encouraged the developing nations to borrow money, contributing to a higher growth rate of the world's economy. "As late as 1981 many of these nations were upheld by the international financial institutions as the very model of economic management, precisely at a time when they had already accumulated vast debts,"[93] according to one observer.

The question of long-term responses has also been discussed at some length. Even if the quite substantial debts of the developing nations could simply be erased, the problem would not be solved. This statement applies equally well to present-day debt renegotiations, in which the developed nations—and financial institutions in those nations—lend the developing nations more money to cover their present payments, or allow them to postpone payments on part of the principal and interest that they owe at the present time. These actions do not solve the problem; they simply postpone the problem; the debts will still be there, and the developing nations are hardly likely to be able to make the payments any more easily in the future (when in fact their debts will be greater) than they can today (see Table 3.4).

Even if the debt were done away with, the more fundamental problems would remain. There is a developmental problem that has to do with a substantial proportion of the world's nations not having sufficient resources, or sufficiently developed resources, to offer their populations what they consider the basic require-

Table 3.4
Debt Figures for Six Developing Nations (in billions of dollars)

Nation	Total External Debt	Economic Growth Rate[a]
Brazil	$120.1	4.8%
Mexico	107.4	0.2
Argentina	59.6	1.4
Venezuela	35.0	1.2
Nigeria	30.5	−0.3
Philippines	30.2	−0.1

[a]Computed by calculating the average annual growth in the gross domestic product between 1982 and 1988.

Source: Adapted from *The New York Times*, July 8, 1989, p. 15.

ments of life. The solution to this problem will require a wide range of actions, including increasing trade with the developing world, increasing investments in the developing world, restructuring of tariff barriers affecting trade with the developing world, increasing the resources available to the developing world, and so on.[94]

The Future for Developing Nations

The more one studies the developing world, the more serious the perceived problems become. The nations of the developing world face a number of crises, one more serious than the other. Often in situations of having shortages of food, raw materials, and a lack of industrial development, as well as an excess of population, these nations face almost insurmountable odds in the contemporary world. Even if one or two of these crises could be resolved, there would still be other problems, equally difficult to resolve, that would need to be overcome.

Among other things, there needs to be institutional development in these countries. That is, if we define development as "an increased capacity for problem solving,"[95] then one of the most desperately needed quantities in the developing world is an increase in the governmental institutions to assist in this increased capacity for problem solving. "Institutional change is primarily an entrepreneurial activity depending very much on the ability of practitioners to gain and retain the interest and attention of top decision makers."[96]

The real challenge for the developing world will be to see whether the resource and institutional growth that are so necessary for political and economic stability can take place in time, before the nations involved are absolutely overwhelmed by the crushing burden of debt, poverty, and population.

Notes

1. Wilfred L. David, *Conflicting Paradigms in the Economics of Developing Nations* (New York: Praeger, 1986), p. 3.
2. John Kautsky, *The Political Consequences of Modernization* (New York: Wiley, 1972), pp. 19–20.

3. Jacqueline Braveboy-Wagner, *Interpreting the Third World: Politics, Economics, and Social Issues* (New York: Praeger, 1986), p. 165.
4. Dudley Seers, "What Are We Trying to Measure?" in Nancy Baster, ed., *Measuring Development: The Role and Adequacy of Development Indicators* (London: Frank Cass, 1972), p. 22.
5. Michael P. Todaro, *Economic Development in the Third World* (New York: Longman, 1989), p. 62.
6. W. W. Rostow, *The Stages of Economic Growth* (Cambridge: Cambridge University Press, 1962).
7. Vicky Randall and Robin Theobald, *Political Change and Underdevelopment: A Critical Introduction to Third World Politics* (Durham, N.C.: Duke University Press, 1985), p. 19.
8. This summation of Rostow's framework is found in J. Faaland and J.R. Parkinson, *The Political Economy of Development* (New York: St. Martin's Press, 1986), pp. 5–6.
9. Samuel P. Huntington, "Political Development and Political Decay," *World Politics* 17 (1965): 386–430.
10. Samuel P. Huntington, *Political Order in Changing Societies* (New Haven: Yale University Press, 1968), p. 35.
11. Braveboy-Wagner, *Interpreting the Third World*, p. 2.
12. Todaro, *Economic Development*, p. 27.
13. Christopher Clapham, *Third World Politics: An Introduction* (Madison: University of Wisconsin Press, 1985), p. 3.
14. The "middle income" group itself has an extremely broad range, and it is divided into a "lower middle income" group and an "upper middle income group." The "lower middle income" group has an average income of $840 per capita, ranging from $440 (Sudan) to $1,500 (Colombia) per capita. The "upper middle income" group has an average income of $2,500 per capita, ranging from $1,680 (Syria) to $6,840 (Trinidad and Tobago) per capita. David, *Conflicting Paradigms*, p. 4–5.
15. Braveboy-Wagner, *Interpreting the Third World*, p. 19.
16. Clapham, *Third World Politics*, p. 12.
17. Braveboy-Wagner, *Interpreting the Third World*, pp. 21–22.
18. Clapham, *Third World Politics*, p. 25.
19. Todaro, *Economic Development in the Third World*, pp. 3–4.
20. David, *Conflicting Paradigms*, p. x.
21. Gabriel Almond and G. Bingham Powell, eds., *Comparative Politics Today: A World View* (Glenview, Ill.: Scott, Foresman, 1988), p. 19. Data come from *The World Almanac and Book of Facts, 1991* (New York: World Almanac, 1991), pp. 756, 762.
22. Beverly May Carl, *Economic Integration Among Developing Nations: Law and Policy* (New York: Praeger, 1986), p. 1.
23. David, *Conflicting Paradigms*, p. x.
24. Carl, *Economic Integration*, p. 1.
25. Braveboy-Wagner, *Interpreting the Third World*, p. 227.
26. Frances Stewart, *Basic Needs in Developing Countries* (Baltimore: Johns Hopkins University Press, 1985), p. 1.
27. Paul Cammack, David Pool, and William Tordoff, *Third World Politics: A Comparative Introduction* (Baltimore: Johns Hopkins University Press, 1988), p. 250.
28. Anne O. Krueger, "Problems of Liberalization," in Armeane M. Choksi and Demetris Papageorgiou, *Economic Liberalization in Developing Countries* (New York: Basil Blackwell, 1986), p. 19.
29. Carl, *Economic Integration*, p. 2.

30. James Brooke, "Brazil Says There Is No Moratorium," *The New York Times,* July 8, 1989, p. 17.
31. Tri Q. Nguyen, *Third-World Development: Aspects of Political Legitimacy and Viability* (Rutherford, N.J.: Fairleigh Dickinson University Press, 1989), p. 115.
32. Almond and Powell, *Comparative Politics Today*, p. 23. United Nations, *1983 International Trade Statistics Yearbook* (New York: United Nations, 1985).
33. Wilfred Beckerman, "Stagflation and the Third World," in Sanjaya Lall and Frances Stewart, eds., *Theory and Reality in Development* (New York: St. Martin's Press, 1986), p. 38.
34. Peter J. Burnell, *Economic Nationalism in the Third World* (Boulder, Col.: Westview Press, 1986), p. 16.
35. Ibid., p. 41.
36. Braveboy-Wagner, *Interpreting the Third World*, pp. 52–70.
37. Burnell, *Economic Nationalism*, p. 150.
38. David Roth, Paul Warwick, and David Paul, *Comparative Politics: Diverse States in an Interdependent World* (New York: Harper & Row, 1989), p. 107.
39. Glynn Cochrane, *Reforming National Institutions for Economic Development* (Boulder, Col.: Westview Press, 1986), p. 2.
40. Nguyen, *Third-World Development*, p. 30.
41. Cochrane, *Reforming National Institutions*, p. 57.
42. Faaland and Parkinson, *The Political Economy of Development*, p. 83.
43. Todaro, *Economic Development*, pp. 177–181.
44. G. Shabbir Cheema and Dennis A. Rondinelli, eds., *Decentralization and Development: Policy Implementation in Developing Countries* (Beverly Hills, Calif.: Sage Publications, 1983).
45. Hidehiko Sazanami, "Introduction," in Cheema and Rondinelli, eds., *Decentralization and Development*, p. 7.
46. Dennis Rondinelli and G. Shabbir Cheema, "Implementing Decentralization Policies: An Introduction," in Cheema and Rondinelli, *Decentralization and Development*, p. 18. © 1983 by Sage Publications. Quotations from this work are reprinted by permission of Sage Publications, Inc.
47. Ibid., pp. 14–17.
48. Harry J. Friedman, "Decentral Development in Asia: Local Political Alternatives," in Cheema and Rondinelli, *Decentralization and Development*, p. 36.
49. Kuldeep Mathur, "Administrative Decentralization in Asia," in Cheema and Rondinelli, *Decentralization and Development*, p. 61–62.
50. See Dennis Rondinelli, "Decentralization of Development Administration in East Africa," in Cheema and Rondinelli, *Decentralization and Development*, pp. 77–83. Discussion of North Africa in this context can be found in the article by John Nellis, "Decentralization in North Africa: Problems of Policy Implementation," in Cheema and Rondinelli, *Decentralization and Development*, pp. 127–182.
51. Richard Harris, "Centralization and Decentralization in Latin America," in Cheema and Rondinelli, *Decentralization and Development*, p. 183.
52. Ibid., pp. 186–187.
53. Ibid., p. 191.
54. Allan Kornberg and Lloyd Musolf, "On Legislatures in Developmental Perspective," in Allan Kornberg and Lloyd Musolf, eds., *Legislatures in Developmental Perspective* (Durham, N.C.: Duke University Press, 1970), p. 28.

55. Chong Lim Kim, Joel Barkan, Ilter Turan, and Malcolm Jewell, *The Legislative Connection: The Politics of Representation in Kenya, Korea, and Turkey* (Durham, N.C.: Duke University Press, 1984), pp. 5–6.
56. Each of these is discussed in some detail in Kim, Barkan, Turan, and Jewell, *The Legislative Connection*.
57. Joseph LaPalombara, "An Overview of Bureaucracy and Political Development," in Joseph LaPalombara, ed., *Bureaucracy and Political Development* (Princeton, N.J.: Princeton University Press, 1967), p. 17.
58. Myron Weiner and Joseph LaPalombara, "The Impact of Parties on Political Development," in Joseph LaPalombara and Myron Weiner, eds., *Political Parties and Political Development* (Princeton, N.J.: Princeton University Press, 1966), p. 400.
59. Ibid., p. 401.
60. Ibid., p. 414.
61. Lucian Pye, ed., *Communications and Political Development* (Princeton, N.J.: Princeton University Press, 1968).
62. James S. Coleman, ed., *Education and Political Development* (Princeton, N.J.: Princeton University Press, 1968).
63. Lucian Pye and Sidney Verba, eds., *Political Culture and Political Development* (Princeton, N.J.: Princeton University Press, 1968).
64. Cochrane, *Reforming National Institutions*, p. 85.
65. Clapham, *Third World Politics*, p. 91.
66. David, *Conflicting Paradigms*, p. 23.
67. Braveboy-Wagner, *Interpreting the Third World*, p. 265.
68. Elbaki Hermassi, *The Third World Reassessed* (Berkeley: University of California Press, 1980), p. 35.
69. A good example of this kind of scholarship is the article by J. Samuel Valenzuela and Arturo Valenzuela, "Modernization and Dependency: Alternative Perspectives in the Study of Latin American Underdevelopment," *Comparative Politics* (July 1978): 535–557. See also James Caporaso, "Dependence, Dependency, and Power in the Global System: A Structural and Behavioral Analysis," *International Organization* 32 (1978): 13–43.
70. Atul Kohli, ed., *The State and Development in the Third World* (Princeton, N.J.: Princeton University Press, 1986), p. 15.
71. A very good review of political development theory can be found in the book by that title by Richard A. Higgott, *Political Development Theory: The Contemporary Debate* (New York: St. Martin's Press, 1983).
72. Discussion of these four approaches is based upon a much longer discussion in Hermassi, *The Third World Reassessed*, pp. 17–40.
73. Ibid., p. 20.
74. See Samuel Huntington, "Political Development and Political Decay," *World Politics* 17 (1965): 386–430.
75. Hermassi, *The Third World Reassessed*, pp. 30–31.
76. David, *Conflicting Paradigms*, p. 137.
77. Nguyen, *Third-World Development*, p. 19.
78. Todaro, *Economic Development*, p. 187.
79. Ibid., p. 217.
80. Faaland and Parkinson, *Political Economy of Development*, p. 168; Todaro, *Economic Development*, p. 191.
81. Todaro, *Economic Development*, p. 265.
82. Faaland and Parkinson, *Political Economy of Development*, p. 180.
83. Ibid., p. 181.
84. Todaro, *Economic Development*, p. 231.

85. Ibid., p. 33.
86. Ibid., pp. 332–333.
87. Ibid., p. 35.
88. Ibid., p. 354.
89. Faaland and Parkinson, *Political Economy of Development*, p. 123.
90. Nurul Islam, "World Food Security: National and International Measures for Stabilisation of Supplies," in Lall and Stewart, *Theory and Reality in Development*, p. 192.
91. Faaland and Parkinson, *Political Economy of Development*, p. 152.
92. See Malcolm Gillis, Dwight Perkins, Michael Roemer, and Donald Snodgrass, *Economics of Development* (New York: W.W. Norton &Co., 1987), pp. 568–586.
93. Mahbub Ul Haq, "Proposal for an IMF Debt Refinancing Subsidiary," in Lall and Stewart, *Theory and Reality in Development*, p. 88.
94. A tentative solution to the problem can be found in Mahbub Ul Haq, "Proposal for an IMF Debt Refinancing Subsidiary," in Lall and Stewart, *Theory and Reality in Development*, pp. 91–94.
95. Kornberg and Musolf, "On Legislatures in Developmental Perspective," p. 26.
96. Cochrane, *Reforming National Institutions*, p. 87.

4

Legislatures and Legislative Structures

Introduction

In 1690 John Locke published his *Second Treatise on Civil Government* in which he discussed the "true original, extent, and end of civil government." In his discussion of *why* individuals would leave the "state of nature" and join society, Locke suggested that the prime motivation for people doing such a thing was the preservation of "their lives, liberty, and estates, which I call by the general name, property."[1] (This phrase was subsequently amended by Thomas Jefferson in the Declaration of Independence to read "life, liberty, and the pursuit of happiness.")

There are "many things wanting" in the state of nature, Locke suggested, and it was these missing structures that would prompt individuals to join society:

[Section 124] First, there wants an established, settled, known law . . .

[Section 125] Secondly, In the state of nature there wants a known and indifferent judge, with authority to determine all differences according to the established law . . .

[Section 126] Thirdly, In the state of nature there often wants power to back and support the sentence when right . . .

[Section 127] Thus mankind notwithstanding all the privileges of the state of nature, being but in an ill condition while they remain in it, are quickly driven into society. . . . And in this we have the original right and rise of both the legislature and executive power as well as of the governments and societies themselves.[2]

Legislatures have come to be among the most popular subjects of analysis by political scientists in recent years[3]; indeed, a new journal has come into existence devoted entirely to the study of legislatures: *Legislative Studies Quarterly.* Among other reasons for this phenomenon is the fact that legislatures are usually important structures in their respective governmental systems.[4] In addition, legislatures are among the oldest political institutions known to society. As we will see throughout this book, although the functions and powers of legislatures within their respective political systems have varied, and continue to vary today on a country-by-country basis, they continue to be almost universally regarded as significant institutions.[5]

Many reasons have been suggested as providing a rationale for the study of legislatures, including the fact that the "function of a legislature is to make the values, goals, and attitudes of a social system authoritative in the form of legislative decisions," the fact that the legislators serve as role models for the public and in this way serve an educative function for society generally, and the fact that legislatures can be useful to society "by allowing for the expression of grievances in a public forum."[6] As a very general rationale, we may assert that "the very prevalence of legislative institutions . . . may be construed as affording *prima facie* evidence of their relevance for inquiry."[7]

It has been suggested that legislatures may be more important in some contexts than in others, much as we suggested at the end of the second chapter might be the case in relation to constitutions. One example of this can be seen in the central role parliaments play in promoting regime stability,[8] or their effectiveness, or lack of it, in developing nations.[9] Another example of such a context is the process of modernization: Legislatures are important to study in this regard "because of their affinity to aspects of modernization itself."[10] Although legislatures may have more direct impact upon some subjects or processes (e.g., regularizing group interaction in society) than others (e.g., land reform), it is not difficult to imagine ways in which legislatures can affect wide areas of human concern. The almost universal acceptance of the existence of legislatures in contemporary politics should in itself afford a sufficient rationale for their study.

One House or Two?

One of the initial characteristics of the legislative institution that we note when we look at a given legislature is whether it is *unicameral* or *bicameral*, whether it has one house or two houses. One recent cross-national study of legislatures indicated that the number of unicameral and bicameral legislatures around the world is about even. Jean Blondel found that of 107 nations which he studied that had legislatures, 52 had bicameral legislatures and 55 had unicameral legislatures.[11] The distribution of unicameral and bicameral legislatures around the world is not random: Bicameral legislatures are much more prevalent in some areas than in others, as Table 4.1 indicates.

If we want to explain why some nations have bicameral legislatures while others have unicameral legislatures, we must be very careful about making broad and sweeping generalizations. Political structures, as we have already seen, are not always what they appear to be, and legislatures are not exceptions to this rule. We *cannot* say "legislatures serve function X" in all political

Table 4.1
Houses in Legislatures

Area	Unicameral	Bicameral
Atlantic area	7	15
East Europe and North Asia	10	3
Middle East and North Africa	6	4
South and East Asia	8	9
Sub-Saharan Africa	17	8
Latin America	7	13

Source: Data come from Jean Blondel, *Comparative Legislatures* (Englewood Cliffs, N.J.: Prentice Hall, 1973), pp. 144-153.

systems, because we cannot be sure that in *all* cases that is true. The "levels of analysis" problem that we introduced in Chapter 1 is relevant here.

Why are some legislatures bicameral while others are unicameral? What do the second chambers do, where they exist? Before we can answer these questions, we must introduce a very important distinction in conceptual terms, one that will be used again and again throughout our study. This is the distinction between that which exists by legal establishment, by law, and that which exists by actual fact, although not by legal establishment. We refer to the former situation, establishment in law, as a *de jure* case, and to the latter situation, establishment in fact, as a *de facto* case.

In a number of instances throughout this book we will see political structures that simply are *not* the same *in fact* as they are *in law*. We will see, for example, that *de jure*, in law, an upper house of a given national legislature may have the power to veto a bill passed by the lower house. It may be the case, however, that although the power exists *de jure*, it does *not* exist *de facto*; that upper house has not used its power of veto in over 200 years, and in the "real world," *de facto*, no matter what the law says it *may* do, custom and tradition prohibit the upper house from exercising what may be its legitimate legal power. In many cases, the *de facto* rule of custom and tradition is stronger than any rule *de jure*.

It should be clear now that it will be almost impossible to answer the questions that we posed earlier with any kind of broad single answer, without stepping into the twin traps of the "ecological fallacy" and the "individualistic fallacy" that were introduced in Chapter 1. Bicameral legislatures may exist in a number of political settings for reasons that are completely inappropriate to one or two other nations (the ecological fallacy); we might find an explanation for the existence (or absence) of a legislature in a political system that simply would not be true for other nations (the individualistic fallacy). In short, we must proceed with caution when we generalize.

Countries that are small in size are more likely to have one chamber than two, because "the problem of the balance of political power is less difficult to solve in them than it is in big countries."[12] Bicameral systems are often regarded in socialist countries as leading to complications and delays, and as contributing few advantages to offset these costs. With the exception of Norway, all of the Scandinavian countries have, in the twentieth century, replaced bicameral systems with unicameral ones.

According to a study undertaken by the Inter-Parliamentary Union, the earliest example of a bicameral system occurred in England toward the end of the thirteenth century:

> It began with the institution of a Chamber for the high aristocracy and brought together the feudal magnates, the Lords Spiritual and Temporal. This arrangement has been maintained to the present day, although the aristocratic characteristic of the House of Lords has been reduced by the appointment to it of Life Peers. [These appointments are good only for the life of the holder, and cannot be passed from one generation to another, as can be the traditional Peerage.] Furthermore, the power of the House of Lords has been greatly restricted in favour of the popular House, the House of Commons.[13]

At present, the Inter-Parliamentary Union asserts, the bicameral system can no longer be explained by the need for a separate aristocratic representation. Bicameral systems are justified primarily by two arguments. First, in federal states (as we shall further develop shortly) bicameralism reflects the split-government nature of the state. Second, in unitary states, bicameralism provides a "revising" chamber for legislation.

Why would a second house exist in a political system? There are a number of possible explanations. A second house might be critical to the general political framework of the regime. It might be necessary that a federal political system be established, for example, in order to meet the conditions set by various member units of the future nation. If this is the case, one condition for national unification may be a bicameral legislature. The American "Great Compromise" in Philadelphia in 1787 is certainly one example of this genesis of a bicameral legislature. The large states wanted a representative legislature based upon population, whereas the small states wanted a representative legislature based upon "equal representation" for the member units (e.g., an equal number of representatives per state). The Great Compromise meant that there would be a bicameral legislature, with one house based on population and the other based on an equal number of representatives for each state.[14]

To take another example, what today is the Province of Quebec in Canada refused to join the Canadian confederation in

1867 without a guarantee that the future Dominion would be federal; Quebec wanted assurances that it would continue to control certain areas of policy jurisdiction as only a federation would permit. Once this was decided, it was inevitable that the new national legislature would be bicameral, with one house (the House of Commons) based upon population, and the other house (the Senate) *not* based upon population, but instead based upon equal representation for the regional units of Canada.

Where we find federal states we will almost always find a bicameral legislature in which the "lower" house represents the national, popular jurisdiction, while the "upper" house represents the intermediate political structures or territories.[15] The United States, Canada, and Germany are all examples of federal states with bicameral legislatures in which the lower houses are "national" and the upper houses are "regional."

Although federal regimes are virtually always bicameral (the sole exception being Swaziland),[16] the association does not work in the other direction: Not all bicameral systems are federal. There are other reasons for bicameral structure than federal status. A new nation might adopt a bicameral legislative structure because that is the structure that its colonial "parent" had, and that structure simply seemed the most "normal" alternative after independence was achieved. We will see that this "imitation" procedure is not at all uncommon for a variety of political structures, including executives and legal systems, when we start to examine political structures in a number of settings around the world. (See Table 4.2)

Furthermore, simple size of a nation may suggest a bicameral legislative structure to a political system. There may be such diversity in a political system that a second legislative house is felt to be needed, regardless of the fact that the political system is unitary, and not federal.

The fact that virtually all federal systems are bicameral, but not all bicameral systems are federal, is illustrated in Table 4.3. We can see in this table that (1) federal systems are in a clear minority, and (2) unicameral and bicameral systems are just about evenly divided.

Where upper houses exist, the representational bases of the legislative chambers vary. They may represent assorted territorial units. (In Canada the Provinces of Ontario and Quebec each receive twenty-four senators, while all of the four Western Prov-

Table 4.2
Some Bicameral Systems

Nation	Lower House	Represents	Upper House	Represents
United States	House of Representatives	Districts (people)	Senate	States
Canada	House of Commons	Districts (people)	Senate	Regions
India	Lok Sabha	Districts (people)	Rajya Sabha	States
Australia	House of Representatives	Districts (people)	Senate	States
Bahamas	House of Commons	Districts (people)	Senate	Appointed
Britain	House of Commons	Districts (people)	House of Lords	Appointed

inces together receive twenty-four senators, and all of the Maritime Provinces together receive twenty-four senators, excluding Newfoundland, which joined the confederation last and therefore received six senators of its own.) Upper houses may provide equal representation for member units of a federation (for example, two senators each for American states), or weighted representation for member units of a federation (for example, in the German system, some Länder have three deputies in the Bundesrat, some have four, some have five, and some have six, depending upon their size). Upper houses may simply provide an extra house in the legislature for a "sober second thought" on legislation, a house that is elected in the same manner as the lower house (such as the Italian case, for example, in which both houses are elected to represent the same constituency—the national population—with no geographic districts). Finally, they may provide several jurisdictions at once; the upper house in Japan represents *both* local and national units, and the British House of Lords represents hereditary positions, as well as new political positions, and judicial and ecclesiastical positions.

The terms "upper" and "lower" as adjectives for legislative houses are today strictly a product of convention. The terms date from early in British parliamentary history, when the House of

Table 4.3
Systems and Houses

Area	Unicameral	Bicameral	Total
Unitary:			
Atlantic area	7	9	
East Europe and North Asia	10	—	
Middle East and North Africa	6	4	
South and East Asia	8	7	
Sub-Saharan Africa	16	8	
Latin America	7	10	
Total	54	38	92
Federal:			
Atlantic area	—	6	
East Europe and North Asia	—	3	
Middle East and North Africa	—	—	
South and East Asia	—	2	
Sub-Saharan Africa	1	—	
Latin America	—	3	
Total	1	14	15
Total	55	52	107

Source: Data come from Jean Blondel, *Comparative Legislatures* (Englewood Cliffs, N.J.: Prentice Hall, 1973), pp. 144–153.

Lords was felt to be superior to the House of Commons, even though (or perhaps because of the fact that) it was not elected by the people. It was felt that the aristocratic nature of the House of Lords, the fact that it was *not* chosen by the public, made it the superior, or "upper" house. Today, we use the term "lower" house to describe that house in a bicameral system (most) directly elected by the people, and "upper" house to describe that house further from direct public control, although today many "upper" houses are also elected directly by the public.

Relations Between Houses

Where we find a unicameral legislature, for obvious reasons we do not have to inquire into the nature of the power relationship between legislative houses. Where there is only one house, only one house can have legislative power; whatever power may reside in the legislature in that particular system resides in the single house. In bicameral settings the situation is not so simple. We may find instances in which the two houses act as equal partners in a cooperative venture, in which the two houses have equal powers but are constantly feuding so that little is ever accomplished, or in which power is not balanced, and one house dominates the other. All of this confusion is exacerbated, made worse, by the *de facto–de jure* distinction mentioned earlier. In many instances the real (*de facto*) relationship between the two houses is not the same as that written in law (*de jure*).

When we speak of a power relationship between any two actors (we can call them *A* and *B*), three possibilities appear. *A* can have more power than *B*, *A* can have the same power as *B*, or *A* can have less power than *B*. The same options can be said to exist if *A* and *B* are two houses of a national legislative body. Let us briefly examine each of these possibilities, where bicameral legislatures exist. Table 4.4 shows us the frequencies with which these alternatives exist in the "real world" today.

The first relationship, in which the lower house is stronger than the upper house, is the most common relationship, both in theory and in practice. Since many second chambers are not elected by the mass electorate, but are either appointed or hereditary bodies, many theorists argue that in principle upper houses *should* be weaker than lower houses; they are in essence "undemocratic" institutions. As Table 4.4 shows, Blondel's study of legislatures around the world found many instances in which the upper houses were *legally*, as well as behaviorally, weaker than lower houses.

Table 4.4
Powers of Upper Houses

Category	No. Countries
Upper house weaker than lower house	26
Upper house equal to lower house	22
Upper house stronger than lower house	0
Upper house only advisory	1
No upper house	58

Source: Data come from Jean Blondel, *Comparative Legislatures* (Englewood Cliffs, N.J.: Prentice Hall, 1973), pp. 144–153.

It must be noted, however, that many of the political settings described in Table 4.4, in which the upper houses are *indicated* as being legally equal to the lower houses, do not *practice* this relationship. For example, although the Canadian Senate is "legally" equal to the House of Commons, and must approve all bills before they become laws, it has been described as having "retained a full set of legislative muscles, but consistently has refused to make real use of them."[17]

In 1988, when the Canadian Senate (controlled by the Liberal party) refused to pass a Free Trade Bill (introduced by the Conservative Government and approved by a Conservative majority in the House of Commons) that would affect Canadian and American trade, the prime minister protested that the Senate's action was unacceptable because senators were not elected and thus they had no legitimacy. (It is worth noting that the senators held their ground and insisted that they would not pass the bill unless the prime minister resigned, called for a new election, and received a new "national mandate." Prime Minister Brian Mulroney did just this, was reelected with a substantial majority in November 1988, and then the Liberal-dominated Senate passed the bill reintroduced by the new Conservative Government of Mr. Mulroney.) This situation has evolved to the point at which the Canadian Senate almost never exercises its power, and when it does it is accused of being undemocratic. Thus, in Canada at least, the legal (*de jure*) status of the upper house does not reflect correctly the real (*de facto*) status of the upper house, that of being a rubber stamp.

In these legislative bodies, then, either the upper chamber legally has fewer powers than does the lower house—as is the case in France, Turkey, India, or Norway—or it consistently chooses to exercise fewer powers than does the lower house, owing to political tradition or political culture, as we saw to be the case with the Canadian Senate.

In other legislatures, the upper house is both legally *and* behaviorally an equal partner in the legislative process. Certainly among the best examples of this type of relationship is the case of the United States Senate. Although the Senate is legally prohibited from certain legislative acts (under the Constitution, for example, it cannot introduce tax bills), overall it is an equal partner in the legislative process. A bill simply cannot become law without the Senate's approval. Similar situations, both *de jure* and *de facto*, may be found in Italy, Switzerland, Yugoslavia, Liberia, Mexico, and Jordan.

Although in theory we might find a legislature in which the upper house is actually stronger than the lower house—and we can find historical instances in which this was the case—in practice this has not proven to be common today. In some cases people might argue that the U.S. Senate is stronger and more important than the House of Representatives. The focus of attention, however, must be the question "Can the Senate pass laws without the approval of the House?" The answer is clearly no. Blondel found *no* contemporary cases (remembering that if we go back far enough in history it is true that at one time the House of Lords dominated the House of Commons in Britain, for example) in which the power relationship was dominated by the upper house.

Finally, there are a few "variable" cases. The German instance is a good example of this type of structure. In cases in which legislation affects the German Länder, or states, the upper house has an absolute veto over legislation. Members of the upper house, the Bundesrat, are not directly elected by the public, but are chosen by the governments of the German states. Accordingly, if a bill that will affect the states (such as a bill on transportation policy, for example) is not approved by a majority of the representatives of the states, it cannot become law. In cases in which legislation does *not* affect the states, such as bills focusing upon foreign policy, the negative vote of the upper house may be overridden by the lower house. We shall examine this process in more detail later in this volume.

Some upper houses, then, can be seen to have an *absolute veto* in the legislative process (e.g., the American case), in which their refusal to approve legislation results in failure of the legislation in question. Other upper houses can be said to have *suspensory vetoes*, in which their refusal to approve legislation is only guaranteed to slow down the legislative process a bit; subsequent repassage by the lower house either with a regular majority (e.g., Britain) or a special majority (e.g., Germany) can create laws without the approval of the upper house. Still other upper houses can be said to have *rubber stamp* power only; for example, the Canadian instance in which the upper house legally has power to affect legislation but traditionally and culturally is prohibited from using that power.

Sizes of Legislatures

Legislatures vary in terms of the number of houses they have, and they vary even more in terms of the number of members they have. Recent studies have found that houses of national legislatures range from a minimum of 16 in the Caribbean island-nation of St. Vincent, and 24 in Barbados, to a maximum of about 3,000 (in China); upper chambers ranged from 6 (Equatorial Guinea) to 1,174 (Britain).[18]

Size of a legislative body may be determined by a number of factors, some philosophical and intentional, others accidental. Some legislative bodies continue to grow until it is clear that there simply is no *room* for them to grow more, and their size (number of members) is then "frozen." The U.S. House of Representatives is a good example of this. From an initial representative-to-population ratio of one for every 30,000 people in 1787 to approximately one for every 500,000 people in 1970, the ratio has been changed because the size of the House was "frozen." In 1787 there were 66 members in the House; there were 242 in 1833. In 1921 a reapportionment based on the 1920 Census would have pushed the size of the House to 483. The House decided at that time to keep its membership at 435, arguing that "the great size of the membership had already resulted in serious limitations on the right of debate and an overconcentration of power in the hands of the leadership."[19] It took eight years until this view came to be incorporated in law, but in 1929 a law was passed and signed by President Herbert Hoover establishing the maximum size of the House of Representatives at 435 members.

The size of Canada's House of Commons has grown over the years, following this pattern of having a census every ten years and adding seats in the legislature to accommodate new population. In the last two decades the size of the House of Commons has grown from 263 members to 295. Some voices in Canada are now calling for a "freezing" of the size of the House of Commons, as was done to the American House of Representatives in 1929. It seems likely that this will eventually happen, but it must be recalled that the British House of Commons grew to 630 members before *its* size was frozen.

In other settings, the size of a legislative body may be symbolic. The unicameral Israeli Knesset has 120 members. Its size was determined by historic precedent: The Great Assembly, the first supreme legislative authority elected by the Jews in the fourth and fifth centuries B.C., had 120 members, ten representatives for each of the "twelve tribes" of Israel.[20] Size may also be intentionally determined by a formula, such as the case in Germany's upper house in which states have three, four, five, or six representatives each, depending upon their population size.

Political Parties in Legislatures

One of the legislative structures about which we *can* generalize is the political party. Parties are, as a general rule, highly significant structures in legislative systems, both in terms of their organizational influence and in terms of their influence over individual legislative behavior.[21] Both of these aspects of party influence merit some discussion here.

Although legislative bodies vary in both the nature and degree of their internal organization, *all* legislatures have *some* organization. One of the major tools for the process of this organization is the political party. Parties provide candidates for formal legislative positions, such as the Speaker, deputy speakers, committee chairs, and the like. Parties provide the basis around which formal organization of legislatures takes place.

Parties also affect individual legislative behavior. In this context the concept of *party discipline* is central. The concept of party discipline relates to the cohesion of the body of party members within the legislature. In a legislature with high party discipline, we can expect legislators to act (and this can include voting, debating, making speeches outside the legislature, introducing bills, or a number of other possible activities as well) in concert with their party leader's directions.[22] In legislatures with low party discipline, the concept of party label is less significant in terms of its usefulness in helping us to predict legislative behavior; individuals will act as they see fit, with little regard for directions from party leaders.

We can take two examples to illustrate the idea of party discipline. In the British House of Commons, party discipline is very great. All members of the House of Commons invariably vote exactly as their leaders tell them to vote. We would expect, for example, all members of the majority Conservative party to vote as a bloc, all the time. Any member who votes against his or her party may be subject to sanctions, including withdrawal of campaign funds, being given poor committee assignments in the legislature (or no assignment at all, for that matter), and the like.[23] On occasion "free votes" take place in the House of Commons, during which time the member of Parliament (MP) may vote as he or she wants,[24] but this is the only time the MP is expected to follow his or her own will in voting.

The United States offers a good example of a legislature with considerably weaker party discipline. This is not to say that there is *no* party discipline in the Congress, for as a general rule, if we know legislators' party identifications, and if we know the position of the party leaders on a bill, we will be correct more often than we will be incorrect in predicting how legislators will behave. However, it is not at all uncommon to find a group of Southern Democrats voting with the Republicans, or a group of liberal Republicans voting with the Democrats.

The concept of party discipline is very important to any discussion of legislative behavior, and even more important in some settings than in others, as we shall see later in this book. We shall return to this concept when we discuss political executives and their relationships to legislatures.

Legislative Committees

Another of the major structures that we find in legislative bodies is that of the committee.[25] Committees exist to meet a real need in legislatures: Legislative bodies as a whole are generally too large and unwieldy to enable serious and complex discussion on highly specialized matters to take place. Additionally, the aspect of specialization is important in its own right. *Every* legislator cannot be an expert on *every* subject. If, however, the entire legislative body is divided into groups, with each group specializing in a different aspect of the legislature's business, the work of the legislature can be performed more efficiently and more accurately. The idea of a division of labor and specialization serves as the primary justification for the legislative committee's existence.

For an example, let us take an imaginary legislature with 200 members. Each of those 200 legislators could not possibly develop and maintain sufficient expertise in all of the disparate business of the legislature (everything from defense weapons systems to tax legislation to national parks policy to agriculture subsidies) to enable the legislature to function at peak capacity. Accordingly, the 200 members will establish, say, twenty committees dealing with the various issues that the legislature must address. Each member may serve on two committees, and each committee will have twenty members. It is usually the case, as well, that the individual committees engage further in the "division of labor–specialization" behavior, too, forming a number of subcommittees so that committee members can specialize in very narrow aspects of the committee's work.

Thus our imaginary legislature might have a Committee on Agriculture, a Committee on Defense, and a Committee on Finance, to take three examples. These committees, as we noted, will have subcommittees, so that members of the Agriculture Committee, who will all be generally well informed about all aspects of agriculture, will each be very well informed about some specific aspects of the Agriculture Committee's work, such as the wheat crop, or price subsidies, for example.

Legislatures tend to have a number of different *types* of committees. *Standing*, or *permanent*, committees are committees that are established at the opening of the legislative term and that last for the life of the legislature. *Select* committees are committees that tend to be given specific scopes of inquiry, or special problems, to address, as well as specific durations. Some bicameral systems have *joint committees*, which are made up of members from both houses. The *Committee of the Whole*, often found in legislatures, is a technical device used to establish a different set of procedural rules; a legislative body can "dissolve itself" into a Committee of the Whole, and without anything physically changing (the same legislators are still sitting in the same seats) there is a different set of rules governing debate time, how motions may be introduced, and so on, that applies to their proceedings.

The relative importance of committees varies on a legislature-by-legislature basis. In some systems, such as the American legislature, for example, legislative committees are very important and have a significant role in the legislative process. In other systems, such as that of Britain, for example, the role of committees is quite weak; they are not as active in the "oversight" function as are American committees, and they do not play as significant a role in the legislative process as their American counterparts. The ability of committees to examine, modify, delay, or even "kill" legislative proposals is very significant and can be quite important in determining the amount of power the executive branch can exercise over the legislative branch of government.

How Legislators Are Selected

There are a number of different "pathways to parliament."[26] Legislators may ultimately arrive in their legislative positions in any of a number of ways. Some legislators, of course, are not elected by the public at all, but are appointed by some individual or political body. Others *are* elected. In this section we want to examine *how* legislators are selected to play the roles that they play.[27]

There are two major methods by which the public elects legislators, whether the legislators involved are in the upper house or the lower house of the legislature involved. One method we can refer to as "district-based" elections; the other method can be called "proportional representation" elections. There are a number of variations for each of these general methods, which vary on a country-by-country basis, that we will see in the next section of this book, but the broad principles are the same.

Single-Member-District Voting

Among the most common forms of district based representation is the system that is referred to as a "single-member-district, plurality voting" system. In this type of system, the entire nation is divided into a number of electoral boxes, or districts. Each district corresponds to a seat in the legislative house. Within each district, an electoral contest is held to determine the representative for that district, with the individual receiving the most votes being elected. Usually all of the districts in the nation hold their elections on the same day, although special elections may be held to replace a representative who has resigned or died.

The single-member-district, plurality (SMD-P) system, existing in the United States, Canada, Britain, Mexico, the USSR, and most other nations, does *not* usually require that any of the candidates win a *majority* of the vote. (A majority is defined as one vote more than 50 percent of the total votes cast.) All that is required for an individual to win is that he or she wins *more* votes than anyone else (a plurality); this is why it is sometimes called a "first past the post" system. So, in a given contest with three or four candidates, it would be possible for an individual to be elected with only 30 or 32 percent of the vote, if the other three candidates each received less (e.g., 25, 23, and 20 percent).

Like every other political structure we might examine, the single-member-district system has both advantages and disadvantages. A major advantage is that representatives have specific districts that are "theirs" to represent, and people know who "their" representatives are.[28] A major disadvantage is that the SMD-P system overrepresents majorities, hides minorities, and promotes a two-party system at the expense of third and minor parties. Three examples will help to make this clear.

In the first illustration, let us take four imaginary electoral districts, each with 100 voters, as illustrated in Table 4.5. Let us suppose that in *each* of these districts, in which for simplicity's sake there are two political parties, Party A wins 51 votes and Party B wins 49 votes. When we total the results, Party A will have won 204 votes to 196 for Party B, a 51–49 percent margin, but Party A will have won 4 seats in the legislature to 0 for Party B, a very slight majority in popular votes turning into an overwhelming majority in legislative seats. In short, the votes for Party B will be "unrepresented." This is an extreme mathematical example, yet the principles it represents are not at all uncommon.

The second example, shown in Table 4.6, illustrates how in a multiparty system (in this case three parties, but the same principles would apply to four, five, or more parties) a very small

Table 4.5
A Two-Party, Single-Member-District System

District	Party A	Party B	Total
District 1	51	49	100
District 2	51	49	100
District 3	51	49	100
District 4	51	49	100
Total votes	204	196	400
Total seats	4	0	4

Table 4.6
A Three-Party, Single-Member-District System

District	Party A	Party B	Party C	Total
District 1	34	33	33	100
District 2	34	33	33	100
District 3	34	33	33	100
District 4	34	33	33	100
Total votes	136	132	132	400
Total seats	4	0	0	4

margin—in this case bare pluralities in place of bare majorities—in a number of districts can make a party *appear* very strong, when, in fact, that is not the case at all. Here, although the plurality party wins only 34 percent of the popular vote, that 34 percent will yield 100 percent of the seats in the legislature.

The third example, seen in Table 4.7, uses the same setting as Table 4.6: four districts of 100 voters, and three parties. We can see that in the most mathematically extreme case a shift of only *two votes* (or one-half of 1 percent, in this case!), from Party A to Party B, results in Party B winning two seats—that is, 50 percent—in the legislature where it previously had none. In other words, a shift in popular support of as little as one-half of one percent of the "popular vote" has the potential to change the composition of the legislature by 50 percent. Party C is still shut out of the legislature, despite the fact that it received 33 percent of the vote, one vote out of three, and only one-half percent less

Table 4.7
A Three-Party, Single-Member-District System

District	Party A	Party B	Party C	Total
District 1	34	33	33	100
District 2	34	33	33	100
District 3	*33*	*34*	33	100
District 4	*33*	*34*	33	100
Total votes	134	134	132	400
Total seats	2	2	0	4

than either Party A or Party B! Clearly this is the most extreme example we could design in a 100-person district, but the principles it illustrates would apply just as forcefully in an electoral district with 100,000 voters.

Although these examples clearly are far simpler than the reality of electoral politics, the patterns of bias that they demonstrate *are* real. In the November 1988 Canadian federal elections, the Progressive Conservative party won 57 percent of the seats in the House of Commons with less than 44 percent of the votes; that is, over 55 percent of the Canadian population voted *against* the incumbent government, and it still won a strong majority.

The problem with the SMD-P system is that if a party cannot get more votes than any other party in a district, it might as well not run there, because it will get no representation at all. In the February 1980 election in Canada, the New Democratic party won 19.8 percent of the national vote—almost one out of every five votes—yet it received only 11.3 percent of the seats in the House of Commons, just about half of what it "deserved." This happened because, although it could count on votes from many districts, in most districts although it had *some* votes, it did not have *more* votes than its competitors, so it ended up with no representation. One by-product of the SMD system is a two-party system, because generally speaking it is extremely hard for third parties to win seats in SMD systems; thus, two major parties tend to dominate the political landscape.

Proportional Representation Voting

There is an alternative electoral system to the SMD system, which is called the *proportional representation* (PR) system. The PR system is not based upon geographical districts at all. Rather, the entire electorate votes for the single *party* it prefers, not for candidates. The proportion of votes that a party receives in the election (e.g., 23 percent of the total votes cast) determines the proportion of seats it will receive in the legislature (e.g., 23 percent of the legislative seats).

An example may help to clarify this. The Israeli system has a "pure" PR electoral framework. At election time, voters cast their ballots for the political party they support. After the election, if the Labour party has received 25 percent of the votes, it receives

25 percent of the 120 seats in the Israeli parliament, the Knesset. How are the individual winners determined? The process is simple. Prior to the election, all parties deposit "lists" of their candidates with a national election board, and these "lists" are made public. The parties usually submit lists of 120 names, one for each possible seat in the Knesset, although they can be sure that they will not win 100 percent of the vote. After the election, if Labour has won 30 seats (25 percent of 120 seats), it simply counts down the top thirty names on its electoral list: Positions 1 through 30 are declared elected, positions 31 through 120 are not elected. This system has an added advantage: If a member of the Knesset dies during the term, or if someone resigns for some reason, a special election is not necessary; the next name on the party list enters the Knesset.[29]

The PR system, like the SMD system, has its advantages and disadvantages.[30] Its advantages center around the fact that it is highly representative. Parties in Israel need to win only 1 percent of the vote to win a seat in the legislature. This means that groups that are not pluralities can still be represented in the legislature. (To take our example in Table 4.5, if all districts in a 100-seat legislature voted in the same 51–49 manner as the four districts we have drawn, in a PR system Party A would receive 51 seats and Party B would receive 49 seats. In a comparable SMD system, Party A would receive 100 seats, and Party B would receive none.)

The disadvantage of the PR system is that PR legislatures tend to be multiparty legislatures—since it is so easy for smaller parties to win representation—which means that they tend to be more unstable and to contain more radical and extreme groups than SMD-two-party legislatures.[31] To use our example from Table 4.6, in a PR system Party A would win 34 of 100 seats in the legislature, Party B 33 seats, and Party C 33 seats. This would require the formation of a coalition government, something we shall discuss later in this chapter. On the other hand, we might want to argue that this is not really a disadvantage at all, it is a real advantage, since groups that exist *should* be represented in the legislature.

There are variations on both the SMD and PR models described above. One variation on the SMD-plurality requires a *majority* for election (SMD-M). The single-member-district, majority system invariably involves runoff elections, since, given the many political parties that might exist, few districts give a majority to a candidate on the first round of voting. Voting might be scheduled on two consecutive Sundays, with the top two vote-getters from the first round having a runoff election on the second Sunday. Generally, few districts would elect candidates on the first round (that is, have candidates that can win majority margins); the other 85 to 90 percent of the districts have runoff elections.

Another variation on the district-based model involves the number of representatives per district. In a number of legislatures we can find "multiple-member districts" (MMD), in which the top vote-getters are elected. In elections for the lower house in Japan (the House of Representatives), each district elects from three to five representatives, depending upon the size of the district. Voters vote for one candidate, and the top three (or four, or five) vote-getters are elected. Japan utilizes an even more complex multiple-member-district scheme for its upper house—the House of Councillors. We will look at this system in more detail later in this book. Technically, American states fall in this "multiple-member" category, since each state is represented in the U.S. Senate by two senators, and is, therefore, not a single-member district but rather a multiple-member district. The method of selection of senators is the SMD method, not the MMD method, however, since election of senators is "staggered," and we elect only one senator at a time.

We will see in the second part of this book—where we shall look at some of these cases and others in much greater detail—that there are a number of variations on the common theme when we study electoral processes. The complication is made even worse when we remember that many legislatures are bicameral, and the method of selecting the second house is rarely the same as the method of selecting the first house. Some nations have second chambers that are elected by the people (e.g., the United States, the USSR, Italy, Australia, and Japan). Some second chambers are appointed by the Head of State, usually on the "advice" of the Chief Executive (e.g., Canada). Some second chambers are elected by some other body (e.g., France, Norway). Some second chambers have members chosen by more than one method (e.g., Britain). In short, it is a complex subject, but one that will become clearer as we examine case studies later in this text.

Legislative Functions

There is a great deal of consensus in the discipline as to the structures and functions of legislatures, as well as their common attributes.

> Manifestations of parliament do share at least two identifying structural characteristics: . . . (1) their members are formally equal to one another in status, distinguishing parliaments from hierarchically organized organizations; and (2) the authority of their members depends upon their claim to be representing the rest of the community.[32]

In general, five broad functions that legislatures perform for political systems may be sifted from the many lists suggested in the literature. These are, not necessarily in order of importance: (1) criticism and control of the other branches of government, most notably the executive; (2) debate; (3) lawmaking or legislation; (4) communication with the public, representation, and legitimation; and (5) recruitment, education, and socialization.

It is, of course, true that not all legislatures can be said to perform all of these functions. Nor, if they do, can it be said that they perform them all equally well. On the other hand, some legislatures, because of idiosyncratic characteristics of the systems in which they can be found, may be said to perform functions in addition to the five outlined here. Because a legislature fails to perform *all* of these functions does not mean that it performs *none* of them. As has been suggested, "if an assembly exists, it must serve some function in its policy, or it would not be able to survive."[33]

Much research on legislatures mentions the *criticism and control* function as being necessary for the maintenance of a stable political system. Such phrases as "criticizing and checking executive powers"[34] may frequently be found in the literature. This function of the legislative branch of government has its roots in seventeenth- and eighteenth-century democratic political theory, when the role of the legislature as a check upon the arbitrary powers of monarchs was first really practiced. An outgrowth of this function has been the recent "decline of legislatures" literature,[35] suggesting that legislatures have, in modern times, been less and less able to perform this very important function satisfactorily. This is a subject to which we shall return later.

A second function ascribed to legislatures is that of *debate*, or discussion of values and rules for the political system. This has been variously described in the literature as "proposing, deliberating, and deciding about public policy,"[36] or as "providing a forum for discussion and criticism of government policies,"[37] to cite but two examples. While this function is closely related to both the lawmaking/legislating and the criticizing functions, it is easy to imagine situations in which it would *not* fit within those functional categories. For example, in many nations the legislature's role in the legislative process is rather modest. It might discuss a bill proposed by the executive or the bureaucracy, but the bill might become law even if it is never actually voted on and passed by the legislature. Alternatively, a legislature might have the power to vote on a bill *in toto*, but not to amend it, or it may vote to reject a bill and the bill might still become law by executive decree. In such instances, a legislature may appear to be performing both a debating and a legislating function, but *de facto* its function is limited to debate.

The function most frequently ascribed to legislatures in Western countries is that of *lawmaking*. As Jean Blondel observes: "From the theorists of the 17th Century to those of the contemporary world, it has been held as axiomatic . . . that the function of legislatures was to make laws."[38] This legislative function is one that is almost universally attributed to legislative bodies—even if they only ratify or rubber-stamp legislation introduced from outside the legislature. Increasingly, however, the lawmaking function is no longer being considered the litmus test by which a legislature is judged. One student of legislatures has observed that "in formal terms, the principal function of the Parliament . . . is to pass legislation. But, legislation is only a part of the Parliament's business."[39] Ultimately, the question of *how much* of a legislative function a legislature plays in a given political system is an empirical question and one that varies on a country-by-country basis.

The fourth function of a legislature is that of *communication with the public, representation, and legitimation*. Included in this function are actions such as appraising and explaining to constituents actions taken within the legislature; answering mail and other forms of communication; interceding with members of a bureaucratic agency on behalf of individuals or groups; having resources allocated to a constituency, and so forth. Much of a legislator's individual authority derives from his or her ability to undertake these activities[40] and to perform them successfully. The collective actions of legislators in these matters, it has been argued, help build support not only for the legislature as an institution but also for the regime itself. By doing so, the legislature also helps clothe the actions of a regime's leaders with legitimacy.[41]

There is a chain of three interconnected concepts at work here. First, legislators are necessarily aware of communications, both supportive and demanding, from their constituents. Second, by performing actions in response to these communications, the legislators can be said to be acting in a representative manner. Finally, by acting in a representative manner, the legislator can contribute significantly to the legitimacy of the governmental structure. We shall return to the theme of representativeness shortly.

The fifth function that has been attributed to legislatures is that of *recruitment, education, and socialization.* Through the process of attracting individuals to politics, giving them political experience, and enabling them to attain higher office, legislatures engage in the recruitment process—drawing people into the political arena. By engaging in open and publicized debates, by undertaking investigations, and participating in well-reported discussions, legislators help to educate the public both as to issues that are important and to the possible positions to take on such issues. By serving as role models and by developing and maintaining political norms, legislatures actively participate in the process of political socialization, the transmission of political values.

In some circumstances legislatures are vested with special functions as a result of a particular constitutional framework or historical background. For example, in addition to the other functions it performs, the British Parliament (and many parliaments like it) also has an elective function—choosing the Prime Minister. The U.S. House of Representatives has a similar elective function (choosing the president), but because of the nature of the electoral college and the historical situations faced by the United States, the House has only rarely been called upon to perform this task.

In addition to a consensus related to the functions just described, there is also some degree of consensus as to structures and other common attributes of legislatures. Legislatures are assemblies. They are assemblages of individuals, elected or appointed, who come together to perform some or all of the functions discussed above. These assemblies are governed by rules, either written or unwritten, perhaps encoded in a national constitution or perhaps encoded elsewhere, regarding the method of selection of legislators, their rights and duties, their roles in the political system, and their relationship with other branches of government. These assemblies may have many or few officers, and may have greater or lesser degrees of individual opportunities for action, such as introducing legislation, for example.

Legislatures and Representation

It was indicated earlier that one of the most important functions usually ascribed to the legislature as an insitution is that of *representation*.[42] Whether or not legislatures are truly representative in a demographic sense, the need for legislatures to *appear* representative is central to their mission.

Central to this issue, however, is the very idea of "representative." In the late eighteenth century the British member of Parliament Edmund Burke introduced the idea of "virtual representation" in which he claimed that he could represent the views of the American colonies in the "no taxation without representation" controversy without actually *being* from the colonies. After all, he claimed, he knew what their view was, and he was capable of presenting it to the British Parliament. The question of how much representation is "enough" is central in a discussion of how "representative" a national legislature is.

For example, must a legislature be demographically representative? Must the distribution of population groups in the legislature accurately reflect their distribution in the general population? It is clear wherever we look that legislatures do not accurately reflect the demographic makeup of their settings.[43] To take the most obvious example, women are grossly underrepresented in their national legislatures.[44] In one recent cross-national study, nowhere did women exceed 10 percent of the membership of national legislatures[45] (although today women in both Norway and Sweden make up more than 10 percent of the total membership of parliament) and in most of the parliaments studied they numbered under 5 percent of the total membership!

Similarly, ethnic, religious, and racial minorities also tend to be significantly underrepresented in national parliaments. Even in settings in which there are no legal barriers to representation, this is a function of educational, financial, career, and other sociological patterns of bias reflected in the electoral machinery of the nation.

Many argue that the important point is not the gender, ethnic identity, age, religious, or racial characteristic of the representative, but the degree to which he or she understands the views of his or her constituency.[46] The true role of the representative, some would argue, is to represent the interests of his or her constituency, since obviously one representative cannot actually belong to all of the many demographic groups he or she represents.

Legislative Roles

Legislative behavior is important to study because of the nature of the legislature itself, and because of the functions that the legislature serves in the political system of which it is a part. The nature of the legislature in virtually all political systems dictates that the output of the legislative body will be a function, to greater and lesser degrees, of the interaction between and among individual legislators, as well as between and among individual legislators and bureaucracies, societal needs and demands, and other extralegislative factors.

The role that legislators play in the generation of legislative output varies in different political systems. According to many theorists, the manner in which legislators perceive roles in different subsystems of the political world will influence the way they behave politically. A political role, as the term is used here, consists of "a pattern of expected behavior for individuals holding particular positions in a system."[47]

> Legislative role orientation, and hence behavior, is thus a product of both initial expectations held by an individual for the legislative position, and attitudes and perspectives subsequently developed

in response to the expectations and requirements of significant others' interaction with him in the legislative system.[48]

Research indicates that in those situations in which legislators perceive their role in the legislative process to be of minimal importance or significance for the political system, they will behave accordingly and are much more likely to become alienated, apathetic, or cynical than legislators who feel highly efficacious. Studies of the cases of Israel and Thailand, both cases of "minimal legislative roles," illustrate this.[49]

Various lists, typologies, and frameworks of legislative roles have appeared in the literature. One author lists seventeen possible roles for legislators to play; others list twenty-three.[50] Rather than debate the exact number of roles that a political actor, in this case a legislator, could assume (if, indeed, such an exhaustive list is even possible), we shall simply state that the possibilities are numerous. The literature seems to be in agreement that variations in role perceptions can affect role behavior, which in turn can affect legislative behavior.

Certainly one of the major distinctions in legislative roles comes in the description of a legislator as a "frontbencher" or a "backbencher." The names derive from positions in the British House of Commons, in which seats were, and still are, arranged in two sets of rows facing each other. Party leaders sit on the front benches of their respective sides. Nonleaders, or followers, sit on the back benches. Hence, "frontbenchers" for leaders and "backbenchers" for followers.

The Prime Minister and members of the cabinet sit on the front bench of the Government side of the House. Members who sit on the front bench of the Opposition side of the House are party leaders who *would* be in the cabinet were their party in power.

Although the terms "frontbencher" and "backbencher" are positional terms, designating only *where one sits*, they are also terms of power. This is true because as legislators' seniority and power increases, they tend to move to the front bench. Those seated on the front bench have power and influence.

Although the British model of legislature places an emphasis—because of its physical organization—on the "Government versus the Opposition" conflict in the legislature, not all legislatures are organized in this way. We noted in our discussion of ideology that "left" and "right" were simply holdovers from 1798,

Interior of the British House of Commons. General view from the Opposition benches looking toward the Speaker's Chair (rear center) and the Government benches (left). The Clerk's table is in the center. (British Official Photograph: Crown Copyright Reserved. Issued by the Central Office of Information, London.)

at which time the French Council of 500 was arranged in a semicircular hall of representatives according to their self-determined place in the political spectrum[51]; those generally supporting the monarch's policies sat on his right, while those who proposed changes in his policies sat on his left; hence, we noted that "leftists" today favor change and "rightists" prefer the status quo. American legislative bodies also sit in a semicircular hall.

All legislative behavior, and thereby legislative output, is influenced by many factors in the legislative system,[52] including the constitutional system in which the legislator acts,[53] sub-structures within the legislative system, including committees,[54] legislative staff and services,[55] legislative buildings and facilities, including office space,[56] party organization and leadership inside the legislature,[57] legislators' backgrounds and socialization,[58] legislative recruitment,[59] constituency and interest group pressures,[60] and party organization outside of the legislature.[61]

All of these structures and subsystems of the "legislative system" influence legislative action, which in turn affects the larger political system. These structures and subsystems are of two types, those included within or are related to the legislative assembly itself, and those found outside of the legislative assembly itself.

The Legislative Process

As David Olson argues, the most common pattern among parliaments in the process of handling legislation is to alternate the focus of activity between the *plenum*—the floor of the legislative house—and committee stages of legislation.[62] Table 4.8 shows the procedures for handling legislation in a typical legislative body; the description is generalized from actual procedures in a number of legislative bodies.[63]

Table 4.8
Steps in Legislative Procedure in a Hypothetical National Legislature

Introduction
  First reading: presentation of bill and discussion of its contents
  Debate
  Vote
  To committee(s)

When (and if) bill emerges from committee(s):
  Second reading: often presented by members of committee(s) that held hearings on the bill
  Debate
  Vote

Third reading
  Debate
  Final vote

In a bicameral system, the bill would then go to the second house, and usually go through the same procedure there.

Certainly one of the most important ingredients in the legislative process has to do with the sponsor of a bill. In systems with a high degree of party discipline, bills sponsored by the majority party are almost certain to pass, and bills sponsored by the minority party are comparably destined to fail. In parliamentary systems in which the leader of the executive branch (e.g., the prime minister) is also the leader of the legislative branch (a theme we will develop and explain in the next chapter) Government bills invariably become law, and Opposition bills invariably do not.[64]

When we speak of legislation, we do not just distinguish between frontbenchers and backbenchers, because this would group the Government frontbench with the Opposition frontbench, and the Government backbench with the Opposition backbench. Instead, we leave the Government frontbench standing alone, and group the Government backbench with the Opposition frontbench and backbench. Bills originating in the Government frontbench—where the members of the cabinet sit—are called Government bills. Bills originating from any other member of parliament, either in the Government backbenches or the Opposition frontbenches or backbenches, are called private members' bills.

In a now-classic study of the relative difference in efficacy between Government bills and private members' bills, Sheva Weiss and Avraham Brichta found a startling, though predictable, difference in legislative effectiveness between the chances of passage of Government bills and private members' bills.[65] Bills introduced by the Government invariably pass and become law; bills introduced by private members do not usually enjoy the same fate.

The reason that bills suggested by Government backbenchers do not have the same success rate as Government bills has to do with party discipline, a concept we have already met. Because of party discipline, all Government bills will receive the support of all members of the Government side of the House, a majority. An individual backbencher on the Government side might have an idea for a bill that the Government does not support, but may not oppose. In this case, the Government might not invoke "tight party discipline" to have the bill passed. The

Government, however, would invoke party discipline to defeat most proposals coming from the Opposition side of the house.

Legislatures and Executives

Much has been made in recent years about the "decline of the legislature" as a viable political structure,[66] effectively able to counterbalance the growing structure of the political executive. The argument is made that in the modern political world the executive structure has grown at an alarming rate in terms of the increase in and centralization of its power, and the legislative structure has correspondingly lost power. This means that the legislature is less able today to provide a meaningful check on the power of the executive.

Some have argued that there is nothing wrong with this scenario at all, and have gone so far as to suggest that the legislature *ought* to expedite this process by voluntarily ceding to the executive many of its own powers. The legislature can remain as an institution, according to these advocates, but it should permit the executive to lead, with the legislature's proper role being to follow.[67]

The question of the relationship between the legislature and the executive is one that can be addressed on two levels. On the normative level, we can ask about what the relationship *should* be. More precisely, which alternative best promotes democratic, representative government? On the empirical level, we can ask about the validity of the observations that legislatures are declining in significance while executives are on the ascent. Is it true? What happens to the executive structure when the legislature loses its power?

Evidence seems to show without fail that the executive institution is winning the battle with the legislative branch, generally speaking. There simply is no way that a legislative body can keep up with a rapidly expanding executive bureaucracy in terms of information, personnel, and ability to formulate policy. To take the example of foreign policy, it simply is not possible for the British House of Commons Committee on Foreign Affairs (with a staff of less than a dozen) to oversee successfully the Ministry of External Affairs (with a staff of literally thousands); the same could be said of the Israeli Knesset's Foreign Affairs and

Security Committee's ability to oversee its Ministry of External Affairs, or the ability of the U.S. Senate's Foreign Relations Committee to oversee the policy of the U.S. State Department (although the U.S. Senate committees have *far* more in the way of committee staff than do committees of other national legislatures). In fact, what often ends up happening is that legislative committees become dependent upon executive agencies—whether they are Ministries of External Affairs, Defense, or Agriculture—to supply them with information, and the ability to control the information to which the legislature will have access gives the executive branch of government a permanant and overwhelming advantage in the legislative-executive power competition.

Legislative Reform

Although it may be the case that legislatures are generally regarded as having lost the battle to executives, that does not mean that they have surrendered completely. Indeed, in recent years we have seen a number of calls for reform, and in many instances some substantial changes have been made in the legislative process that have been designed to strengthen the legislature in relation to the executive, to regain some of the traditional powers of the legislature, although there have been some very clear limitations to this reform.[68]

Indeed, we should note that the subject of legislative reform is not a new one; it has been discussed by legislatures for well over a hundred years.[69] The problem has been, of course, that parliamentary reform—that is, an increase in the *de facto* power of parliament in relation to the executive—is seen as being in a zero-sum game with the executive: Any gains on the part of parliament must come at the expense of the executive. It has been demonstrated in recent years[70] that some reforms are possible without undermining the basic pillars of the parliamentary establishment, and that members of parliament may be given the opportunity to contribute to the legislative process without fear that this may cause the collapse of parliamentary government.[71]

It is to an examination of the executive structure that we now turn our attention.

Notes

1. In Sir Ernest Barker, ed., *Social Contract: Essays by Locke, Hume, & Rousseau* (New York: Oxford University Press, 1970), p. 73.
2. Ibid., pp. 73–77.
3. What has become a "definitive" resource in the field appeared in 1985, which reviewed the state of the art of legislative studies until that time. See Gerhard Loewenberg, Samuel Patterson, and Malcolm Jewell, eds., *Handbook of Legislative Research* (Cambridge: Harvard University Press, 1985).
4. Jean Blondel once wrote that "of the 138 countries which exist in the world today, only five, all in the Middle East, have never had a legislature." In Jean Blondel, *Comparative Legislatures* (Englewood Cliffs, N.J.: Prentice Hall, 1973), p. 7.
5. A very good recent study is that by Ezra Suleiman, *Parliaments and Parliamentarians in Democratic Politics* (New York: Holmes and Meier, 1986).
6. Allan Kornberg, *Canadian Legislative Behavior* (New York: Holt, Rinehart, & Winston, 1967), p. 2.
7. Allan Kornberg, Harold Clarke, and George Watson, "Toward a Model of Parliamentary Recruitment in Canada," in *Legislatures in Comparative Perspective*, ed. Allan Kornberg (New York: David McKay, 1973), p. 271.
8. Joseph LaPalombara, *Politics Within Nations* (Englewood Cliffs, N.J.: Prentice Hall, 1974), p. 177.
9. See Michael Mezey's essay "The Functions of Legislatures in the Third World," in Loewenberg, Patterson, and Jewell, *Handbook*, pp. 733–772.
10. Kornberg, Clarke, and Watson, "Toward a Model," p. 276.
11. Data come from Blondel, *Comparative Legislatures*, pp. 144–153. To illustrate different nation-counts, note that Michael Curtis says that 47 out of 144 nations in the world are bicameral. See Michael Curtis, *Comparative Government and Politics* (New York: Harper & Row, 1978), p. 195.
12. Valerie Herman, ed., *Parliaments of the World* (London: Macmillan, 1976), p. 3.
13. Ibid.
14. See James Madison, *Notes of Debates in the Federal Convention of 1787*, Introduction by Adrienne Koch (Athens: Ohio State University Press, 1966), pp. vii–xxiii.
15. See the data in Table 3.2.
16. Data come from Blondel, *Comparative Legislatures*, p. 152.
17. Kornberg, *Canadian Legislative Behavior*, p. 19. See Colin Campbell, *The Canadian Senate: A Lobby From Within* (Toronto: Macmillan of Canada, 1978).
18. Blondel, *Comparative Legislatures*, pp. 144–153. Blondel's data are out of date, and also a bit inaccurate. Caribbean data come from my research there; for the British upper house a publication by the House of Lords itself gives its total membership as 1,174. See Nicholas Baldwin, *The House of Lords: Its Constitution and Functions* (Exeter: Exeter University, Teaching Services Centre, 1982), p. 7.
19. Robert Diamond, ed., *Origins and Development of Congress* (Washington, D.C.: Congressional Quarterly, 1976), pp. 127–128.
20. Asher Zidon, *The Knesset* (New York: Herzl Press, 1967), p. 27.
21. A very good review essay is that by David Brady and Charles Bullock III,

"Party and Factions Within Legislatures," in Loewenberg and others, *Handbook*, pp. 135–189.

22. See Richard Rose, "British MPs: More Bark than Bite," in Suleiman, *Parliaments*, pp. 8–40.

23. Mark Franklin, Alison Baxter, and Margaret Jordan, "Who Were the Rebels? Dissent in the House of Commons, 1970–1974," *Legislative Studies Quarterly* 11:2 (1986): 143–160; and Edward Crowe, "The Web of Authority: Party Loyalty and Social Control in the British House of Commons," *Legislative Studies Quarterly* 11:2 (1986): 161–186.

24. John R. Hibbing and David Marsh, "Accounting for the Voting Patterns of British MPs on Free Votes," *Legislative Studies Quarterly* 12:2 (1987): 275–298.

25. A good review of the literature in this area can be found in the essays by Heinz Eulau, "Committee Selection," in Loewenberg and others, *Handbook*, pp. 191–238; and Heinz Eulau and Vera McCluggage, "Standing Committees in Legislatures," in Loewenberg and others, *Handbook*, pp. 395–470.

26. See Austin Ranney, *Pathways to Parliament* (Madison: University of Wisconsin Press, 1965).

27. A very good review essay dealing with elections is by Lyn Ragsdale, "Legislative Elections and Electoral Responsiveness," in Loewenberg and others, *Handbook*, pp. 57–96. See also Andre Blais, "The Classification of Electoral Systems," *European Journal of Political Research* 16:1 (1988): 99–110.

28. An example of this is John R. Hibbing, "Representing a Territory: Constituency Boundaries for the British House of Commons of the 1980s," *Journal of Politics* 48:4 (1986): 992–1005.

29. See Gregory Mahler, *The Knesset: Parliament in the Israeli Political System* (Rutherford, N.J.: Fairleigh Dickinson University Press, 1981), especially chap. 2.

30. Rein Taagepera and Bernard Grofman, "Rethinking Duverger's Law: Predicting the Effective Number of Parties in Plurality and PR Systems— Parties Minus Issues Equals One," *European Journal of Political Research* 13:4 (1985): 341–352.

31. This was a major concern when the French changed from an SMD system to a PR system in 1985, but the concerns did not materialize. Andrew Knapp, "Proportional But Bipolar: France's Electoral System in 1986," *West European Politics* 10:1 (1987): 89–114.

32. Gerhard Loewenberg, *Modern Parliaments: Change or Decline?* (Chicago: Atherton, 1971), p. 3.

33. Fred Riggs, "Legislative Structures: Some Thoughts on Elected National Assemblies," in Allan Kornberg, ed., *Legislatures in Comparative Perspective*, p. 74.

34. Kornberg, *Canadian Legislative Behavior*, p. 1.

35. See, among others, Loewenberg, *Modern Parliaments*.

36. John Wahlke and others, *The Legislative System* (New York: Wiley, 1962).

37. Michael Mezey, "The Functions of a Minimal Legislature: Role Perceptions of Thai Legislators," *Western Political Quarterly* 25 (1972): 686–701.

38. Blondel, *Comparative Legislatures*, p. 4.

39. Laxmi Singhvi, "Parliament in the Indian Political System," in Allan Kornberg, ed., *Legislatures in Developmental Perspective* (Durham, N.C.: Duke University Press, 1970), p. 217.

40. Loewenberg, *Modern Parliaments*, p. 3.

41. David Easton, "A Re-Assessment of the Concept of Political Support," *British Journal of Political Science* 5 (1975): 435–457.
42. Malcolm Jewell covers the literature in this area in his essay "Legislators and Constituents in the Representative Process," in Loewenberg and others, *Handbook*, pp. 97–134.
43. A good example of such an issue is the discussion found in Augie Fleras, "From Social Control Towards Political Self-Determination? Maori Seats and the Politics of Separate Maori Representation in New Zealand," *Canadian Journal of Political Science* 18:3 (1985): 599–608.
44. Wilma Rule, "Electoral Systems, Contextual Factors, and Women's Opportunity for Election to Parliament in Twenty-three Democracies," *Western Political Quarterly* 40:3 (1987): 477–498. See also Donald Studlar and Susan Welch, "Understanding the Iron Law of Andrarchy: Effects of Candidate Gender on Voting in Scotland," *Comparative Political Studies* 20:2 (1987): 174–191.
45. Walter S. G. Kohn, *Women in National Legislatures: A Comparative Study of Six Countries* (New York: Praeger, 1980), p. 234.
46. An entire issue of *Legislative Studies Quarterly* was recently devoted to this topic, including the following: Heinz Eulau, "Converse and Pierce on Representation in France: The Congruence Model Revisited," *Legislative Studies Quarterly* 12:2 (1987): 171–214; John C. Wahlke, "Converse and Pierce on Representation in France: Legislative Behavior, 1967–1968," *Legislative Studies Quarterly* 12:2 (1987): 215–226; Mark Franklin and Thomas Mackie, "Converse and Pierce on Representation in France: Electoral Behavior," *Legislative Studies Quarterly* 12:2 (1987): 227–236; and Jean Charlot, "Converse and Pierce on Representation in France: The Responsible Party Model," *Legislative Studies Quarterly* 12:2 (1987): 237–242. See also Chan Wook Park, "Constituency Representation in Korea: Sources and Consequences," *Legislative Studies Quarterly* 13:2 (1988): 225–242; David Wood, "The Conservative Member of Parliament as Lobbyist for Constituency Economic Interests," *Political Studies* 35:3 (1987): 393–409.
47. Raymond Hopkins, "The Role of the M.P. in Tanzania," *American Political Science Review* 64 (1970): 754.
48. Kornberg, *Canadian Legislative Behavior*, p. 8. For an example of a diagrammatic depiction of role orientations, see Malcolm Jewell and Samuel Patterson, *The Legislative Process in the United States* (New York: Random House, 1973), p. 408.
49. Mezey, "Thai Legislators," and Mahler, *The Knesset*, especially chap. 8.
50. LaPalombara, *Politics Within Nations*, pp. 180–182, and Jewell and Patterson, *Legislative Process*, respectively.
51. Curtis, *Comparative Government and Politics*, p. 158.
52. See Ronald Hedlund, "Organizational Attributes of Legislative Institutions: Structure, Rules, Norms, Resources," in Loewenberg and others, *Handbook*, pp. 321–394.
53. See M. Cormack, "The Australian Senate," *Parliamentarian* 53 (1972): 175–185; J. Lynsky, "The Role of the British Backbencher in the Modification of Government Policy," *Western Political Quarterly* 23 (1970): 333–347; and Sheva Weiss and Avraham Brichta, "Private Members' Bills in Israel's Parliament," *Parliamentary Affairs* 23 (1969): 21–33.
54. See J. Pettifer, "Privilege in the Parliament of the Commonwealth of Australia," *Parliamentarian* 53 (1972): 288.
55. See Susan Webb Hammond, "Legislative Staffs," in Loewenberg and others, *Handbook*, pp. 273–320; M. Limaye, "On Private Members' Bills,"

Journal of Constitutional and Parliamentary Studies 3 (1969): 110–113; J. Ley, "Strengthening the Position of the Backbencher in Papua, New Guinea," *Parliamentarian* 53 (1972): 303–308; or J. Robinson, "Staffing the Legislature," in Kornberg, *legislatures in Developmental Perspective*, pp. 367–390.

56. See A. McMullin, "Proposed New and Permanent Parliament Houses for the Australian Parliament," *Parliamentarian* 51 (1970): 263–269.
57. See Robert Peabody, "Leadership in Legislatures: Evolution, Selection, and Functions," in Loewenberg and others, *Handbook*, pp. 239–272.
58. Kornberg, *Canadian Legislative Behavior*, pp. 49–51.
59. See Donald R. Matthews, "Legislative Recruitment and Legislative Careers," in Loewenberg and others, *Handbook*, pp. 17–56.
60. Singhvi, "Parliament in the Indian Political System," pp. 207–213.
61. Jewell, "Legislators and Constituents," p. 118.
62. See David Olson, *The Legislative Process: A Comparative Approach* (New York: Harper & Row, 1980), p. 346, for a discussion of specific procedures in a number of nations.
63. A good theoretical essay is that by William Panning, "Formal Models of Legislative Processes," in Loewenberg and others, *Handbook*, pp. 669–700.
64. See Melissa P. Collie, "Voting Behavior in Legislatures," in Lowenberg and others, *Handbook*, pp. 471–518.
65. See Weiss and Brichta, "Private Members' Bills," p. 25.
66. See Bert Rockman, "Legislative-Executive Relations and Legislative Oversight," in Loewenberg and others, *Handbook*, pp. 519–572; Keith Hamm, "Legislative Committees, Executive Agencies, and Interest Groups," in Ibid., pp. 573–620; and Bruce Oppenheimer, "Legislative Influence on Policy and Budgets," in *Ibid.*, pp. 621–668.
67. See especially the classic argument of Samuel P. Huntington, "Congressional Responses to the Twentieth Century," in *Congress and the President*, ed. Ronald Moe (Pacific Palisades, Calif.: Goodyear Publishing Co., 1971), pp. 7–31.
68. Kevin J. O'Brien, "China's National People's Congress: Reform and Its Limits," *Legislative Studies Quarterly* 13:3 (1988): 343–374.
69. On this note see David Judge, "Why Reform? Parliamentary Reform Since 1832: An Interpretation," in David Judge, ed., *The Politics of Parliamentary Reform* (Rutherford, N.J.: Fairleigh Dickinson University Press, 1984), pp. 9–36.
70. Here I would recommend several essays, including the following: Philip Norton, "Behavioural Changes: Backbench Independence in the 1980s," in Philip Norton, ed., *Parliament in the 1980s* (Oxford: Basil Blackwell, 1985), pp. 22–47; Stephen Downs, "Structural Changes: Select Committees: Experiment and Establishment," in Ibid, pp. 48–68; or Michael Rush, "Parliamentary Reform: The Canadian Experience," in Judge, *Parliamentary Reform*, pp. 147–164.
71. One example of this type of reform can be found in an article by Audrey O'Brien, "Parliamentary Task Forces in the Canadian House of Commons: A New Approach to Committee Activity," *The Parliamentarian* 66:1 (1985): 28–32.

5

The Executive

Introduction

When John Locke wrote that the state of nature was wanting power to back and support the sentence of a national judiciary,[1] he was speaking of an executive power. There is a great deal of difference, however, between the kind of executive power that Locke had in mind and the kind of political executive that we find in contemporary political systems. What are the power situations in which contemporary political executives find themselves? How do they get where they are? What kind of relationships do they have with the legislatures of their respective political settings? It is to these questions that we shall try to respond in this chapter.

The Executive Roles

What does an executive do in a political system? In his classic study of the American presidency, Clinton Rossiter listed ten distinct, identifiable roles that the president is expected to play in the American political arena. They are:

1. Chief of State	6. Chief of Party
2. Chief Executive	7. Voice of the People
3. Commander-in-Chief	8. Protector of Peace
4. Chief Diplomat	9. Manager of Prosperity
5. Chief Legislator	10. World Leader[2]

When we look at this list of duties that the president must perform, we must marvel that anyone is able to handle the demands of the office. Indeed, this was one of the major themes of Rossiter's study. Wouldn't a political system be more efficiently run if it hired a *crew* of executives to handle all of these jobs, one job to a person? Actually, the concept of a *multiple executive* is not new at all, and in a number of different political contexts in the history of political systems the multiple executive has been tried out. At the Federal Convention in Philadelphia in 1787 where the American Constitution was created, the idea of a multiple executive was suggested but was rejected because history had shown that it might tend to (1) cause divisiveness when a difficult decision needed to be made, and (2) obscure responsibility, or culpability, in that blame for a bad decision might be difficult to attribute to a single individual.[3]

In point of fact, Rossiter's list of ten roles of the president may be more detailed than is necessary. Political history has shown that we really only need to separate the executive role into two components: a symbolic role and a political role.[4] In the former, the executive represents the dignity of the state. The executive lays wreaths on tombs, attends funerals, sponsors Easter egg hunts, lights the national Christmas tree, makes national proclamations, and generally serves a ceremonial function. In the latter, or political, role, the chief executive "manages the national business," and makes the hard political decisions that need to be made. In this context the chief executive can be seen to be chief of the executive branch of government, the ultimate decision maker in a huge pyramid of decision-makers, the owner of the desk where "the buck stops."

There are, generally speaking, four approaches to the executive institution that are found in political systems around the world, two of which we shall examine at this time. This is *not* to suggest that all political systems are identical to one or the other of these four models; but rather it suggests that *virtually all* political systems are *modelled after* one or the other of the four general plans. We will see in the second part of this book that *all* political systems have their idiosyncratic differences, but at this stage of our study we are only concerned with explaining the *general* models.

One general type of political executive can be referred to as the *presidential* model of executive, and the other type of political executive can be referred to as the *"Westminster" parliamentary-cabinet* form of executive. Later in this text we will add discussion of the *French parliamentary-cabinet* model and the *Soviet–East European collective executive* model (although the Soviet–East European model has become virtually extinct within the last year), which really are variations on the two models we shall discuss here. As we did with our discussion of legislatures, we will preface our descriptions of executives by saying that what we are about to describe will vary in specific detail from country to country.

The Presidential Executive

The type of political executive with which American students are most familiar is the presidential executive. American students are often surprised to learn, however, that the presidential model of executive behavior is in a minority once we look beyond the borders of the United States. The model was developed in the United States and has been copied by a number of political systems outside of the United States, primarily in Central and South America but also in Africa and Asia.

The presidential model centralizes both political power and symbolic authority in one individual, the president. The president is the individual presiding at ceremonial functions, and it is the president who symbolizes the nation in the eyes of the rest of the world. The president is the head of state. Foreign diplomats present their credentials to him (and, in a number of countries in the world, to *her*). He presents the State of the Union message to the Congress each year. He throws out the first ball to open the baseball season.[5]

Presidential systems do not separate the dignity and the business functions of the office, although such suggestions have been made in the past. For example, some have suggested that since American government has the institution of the vice presidency, which has few constitutional duties and whose primary significance is not in what it is but in what it might become, a good use of the vice president might be to assign to him (or someday *her*) the ceremonial duties of office and leave the president to important decision-making duties. The problem is that vice presidents do not jump at the idea of spending all of their time at funerals and ceremonies. Moreover, the public does not accept the idea either; the vice president is, after all, the second officer of American government, not the first, and the public wants to see the president.[6]

The strength of the presidency is in its independence. In the American presidential system, which is the model for presidential systems elsewhere, the president is elected independently from the legislature. Presidential elections in the United States are held every four years, no more frequently, and no less frequently.

As indicated in Figure 5.1, the president is independently elected on the basis of popular election. The American political system has an additional structure inserted between the populace and the president, the electoral college, which officially elects the president. The genesis of the electoral college is based upon the distrust of the Founding Fathers of the popular will; the founders were suspicious of popular opinion, and it was felt that by having voters choose electors, who would subsequently cast ballots for the presidency, their concern could be resolved.[7] Recent American political history has shown the electoral college to be an anachro-

Figure 5.1
Presidential Systems' Bases of Power

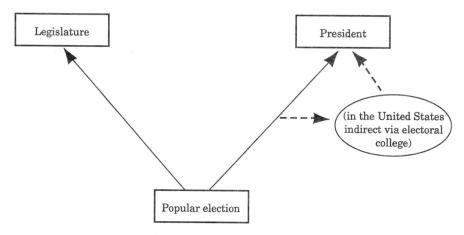

nistic institution, and efforts are regularly undertaken to do away with the institution and to have the president directly elected by the public.

The fact that the American public votes in several different electoral contests, once for the president and vice president, and once for the House of Representatives (all seats in the House of Representatives come up for reelection every two years), and, where a contest is held, once for the Senate (Senate seats have six-year terms and are staggered so that both seats in any given state are not up for election at the same time) is quite significant for a number of reasons. First, it gives the president an independent power base. Short of the process of impeachment, which history has shown can be instituted only for high crimes and treason, not simply for reasons of political opposition, the president does not depend on either the legislature or public opinion for continuation of his (or her) four-year term. Once the president is in office, this individual remains in office until the term is completed. This allows the president to take actions that may be unpopular with both the public and the legislature in the short term, but which the president feels, nonetheless, are the right actions to take.

A second significant point is that this relationship also works in the other direction. That is, American legislators are chosen by the people, not by the president, and as long as they keep their constituencies happy they can act independently of the president, and there is virtually nothing that the president can do to them. As already indicated, members of the House of Representatives are elected for two-year terms, and although the president may threaten not to campaign for them in the next electoral campaign if they don't do what he wants them to do, the president cannot directly affect their time in office, cannot "fire" them. Senators are elected to six-year terms, and they, in a similar manner, are secure in their office.[8] A president might be angry when a senator from his party fails to support the president's legislation in the Senate, but there is little the president can do to directly "punish" a recalcitrant senator short of threatening to withhold future support.

A third significant point to note is that this structural independence of the branches of government (which is depicted in Figure 5.1) can have some negative consequences. By virtue of the fact that both the executive and legislative branches of government have secure tenure in office, they can frustrate each other, but that is all they can do. The president can veto acts of Congress, but Congress can override the presidential veto. (The president does *not* have an "absolute" veto that is impossible to override.) Congress can refuse to pass a legislative request of the president, and the president can try to accomplish his goals through executive decrees, executive agreements, and similar unilateral executive actions.

It is important to keep in mind that the president is *not* part of the legislative branch of government, and cannot, literally, take part in the legislative process. Only senators can introduce bills in the Senate, and only representatives can introduce bills in the House. If the president is unable to find a legislative "sponsor" for a bill (something that, realistically, is unimaginable!), he or she would be unable to introduce new legislation. This means that the situation can deteriorate to one that we can label as a point of *immobilism*; each actor has the power to frustrate and block the other, which means that it is possible that *nothing* will get done.

This situation is most evident when the two branches of government are controlled by the two major political parties. When Richard Nixon (a Republican) was president he faced a Senate and House controlled by Democrats; the relationship between the two branches of government was frequently tense, with presidential vetoes and legislative defeats of presidential proposals flying back and forth. This situation was repeated during the term of (Republican) Ronald Reagan in the 1980s, part of the time with a Congress partly controlled by Democrats (a Republican Senate and a Democratic House), and part of the time fully controlled by a Democratic majority in both houses. Although it is true that both Nixon and Reagan were able to get the support of some Southern (and other more conservative) Democrats, as a general rule much tension existed between the two branches.

Party difference is not a *requirement* for this kind of tension, however. The four years of Jimmy Carter (a Democratic president with a Democratic Congress) were not terribly productive, either, and often witnessed the same tension. After his inauguration, Carter proposed a national energy program, which he labelled "the moral equivalent of war." By the time the Congress acted, (over two years later), Carter's original legislative proposals were almost unrecognizable when compared with the legislation produced by the Congress.

In brief, although the executive and legislative branches of government *may* pull in tandem, they do not *necessarily* do so, and the structure of the independently selected presidency and legislative branch does enable the state of *immobilism* to develop.

The Parliamentary Executive

The parliamentary executive is more complex than its presidential alternative, if for no other reason than it is in reality a *multiple executive*. The head of state function and the chief executive function are performed by two separate individuals, whose titles vary by political system (see Table 5.1).

The function of the head of state is to symbolize the state and the dignity of the political regime. The head of state will receive ambassadors, host receptions, lay wreaths at tombs, and, generally, perform many of the ceremonial tasks government requires. Heads of state, generally speaking, are chosen one of three ways. First, in a number of political systems—about one third of all parliamentary systems—the head of state is a hereditary position, one that "belongs" to the royal family. Certainly among the

Table 5.1
Executive Titles

Nation	Presidential/ Parliamentary	Head of State	Chief Executive
Australia	Parl.	Governor-General[a]	Prime Minister
Canada	Parl.	Governor-General[a]	Prime Minister
India	Parl.	President	Prime Minister
Israel	Parl.	President	Prime Minister
Italy	Parl.	President	Prime Minister
Japan	Parl.	Emperor	Prime Minister
Mexico	Pres.	President	President
United Kingdom	Parl.	Queen	Prime Minister
United States	Pres.	President	President
Germany	Parl.	President	Chancellor

[a]Serving on behalf of the monarch in his or her absence.

best-known examples of this manner of selection is the British monarchy, with a clearly delineated line of succession.

A second pattern of selection is one in which the head of state is selected by a governmental body, often the legislature. The president of Israel is elected by the Israeli parliament, the Knesset, and the president of India is elected by the Indian parliament, the Lok Sabha and the Rajya Sabha. Finally, a third method of selection has been referred to as "self-selection," and is characteristic of political systems in which power has been seized, such as the position of Fidel Castro in Cuba, or the now-toppled position of Idi Amin as president-for-life in Uganda.[9]

The chief executive, on the other hand, is precisely what his or her title implies: the chief of the executive branch of government. The chief executive is a full-time politician, devoting little time to ceremonial duties of office. Generally speaking, the chief executive in a parliamentary regime performs the same tasks as the chief executive in a presidential regime, but not the symbolic activities. Both executives coordinate government policy-making. Both executives are assisted by cabinets of individuals heading separate departments or ministries of government. Both executives are responsible for the day-to-day operation of government.

In many political systems the position of chief executive is totally without legal basis, but instead is founded upon years of political custom and tradition, which we have already noted can be just as important as written constitutional measures. The manner in which the office of the chief executive in parliamentary systems was created is significant in that it tells us a great deal about both the position of the chief executive and the manner in which that position relates to the position of the head of state.

The Changing Role of the Monarchy

Even though we will not focus solely upon British politics until later in this volume, when we discuss the development of parliamentary government we *are*, in fact, discussing British political history, just as we are discussing American political history when we speak of the development of the presidential model of government. Although many parliamentary systems today differ to varying degrees from the contemporary British system, the parliamentary system of government as we know it was born in

England, and is generally regarded as starting with Robert Walpole as prime minister in 1741. An exceedingly brief survey of nine centuries of political history is in order here to help us understand and appreciate the role of the British monarchy today.[10]

When William, Duke of Normandy, took the English throne in 1066 there already existed a political structure called the *witenagemot*, a legislative assembly of sorts, which formally elected him king. William the Conqueror (as he became known) extended and formalized the continental feudal system during his tenure and institutionalized the *Curia Regis*, the King's Court, as a political body. At this time there was no distinction among the legislative, executive, and judicial functions of government (John Locke was not to come onto the scene for another 600 years!): All government was the king. The king used both the Curia Regis and the witenagemot as sources of funds, and in return for members' financial support he listened to their counsel and advice, although he was clearly not bound to accept it.

In 1215 the group of barons of the realm that had made up the Curia Regis drew up a document that was called the *Magna Carta*, this document described what the barons considered to be the proper relationship between the king and the barons of the realm. It is important to note that this was not a declaration of *new* rights and privileges, but rather was an expression of what the barons asserted *to have been* the relationship for some time, arguing that the king had been forgetting some of the powers and rights that kings had already given to barons and the public. This "Great Charter" was a significant constitutional document. It expounded upon political obligations of the time: peoples' obligations to the king, the king's obligations to the people, and how law and justice should be administered.

During the thirteenth century the resources of the barons of the Curia Regis were not sufficient for the needs of government, and the Curia Regis called upon representatives of towns and counties for "aids"—financial help. In exchange for their financial contributions, the representatives of the towns and counties were admitted to the Curia Regis alongside the barons, thus giving the Curia Regis two classes of members: the earlier baronial membership, which became the House of Lords, and its new (and often elected) membership, which became the House of Commons. The term "parliament," which refers to these bodies, was first used during the thirteenth century to refer to their debating function.

Because the king was receiving financial assistance from both groups, he was now obligated to discuss public affairs not only with the baronial nobility but also with the representatives of the commoners. The public's representatives had an important weapon in their hands to ensure that they were listened to: the right to assent, or refuse to assent, to the king's proposals for raising money. Parliament, especially the House of Commons, used this power as a condition with the king: its approval of royal financial proposals in exchange for the king's attention to public grievances. By about the year 1500 the Commons had grown in political strength to the point at which it could introduce proposals on its own to change laws, and could offer amendments to bills that had originated in the House of Lords, the previously superior house of the legislature.

The seventeenth century saw the legislature's power grow in relation to the monarch, and it was a period of much stress. King James I (1603–1625) was an advocate of the "Divine Right of Kings" theory,[11] which argued that the monarch derived his power directly from God, not from the people. James had little need for Parliament as an institution, and he argued that any privileges of Parliament were gifts from the King, not rights of Parliament. During James's twenty-two-year reign, Parliament sat for only eight years. On a number of occasions the king "dissolved" the House of Commons, declared that members were not "truly" elected, and sent them home—in effect, he fired them.

Charles I succeeded his father, James I, in 1625, and followed his father's practice of imprisoning members of Parliament (especially, of course, members of the House of Commons) who opposed him. When Charles could not control Parliament, he dissolved it and called for new elections after a period of time. By 1640 Charles was in need of funds and convened Parliament to authorize new taxes. The Commons refused; three weeks later Charles again dissolved Parliament. This became known as the "Short Parliament."

Six months later another Parliament assembled, which became known as the "Long Parliament." The issue upon which the election for the House of Commons had been held was the question of whether the king should rule Parliament, or whether

Parliament should rule the king. Within two years an armed struggle ensued between supporters of the king and supporters of the Parliament; eventually the royal army was defeated and Charles was captured and sentenced to death (1649) as "a tyrant, traitor, murderer, and public enemy." The Commons dissolved the British monarchy and established a republic. In 1660 the Long Parliament dissolved itself, and the Convention that was elected to take its place restored the Stuart family to the throne. Charles II became king of England.

Through the reign of Charles II (1660–1685) and James II (1685–1688) the Parliament-monarch tensions grew again, and in 1688 James II was pressured into abdicating—resigning his position as monarch. Parliament then invited William, Prince of Orange, and grandson of Charles I, to rule, and William and his wife, Mary, were proclaimed king and queen by Parliament in 1688.

During the reign of William and Mary the English constitutional system became much more stable; indeed, it laid much of the groundwork for stable constitutional government to come. The British *Bill of Rights* (1689)—which asserted that taxes could be raised only with the assent of Parliament, guaranteed the people the right to petition the king, limited the use of the army without the consent of Parliament, guaranteed free elections and freedom of speech and debate in Parliament, limited excessive bail, prohibited "cruel and unusual punishment," and asserted that Parliament ought to meet frequently—became law. Parliament became institutionalized as a significant political actor in the English system of government.

Constitutional Monarchy

Over nearly the last three centuries, the relationship between the king and the Parliament has evolved to a point that not even William and Mary would recognize. *De jure*, under law, most powers of the British government (and parliamentary governments, generally) are still exercised in the name of the king or queen, but today they are invariably exercised "on the advice" of the chief executive.

In the eighteenth and nineteenth centuries, the king relied more and more on his cabinet, a group of advisors, for guidance. In the early eighteenth century the role of the cabinet was *only* that of providing *advice*; the king still could do as he pleased. As ideas of democratic and republican government grew over the next two centuries, the power relationship had changed so that the king was now *obligated*, although not *legally required*, to accept the advice of cabinet members, who by now were primarily chosen from that house of Parliament elected by the public, namely the House of Commons. Now the cabinet was in reality governing in the name of the king, and without consulting him.

Among the most striking characteristics of parliamentary government today, wherever we find it, is the duality of its executive leadership that we referred to earlier. The monarch is the official (*de jure*) head of state, but the active (*de facto*) head of government is the prime minister. Appointments are made, acts of parliament or the legislature are proclaimed, and all government is carried on in the name of the monarch, although it is the prime minister and his or her cabinet who make all of the selections for appointments, who author or sponsor legislative proposals, and who make the administrative decisions that keep government running.

The legal bases for the prime minister and cabinet are rare, and in many political systems both the prime minister and cabinet are constitutionally nonexistent institutions. In the case of Great Britain (and many Commonwealth nations), the legal claim to power of the cabinet rests in the fact that, ever since the seventeenth century, the monarch has had a Privy Council to advise him or her—a kind of present-day cabinet. Today, although the Privy Council is no longer active, cabinet members are *first* made members of the Privy Council, and *then* are appointed to the cabinet. The cabinet meets as a "subcommittee" of the (inactive) Privy Council, and acts in the name of the Privy Council, a body that *does* have constitutional and legal status. Discussing the relationship between the Canadian cabinet and the Queen's Privy Council for Canada, R. MacGregor Dawson has noted:

> Those appointed to the Privy Council remain members for life, and hence will include not only ministers from the present Cabinet, but also all surviving ministers of past Cabinets as well. The Privy Council would therefore, if active, be a large and politically cumbersome body with members continually at cross-purposes with one another; but is has saved itself from this embarrassment by the simple device of holding no meetings.

The Cabinet, lacking any legal status of its own, masquerades as the Privy Council when it desires to assume formal power; it speaks and acts in the name of the entire Council.[12]

The Selection of the Chief Executive

Although the British monarch may have felt free to chose whomever he or she wanted as advisors in the seventeenth and eighteenth centuries, such is no longer the case today. The process by which the head of state in a parliamentary political system selects the chief executive is another one of those patterns of behavior that may legally (*de jure*) be entirely up to the head of state, but practically and politically (*de facto*) the head of state usually has little or no choice in the matter at all.

In parliamentary systems of government, unlike their presidential counterparts, there is no special election for the chief executive. The chief executive is elected as a member of the legislature, just as all the other members of the legislature are elected. Elections for the legislature are held on a regular basis that varies with the political system. In Britain the term of the House of Commons is limited to five years. (Keep in mind, of course, that the upper house, the House of Lords, is appointed, not elected, and hence has nothing at all to do with the selection of the executive.) In Israel, to take another example, elections must be held at least every four years.

After the elections for legislative seats have taken place, it is the duty of the head of state to "invite" someone to create a Government. (It should be noted at this point that the term "Government" with a capital *G* has a specific meaning in this volume, namely the prime minister and the cabinet; "government" with a small *g* refers to the general political system.) Although the head of state in most systems is technically free to select whomever he or she wants for the Government, in practice and custom (*de facto*) heads of state are "required" to invite the leader of the largest political party in the legislature—a recognition of the will of the people—as indicated in Figure 5.2.[13]

Once the head of state designates an individual to create a Government, that individual will subsequently "advise" the head of state as to whom to appoint to the cabinet. When the Government (prime minister and cabinet) is assembled, in most political systems that Government must first receive a *vote of confidence* from the legislature before it assumes office. The vote of confi-

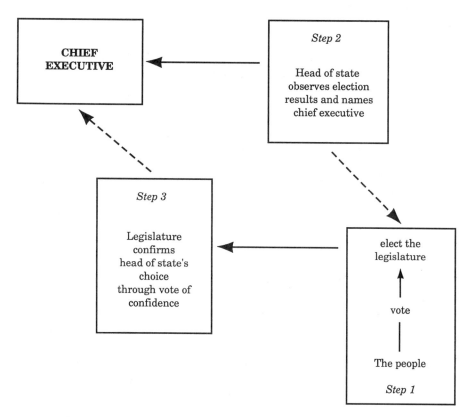

Figure 5.2
The Selection of the Parliamentary Chief Executive

dence is simply a vote by a majority of the legislative house indicating its confidence in, or support for, the prime minister and his or her cabinet.

In most political systems if the Government does not receive a vote of confidence—if it receives the support of less than a majority of the legislature in a vote—it cannot take office, and another Government must be designated by the head of state. The British case is an exception to the general rule that newly designated Governments need votes of confidence. In the case of Britain, and many other Commonwealth nations, the designation by the head of state *assumes* legislative confidence (e.g., the head of state wouldn't make the appointment without making sure of legislative support first), and the Government assumes power immediately, without first needing an expression of confidence of the legislature.

The institution of the vote of confidence is an indication of *legislative supremacy* in the political system. That is, the legislature "hires" the executive (although the head of state may "nominate" him or her). The chancellor in Germany, as well as the prime minister in Israel or Japan or India, to cite just a few examples, assumes power only *after* this individual has received a majority vote of support in the legislature.

This legislative power also works in the other direction. Just as the legislature "hires" the executive, by expressing support in one of its members forming a Government, it can "fire" the executive by expressing a *lack* of confidence in the Government. Whenever the chief executive loses the confidence of the legislature, whenever the legislature passes a resolution of *no confidence* (or, conversely, fails to pass an expression of confidence), the chief executive is in fact fired. If the legislature expresses a lack of confidence in the chief executive only a week after that person has assumed office, he or she must resign. In some systems this resignation is a legal requirement; elsewhere it is simply a custom that has the force of law. In some political systems a vote of no confidence is not even required to fire a chief executive: If the Government is defeated on *any* major piece of legislation, that is *considered* as an expression of a lack of confidence in the Government. It should be added that in most parliamentary systems, with their strong tradition of party discipline and the ability of the prime minister to muster a majority, votes of no confidence are very rare. They do, however, happen.

When the Government (that is, the prime minister) resigns, we say that the *Government has fallen*. A Government falls when either of two things happens: It loses on a question of confidence or a major piece of legislation, or the prime minister dies or resigns for some reason. The resignation of an individual minister does not cause a Government to fall, but the resignation of the prime minister does cause the Government to fall.[14]

The prime minister in a parliamentary system, then, does not have the job security that a president in a presidential system does. The prime minister is selected by the head of state to be chief executive *precisely because* he or she is the leader of the largest party in the legislature. If this individual's party controls a *majority* of the legislative seats, and if the prime minister can maintain that majority through party discipline, this peson should be able to remain prime minister for the entire term of the legislature (and perhaps several terms of the legislature). If, however, the prime minister does not control a majority, or if the prime minister is not able to retain the support of a majority of the legislature, his or her tenure might be brief.

Of course, if there is a party with a majority, the head of state will appoint its leader to be prime minister. (Obviously, if the head of state appointed anyone else, the majority party would make sure that the new Government failed to receive a vote of confidence.) If there is no majority party, one of three situations is possible. First, the head of state may appoint someone to head a *minority government*, one in which the prime minister does not control over 50 percent of the seats in the legislature. Minority governments tend to be short-lived. They usually obtain an initial vote of confidence through a temporary understanding among a number of parties who do not want another election right away, and who see a minority government as the least of several evils. These initial understandings usually break down after a short while and result in a no-confidence vote and the Government falling.[15]

An example of such a government occurred in 1979 in Canada. The Conservative party, headed by Joe Clark, won slightly less than half of the seats in the House of Commons, capturing 48.2 percent of the House seats (136 of 282) based upon 35.8 percent of the popular vote. (Based upon our discussion of electoral systems in Chapter 4, it should be clear how in a single-member-district system like Canada 35.8 percent of the popular vote could yield 48.2 percent of the seats in the legislature.) The two left-of-center parties, the Liberals (114 seats) and the (socialist) New Democratic Party (26 seats) combined, controlled 49.6 percent of the seats in Parliament, with a small conservative faction, the Social Credit party, controlling about 2 percent (6 seats). Clark vowed to run the government "as if he had a majority," believing that the (conservative) Social Credit party would prefer his (Conservative party) leadership to that of the Liberal and socialist opposition, giving him a practical working arrangement of 142 seats out of 282 in any parliamentary vote, a clear (but bare) majority. The Conservative and the Social Credit parties never entered into a formal coalition, however.

Approximately six months after the election, Clark introduced his first budget in the House of Commons, and the Social Credit party announced that it found some of the tax measures in the budget so objectionable that it intended to abstain on the budget vote, leaving a 136-member Conservative party to face a 140-member opposition. A motion of no confidence was introduced by the opposition parties, and the Clark Government fell.

A second alternative when there is no majority party is for the head of state to appoint someone to form a *coalition government*. A coalition government is one in which two or more non-majority parties pool their resources (in this case, seats in the legislature) to form a majority parliamentary bloc. There may well be a formal agreement drawn up among the participants in the coalition, in which they agree to team up and create a majority in the legislature to support a Government. We will discuss coalition governments shortly.

The third alternative, and one usually not taken right away, is for the head of state to not form *any* Government, but instead to *dissolve the legislature*—fire the newly elected legislators—and call for new elections in the hope that the next one will result in one party winning a clear mandate. This usually is not taken as a first resort, but if the head of state appoints a minority government, which falls within a short period of time, it may be clear to that person that political stability is simply not possible with the legislature constituted in its current form. If such is the case, the head of state may dissolve the legislature and call for new elections.[16]

The chief executive, then, is selected by the head of state *from* the legislature. The chief executive retains his or her position as long as the legislature continues to express support for the Government by approving the proposals of the Government. The concept of party discipline is very important in this regard, for it is party discipline that enables the prime minister to control the legislature. There is a circular relationship at work here: The prime minister is selected to be prime minister precisely because he or she is the chosen leader of the largest party in the legislature. This person will remain prime minister as long as he or she can control a majority of the legislature. When a majority *cannot* be controlled, a motion of no confidence will be passed, and the prime minister will be forced (through either law or custom) to resign.

At this point it is *not* necessary that new elections be held. The head of state must now reassess the situation and may invite someone else (or perhaps even the same person who last failed) to try to form a Government and receive an expression of legislative confidence. This process—a Government being designated, receiving a vote of confidence, surviving for a period of time, receiving a vote of no confidence and falling, a new Government being designated, and so on—can go on, over and over again, until the head of state decides that there is no point in trying again. At that point the head of state will issue a *writ of dissolution*, "dissolving" the legislature (much as we noted Charles I did in 1640), and call for new elections. Thus the entire process starts again, as indicated in Figure 5.3.

It occasionally happens that a chief executive will *cause* his or her own Government to fall, for reasons of electoral advantage. Let us suppose that in a hypothetical political system the constitution requires that elections be held at least every five years (as is the case in Great Britain), and elections are held in January 1990 that result in the Liberal party winning 56 of the 100 seats in the legislature, and the Conservative party winning the remaining 44 seats. The leader of the Liberal party, I. Maginary, becomes prime minister. As time goes by, Maginary's popularity, and correspondingly the popularity of his Liberal party, fluctuates up and down, depending upon economic factors, world events, and so on.

Prime Minister Maginary knows that if the present Government can keep the majority in the legislature satisfied, the constitution will require that elections be held *by* January 1995 (five years after the last election). In early 1993, three years into the term of the legislature but almost two years *before* elections must be held, Maginary's popularity is at an all-time high, as depicted in Figure 5.4. After some discussion with political advisors, the Maginary Government resigns and asks the head of state to dissolve the legislature and to call for new elections. They do this because they feel that if the elections are held now, they may win control of the legislature by an *even bigger* margin than they did in 1990. The head of state has no real choice in the matter: Maginary's Liberal party controls a majority in the legislature and supports Maginary's decision to call for early elections. If the head of state were to refuse to dissolve the legislature and tried to name some other leader (such as the head of the opposition Conservative party) to form a Government, the Maginary-Liberal group would vote the new Government down by a 56–44 vote. The head of state, then, grants Prime Minister Maginary a dissolution

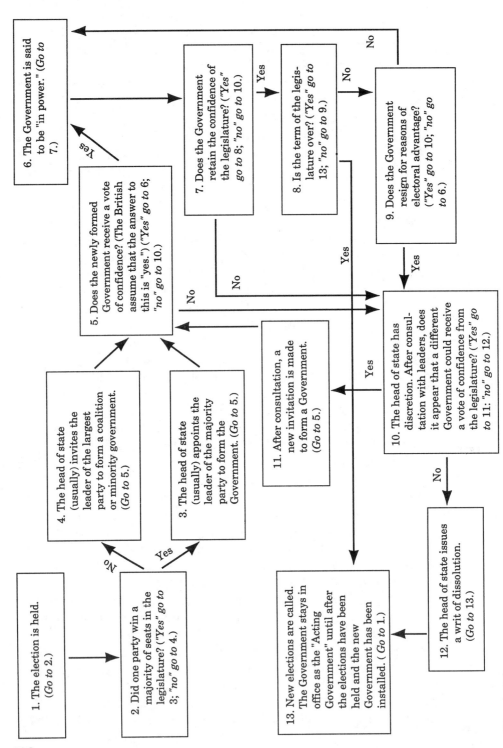

Figure 5.3
The Government-Formation Process: A Flowchart Presentation

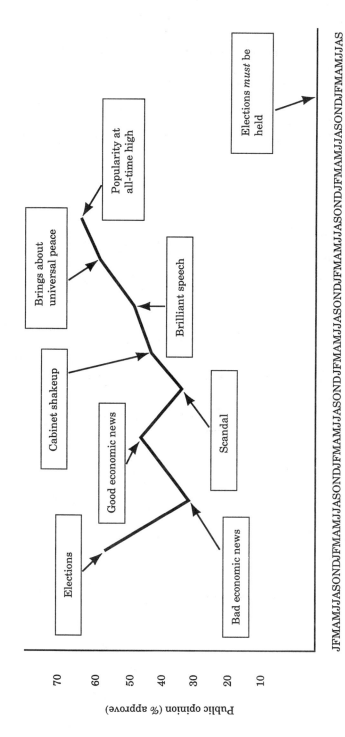

Figure 5.4
Government Falling as a Result of Fluctuations in Public Opinion

137

and calls for new elections to be held, typically in eight to ten weeks. During the interim period, the Maginary Government continues in office as the "Acting" Government, and Maginary's title is "Acting Prime Minister" until the next election is held and a new prime minister is designated by the head of state.

Although the example just presented is hypothetical, the situation it depicts happens *regularly* in parliamentary systems. In recent years, dissolutions of this type have taken place in Japan, France, Great Britain, Israel, Belgium, and India, among other nations.

Coalition Governments

In political systems that have more than two major political parties it regularly is the case that no single party controls a majority in the legislature. (Clearly, in a two party system we don't have this problem. Unless there is a tie—which turns out to be quite rare—one of the two parties must, by definition, have more than half of the legislative seats.) Where no party has a majority, as was indicated previously, several options are available to the head of state in the creation of a Government. The most commonly utilized option is the creation of a *coalition government*.

Let us take a hypothetical newly elected legislature to use as an example as we discuss the process of coalition formation. Imagine a 100-seat legislature with five political parties, as described in Table 5.2. In this instance, the head of state would most likely invite the leader of Party A to form a Government, since Leader A has the largest popular mandate. We should note, however, that in most systems the head of state is not *required* to invite Leader A; the head of state can invite anyone that he or she

Table 5.2
A Hypothetical Legislative Composition

Party A	33 seats
Party B	20 seats
Party C	18 seats
Party D	16 seats
Party E	13 seats

feels has the best chance to form a coalition successfully. Leader A needs to find an additional 18 seats in order to form a majority of 51 to support his Government in the legislature. In this case, Leader A could go to either the leader of Party B, or the leader of Party C, to find a partner. As well, of course, Leader A could go to *more* than one other party to try to form an ABC coalition, for example.

Usually, Leader A will have to promise the leader(s) of other parties involved in the coalition some reward for joining the coalition. In most instances, this reward is a cabinet position (or several cabinet positions). Sometimes the payoff is a promise that a certain piece of legislation that the prospective coalition partner has drafted will be passed as part of the Government's program.[17]

If Leader A can reach an agreement with one or more partners to form a coalition that will control a majority of the seats in the legislature, then Leader A will receive his or her vote of confidence, and the Government can be said to be installed. If, however, Leader A *cannot* find sufficient coalition partnership within a constitutionally mandated period of time, usually two to three weeks, then Leader A must return his or her "mandate" to the head of state and inform the head of state of the leader's inability to form a coalition.

At this point, as indicated earlier, the head of state makes a decision. The head of state could either dissolve the legislature and call for new elections, with the hope that in another election a party in the next legislature might win a majority, or at least a large enough plurality to be able to form a coalition easily; or the head of state could invite some other party leader to try to form a government. In our hypothetical example, the head of state at this point might turn to Leader B to see whether that person could form a coalition.

The process then goes on and on in this fashion. At each occasion that a Government fails to retain the confidence, or support, of a majority in the legislature—that is, a motion of no confidence introduced by the opposition passes, or a motion of confidence introduced by a Government supporter fails—the head of state must decide whether *another* leader might be able to succeed. Elections, after all, are expensive, and possibly divisive, and one doesn't want to have a national election every six months.

Coalition majority governments *tend* to be less stable than single-party majority governments in parliamentary systems.[18]

In a single-party majority system, the prime minister must be concerned with party discipline keeping party followers in line. In a coalition system, the flow of power is more diffuse. The prime minister exercises party discipline over his or her party followers, and counts on the leader(s) of the partner coalition party or parties to do the same. Coalitions fail usually because of differences between party leaders—in our example above, because Leader B has a disagreement with Leader A and pulls the support of Party B out of the AB coalition—*not* because of a failure of party discipline within either Party A or Party B.[19]

As might be expected, the complexity of the coalition-formation process is a direct function of the number of political parties in a legislature.[20] In the example in Table 5.3, it is clear that Situation I is most simple, Situation II more complex, and Situation III even more complex. The more parties there are, the more possibilities there are for a winning coalition to form, and the

Table 5.3
Complexity of the Coalition-Formation Process

Party	Seats	Majority Possibilities
Situation I: Simplest		
Party A	44 seats	AB, AC, BC, ABC
Party B	42 seats	
Party C	14 seats	
Situation II: More Complex		
Party A	38 seats	AB, AC, AD, ABC, ABD,
Party B	20 seats	ABE, ACD, ACE, etc.
Party C	17 seats	
Party D	15 seats	
Party E	10 seats	
Situation III: Most Complex		
Party A	30 seats	ABC, ABD, ABE, ABF, ABG,
Party B	19 seats	BCDE, CDEFGH, etc.
Party C	12 seats	
Party D	9 seats	
Party E	8 seats	
Party F	8 seats	
Party G	7 seats	
Party H	7 seats	

more partners there are in a coalition, the more possibilities there are for a coalition to fall apart.

The study of coalitions has been interesting to many observers in recent years because of cabinet instability in many political systems.[21] Coalition governments in Italy, Israel, Japan, Belgium, and related minority government problems in France, Britain, and Canada, among other nations, have stimulated an interest in many political scientists in how and why coalitions are created.[22]

As we indicated in Chapter 4, coalition governments often become necessary as a result of a nation's electoral system: Where proportional representation elections exist, there almost inevitably results a multiparty system in the legislature, which often means that no single party will control a majority of the seats in the legislative assembly. This necessitates, as we have indicated here, that a coalition be formed. The motivations involved in the selection of coalition partners vary as a result of ideology and political culture.[23] Often economic issues provide the central concerns upon which parties coalesce.[24] In any event, the existence of coalitions adds a note of uncertainty and instability to a political equation *in addition to* whatever uncertainty or instability may have already existed.

The Executive Function: Public Administration and the Bureaucracy

Apart from the creation of a cabinet, the other manifest function of the political executive is to administer policy. In this respect, this volume would be seriously remiss if we did not discuss, albeit briefly, the comparative study of public administration and a comparative analysis of the structure that has come to be called "the bureaucracy." Public bureaucracies are perhaps the *most common* political structures in the world today; they exist in all political systems, whether they are democratic or authoritarian, "presidential" or "parliamentary," "developed" or "underdeveloped." They are as nearly a universal political structure as one can find: As a specialized structure, "bureaucracy, is common to all contemporary nation-states."[25]

The term "bureaucracy" itself is something of a problem because it has a number of definitions, some value free and some

quite judgmental. The scholar whose work is most closely associated with the term, and who contributed most to its development,
is Max Weber (1864–1920). Weber's concern was "less with organizational efficiency than with the expansion of bureaucratic
power, and with the implications of that expansion for fundamental liberal values."[26]

Weber saw "modern officialdom" as having six characteristic
patterns of behavior:

1. It has "fixed and official jurisdictional areas," which are "generally
   ordered by rules or administrative regulations;
2. The authority to give orders is also limited by rules, and officials
   have "coercive means" that they may use to enforce those rules;
3. The management of the office "is based upon written documents
   ('the files')," which requires a substantial staff to keep records;
4. Management "presupposes thorough and expert training";
5. Office activity requires the full attention of the official;
6. "The management of the office follows general rules."[27]

Generally, bureaucracies have been studied from several
different perspectives.[28] First, they can be studied from an *organizational* perspective, focusing upon structures, organizational
charts, lines of communication, hierarchical organization, its
formal rules, and how it operates.[29] Second, bureaucracies can be
studied from a *behavioral* perspective, seeking to understand
what bureaucracies do, how they behave, and what behavioral
characteristics distinguish bureaucracies from other hierarchi-
cally organized structures.[30] A third approach focuses upon how
well bureaucracies *achieve their goals* and discusses their efficiency, specialization, rational activity, and their role in the
framework of democratic government.[31]

Bureaucracies (and here we speak of *public* bureaucracies,
although most of what we say about public bureaucracies also
applies to private bureaucracies) are typically complex systems
of personnel, usually organized in a hierarchical fashion. That is,
bureaucracies are usually *pyramidally* shaped, with the number
of employees in higher positions being fewer than those in lower
positions.

The nature of a bureaucracy is usually that specialized jobs
are performed by different divisions of the organization, and the
organization is divided into *functional* categories. Bureaucracies
are also well known for having well-institutionalized sets of *rules*,

or *procedures*, and a relatively rigid set of *precedents* that govern their behavior.

Bureaucracies often claim to be based upon some kind of merit system, in which one takes an examination to receive a position, or receives a position based upon some perceived objective skills. This is characteristic of more developed nations[32] and is a reaction to practices dating back to the early years of the American Republic when President Andrew Jackson coined the phrase the "spoils system," referring to a chief executive's right to appoint public personnel as one of the "spoils" of an electoral victory.

It is often the case in political bureaucracies that some type of *civil service* system exists that protects the lower-level bureaucrats from political interference in their jobs; if they have been working for several years under the direction of one political party, they do not need to fear that they will lose their jobs should the opposition party gain control of the government. The other side of this coin, of course, is that a party that is new to government does not have the ability to put an unlimited number of its followers into positions of power when it wins an election. They must compete for positions through the established civil service system that exists at the time. Parties that have been out of power for a long time often claim that the bureaucracy "represents" the interests of the "old order," and that it is "resisting" their proposed changes. Often this is the case.

Top-level positions in the bureaucracy often are *political appointments*; there *is* an expectation that after an election is held all officials at this level will submit their resignations and permit a new cohort of political appointees to direct the administration of policy. Thus in a typical government ministry the minister and the deputy ministers will clearly be political appointments, with the minister being an MP and the deputy ministers being party loyalists, but the director-general (or an official with a similar title) will be a civil servant who remains in office even with a change of administrations.

The function of the bureaucracy is theoretically to *administer* the policy of the executive and to *offer specialized advice* to the executive,[33] not to make policy of its own, although as we indicated earlier one of the frequent complaints about bureaucracies is that they *do*, in fact, make policy in an "irresponsible" way—

"irresponsible" because nobody elected them.[34] As society has grown more and more complex, resulting in the gradual expansion of the executive branch of government over the legislative branch of government—something we discussed in Chapter 4—this administration has required more and more personnel, leading to a rapid growth of public bureaucracies.[35] Often the growth of bureaucracy in modern society is decried, but it simply has been demonstrated to be *necessary* to administer more and more complex social policy.

Presidential and Parliamentary Systems: Some Comparisons

Clearly there are a number of major and significant differences in structure between the presidential and the parliamentary-cabinet system. A question for us to ask at this time is: What are the *behavioral* implications of the differences between the two systems, and how will the two systems differ in terms of policy output and day-to-day operation? Several significant dimensions of difference are mentioned here.

The first distinction has to do with the idea of *responsible government*. Responsible government in this context does not mean trustworthy or rational government, but instead refers to the Government's ability to *deliver* on its promises. Responsible government comes about in parliamentary systems through some of the structural characteristics we have already met. The idea of party discipline suggests that legislators will vote (and speak and act) in the manner that their party leader suggests. The selection of the prime minister as leader of the largest party in the legislature and the notion of the vote of confidence ensure that the prime minister will always have the support of (and therefore because of party discipline be able to control) a majority of the legislature. Consequently, whatever the prime minister wants will have the approval of a majority of the legislature. If the prime minister's proposals do *not* receive a parliamentary majority, of course, the prime minister will have to resign.

This means that when the prime minister promises the public that his or her Government will act in a certain way, that person is in a position to follow through on that promise. In addition to being the leader of the executive branch of government, the prime minister is *also* (by definition) the leader of the legislative branch of government.

Contrast this with the presidential system in which the notion of separation of powers and checks and balances—something that explicitly does *not* apply in a parliamentary system—is so important. One of the central principles of presidential government is that the legislature is free to say no to requests of the president. Consequently, although a presidential candidate may run for office on the basis of the his or her position on a single issue, or a number of issues, in most cases the candidate cannot guarantee delivery of campaign promises. To enact policy, the legislature *must* be convinced that the president's policy preferences are the right ones.

Which system is "best"? It is hard to say, and the answer depends upon certain value judgments, since each system has its own strengths and weaknesses. On one hand, the parliamentary system does have a real advantage in rapid policy delivery, through the notions of party discipline and cabinet leadership. On the other hand, if *good* policy can be passed quickly, so can *bad* policy. However, many in parliamentary systems bemoan the overwhelming influence of party discipline, and some have even suggested that their respective systems consider changes to the presidential model.[36]

The corresponding weakness/strength of the presidential system is precisely its slower, more deliberative legislative process. The argument that is suggested is that whereas it may (and almost always does) take longer to pass policy, groups that are in a minority on a particular issue have more opportunity to protect their interests, and the policy that is ultimately passed is more likely to be a good one. Put slightly more cynically, the policy that is ultimately passed is likely to offend as few as possible. On the other hand, a policy decision that is *urgently needed* may go unanswered for a long period of time while the legislature deliberates.

Another major area of difference between the two systems has to do with stability and tenure of office. In the presidential system, both the president and the legislature have fixed terms of office. They can be secure in these positions, barring extraordinary occurrences (such as impeachment and conviction of the president in the United States, for example). This security permits both the president and the legislature to take either an unpopular position or an antagonistic position in relation to the other branch of government if it is believed that such a position is the proper one to take.

The parliamentary system offers no such job security. The chief executive can lose this position at any time, depending upon the mood of the legislature. A chief executive worried about keeping his or her job, then, would be less likely to take a position that is clearly disapproved by the legislature than would a president. Moreover, the legislature would be less likely to "rebel" against executive leadership: Party discipline would tend to force party members to follow the instructions of their leader (and the leader of the majority party, of course, would be the chief executive), and if the legislature became too contentious, the chief executive could request a writ of dissolution from the head of state, effectively "firing" the legislature and calling for new elections.

As we indicated earlier, it is easy to see that each of these systems has advantages and disadvantages as far as stability, policy output, protection of minority rights, ability to deliver on campaign promises, responsiveness to public opinion, and so on are concerned.[37] Some of these values are simply the inverse of others: Responsiveness to public opinion may infringe on minority rights, for example. What is seen as an advantage to one observer may be a distinct disadvantage to another.

Both the presidential and the parliamentary models of executive structure are conducive to democratic government. Both models can be responsive to public opinion, both can provide effective leadership, and both can provide for the general welfare of the political system. The differences between the two types of systems are differences of structure and process, not ideology. As such, it is difficult to argue that one type of system is, overall, *better* than the other. They are simply *different*.

Notes

1. See Locke's Section 126 in Sir Ernest Barker, ed., *Social Contract: Essays by Locke, Hume & Rousseau* (New York: Oxford University Press, 1970).
2. Clinton Rossiter, *The American Presidency* (New York: Mentor, 1960), pp. 14–40 passim.
3. See James Madison, *Notes on Debates in the Federal Convention of 1787* (Athens: Ohio University Press, 1966), passim.
4. See J. LaPalombara, *Politics Within Nations* (Englewood Cliffs, N.J.: Prentice Hall, 1974), pp. 190–196.
5. For descriptions of the American presidency, see Rossiter, *American Presidency*, or Richard Neustadt, *Presidential Power* (New York: New American Library, 1964).
6. On the powers of the vice president, see Rossiter, *American Presidency*, pp. 129–135.
7. *Federalist* Number 68 by Alexander Hamilton discusses the rationalization of this structure. See *The Federalist Papers* (New York: New American Library, 1961), pp. 411–415.
8. See Ronald Moe, ed. *Congress and the President* (Pacific Palisades, Calif.: Goodyear Publishing Co., 1971).
9. LaPalombara, *Politics Within Nations*, pp. 192–194. See also the data in Jean Blondel, *Comparative Legislatures*, Englewood Cliffs, N.J.: Prentice Hall, 1973, pp. 144–153, column 39.
10. This section is based upon a much longer discussion of the same subject in the now-classic study by Sydney Bailey, *British Parliamentary Democracy* (Boston: Houghton Mifflin, 1958), pp. 12–20.
11. This argument was expounded at length in his *True Law of Free Monarchies* in 1603.
12. R. M. Dawson, *The Government of Canada* (Toronto: University of Toronto Press, 1965), pp. 184–185.
13. In fact, most cabinet members come from the legislative body. See Blondel, *Comparative Legislatures*, pp. 144–153, column 40.
14. Ibid., pp. 144–153, column 42.
15. See Kaare Strom, "Deferred Gratification and Minority Governments in Scandinavia," *Legislative Studies Quarterly* 11:4 (1986): 583–606.
16. Blondel, *Comparative Legislatures*, pp. 144–153, column 41.
17. Ian Budge and Michael Laver, "Office Seeking and Policy Pursuit in Coalition Theory," *Legislative Studies Quarterly* 11:4 (1986): 485–506; Robert L. Peterson and Martine M. DeRidder, "Government Formation as a Policy-Making Arena," *Legislative Studies Quarterly* 11:4 (1986): 565–682.
18. John Frendreis, Dennis Gleiber, and Eric Browne, "The Study of Cabinet Dissolutions in Parliamentary Democracies," *Legislative Studies Quarterly* 11:4 (1986): 619–628.
19. A very good comparative study is by Lawrence C. Dodd, *Coalitions in Parliamentary Government* (Princeton, N.J.: Princeton University Press, 1976).
20. Hans Daalder, "Changing Procedures and Changing Strategies in Dutch Coalition Building," *Legislative Studies Quarterly* 11:4 (1986): 507–532.
21. Eric C. Browne and Mark N. Franklin, "New Directions in Coalition Research," *Legislative Studies Quarterly* 11 (1986): 469–484.
22. See, for further reading on coalitions, A. DeSwann, *Coalition Theories and Cabinet Formations* (San Francisco: Jossey-Bass, 1973); William Gamson.

"A Theory of Coalition Formation," *American Sociological Review* 26 (1961): 373–382; or Gregory Mahler and Richard Trilling, "Coalition Behavior and Cabinet Formation: The Case of Israel," *Comparative Political Studies* 8 (1975): 200–233.

23. William Reisinger, "Situational and Motivational Assumptions in Theories of Coalition Formation," *Legislative Studies Quarterly* 11:4 (1986): 551–564.

24. John Robertson, "Economic Polarization and Cabinet Formation in Western Europe," *Legislative Studies Quarterly* 11:4 (1986): 533–550.

25. Ferrel Heady, *Public Administration: A Comparative Perspective* (New York: Marcel Dekker, 1984), p. 59.

26. David Beetham, *Bureaucracy* (Minneapolis: University of Minnesota Press, 1987), p. 58.

27. Max Weber, "Bureaucracy," in H. H. Gerth and C. Wright Mills, eds., *From Max Weber: Essays in Sociology* (New York: Oxford University Press, 1978), p. 196. See also Claude Lefort, *The Political Forms of Modern Society: Bureaucracy, Democracy, Totalitarianism* (Cambridge: M.I.T. Press, 1986), p. 96.

28. This section is based upon much more detailed analysis in Heady, *Public Administration*, pp. 61–64.

29. This is the approach of B. Guy Peters, *The Politics of Bureaucracy: A Comparative Perspective* (New York: Longman, 1978).

30. To a substantial degree this approach is illustrated by Eva Etzioni-Halevy, *Bureaucracy and Democracy: A Political Dilemma* (London: Routledge and Kegan Paul, 1983).

31. An example of this kind of study might be John Burke, *Bureaucratic Responsibility* (Baltimore: Johns Hopkins University Press, 1986).

32. See the discussion by Heady, "Relating Bureaucratic and Political Development" in his *Public Administration*, pp. 409–17.

33. A very good study of the *advising* function is edited by William Plowden, *Advising the Rulers* (Oxford: Basil Blackwell, 1987).

34. A very good discussion of some of the philosophical dimensions of this problem, and how democratic control can coexist with bureaucracy, can be found in the volume by Judith Gruber, *Controlling Bureaucracies: Dilemmas in Democratic Governance* (Los Angeles: University of California Press, 1987).

35. This point is discussed at some length in the study by Peters, *The Politics of Bureaucracy*. Peters' second chapter is entitled "The Growth of Government and Administration," and he discusses the growth of administration not only in the executive branch, but also in the legislature and in other areas of the government.

36. See, for example, Avraham Brichta and Yair Zalmanovitch, "The Proposals for Presidential Government in Israel: A Case Study in the Possibility of Institutional Transference," *Comparative Politics* 19:1 (1986): 57–68.

37. Some discussion of this may be found in Jaakko Nousiainen, "Bureaucratic Tradition, Semi-Presidential Rule and Parliamentary Government: The Case of Finland," *European Journal of Political Research* 16:2 (1988): 229–249.

6

Judiciaries and the Legal Order

On the Comparative Study of Judiciaries

After our discussion of legislative and executive structures, the structure of government suggested by John Locke in 1690 that remains to be discussed is "a known and indifferent judge, with authority to determine all differences according to the established law."[1] One of the functions that was ascribed to constitutions in our discussion in Chapter 2 was that they serve as an expression of the basic laws of the regime. At this point of our inquiry we should say something about the function of legal systems in political processes and the importance of legal culture in general, and also something about the role of judges in political systems.

Of the three major Lockean governmental structures—the legislature, the executive, and the judiciary—that can be observed on a cross-national basis, courts and legal systems generally continually receive the least attention in introductory texts and comparative studies,[2] unless, of course, the study in question explicitly focuses upon the judiciary or the law.[3] Why is this the case? Two possible suggestions are offered here.

First, as far as systemic characteristics and political institutions go, legal systems and courts may be most *system-specific*. That is, although both executives and legislatures have structural idiosyncrasies, and have behavior that varies on a country-by-country basis, we can still make a number of useful generalizations about both their structures (e.g., "presidential" systems as compared with "parliamentary" systems) and their behavior (e.g., a system with high party discipline compared with a system with low party discipline). This level of generalization is hard to achieve with legal systems and courts. Although we can speak of constitutional regimes—governments of laws, not ruled by individual whim—we very quickly get to the point at which individual system-level characteristics of judiciaries must be discussed; consequently, generalizability is low.

Second, while executives and legislatures are undoubtedly part of the political process, in *many* political systems the courts are explicitly *excluded from* the political arena. This is not a refutation of Locke's argument that courts (judges) are necessary to *society*; it simply limits the role of the judges and the courts to one of arbitration or mediation. They are not part of the lawmaking process, specifically, or the political arena, generally. (It should be noted, in fact, that Locke suggested the function of the judge was to "determine all differences according to the *established* law," [emphasis added] *not* to make the law or public policy.) Accordingly, many political scientists have left the judiciary out of their studies of the political arena and the policy-making process generally.

In explaining the almost-nonpolitical role of the courts, one recent study pointed out that courts "logically and historically have been undemocratic institutions. An increased role for the courts, then, could render a political order less democratic."[4] Thus although the courts have often been significant in maintaining individual rights, they have often kept a "low profile" in their respective polities, thereby generating relatively little scholarship on their *comparative* political impact.

Although courts are often "nonpolitical" in nature, they *do* play a significant role in political systems. As we shall see, in many systems courts play a role through *judicial review* in shaping the law. In other systems the role of the courts may be more circumscribed, but courts still interpret statutes, hear cases involving government leaders, and, generally, participate in official government action.

> Courts are, in sum, part of every political system, and the politics of none can be understood without an appreciation of their role. Yet modern political science has tended to downplay or even ignore judicial institutions, and to the extent that it has done this, its analyses of politics remain incomplete. As we more fully comprehend the roles of courts in each modern democracy, we will be in a better position to construct genuine comparative theories both about courts themselves and modern political development.[5]

The Idea of Law

The idea of law tends to be assumed whenever we think of politics. That is, there is an implicit assumption that political systems are based, to varying degrees, upon the rule of law. This assumption is made because so many of our contacts with government come in relation to governmental rules, regulations, and administrative guidelines. It is almost impossible to think of government existing without laws; the "authoritative allocation of values" with which politics is concerned deals with laws.

Law is generally regarded as one of the greatest achievements of civilization. It is concerned with basic rules of conduct that reflect to some degree the concept of justice. These rules concern the relationships of the individual with government and with other individuals. An ideal of justice frequently expressed is that the government should be a government of laws and not of men. Whether this goal can be achieved is questionable, as laws are made and administered by human beings. But in practice this ideal is generally interpreted to mean a legal system that treats everyone equally and that is not subject to change through the arbitrary acts of a dictator, or even the whim of transient majorities.[6] Hence, even in the seventeenth century, John Locke saw *law* as being the principal attraction of society: Thus mankind, notwithstanding all the privileges of the "state of nature, being but in an ill condition while they remain in it, are quickly driven into society . . . [they] take sanctuary under the established laws of government."[7]

There are a number of different *kinds* of law to which the interested student can find reference, including positive law, divine law, moral law, natural law, and scientific law.[8] Scientific laws refer to observations and measurements that have been empirically determined and that focus upon physical, biological, and chemical concepts, not social questions. Moral laws refer to precepts or guidelines based upon subjective values, beliefs, and attitudes, focusing upon behavior: the *proper* way of doing things. Clearly moral laws, unlike scientific laws, will vary depending upon the value system used to construct them. Divine law, as well, will be seen to vary depending upon the religious or theological conceptual framework from which it is said to be derived.

The two major approaches to law with which we as social scientists are concerned are natural law and positive law. *Natural law* refers to a body of precepts governing human behavior that is "more basic than man-made law, and one that is based on fundamental principles of justice."[9] The type of law with which governments are most concerned is *positive law*, which can be said to have three major identifiable characteristics: (1) it is manmade law, (2) it is designed to govern human behavior, and (3) it is enforceable by appropriate governmental action.

Conflict has erupted throughout human history when natural law and positive law appear to conflict. Political philosophers from the time of Cicero (106–43 B.C.), including John of Salisbury, Thomas Aquinas, Thomas Hobbes, John Locke, Jean-Jacques Rousseau, David Hume, Jeremy Bentham, and Karl Marx, through philosophers of the present day have dealt with this thorny issue.[10] What is the individual to do when the law of the state tells an individual to do one thing, but one's perception of natural law, of the *fundamental* standard of "rightness," says to do something else? Many have argued that human laws (positive laws) that conflict with natural laws are null and void. St. Augustine's "two sword" theory in the early fifth century was one attempt to resolve this conflict.[11] Augustine argued that natural law and divine law were the same thing: The laws of nature are God's laws. Individuals are required to obey earthly (positive) law only insofar as it does not conflict with natural law. When natural law and positive law conflict, it is the law of God that must be obeyed.

Legal Cultures

The concept of a "culture" is one that has been developed primarily by sociologists and anthropologists. A legal culture can be considered to be:

> a set of deeply rooted, historically conditioned attitudes about the nature of law, about the role of law in the society and the polity, about the proper organization and operation of a legal system, and about the way law is, or should be made, applied, studied, perfected, and taught. The legal tradition relates the legal system to the culture of which it is a partial expression.[12]

The concept of a legal culture, then, focuses upon the beliefs, attitudes, and values of society *relative to the law and politics*.

These values have to do with the nature and process of justice in the political system, the concept of equality, and, more basically, the nature of law in the regime itself. The latter includes the very fundamental question of law and its influence on government policy.

We mentioned earlier the idea that political systems should be "governments of law and not of men." This reflects one of the most central questions of any political regime: Is the government bound to obey its own laws, or is it permitted to go beyond the laws in its execution of public policy? The reader will recall that in our discussion of constitutions and constitutional government one of the dividing lines between (behaviorally) constitutional and unconstitutional regimes was the degree to which the behavior of regimes was *limited*, controlled by law. Are there limits beyond which the government absolutely may not go? Or, conversely, is the function of law perceived to be primarily that of controlling individual behavior, keeping individuals "under control," while the government may do whatever it wishes?

It is precisely this type of normative, philosophical question that is addressed by the concept of the legal culture. This explains why legal cultures are so difficult to study: They are blends of philosophy, sometimes quite complex, and cannot readily be described in only a few words. To appreciate fully the legal culture of a political system, we must understand its political and social history, its political structures, and the political values and attitudes dominant in that political system at any given time.

A nation's legal culture will shape the role that the law and legal institutions play in the political realm. For example, the fact that the United States is "the most litigious country in the world"[13] suggests that Americans are more likely to look to the courts than might citizens of other polities. On the other hand, "the Japanese legal culture puts a premium on informal settlement of legal disputes based on informal controls and social sanction without legal procedure," so Japanese citizens are hesitant to resort to the courts to resolve political issues, although "when the traditional means of conciliation and mediation fail, the Japanese become very determined to exhaust all avenues of legal device and remedy."[14]

Although political cultures do vary on a nation-by-nation basis, there are certain "families" or groupings of legal cultures that may be suggested here for purposes of generalization. These are: (1) the Romano-Germanic family; (2) the family of the common law; (3) the family of socialist law; and (4) the non-Western legal families.[15]

The *Romano-Germanic* approach to law, sometimes referred to as "code" law, has developed from the basis of Roman law at the time of Justinian (A.D. 533).[16] This type of law, as contrasted with common law, is based upon comprehensively written legislative statutes, often bound together as "codes." The *Code Napoléon* was just such a bound collection; the Emperor Napoleon (ruled 1804–1815) decided that law throughout his empire needed to be standardized, and he had a single, comprehensive set of laws assembled and disseminated. The *Code Napoléon* influenced legal structures from North America through Asia. The French legal system is characteristic of a code law system, and the legal systems of Louisiana and Quebec in North America have similar characteristics, evidence of their colonial heritage.

The *common law* system, found in England and countries modelled on English law (including the United States), is sometimes called "Anglo-American" law,[17] and has been referred to as "judge-made law." This is not to suggest that today laws in these political systems are not made by the legislatures of those systems, but, rather, suggests that when the science of the law was being developed in England in the twelfth century, it was the judges who made decisions. Today *judicial precedent* plays a major role in common-law nations—the process is referred to as *stare decisis* (to stand by things decided). A judge may use a previously adjudicated case as a guide for his or her decision, but the judge may also decide that there are new characteristics involved in the case being considered that require deviation from earlier decisions. Of course, today the legislature plays a highly significant role in designing the laws the judge is applying to the specific situation.

The differences between the code law systems and the common law systems can be overstated, but two main characteristics should be pointed out. First, judges play a slightly less significant role in decision making in the code law systems, with correspondingly greater influence exercised by the legislature. Second, the common law system, characteristic of Anglo-American nations, tries to minimize the likelihood of an innocent person being convicted by setting up various procedural and substantive safeguards. The code law systems, characterized by the system found in France, "lays more stress on preventing a guilty person from escaping punishment.[18]

Socialist law derives from a different philosophical root. Karl Marx and his philosophy assumed that law was a tool of the state in capitalist societies that was used to oppress the working class. Marx argued that in a perfect socialist state there would be no need for law at all, once the economic ills of society were cured. In fact, of course, things have not turned out to be quite as simple as Marx thought they would. Law in the USSR, characteristic of socialist systems, plays, if anything, a *greater* role than in Western democracies.

Modern Soviet Marxists have seen law as a tool of the state, to be used to work toward a socialist society. The state can (and should) *use* law to further its ends. This results in a kind of twisted logical circle; law exists to further the interests of citizens. The state knows better than any individuals what the interests of the citizens are. Anything the state does, therefore, must be legal, since it is the state that writes the laws defining what, exactly, legal behavior is. Thus law becomes simply another instrument of state policy. When we discussed the Soviet constitutional system in Chapter 2 we indicated the difference in approaches to civil and political rights in the USSR and Western democracies. This illustrates the differences in legal cultures between the USSR and other "socialist" regimes on one hand, and code and common law nations on the other.

In *non-Western legal systems*, such as those of some developing nations, legal cultures are quite different and depend upon (1) local traditions and customs, (2) the legal culture of the colonizing power (if any) that controlled the political infrastructure prior to independence, and (3) the degree to which the colonizing power permitted autonomy and development during the colonial era. In some non-Western systems religious law, especially Islamic law, has a major role in the general legal framework of the regime. In others, religious and tribal laws are blended with colonial legal values. Elsewhere, developing nations have completely forsaken their traditional legal cultures and have opted instead for modern legal structures and processes. To take just one example, the legal culture found in Israel today is a blend of Turkish law and British law (former colonial powers in the Middle East), religious law (including Jewish, Moslem, and Christian components), as well as contemporary legal and judicial values.

Sources of Law

For as long as political systems have been based upon the rule of law, there have been a variety of sources for the laws that have existed. In the Middle Ages, the sole source of law might have been the monarch in power, or perhaps the monarch in combination with religious guidelines. A number of different sources can be singled out and mentioned here.

Prior to the creation of society, with its rules and regulations and formal legal structures, patterns of behavior were governed by *religious* or *moral values*. This type of law generally comes in entire bodies, often in a specifically delineated set. Thus the Mosaic law—the Ten Commandments brought down from Mount Sinai by Moses—was a *body* of law. Similarly, the Koran, the sacred book of the Moslem religion, contains a *body* of laws. This religious law often is interpreted to be natural law, as we distinguished the terms earlier, although some might want to argue that religious law may contain elements much more specific than natural law. Religious laws may prohibit the consumption of certain foods, or working on a certain day of the week, when there is no immediately apparent reason why this should be considered to be a "law of nature." Depending upon the nature of a society, this type of religious or moral value may become entrenched in the legal framework of a political system.

Some monarchs, notably James I of England (1603–1625), used religion as a basis of their power. In his *True Law of Free Monarchies,*[19] James I developed his theory of "divine right of kings," arguing that rulers derived their powers from God, and what they wanted was law. James I was not the only monarch to believe this, and *the will of the monarch* became a major source of law for a long time.

Another source of law is *tradition* or *custom.* We made the distinction in our discussion of legislatures and executives between *de jure* (in law) and *de facto* (in fact) political power, and argued that tradition may develop the *force* of law, even if it never *becomes* law. The tradition in England, for example, that the monarch selects the leader of the largest party in the House of Commons to be prime minister has become so established that it is taken as part of the "Westminster model" constitutional regime there.

Sometimes traditions are left unwritten, as the case of the head of state acting "on the advice" of the chief executive illustrates. On other occasions, however, traditions are actually formalized and made part of the constitutional or legal framework of a political system. For example, the tradition of American presidents serving only two terms of office was firmly entrenched in American politics prior to World War II. George Washington started the tradition, and if a president did not bow out of politics at the end of his first term of office, he inevitably did so at the end of his second term. When Franklin Delano Roosevelt violated this tradition and ran for a third term, and then a fourth term, some reacted quite strongly. This reaction eventually resulted in passage of the Twenty-second Amendment to the Constitution, limiting presidential terms of office.

Certainly a major source of law in contemporary regimes is the *constitution* of the regime. Some national constitutions include specific legal proscriptions that must be followed in the political system, as well as more general descriptions of the structures and institutions to be found in the regime. The U.S. Constitution, for example, contains a number of specific limitations and guidelines that are not only laws in their own right (e.g., "Congress shall make no law . . . abridging the freedom of speech . . .") but have also generated an entire body of supplementary law.

This happens through yet another source of law, *the judiciary*. Judicial decision making, including the interpretation of constitutional dogma and legislative statutes and the application of judicial precedents to new circumstances, has resulted in a great deal of "judge-made" law. Judge-made law is derived from, based upon, what is in the constitution, supplementing constitutional parameters and helping the court to be more "relevant" to contemporary times.

Another governmental structure directly concerned with the creation of law is, of course, *the legislature*. The legislature as an institution derives its name from the law (*legis*), and certainly one of the functions most commonly attributed to the legislature is the lawmaking function. We have already seen that this may not, in fact, be the case in every political regime. Often the legislature is more important in a specific political system in some *other* capacity—its legislative function may be primarily that of a rubber stamp.

More and more often today we see arguments that legislatures are in decline as far as their legitimate legislative powers are concerned. The argument suggests that, in both presidential and parliamentary systems of government, legislatures are surrendering their legislative powers to the executive branch in exchange for the rubber stamp function. The question important to ask is, Why is this so?[20]

Theodore Lowi has argued that part of this problem stems from the complexity of modern society and government. It was easy for legislatures in 1690, for example, to pass laws forbidding poaching on the king's land. It is much harder for legislatures to address the complex social problems of the 1990s that governments must address: For example, how can a legislature fight poverty? It could pass a law making it illegal to be poor, but that would not solve the problem. Lowi suggests in his book *The End of Liberalism* that problems such as these may be beyond the competence of legislatures. Often the only response to these complex problems that is available to a legislature is to pass the buck to an executive agency, appropriate some money, and give the executive agency authority to set rules and policy by itself.[21]

This has led to yet another source of law—*administrative decisions*. A legislature may decide, for example, that it does not have either the time or the capacity to make highly specialized policy decisions regarding food and drugs. Its response to this quandary, given a feeling that some regulation in this area is clearly necessary, might be to establish, say, a National Food and Drugs Agency, giving commissioners on the agency authority to set standards and regulations ensuring a constant quality of both food and drugs. The actions of a majority of commissioners, then, may have the force of law (violations of their decisions and rules could result in fines or imprisonment) and could have the same *effect* as legislated laws, even though the legislature really was not responsible for specific policy set by the agency.

We can see, then, that although positive laws may derive from a number of sources, their effects can be the same. Whether these laws stem from religious or moral values, tradition or custom, a constitution, judicial interpretation, legislation, or administrative actions and decisions, all serve the functions of regulating behavior in society.

Structures in Legal Systems

The heart of a judicial system's structure is to be found in its network of *courts*. Theodore Becker, a significant contributor to the cross-national literature on judiciaries, has characterized courts as having seven components. A court is:

1. An individual or group of individuals;
2. With power to make decisions in disputes;
3. Before whom the parties or their advocates present the facts involved in the dispute and cite principles (in statutes, or other forms) that
4. Are applied by that individual or those individuals;
5. Who *believe* that they should listen to the facts and apply cited principles impartially, and;
6. That they may so decide, and;
7. As an independent body.[22]

The main service of the courts, then, is to serve as an *arena* in which *controlled* conflict may take place. The controls exercised upon this conflict are very rigid, emphasizing verbal, conceptual, legal, and philosophical strengths rather than physical prowess.

Martin Shapiro has suggested that the basic concept explaining the role of courts in the resolution of conflict is that of the "triad."

> Cutting quite across cultural lines, it appears that whenever two persons come into a conflict that they cannot themselves solve, one solution appealing to common sense is to call upon a third for assistance in achieving a resolution. . . . [F]rom its overwhelming appeal to common sense stems the basic political legitimacy of courts everywhere. . . . [This is] a logic so compelling that courts have become a universal political phenomenon.[23]

To process the disputes as smoothly and efficiently as possible, judicial structures are established in political systems. These frameworks include not only the body of laws of a political regime but also a series of courts to make decisions based upon these laws. The actual structures of these courts vary tremendously on a system-by-system basis. Federal political systems may have legal infrastructures that reflect their federal makeup; unitary systems may be more simple. Some systems may have very specialized courts as part of their judicial structure, while others may not.

Judiciaries *tend* to be organized in a pyramidal fashion, with a large number of courts of initial adjudication, fewer appeals courts, and a single, ultimate, supreme court. In many judicial systems, *all* cases must begin on the "ground floor" and work their way up through the judicial system, although there are instances in some judicial systems in which the appeals courts and supreme court may have some *original jurisdiction*—some cases may *start* at the intermediate or top level, and not have to work their way to that point.

The question of jurisdiction, of which court (or level of court) has authority to adjudicate a specific question, can be quite complex. For example, in the American judicial system, jurisdiction is divided between federal courts and state courts, reflecting the federal nature of the polity. The initial determination that must be made in any exercise in litigation is where jurisdiction lies: Is the matter a federal case or a state case? Sometimes jurisdiction might overlap: In the United States today, for example, it is not a federal crime to rob a bank, but a state crime. It is, however, a federal crime to rob a bank insured by the federal government (and, it turns out, virtually all banks today are federally insured).

So, the individual who robs a federally insured bank actually commits *two* crimes: robbing a bank (a state crime), and robbing a federally insured bank (a federal crime), and can, accordingly, face two trials. (Parenthetically, it should be noted that this liability to face two trials is not the same thing as "double jeopardy" against which the individual is protected under the Fifth Amendment to the U.S. Constitution. The Fifth Amendment says that no person shall "be subject for the same offense to be twice put in jeopardy of life or limb. . . ." If a person commits two offenses, even in the same act, he may be tried twice; he may not be tried twice for the same offense.)

The American federal judicial structure, then, consists of a single federal judicial pyramid and fifty separate state judicial pyramids. This double-structured judicial framework was designed to accommodate the federal nature of the American political arena, although it does occasionally make determination of jurisdiction more difficult.

Other political systems manage to allow for reflection of their federal character in their judicial systems without this parallel structure. In the case of Canada, for example, there is no "double-pyramid" structure.[24] Courts are "constituted, maintained, and organized" by the provinces in both the areas of civil and criminal law. At the same time, however, to balance the grant of exclusive power over civil *procedure* given to the provinces, the federal government has exclusive jurisdiction over criminal *procedure*, and it is the federal government that controls the appointment, salary, and tenure of the judges in the courts that are established by the provinces. Thus the Canadian federal judicial structure appears as ten separate provincial pyramids, designed by the provinces and staffed by federal appointments, with civil procedure established by the provinces (so that, for example, civil procedures in Ontario might be different from civil procedures in British Columbia), but criminal procedure will be standardized through its control by the federal government. There is, moreover, a single Supreme Court of Canada that acts as an appeals court for the entire nation.

Australia, similarly, has a federal political system reflected in its judicial structure. The High Court of Australia can hear appeals from the Federal Court of Appeal or Court of Criminal

Appeal, and can also hear appeals from state and territory supreme courts. Federalism, it has been suggested, has been "largely responsible for [the] Australian profusion of legalism."[25]

It can be seen, then, that the actual structural design of judicial systems varies on a nation-by-nation basis. Questions of jurisdiction, appeals, and procedure are so tailored to individual national characteristics that even members of the same legal "families" that we saw earlier—the common law family, for example, or the code law family—may differ significantly in terms of specific political structures. Not only do Canada and the United States differ significantly in the manner in which their judicial structures reflect their federal natures, but even within a nation the judicial structures can vary. For example, the court structure in Massachusetts differs from courts in California, and courts in Alberta differ from courts in Newfoundland.

Judicial Functions

The judicial function has been characterized as:

> the determination of the meaning of laws and rules, the imposition of penalties for violating those rules, the deciding on the relative rights and obligations of individuals and the community, the determination of the area of freedom to be allowed persons within the political system, and the arbitration of disputes between individuals and officials.[26]

With such a list of functions, it is no wonder that courts or judiciaries are important political structures! Given a focus upon *functions*, it is easy to see that the *structure* of a judiciary can vary, as we have just indicated.

Some of these functions performed by the judiciary are not unique to the judiciary. The legislature may act to clarify its own laws and rules, or mandate specific penalties for violations of rules, thus limiting the freedom of the judiciary. Actions of the executive may serve to arbitrate disputes between individuals and officials. In many instances, however, the judiciary is uniquely qualified to provide services beyond the capabilities of other governmental structures.

Because the courts can be seen as *impartial* to conflicts that come before them, they can be especially influential in both establishing facts and interpreting law. They can mediate in disputes between and among executive agencies and legislative structures, and may be applied to by citizens with complaints that they feel are not being properly addressed by other governmental agencies.

Additionally, judges are often in an invaluable position to protect minority rights. Most judicial systems offer some degree of protection for judges, shielding them from political consequences of their actions. Judges not only can take a nonpolitical view of conflicts but they are also free to act; in most systems judges cannot be fired for unpopular decisions. Judges have the power to hand down decisions that might be so unpopular, socially or politically, that legislators or executives might hesitate to act, and judges need not be worried about losing their positions. Short of treason or a major criminal offense, judges are often "irresponsible" to majority opinion.

An "irresponsible" judiciary, of course, can be seen as either good or bad, depending upon one's view of the policy question under consideration. Some citizens might view a court decision giving individual women the right to decide whether or not to have an abortion as legal toleration of murder; others might see the same decision as a victory for freedom of choice. One constituency might cry that a court's decision banning prayer in public school is an act of atheism, while others might argue that the decision has nothing to do with *religion* at all, simply with *religion in school*, and is, therefore, a protection of the rights of a minority in the school who don't want to follow the majority's religious preferences.

Judiciaries in the Political Arena

The judiciary may, in many political systems, engage in a lawmaking function of a sort, by interpreting laws made elsewhere. As a general rule, however, the courts prefer to stay out of the political arena.

> In some political matters the judiciary is unable or unwilling to act. Courts may be excluded from jurisdiction in certain subjects, as in Switzerland where federal laws cannot be challenged in the

courts, or in France where *actes de gouvernement* remain outside the province of the courts.[27]

Even in the United States, where the U.S. Supreme Court is among the most politically active high tribunals in the world, the Court is hesitant to inject itself into the political arena, often deciding controversial cases in the most "narrow" manner possible to avoid political controversy. In addition to making decisions in politically controversial cases, courts may be involved in the political process by issuing writs, court orders, or injunctions in politically sensitive matters.

Clearly, however, the most direct interaction between the courts and other political structures in a regime comes through the pattern of behavior that we refer to as *judicial review*. Judicial review is the process by which courts are in the position to rule upon the propriety or legality of action of the legislative and executive branches of government. More specifically:

> judicial review refers to the judicial power to decide on the constitutionality of activities undertaken by other governmental institutions, most notably those decisions, laws, and policies advanced by executives and legislatures.[28]

As is indicated in Table 6.1, the concept of judicial review exists in only a clear minority of the approximately 170 nations of the world, and where it *does* exist, the *extent* of its scope and ability to review the actions of other governmental structures varies. That is, not all of the courts listed in Table 6.1 are as powerful in their respective political systems as is the Supreme Court in the United States.

The idea of judicial review, although most strongly institutionalized today in the United States, was not, as some scholars have suggested, "invented" in American colonial days, or with the decision of Chief Justice Marshall in *Marbury* v. *Madison* in 1803. We can go back to the time of Plato to find discussion of judicial review, in a primitive sense, when Plato discussed the establishment of a "nocturnal council of magistrates" to be the "guardians of our god-given constitution."[29] Charles G. Haines, a leading scholar of American constitutionalism, has argued that:

the practice of English colonial administration agencies and of the assertion of authority by the Privy Council influenced the [American] colonists in that they realized the possibility of having their judgments reviewed and in certain instances their statutes invalidated by a superior tribunal.[30]

Although judicial review may not exist at the present time in all judicial systems, there clearly is an ingredient of *change* that we must keep in mind. For example, most studies take it as a given that there is no judicial review in Great Britain, and that the *fundamental* principle underlying the operation of British politics is that of parliamentary supremacy. While this is true, it also has recently been pointed out that the role of the courts in the British political culture has changed, and that this reflects "deep-seated changes occurring in the institutional fabric of British government," especially in the realm of administrative law. It has been shown that "until twenty years ago judges took an extremely restrained position vis-à-vis administrative agencies," but more recently scholars have noted "an embryonic move toward judicial activism."[31] Although this does not suggest that British courts will soon be nullifying Acts of Parliament, it does illustrate the fact that all political institutions, courts included, can change over time.

Table 6.1
Judicial Review in Some Political Systems

Western Europe & North America	Latin America	Asia & the Pacific	Other
Austria	Argentina	Australia	Ghana
Canada	Brazil	India	Israel
Denmark	Colombia	Japan	Nigeria
Ireland	Mexico	Pakistan	Yugoslavia
Norway		Philippines	

Sources: Monte Palmer and William Thompson, *The Comparative Analysis of Politics* (Itasca, Ill.: F.E. Peacock, 1978), p. 136; Theodore Becker, *Comparative Judicial Politics* (Chicago: Rand McNally, 1970), pp. 137, 209, 213, 219–222.

Theodore Becker, in his comprehensive cross-national study of judicial politics, indicates three dimensions along which we can locate judicial systems. First, there are different types of "judicial reviewing organs." Second, there are differences in the processes by which questions of constitutionality can reach the courts. Third, there are differences in the type of proceedings and ranges of jurisdiction of the reviewing courts.[32]

There are two major types of judicial-review mechanisms to be found today. One, in the American model, uses the *regular* courts to make decisions. Judicial review is simply added to the other duties performed by the courts in the political system. The other major type of judicial review structure comes from Europe and provides a *special* constitutional court or reviewing body to perform the judicial-review function.

Political systems vary as well in the question of *who* can initiate suit. In the United States, only someone "injured" by an act can initiate suit. The U.S. Supreme Court will not issue an advisory opinion, or permit an uninvolved party to commence litigation. In some political systems, those affected by an act are specifically *not* permitted to initiate a suit. Rather, only specific governmental agencies may apply for judicial review. In still other systems, the access to the judicial review process is very liberal, and anyone can bring a case into the reviewing process. In Colombia, for example, "anyone could introduce a petition of unconstitutionality directly to the Supreme Court, without even having to prove a case or controversy existed, or that he had any real or personal interest in the constitutionality of the law in question."[33]

The third dimension of distinction according to Becker deals with the scope of jurisdiction of the courts. Americans are familiar with a judicial system that exercises a *very broad* range of judicial review. Elsewhere, this breadth is not necessarily the case. In Israel, for example, although the court may rule on local ordinances as well as actions by the executive branch of government, it will not review laws enacted by the Knesset, Israel's legislature.[34] In Italy, it has been pointed out, although there is no direct judicial review, the strength of the system of administrative courts results in the "potential political impact" of the courts remaining strong.[35]

The justification of judicial review—a practice many condemn as undemocratic in that it permits an (often) unelected and therefore "irresponsible" judiciary to reverse or nullify actions of democratically elected legislators and executives—is basically that there is inevitably some degree of uncertainty about constitutional matters, whether they be powers of an executive or parameters of permissible legislation. Constitutions, as we indicated in Chapter 2, in addition to being structural blueprints of a regime, in effect provide limitations upon what government may or may not do in a political environment. The authors of a constitution do not have unlimited foresight, and therefore it is inevitable that eventually even sincere, honest, ethical individuals of goodwill (not to mention dishonest and unethical individuals) will disagree over what is permissible governmental behavior and what is impermissable governmental behavior. At that time the court is the appropriate organ of government to step into the picture and help to resolve the conflict.

Courts in Comparative Perspective

We began this chapter by observing that courts, as the third of the "standard" three branches of government, tend to not receive the same amount of attention in introductory cross-national studies as do legislatures and executives. It was suggested that this is so primarily because (1) legal systems and legal cultures are more system-specific, and hence more difficult to generalize about, and (2) in many political systems courts and judiciaries are specifically *excluded from* the political process, and, therefore, not really of direct relevance to discussions of political behavior.

Throughout this chapter we have further developed both of these arguments. Once we have gone beyond general philosophical arguments about law, generally, and about the various sources of law, we find it necessary to qualify virtually all of our observations with phrases such as "in some systems . . . while in other systems . . ." Descriptions of the actual structure of courts, as well as powers and jurisdictions of courts, are highly limited: They rarely go beyond national boundaries.

We have seen, however, that judiciaries as well as legal cultures are highly significant to the political systems of which they are a part. The legal culture sets the *tone*, at a minimum, for the operation of the political regime. Even if the legal culture does not describe specific political structures, it does include the essential philosophical and theoretical principles that will underlie the daily operation of the regime. The judiciary, as a governmental structure, may be more or less political in its operation. Even when it is at its *minimum* political dimension, however, it is important for the regime in terms of the services it provides in areas of mediation, conflict resolution, and the promotion of regime legitimacy and stability.

Notes

1. See Locke's Section 125 in Sir Ernest Barker, ed., *Social Contract: Essays by Locke, Hume, & Rousseau* (New York: Oxford University Press, 1970).
2. For example, J. LaPalombara's *Politics Within Nations* (Englewood Cliffs, N.J.: Prentice Hall, 1974) had fourteen chapters, with chapters on legislatures, executives, bureaucracies, interest groups, political parties, participation, and so on, but judiciaries and courts are not discussed.
3. See, for example, Glendon Schubert and David J. Danelski, eds., *Comparative Judicial Behavior* (New York: Oxford University Press, 1969); or Theodore L. Becker, *Comparative Judicial Politics* (Chicago: Rand McNally, 1970).
4. Jerold Waltman and Kenneth Holland, "Preface," in *The Political Role of Law Courts in Modern Democracies*, ed. Jerold Waltman and Kenneth Holland (New York: St. Martin's Press, 1988), p. vi.
5. Jerold Waltman, "Introduction," in Ibid., p. 5.
6. Herbert Winter and Thomas Bellows, *People and Politics* (New York: Wiley, 1977), p. 307.
7. See Locke's Section 127 in Barker, *Social Contract*, p. 74.
8. Dell Hitchner and Carol Levine, *Comparative Government and Politics* (New York: Harper & Row, 1981), p. 217.
9. Winter and Bellows, *People and Politics*, p. 308.
10. See George Sabine, *A History of Political Theory* (New York: Holt, Rinehart & Winston, 1961), p. 942.
11. Ibid., pp. 194–196.
12. John Merryman, *The Civil Law Tradition*, quoted in Henry Ehrmann, *Comparative Legal Cultures* (Englewood Cliffs, N.J.: Prentice Hall, 1976), p. 8.
13. Kenneth Holland, "The Courts in the United States," in Waltman and Holland, *Political Role of Law Courts*, p. 7.
14. Hiroshi Itoh, "The Courts in Japan," in Ibid., p. 211.
15. Ehrmann, *Comparative Legal Cultures*, p. 13. This and the following several paragraphs are based on more extended material in Ehrmann, and Winter and Bellows, *People and Politics*, pp. 309–310 and 319–322.
16. A good discussion of this can be found in Martin Shapiro, *Courts: A Comparative and Political Analysis* (Chicago: University of Chicago Press, 1981), chap. 3; "The Civil Law System and Preexisting Legal Rules."
17. A thorough discussion of the assumptions of the Anglo-American legal process can be found in Mirjan R. Damaska, *The Faces of Justice and State Authority* (New Haven: Yale University Press, 1986).
18. Winter and Bellows, *People and Politics*, p. 316.

19. Sydney Bailey, *British Parliamentary Democracy* (Boston: Houghton Mifflin, 1958), pp. 15–16.
20. See the references to the "decline of legislatures" literature discussed in Chapter 4 of this book.
21. Theodore Lowi, *The End of Liberalism* (New York: W.W. Norton & Co., 1969), esp. chap. 5, pp. 128–156.
22. Becker, *Comparative Judicial Politics*, p. 13.
23. Shapiro, *Courts: A Comparative and Political Analysis*, p. 1.
24. See the British North America Act (Canada Act) of 1867, Section 92 (14), for provincial legislative jurisdictions, and Section 91 (27) for federal legislative jurisdiction. The interested student can find this in J.R. Mallory, *The Structure of Canadian Government* (Toronto: Macmillan of Canada, 1971), pp. 289–97.
25. Roman Tomasic, "The Courts in Australia," in Waltman and Holland, *Political Role of Law Courts*, p. 50.
26. Michael Curtis, *Comparative Government and Politics* (New York: Harper and Row, 1977), p. 102.
27. Ibid., p. 107.
28. Monte Palmer and William Thompson, *The Comparative Analysis of Politics* (Itasca, Ill.: F.E. Peacock, 1978), p. 136.
29. Becker, *Comparative Judicial Politics*, p. 206.
30. C.G. Haines, *The American Doctrine of Judicial Review* (New York: Russell and Russell, 1959), p. 44, cited in Becker, *Comparative Judicial Politics*, p. 218.
31. Jerold Waltman, "The Courts in England," in Waltman and Holland, *Political Role of Law Courts*, pp. 119–20.
32. Becker, *Comparative Judicial Politics*, p. 206.
33. Ibid., p. 208.
34. Hitchner and Levine, *Comparative Government*, p. 236.
35. Giuseppe Di Federico and Carlo Guarnieri, "The Courts in Italy," in Waltman and Holland, *Political Role of Law Courts*, pp. 170–171.

7

Interest Groups, Political Parties, Elections, and Voting

A number of other variables should be considered in the process of political analysis before we can appreciate or understand a specific political system in its entirety. We need to know something about the electoral system of a nation, because it is clear that the electoral system can influence the pattern of selection of legislators and executives, as we indicated in Chapters 4 and 5. Related to this, we need to understand the party system of the political regime under consideration. Whether a polity has one, two, three, or twenty-three political parties has great significance for the operation of constitutional structures in that system, as does the type of behavior exercised by adherents of the party.

Pluralism and Corporatism

Among the most basic concepts in modern political science is the idea of "pluralism." The idea of pluralism suggests that "multiple, competing elites (including interest groups) determine public policy through bargaining and compromise."[1] This same subject, although referred to as "factions" and not called "pluralism" at the time, was present at the establishment of American political institutions, and was the theme of Madison's *Federalist* No. 10.[2] The center of the concept of pluralism includes the idea of individual rationality, and individual choice, and the premise that a rational individual will act in his or her own self-interest.

According to what is called "pluralist theory,"[3] interest groups could be called "advantage groups": People join them because they perceive that it is to their advantage to do so. Interest groups are the focus of pluralist theory; pluralist theorists believe that individuals join groups because they think that they will be better represented and have more political influence if they join a group than if they do not join a group. Policy outcomes, then, are simply perceived as a result of group competition, not necessarily a product of majority rule: A well-organized minority can defeat a less-well-organized majority in the process of competition for policy outcomes.

The original group theorist was Arthur Bentley, whose 1908 work became popular in the 1950s; it was expanded upon by David Truman, whose book *The Governmental Process* became one of the classics of political science in 1951. Truman took the idea of interest groups further than had Bentley, suggesting that individuals belonged to several different interest groups, different group loyalties reflecting different aspects of their interests and personalities; this gave rise to Truman's idea of "overlapping" group affiliations. According to Truman:

> "Interest group" refers to any group that, on the basis of one or more shared attitudes, makes certain claims upon other groups in the society for the establishment, maintenance, or enhancement of forms of behavior that are implied by the shared attitudes.[4]

Not only did Truman consider organized interest groups as part of what he called "the governmental process," but he also considered *potential* interest groups part of the process.

The problem with Truman's theories was that they did not fare very well at the hands of empirical research. Political scientists seeking to test the role of interest groups in the (American) political process found that interest groups "were *not* invariably major actors in any policy dispute" [emphasis added].[5]

Mancur Olson's work *The Logic of Collective Action*[6] helped to explain the problems with Truman's theory, because Olson pointed out that it was not logical, or rational, for an individual to invest his or her time or effort in joining an organization if that organization was working for a *collective good*. He defined a "collective good" as "any good such that, if any person X in a group . . . consumes it, it cannot feasibly be withheld from the others in that group."[7] Thus Olson's work demonstrated that if there already was an interest group to further a certain goal, it might *not* be the case that all individuals interested in that goal would join the group: They could enjoy the benefits of the group without contributing anything to the efforts of the group.

The idea of *corporatism* implies a "close interaction of groups and government."[8] For some, it further suggests "a situation where the interest organizations are integrated in the governmental decision-making process of a society."[9] Modern development of the idea of corporatism, called "neo-corporatism," "emphasizes the characteristics of the interest associations entering a relationship with the state apparatus, and the nature of this relationship, i.e., the ways in which they are recognized and granted a representational monopoly by the state."[10]

Thus, a theory of neo-corporatism takes up where the theory of pluralism leaves off. It suggests that groups *are*, in fact, of significance in the political system, although it accepts Olson's observation that not all individuals with shared interests will necessarily join those groups. There are a number of common elements in the several variations of neo-corporatist theory today:

1. Monopolies of interest representation exist and are important to explain political behaviour and policy outcomes.
2. Hierarchies emerge among associations and they may subordinate and coordinate the activities of whole economic sectors and/or social classes.
3. Membership in associations is not always voluntary . . . arrangements exist both to bind members to "their" associations and to prevent the emergence of competing ones.
4. Interest associations are not just the passive recipients of already formed member interests, but may play an active role in identifying and forming those interests.
5. Interest associations do not merely transmit member preferences to authorities, but may actively and coercively govern the behaviour of their members, especially through devolved responsibility for the implementation of public policy.

6. The state may not be either an arena for which interests contend or another interest group with which they must compete, but a constitutive element engaged in defining . . . the activities of associations. . . .

7. Interest associations are not always autonomous entities pressuring the state from without and seeking access wherever they can find an opportunity. . . .[11]

The idea of *conflict*, then, is to be found at the center of neo-corporatist theory just as it is at the center of pluralist theory. In many respects pluralism and corporatism (or neo-corporatism) are at different ends of a continuum, because both argue for the significance of the *group* in the political process. Where they differ is on the relationship between government and groups; perhaps put another way, the degree to which the government establishes a patron-client relationship with specific interest groups.

Interest Groups

Although political systems may contain political structures designed to ensure popular representation in the governmental policy-making process, most notably the legislature, it is entirely likely that the formal governmental (constitutional) structures of representation will not prove to be sufficient for representing all shades of public opinion.

Two additional structures are available in the political environment to supplement the formal (constitutional) representative structures, and they are quite effective in many political regimes. Both the *interest group* and the *political party* can play significant roles in political systems in assisting formal-legal structures in the processing of political demands and the communication of public beliefs, attitudes, and values.

Although interest groups and political parties have a number of characteristics and functions in common,[12] we should be very careful to distinguish between the two types of structures, for they really are quite different.

As we indicated earlier, group theory suggests that *all* public opinion can be described in group terms and that individual opinion is essentially unimportant, save for the fact that individuals *make up* groups. All public opinion either originates with groups or is articulated by groups, so we do not really need to worry about individual representation as long as a mechanism for group representation exists.[13]

Interest groups are collections of individuals who share common beliefs, attitudes, values, or concerns. The shared concern(s) may focus upon serious issues, such as concern about nuclear weapons, concern about gun control, concern about air and/or water pollution, or concern about a minimum wage or working conditions. The shared concern(s) may also be a bit more frivolous, such as (with due apologies to anyone offended!) love of Angora cats or appreciation of Ford Edsels.

Interest groups come into existence because a collection of individuals sees something to be gained by such an association, either material gains (higher wages by joining a union, or free auto towing and maps by joining an automobile club); psychological gains (a feeling of "brotherhood" by joining a fraternity, or a sense of theological or eschatological satisfaction by joining a church); recreational gains (lower ski-lift fees by joining a ski association, or a sense of pastime well spent by joining an antique car club); humanitarian gains (helping to do away with nuclear proliferation by joining a sit-in group, or promoting civil rights by contributing to a civil rights organization), and so on.[14]

Interest groups might be highly organized, with weekly meetings, dues collection, a monthly newsletter, and membership cards. They might also be quite loosely organized, or not formally organized at all, for that matter.[15] Their scope of concern might be quite broad or quite narrow. Groups might be open to anyone interested or limited in membership. They may, in short, vary greatly.

Group theorists suggest that interest groups play a very important function in the political arena. They can be important as *linkage mechanisms*, some argue, because they are very effective communicators of segments of public opinion. Because interest groups generally are of limited scope, they are able to communicate their collective opinion more effectively than can individuals. The National Rifle Association (NRA) and the American Medical Association (AMA) are two examples of interest groups that, although numerically not overwhelmingly large, are very effective in exerting political pressure in the areas of concern to their members.[16]

The argument for interest group utility suggests that political (formal, constitutional, legislative) representatives simply *cannot* represent all of their constituents. On any given issue in relation to which a legislator takes a position, he or she is bound to alienate some group. An American legislator voting in favor of gun control, for example, is going to irritate constituents who oppose gun control. What is more, once "their" representative has come out on the opposite side of an issue, the anti-gun-control constituents, to use the same example, are no longer (strictly speaking) represented by their representative in the legislature. The existence of an interest group, in this case the NRA, affords these individuals recourse to an *alternative* representational structure, that will voice their concerns and act on their collective behalf.

Many political scientists use the terms "interest group" and "pressure group" interchangeably. Others, however, make a distinction between the two terms, and whether or not the student *chooses* to make this distinction, he or she should be aware of the distinctions that are drawn. Pressure groups, simply put, are said to be a subset of interest groups that are organized exclusively for the purpose of political lobbying. Thus we can say that all pressure groups are interest groups, but not all interest groups are pressure groups.

There are clearly many interest groups ("collections of individuals who share a common belief, attitude, value, or concern") whose activities are oriented around unequivocally nonpolitical themes. For example, the Rocky Mountain Cavy Club is an interest group that meets once a month to have cavy (guinea pig) shows and competitions, give prizes and award ribbons, and which publishes a monthly newsletter, "Cavy Chatter." Theirs is obviously a nonpolitical concern! Other interest groups are *usually* nonpolitical. The American Automobile Association (AAA) has as its primary *raison d'être* auto safety, and it provides its members with a number of benefits: maps, car insurance, tow service, and so on. On occasions, however, the AAA *has* become politically active, such as on the occasion when the Congress was considering an extra tax on gasoline. The AAA, acting on behalf of its members (drivers), lobbied effectively against such a tax.

Still other interest groups are *exclusively* political, having as their primary reason for being a policy objective: the Vietnam Veterans to End the War in Vietnam, Concerned Citizens for Proposition 13, the National Organization of Women lobbying for the Equal Rights Amendment, and so on. Pressure groups are almost invariably very narrow in scope, usually related to a single issue, and ostensibly temporary. Once their policy objective is achieved, they no longer have a reason for being. General interest groups, on the other hand, are much longer-lived, and their reason for being is not as transient.

Political Parties

This political dimension of interest group activity leads us to our next distinction, namely the difference between interest groups (and here the term includes our pressure-group subcategory) and political parties. A number of distinctions have been pointed out in detailed studies, including permanence of organization and levels of organization (political parties tend to be more permanent and institutionalized than are interest groups), and breadth of issue concerns (parties almost invariably are concerned with a large number of issues, whereas interest groups ususaly focus upon a narrower range of issues).

The single most important difference, however, relates to the ultimate *goals* of the organization. The goal of the interest group is to satisfy its members, either through the organization itself (e.g., with the Cavy Club), or through political pressure resulting in a specific policy outcome (e.g., the NRA helping to defeat gun-control legislation). The goal of a political party is to win political office, gain political power, and thereby control the policy-making process. The interest group does not care which party or which individual wins an election as long as its specific policy concern prevails. The political party is much broader in scope and seeks to hold power (to the point of perhaps modifying some of its issue positions if that will help it to control power); the interest group is not so much concerned with power as with policy outcome.[17]

Parties have been said to derive from a number of different sources. One source of party development is factions within a national legislature. American political parties can be seen to be examples of this; they originally formed as groups of legislative supporters of Thomas Jefferson and Alexander Hamilton, which subsequently established formal organizations leading to the creation of the Jeffersonian-Democrats and the Federalists. A second source of party organization is the labor movement. The

British Labour party is a good example of this type of party, in which an already existing labor organization (itself an interest group) decides to develop an explicitly political identity, seeking not only to influence labor policy but also to control power. Still another point of origin of political parties is the national-liberation movement. The Congress party in India was not primarily a political party under British rule; rather, it was organized to help achieve Indian independence and to help drive the British from India. Once the British left, the conversion from liberation movement to political party was easily achieved. Finally, parties may be created for ideological reasons, being created to represent a viewpoint not otherwise represented in the polity.[18]

As organizations, political parties vary greatly in a number of different respects, including membership and size, and structure of organization, not to mention variation in the number of parties active in the system itself.[19] One of the primary structural distinctions among parties is whether they are "mass" parties or "cadre" parties. Maurice Duverger, in his classic work *Political Parties*, suggests that "the difference involved is not one of size but of structure." For mass parties, the recruiting of members is a fundamental activity, "the members are therefore the very substance of the party, the stuff of its activity. Without members, the party would be like a teacher without pupils."[20] Also, mass parties are *financially* based upon the mass; the party finances are, to a large extent, based upon member dues. Thus Duverger suggests that:

> the mass-party technique in effect replaces the capitalist financing of electioneering by democratic financing. Instead of appealing to a few big private donors . . . to meet campaign expenses—which makes the candidate (and the person elected) dependent on them— the mass party spreads the burden over the largest possible number of members, each of whom contributes a modest sum.[21]

The cadre party is of a different sort. As Duverger suggests, "what the mass party secures by numbers, the cadre party achieves by selection; . . . it is dependent upon rigid and exclusive selection."[22] Sometimes the distinction between mass and cadre parties is made less clear because the cadre parties may admit numbers of the mass in imitation of a mass party; there are a few *pure* cadre parties today. American political parties today, for example, are disguised cadre parties. They have democratic constitutions and permit mass participation, but are steered by a much smaller group of individuals. According to Duverger, in 1950 "the Turkish Democratic party claimed before the election that it had 'three or four million members.' Obviously it was referring to supporters, in actual fact it was a cadre party."[23] Generally, then, cadre parties correspond to more caucus-organized types of parties, usually decentralized, whereas mass parties tend to correspond to parties based on branches, more centrally organized and "firmly knit."[24]

The number of political parties in an electoral system is, as was suggested in Chapter 4, a function of several factors, including ideology, political culture, electoral laws, and methods of election. Duverger noted that the relationship between the electoral regime and the number of political parties "can be expressed in the following formula: the simple-majority single-ballot system favours the two-party system."[25] There are a number of different-sized party systems; single party systems, two-party systems, two-party-plus systems, and multiparty systems. Even this classification is too general, though, because a number of different variations of two-party systems may be discerned.[26]

Political parties are an important part of a theory of pluralism. If "political pluralism," as one author has put it, highlights the "existence of a 'plurality of groups that are both independent and non-inclusive,'" then parties are an important part of that pluralistic model.[27] As we saw in Chapters 4 and 5, parties are absolutely crucial as a part of a "responsible government" model: Obviously, "party discipline" could not exist without political parties, and it is party discipline that is the vehicle for responsible government, a government being able to "deliver" on its promises.

Internal party organization, clearly, varies on a party-by-party basis. Some parties are highly unified, wheras others are collections of factions that may not have a great deal in common except their commitment to share power. Some political parties are very democratic organizations, not only permitting but indeed encouraging intraparty competition, while others permit no internal competition at all and are simply organizations dedicated to following and supporting a single individual's political advancement.

Political parties, much as interest groups, serve a number of important functions in the political regime. They are, among other things, rather elaborate personnel services, serving as a mechanism for assisting in the hiring of political leaders.[28] They help to organize political groups.[29] They help to articulate political demands.[30] They serve as a point of reference for bewildered voters who are overwhelmed by the political world: Party label is often the only clue available to voters to guide their behavior, and it is widely used as such.[31]

Another important function served by the political party as an organization is in the process of political development. Parties are important vehicles in the process of political recruitment—we shall discuss this in more detail in the next chapter—helping to "bring individuals into" the political arena by offering a convenient vehicle for participation to the masses.[32]

Parties also serve as structures that mobilize the electorate—"get out the vote" and participation—through competition between parties (or within a party in one-party systems). Through this action, we are told, they contribute to a sense of "national integration"—the "amalgamation of disparate social, economic, religious, ethnic, and geographic elements into a single nation-state,"[33] thus helping to develop a sense of political nationhood on the part of the masses.[34]

In short, research has shown that political parties can play significant roles in five important respects in the process of political development. First, parties encourage and make easier political participation. Second, they help to stimulate a sense of governmental legitimacy through the campaign process and the debate that ensues. Third, they contribute to the development of a sense of national integration. They also play an important role in conflict management within the policy, providing a vehicle by which differences of opinion over policy preferences can be peacefully resolved. Finally, political parties play an important role in the political socialization function in society, helping to transmit attitudes and values from one generation to another.[35]

Much as the interest group was seen to be a political structure that assists in the representation function in the political world, so too the political party serves as a "linkage mechanism"[36] in passing along public opinions from various groups in the electorate to government officials. Of course, the degree to which parties serve these several functions depends upon the individual party organization and the political system within which it is found. Depending on the number of political parties in a system, the degree of party discipline found in the political system, and the ideology and constituency of the party in question, the role of the party will vary.

Scholars have speculated about the future of political parties, and whether they can continue to be as central a political structure in their respective political systems as they have been in the past. The continual growth of executive power in political systems all over the world, combined with greater public attention to politics and increasingly aggressive media, means that traditional assumptions about political parties and political party behavior have to be rethought.[37]

Electoral Systems

We saw in Chapter 4 that the system of representation found in a given nation can drastically affect the composition of its national legislature. Proportional representation elections lead to multipartyism and corresponding instability brought on by necessary coalition governments. Single-member-district elections tend to provide a much greater degree of stability because they lead to the existence of a two-party system (or sometimes what is called a two-party-plus system), but they have the distinct disadvantage of "hiding" minorities. We saw that groups constituting 20 to 30 percent of the population could end up with no representation in the national legislature. So, different systems of electoral representation can make a difference in how *effective* a system of representation is.[38]

In this section of the chapter we shall discuss several aspects of electoral systems other than how (and whether) electoral districts are drawn, and whether representation is based on geographical districts or proportional representation. First, we shall briefly discuss some different classifications of electoral systems. Second, we shall discuss some other structures of electoral systems that can influence the outcomes of elections, such as electoral laws, campaigns, and the like. Third, we shall discuss the more philosophical question of the importance of elections themselves.

Political scientist Robert Dahl has suggested a number of characteristics of an "ideal" election.[39] Before the voting period, all voters would have the opportunity to make sure that their choices were included among the alternatives to be voted upon, and all voters would be equally (well) informed. During an election all eligible voters would vote, all their votes would be counted equally, and the candidate with the most votes would win. After the election the winning choice would be implemented.

Elections have been classified a number of different ways, depending upon degree of choice between parties and degree of choice between candidates.[40] Some political systems are extremely open, and a large number of parties are permitted to compete; examples of this type of system might include Italy, or Australia. Others are less open, with a much narrower range of parties that can compete, such as can be found to be the case in Poland, or Tanzania. Still others do not permit more than one party to compete in any election, such as is the case in Kenya. Similarly, the degree of choice between candidates ranges from a highly competitive system, such as that which we described in Israel, to a system in which there is no choice between candidates for the voters: They vote for predetermined candidates chosen by the competing parties. These different characteristics have suggested four broad types of elections: competitive, dominant-party, candidate-choice, and acclamatory.

In "competitive" elections, voters are presented with a choice between competing parties, and the number of parties presenting alternatives to the voters may range from two to over a dozen. Voters may not have the ability to actually select *which* party candidates they most prefer; this is an option in Japan, but is not in Great Britain.

In "dominant-party" elections, although voters may have the legal right to vote for any party they want, they do not, in fact, have a "real" choice for a variety of reasons. Sometimes actual intimidation is involved, where even "secret" votes are checked and voters not voting for the "correct" party can suffer injury, even death, as was the case in recent elections in Haiti. Elsewhere it is not intimidation, but instead fraud or corruption, which keeps the single dominant party in power, such as was the case in the Philippines under President Marcos, and such as was claimed to be the case in the 1988 elections in Mexico. Still elsewhere a single party stays dominant over a longer period of time simply as a result of its ability to claim that it is the only "real" possible governing party, perhaps wrapping itself up in the national flag, perhaps claiming to be the heir of an independence movement. These "dominant-party" elections "are a surprisingly common and resilient type of election in the third world."[41]

"Candidate-choice" elections are also somewhat common in the developing world. In this type of election, voters are not offered a choice between political parties—there is only one "permissible" political party—but they are given a choice between or among several candidates from that one approved party in any given election. To take one example, in Kenya there may be several KANU (Kenyan African National Union) candidates competing for each race; the voters have a choice between candidates, but not between parties.

Finally, in "acclamatory" elections, voters have no choice either between parties or between candidates. The most frequently cited example of this style of election in recent years has been the Soviet Union, where virtually all of the more than 1,500 members of the Supreme Soviet "ran" for their positions without opposition. Although not all of these "candidates" were members of the Communist party, virtually all of them ran unopposed: A nominating body at the constituency level would nominate a single candidate to run for the office. In the last year radical changes have been introduced in the Soviet Union and across Eastern Europe, and it appears that this style of election is going to become almost nonexistent in these nations.

Whatever the general type of electoral system that exists, it is clear that there are many legal and behavioral characteristics of a political regime that can affect electoral behavior. In some of the cases just cited the regimes actually have laws outlawing opposition parties: In these regimes it is clear that legal behavior of the government affects the type and style of electoral behavior we can witness.

Electoral law can have a profound effect on the outcome of elections, whatever the basis of representation is. There is a very wide range of electoral law that could be examined by an interested student, including regulations governing *who* can be a candidate, *how* campaigns are run, which *parties* can compete, and who the *voters* will be, among others.

Regulations governing *who can be a candidate* in an election vary widely.[42] All systems have some *age* criterion for candidacy, often simply legal majority but often more than that.

(For example, in the United States citizens may vote in federal elections at the age of 18 years; one cannot be a member of the House of Representatives until the age of 25, and one cannot be a member of the Senate until the age of 30. State requirements vary.) Some systems have a *residency* requirement (that one must live in the district one represents), while others do not. Some have *gender, race,* or *ethnic group* restrictions on candidacy, as well.

Some systems have quite stringent sets of laws governing *how the election campaigns are to be run*, which clearly are of great significance in a campaign.[43] Limitations on *fund-raising*, for example, can determine who can afford to run for office and who cannot.[44] This type of limitation can certainly affect who has a greater likelihood to win the election, because it affects the amount of campaigning one can do and the amount of advertising one can buy.[45] Specifically, of course, *the media* are often crucial, and thus are regulated in campaigns.[46] During the last month of the 1988 Israeli election campaign each party was given ten free minutes of prime time televison each evening, six nights a week; parties already having seats in the legislature received an additional four free minutes per seat they controlled.[47]

It is also common to find legislation governing *which parties* can compete in elections. This type of limitation ranges from the most rigid which might indicate that only a single party was legally permitted to submit candidates in an election—the type of situation found in many one-party states—to a much more flexible situation in which there simply are requirements affecting (1) a minimum number of individuals who must sign a party petition before a party may submit a candidate, (2) monetary "deposits" that must be paid by political parties which are returned if they receive a certain percentage of the vote (this is designed to discourage parties from submitting "unrealistic" candidates who will receive very little public support); or (3) deadlines by which parties must submit their candidates.

Finally, it is common to find governmental regulations affecting *who can vote* in an election.[48] These regulations usually include an *age* requirement, a *registration* requirement (e.g., one must register to vote sixty days before an election or one cannot vote), a *residency* requirement (e.g., one must live in the district in which one votes), or a *literacy* requirement ranging from a minimal requirement that an individual be able to read a ballot (although many systems will provide readers if that is a problem) to a much more rigorous requirement that one be able to "pass an examination to demonstrate one's literacy" before one can vote. The latter type of test was used as a vehicle for preventing Southern blacks from voting for many years in the United States. As well, it still happens in some systems that *gender, ethnic group,* or *racial* characteristics also are the subject of regulation in terms of who can vote in an election.

We have addressed some of the issues related to various structures affecting the operation of elections, but we have not yet answered the more general questions: What do elections do? Why bother to have them? What do elections decide?[49] Answers to these questions may seem so obvious that they are not worth asking, but the exercise is probably worth doing so that we can be sure about some of the assumptions we may be making.[50] Probably the most common answer to the question "Why have elections?" involves *choosing representatives*. The idea of representation is a central one in democratic theory and has been discussed by Thomas Hobbes (1651), John Locke (1690), Jean-Jacques Rousseau (1762), Edmund Burke (1790), and John Stuart Mill (1861), among the other great thinkers of modern history. Although representatives may be selected any number of ways, clearly one of the most obvious ways—and most defensible in terms of democratic theory—is through election.

Another function of elections is to offer the (voting) public *a choice* among a variety of political parties, candidates, governments, or policy preferences. In democratic polities, the electorate choose between two or more political parties, and these parties (often) represent different positions on controversial issues of the day. Thus elections may help to resolve some issues dividing society.

Elections also serve as a vehicle for *creating governments* in democratic systems. As we described earlier in this book, most systems in the world are parliamentary, not presidential, so most voters in the world do not actually have an opportunity to vote for a *government*. Rather, they vote for a representative (and, often, a political party) and dynamics within the legislature after the election will determine which government is formed. Although it may still be necessary to create a coalition (as we described earlier in this text) in order to establish a majority in a legislature, elections often serve the function of creating a government by giving an individual candidate a mandate, or giving a specific political party a mandate to govern.

Elections *influence policy* by choosing which politicians will be exercising power. By giving some politicians mandates to rule rather than others, citizens in an indirect way can influence the types of public policy made by the governments that represent them.

Elections also *provide legitimacy* for the government. Governments derive legitimacy by appearing to be responsible and responsive to the public over which they rule, and by appearing to be ruling in a "just" manner; that is, the government that is in power *ought* to be in power. Elections vest legitimacy in governments by providing the "mandates" we mentioned above, and a government perceived as being "legitimate" can rule more easily than a government not viewed that way.

Elections also serve an *educative* function in that during the campaign period there is usually an increased level of discussion of the major issues of the day. Individuals who pay attention to campaign debates and speeches can learn a great deal about their political system, about international affairs, about domestic social or economic issues, or about any of a number of other aspects of the political world.

Finally, elections can *influence political parties*. A party that regularly loses elections will receive a message: "Change the alternatives you are offering us." In the spring of 1989 the British Labour party changed—after years and years of debate and argument—its unilateral nuclear disarmament policy, largely as a result of arguments that Labour would continue to lose to the Conservative party there as long as it held the extreme antinuclear position it had been advocating for the preceding decade. Political parties, as we defined them earlier, are committed to *winning* elections, and will usually try to do whatever is necessary to win. Elections can send messages to parties that will influence what they do and what they think.

Ultimately, of course, the study of elections involves more than the study of electoral *systems*. It focuses upon the relationship between the mass public and the elite that make up the cadre of political leaders of a system. It focuses upon voting behavior, public opinion, and individual political attitudes, as well as questions related to political stability and the process of political recruitment.

Political Participation and Voting Behavior

The act of voting is clearly influenced by much more than only the types of structural electoral characteristics we have been discussing here. While it is clearly the case that if the law says someone must be 21 years of age in order to vote, one simply *cannot* vote at age 19, it does not necessarily follow that if the law says one must be 21 years of age in order to vote one will *always* vote if one has the opportunity. Motivation, attitudes, values, political opinions, etc., all affect participation, whether we are limiting our discussion of political participation to voting in an election, or whether we are including participating in a political demonstration of over a million students in Beijing lobbying for a greater democratization of Chinese politics in May 1989.

Voting is a *kind* of political participation, but we certainly should not be so simplistic as to equate voting with all other types of participation. In a stable Western democracy we may automatically think of election campaigns when we think of "participation," but that is not the case everywhere. It is not hard to imagine situations in which wearing a certain style of clothing would be taken—legitimately—as a political gesture. Going to church in a society that is officially atheistic may have political implications. We certainly would accept making public speeches as political behavior, or burning draft cards, or participating in an organized boycott. In short, although we may use voting as a yardstick by which we measure political behavior here, we must keep in mind that political behavior as a variable may be *culture-* or *system-dependent*, and what is one society's casual entertainment may be another society's politically significant act.

How have social scientists explained the variations in participation from country to country over the years? Several explanations have been offered, some on the *macro*-level, some on the *micro*-level. We shall briefly discuss each of these here.

Micro-level characteristics are those centered on the political individual and his or her beliefs, attitudes, and values. Such characteristics as *resources*—including income, education, and perhaps employment or transportation—and *psychological characteristics*, including political attitudes and orientations, are clearly of great significance in explaining why individuals behave as they do.

Macro-level characteristics affecting political participation include many of those factors suggested above, including electoral rules, opportunities (one cannot vote for a candidate for president, no matter how strongly one supports that candidate, if there is no election scheduled to be held for the next two years), and costs in time, money, and effort. (Participating in a demonstration tolerated by the government on a pleasant day requires a different amount of effort and degree of commitment from participating in a demonstration in a monsoon, or with temperatures at 20° below zero, when you know that the government intends to jail—and/or shoot—all participants in the demonstration.)

Groups, Parties, Elections, and Voting

All three of these terms, "parties," "(interest) groups," and "elections," are central in any discussion of democratic politics, and are even central in discussion of political participation in systems that may not, at any given time, be democratic. After all, the existence of over a million Chinese students in Beijing in May 1989 shows the potential impact of an interest group: The "critical mass" was present and was so large that even calling in the Chinese Army was not able to control students' behavior. Political parties and interest groups—whatever the degree of organization of the latter—are the primary vehicles by which collective public opinion is communicated to the political elite in most political systems.

Studying only the formal organizations of political parties and (organized) interest groups, however, is not adequate to ensure a thorough understanding of the operation of the political system. Analyses of public opinion and voting behavior show us that there are many *micro*-level—that is, varying on an individual-by-individual basis—factors equally important in helping us to understand how political systems operate. We turn our attention to many of these factors in the next chapter.

Notes

1. Harmon Zeigler, *Pluralism, Corporatism, and Confucianism: Political Association and Conflict Regulation in the United States, Europe, and Taiwan* (Philadelphia: Temple University Press, 1988), p. 3.
2. Alexander Hamilton, James Madison, and John Jay, *The Federalist Papers* (New York: New American Library, 1961), pp. 77–83.
3. This section is based upon a much longer analysis in Zeigler, *Pluralism*, pp. 4–11.
4. David Truman, *The Governmental Process* (New York: Knopf, 1951), p. 33.
5. Zeigler, *Pluralism*, p. 7.
6. Mancur Olson, *The Logic of Collective Action: Public Goods and the Theory of Groups* (Cambridge: Harvard University Press, 1965).
7. Ibid., p. 14.
8. Zeigler, *Pluralism*, p. 15.
9. O. Ruin, "Participatory Democracy and Corporatism: The Case of Sweden," *Scandinavian Political Studies* 9 (1974): 171–186, as cited in Gerhard Lehmbruch and Philippe Schmitter, eds., *Patterns of Corporatist Policy-Making* (Beverly Hills, Calif.: Sage Publications, 1982), p. 4.
10. Marino Regini, "Changing Relationships Between Labour and the State in Italy: Towards a Neo-Corporatist System?" in Lehmbruch and Schnitter, ibid., p. 112.
11. Philippe C. Schmitter, "Reflections on Where the Theory of Neo-Corporatism Has Gone and Where the Praxis of Neo-Corporatism May be Going," in Lehmbruch and Schmitter, *Patterns*, pp. 260–61.
12. See *inter alia*, Norman Luttbeg, ed., *Public Opinion and Public Policy* (Homewood, Ill.: Dorsey Press, 1974), especially pages 1–10, 109, and 187.
13. Truman, *Governmental Process*, especially pages 129–139, offers the classic articulation of this argument.
14. See Michael Curtis, *Comparative Government and Politics* (New York: Harper & Row, 1978), pp. 141–143.
15. One of the classic typologies developed for the study of interest groups was done by Gabriel Almond, and can be found in his Introduction to G. Almond and J.S. Coleman, eds., *The Politics of the Developing Areas* (Princeton, N.J.: Princeton University Press, 1960), pp. 33ff.
16. See Luttbeg, *Public Opinion*, pp. 187–188. The articles reprinted in this section of this reader that deal with the pressure groups model of political linkage are all very well done and provide illustrations of the linkage suggested by the theory.
17. For further distinctions, see Curtis, *Comparative Government*, pp. 143–144. A very well written essay that develops this distinction is that by Dennis C. Beller and Frank Belloni, "Party and Faction: Modes of Political Competition," in Frank Belloni and Dennis Beller, eds., *Factional Politics: Political Parties and Factionalism in Comparative Perspective* (Santa Barbara, Calif.: ABC-Clio Press, 1978), pp. 417–450.
18. One of the classic essays in this area is that by J. LaPalombara and M. Weiner, "The Origin and Development of Political Parties," in J. LaPalombara and M. Weiner, eds., *Political Parties and Political Development* (Princeton, N.J.: Princeton University Press, 1966), pp. 3–6. Another classic study is that by Leon Epstein, *Political Parties in Western Democracies* (New York: Praeger, 1972).

19. Probably the best single reference book was compiled and edited by Alan Day and Henry Degenhardt, *Political Parties of the World* (Detroit: Gale Research Company, 1980). This 500-page compendium lists all political parties in the world (at the time), their leadership structures, ideologies, electoral histories, and any other descriptive characteristics readily available.
20. Maurice Duverger, *Political Parties* (New York: Wiley, 1963), p. 63.
21. Ibid.
22. Ibid., p. 64.
23. Ibid., p. 65.
24. Ibid., p. 67.
25. Ibid., p. 217.
26. One of the better theoretical essays in this area is by John G. Grumm, "Theories of Electoral Systems," in *Comparative Political Parties*, ed. Andrew Milnor (New York: Crowell, 1969). pp. 230–250.
27. Giovanni Sartori, *Parties and Party Systems: A Framework for Analysis* (Cambridge: Cambridge University Press, 1976), p. 15.
28. One of the classics in this area is the work of Austin Ranney, *Pathways to Parliament: Candidate Selection in Britain* (Madison: University of Wisconsin Press, 1965). A classic American study would be that by Samuel Eldersveld, *Political Parties: A Behavioral Analysis* (Chicago: Rand McNally, 1964), chap. 22.
29. One of the best essays of this nature is by Samuel Barnes, "Party Democracy and the Logic of Collective Action," in *Approaches to the Study of Party Organization*, ed. W.J. Crotty (Boston: Allyn & Bacon, 1968), pp. 105–138.
30. See Kay Lawson, *The Comparative Study of Political Parties* (New York: St. Martin's Press, 1976), pp. 136–161.
31. Two classic references for party voting are H.A. Scarrow, "Distinguishing Between Political Parties: The Case of Canada," *Midwest Journal of Political Science* 9 (1965): 61–76; and Epstein, *Political Parties*, pp. 80 ff. Epstein argues that "European voting is probably more highly structured than American."
32. A very good study of this nature is by Leonard Binder, "Political Recruitment and Participation in Egypt," in LaPalombara and Weiner, *Political Parties and Political Development*, pp. 217–240.
33. Myron Weiner and Joseph LaPalombara, "The Impact of Parties on Political Development," in LaPalombara and Weiner, ibid., p. 413.
34. See Stein Rokkan, "Electoral Mobilization, Party Competition, and National Integration," in LaPalombara and Weiner, ibid., pp. 241–266; and Rupert Emerson, "Parties and National Integration in Africa," in LaPalombara and Weiner, ibid., pp. 267–302.
35. Myron Weiner and Joseph LaPalombara, "The Impact of Parties on Political Development," in LaPalombara and Weiner, ibid., p. 413.
36. Luttbeg, *Public Opinion*, pp. 109–186. See also Kay Lawson, "When Linkage Fails," in Kay Lawson and Peter Merkl, eds., *When Parties Fail: Emerging Alternative Organizations* (Princeton, N.J.: Princeton University Press, 1988), pp. 13–40.
37. An example of this type of study is the work by Louis Maisel and Paul Sacks, eds., *The Future of Political Parties* (Beverly Hills, Calif.: Sage Publications, 1975).
38. See David Butler, "Electoral Systems," in *Democracy at the Polls: A*

Comparative Study of Competitive National Elections, ed. David Butler, Howard Penniman, and Austin Ranney (Washington, D.C.: American Enterprise Institute, 1981), pp. 7–25. A fairly sophisticated discussion of this is presented in the volume by Richard S. Katz, *A Theory of Parties and Electoral Systems* (Baltimore: Johns Hopkins University Press, 1980).

39. Robert Dahl, *A Preface to Democratic Theory* (Chicago: University of Chicago Press, 1956), pp. 67–71.
40. Much of the discussion that follows is based upon more detailed discussion in Martin Harrop and William Miller, *Elections and Voters: A Comparative Introduction* (New York: Meredith Press, 1987), pp. 2–5.
41. Ibid., p. 4.
42. Many of these issues are discussed in Austin Ranney, "Candidate Selection," in Butler, Penniman, and Ranney, *Democracy at the Polls*, pp. 76–105.
43. See Howard Penniman, "Campaign Styles and Methods," in Butler, Penniman, and Ranney, *Democracy at the Polls*, pp. 107–136.
44. A very good article on this subject is by Benjamin Ginsberg and John C. Green, "The Best Congress Money Can Buy: Campaign Contributions and Congressional Behavior," in Benjamin Ginsberg and Alan Stone, eds., *Do Elections Matter?* (Armonk, N.Y.: M.E. Sharpe, 1986), pp. 75–90.
45. This is discussed by K. Z. Paltiel, "Campaign Finance: Contrasting Practices and Reforms," in Butler, Penniman, and Ranney, *Democracy at the Polls*, pp. 138–172.
46. See Anthony Smith, "Mass Communications," in Butler, Penniman, and Ranney, *Democracy at the Polls*, pp. 173–195.
47. Gregory Mahler, *Israel: Politics and Government in a Maturing State* (New York: Harcourt Brace Jovanovich, 1989), p. 132.
48. This is discussed in Ivor Crewe, "Electoral Participation," in Butler, Penniman, and Ranney, *Democracy at the Polls*, pp. 216–264.
49. This question is asked by Anthony King, "What Do Elections Decide?" in Butler, Penniman, and Ranney, ibid., pp. 293–325.
50. This is based upon much more extensive discussion and analysis in Harrop and Miller, *Elections and Voters*, pp. 245–268.

8

The Individual and the Political Environment

The Political System Revisited

In Chapter 1 we introduced the concept of the political system, a set of related objects connected with one another in an analytic way. We indicated at the time that the relationships of these objects were to be *perceived* by the observer: Sometimes the links between objects are clear and distinct, and sometimes they are not. The links between the U.S. House of Representatives and the U.S. Senate are reasonably clear; the links between multinational corporations and a Third World nation's political stability may be less so.

Thus far in this comparative study we have focused our attention upon the central political structures of regimes: constitutional frameworks, legislatures, executives, bureaucracies, judiciaries, and political parties and interest groups. We must keep in mind, though, that these political structures, however similar or varied they may be and however they may be related to other constitutional structures in their political regimes, all operate within a political context or a political environment, and not in a vacuum. Thus, although it is possible for us to speak abstractly about constitutional structures in presidential systems or parliamentary systems, we cannot be content to end our cross-national political analysis at that point; the political environment also introduces a broad range of variables into our examination.

Although we have now examined a very wide range of political structures that exist in the political system, there are still a number of other variables—some at the individual level, and some at the level of the political system—that should be considered to be part of the political environment within which an individual operates in the normal process of political participation. On the individual level, it is appropriate for us to understand how individual political attitudes are developed and passed from generation to generation—the process of *political socialization*—so as to appreciate the political culture of the regime. Moreover, preliminary examination may indicate a need to understand the process of *political recruitment*. We should ask: How are political leaders and political elites selected from among the ranks of the masses?

At the level of the political system, we need to understand several other possible influences on political behavior. The subject of political recruitment introduces questions related to the relation of the *political elite* to the masses. We know that the recruitment process serves to separate an elite from the masses, but how "open" is the elite? Additionally, although the *military* is not a significant political structure in the United States, in some political cultures it is taken very seriously as a political actor, and we shall briefly discuss its political role here. Finally, we shall briefly discuss the subject of *political violence*, since it is a type of political behavior that is of significance to the political system in the context of "systems maintenance" we discussed in Chapter 1.

All of this is a weighty assignment for the beginning student. The solution to this quandary opted for by many authors of introductory texts is to give short shrift to the constitutional structures and political institutions of any regime, and to focus instead in great detail upon the topics mentioned above. In this text we do the opposite, for reasons that were discussed in the Preface. In the sections of this chapter that follow, we will *briefly* discuss the several individual and systemic structures and behaviors referred to above. We will undertake to discuss their potential impact in the political systems of which they are a part. They will *not*, however, be the *primary* foci for our area studies chapters in the second part of this book. Our assumption here is that the student is better prepared for further cross-national study with an introduction emphasizing political structures and political institutions and placing less emphasis on the many variables in the political environment, than the student would be with an introduction emphasizing the many variables in the political environment but giving short shrift to the decision-making processes of political regimes.[1]

After brief discussion of the several factors that may be of significance in the political environment within which a political system operates, we will turn our attention in the second part of this book to a number of area studies chapters. These chapters will focus primarily upon the structures and processes described in Chapters 2 through 8. Where some of the environmental variables described here are of great significance, they will be discussed as well, but we will not undertake to treat *all* of these factors comprehensively in *all* chapters; time and space simply do not permit such a treatment.

The Study of Political Socialization and Political Attitudes

Contemporary studies focusing upon political actors are often based upon the assumption that *who the actors are* affects the product generated by the systems of which they are a part.[2] This includes the study of values, attitudes, beliefs, and skills that actors bring with them to the political arena and leads us to a discussion of political socialization.[3] Although the concept of political socialization has not yet proven to be as valuable as an explanatory tool as many had hoped when it became a popular subject of study in the 1960s, many people continue to believe that it still has value as a factor contributing to a greater understanding of how individual political behavior is motivated.

Interest in political socialization is not a creation of contemporary political scientists. Plato dealt with the problem of political education in his *Republic*, as did Aristotle in his *Politics* and *Ethics*; the debate has continued from the time of Jean-Jacques Rousseau to B.F. Skinner:

From time immemorial, social philosophers have thought that political education *should* have an early start. For Plato and Rousseau there was also little question about the feasibility of such early instruction; to them it was common sense that young children could be educated in fundamental political matters.[4]

Current interest in the study of political socialization was given a major impetus from the work of Herbert Hyman in 1959, who was perhaps the first modern political scientist to urge the study of political socialization as a subfield of political science.

Political socialization has been conceptualized as the process by which "the individual acquires attitudes, beliefs, and values relating to the political system of which he is a member and to his own role as a citizen within that political system."[5] Elsewhere, socialization has been defined as "those developmental processes through which persons acquire political orientations and patterns of behavior."[6] The important thing to note in these and other conceptualizations is that socialization is conceived as a *process*; that is, it is an ongoing action that is not finished as long as the individual is still able to perceive his or her environment and respond to it.

The process of political socialization may be either direct or indirect, formal or informal.

Much of American civic education takes place informally. From an early age children learn about government and politics and begin to prepare for their adult political roles, through processes which neither they nor those who instruct them are especially conscious of, but which nevertheless provide the basis of democratic political participation.[7]

While the idea of direct, formal political socialization has negative connotations for many because of its similarity to the "indoctrination" of youth in more authoritarian political systems, it is nonetheless the case that there are many societal actions directly politically socializing that exist virtually unopposed even in "democratic" regimes—including civics courses and the Pledge of Allegiance, for example.

Many theoretical gaps still need to be filled in socialization research, and much attention needs to be given to several major questions yet outstanding. In the introductory essay to his now-classic book *Socialization to Politics*, Jack Dennis suggested "ten central problem dimensions" related to contemporary socialization research. These several problem dimensions of socialization research include the system relevance of political socialization; varieties of the content of political socialization; socialization across the life cycle and generations; cross- and subcultural aspects and variations in socialization; the political learning process, the agents and agencies of political socialization, the extent and relative effects of political socialization upon different individuals; and, finally, problems related to specialized political socialization, especially socialization of political elites.[8]

Although researchers concerned with political socialization have been conscious of the need to relate their work theoretically to general theories of political behavior, this task has not yet been performed to the satisfaction of all. Jack Dennis suggested almost two decades ago that "the question about what effects political socialization has upon political life" is "the most important aspect of political socialization research for the development of a theory of politics."[9] If one perceives political phenomena as existing and taking place within a political system, it becomes necessary to prove the relevance of any study of such political phenomena as contributing to a better knowledge of the system itself; if "system relevance" cannot be demonstrated, then the entire body of political socialization literature is of only dubious value, as many people claim.

It has been argued that minimally political socialization is important to the political system because it generates a general support for the political system in which it takes place. What is not known, however, is that proportion of whatever diffuse or general support for a political system exists that may be attributed to socialization. There are other factors that generate diffuse support in a political system—such as popular leaders, popular decisions or policies, and the like—and it has not yet been sufficiently illustrated that it is the process of political socialization itself that plays a meaningful and significant role in the creation of diffuse support. Quite clearly, to measure the effects of socialization upon diffuse support, all other factors would need to be held constant. Since this has not yet been accomplished, the positive effect of political socialization on diffuse support has not yet been proven, although it has been asserted and suggested.[10]

It is interesting to note that *negatively* the effect of socialization upon diffuse support has been illustrated to some degree. In one study, investigators have shown a relationship between the cynicism of parents to government and an increased occurrence of such cynicism in their children, with clear implications for diffuse support for government, generally. This work suggests several theoretical questions that have yet to be resolved or substantiated.[11]

Once it is established that the study of political socialization is relevant to the study of politics, generally, and once we have examined the gaps in the attempt to establish this fact, we can turn our attention to the "what" of the process: What is the object, the content, of political socialization that is supposed to be of significance for the political system? Many subjects are suggested as being taught in this process, including the general political culture, political roles, knowledge of how the political system operates, and the like.

Perhaps the best-known exposition on political culture and the passing of political cultures from one generation to another is to be found in Gabriel Almond and Sidney Verba's *Civic Culture*.

> When we speak of the political culture of a society, we refer to the political system as internalized in the cognitions, feelings, and evaluations of its population. People are induced into it just as they are socialized into non-political roles and social systems.[12]

Similarly, Gabriel Almond has written elsewhere that political socialization is "the process of induction into the political culture. Its end product is a set of attitudes—cognitions, value standards, and feelings—toward the political system.[13]

Political roles, as well as a political culture, are also suggested as being among the objects taught by political socialization. As the term is used here, a political role is "a pattern of expected behavior for individuals holding particular positions in a system."[14] Roles and role behavior are clearly not established from the time of birth, but are taught and learned phenomena. As such, they are a part of the content of political socialization.[15]

A general knowledge of the political system and the manner in which it operates is also included in the content of political socialization. Such subjects as how the system works, the functioning of different branches of the government, what the role of political parties is in the political system, and so on—all are introduced to individuals through the socialization process.[16]

It has also been suggested that the process of socialization may play a significant role in participation in politics itself.[17] That is, not only can socialization help the political system by promoting diffuse support, but it can also help the system by promoting participation within the structures of the political framework.

While many theorists have focused their attention on the "what" of the process of socialization—the content of what is learned—theoretical gaps exist in other areas of their work as well. Another area of study that has been given considerable attention in investigation, and that is by no means resolved, is the "when" of the process, a temporal dimension of socialization, including the individual's development across the life cycle and differences across generations. As indicated previously, political socialization is best conceived as a process, and as such it is not a phenomenon to be studied merely in individuals between the ages of, say, 6 and 16, with no consideration given to earlier and later years. Studies examining the temporal nature of political socialization have focused on such questions as when the process begins, which are the most important years for later political attitudes, and how long the political socialization process can be said to continue.

Research has shown that there is a strong relationship between the time of initial socialization to politics and the agents of initial political socialization. One study found that legislators could be placed along a bidimensional continuum:

> ranging from those who were socialized early (childhood or grammar school) by the family, through those socialized as adolescents by self (self starters), to those whose socialization was delayed until the post-adolescent period and occurred because of external events and conditions.[18]

It has been difficult to show the consequences of this differential socialization, however. While we can say that different agents of socialization are most effective at different times of the age span, problems appear when we try to translate this fact into its effect on legislative behavior, for example.

Different points in the life cycle are significant in terms of *what* will be learned, as well as *by what agent* the socialization will be influenced. It has been clearly demonstrated[19] that children are first aware of executive positions in government, such as the president or a mayor, and not until they grow older do they perceive legislators, such as congressmen for example, as anything but "the president's helpers." Jean Piaget has shown that certain concepts are more difficult than others for a child to learn.[20] For example, in one set of studies there was much confusion for young children as to whether they were citizens of Switzerland or citizens of Geneva; it was not until the youngsters reached a later level of cognitive development that they saw that these two possibilities were not mutually exclusive.

Still other studies have focused upon intergenerational differences in socialization. Although this area of socialization research has not received as much attention as others, it clearly suggests several theoretically interesting questions that are worth further investigation. To take one example, if aging seems to promote greater consistency in partisan orientation in politics,[21] what implications exist for those individuals investigating the agents of socialization? That is, if aging makes an individual more partisan, it seems likely that the individual would also become more sensitive, and responsive, to partisan political stimuli, and thereby tend to be further socialized to follow the party line. This is but one of the several hypotheses that could be investigated in this general area; much work has yet to be done.

What Jack Dennis calls the "spatial"[22] dimension of political socialization research is yet another area among the ten "central problem dimensions" suggested as being keys to contemporary political socialization research. This spatial dimension includes both cross-cultural as well as subcultural and group variations in the socialization process.

Cross-cultural differences and similarities may, in fact, be among the most valuable of the several types of socialization studies, because they have implications for several of the central problem dimensions discussed here.[23] By finding differences in the socialization processes in two different cultural settings, implications can be drawn relating not only to the effectiveness of various agents of socialization but also implications can be drawn relating to system relevance of the study of political socialization.

Within a single national setting, studies of subcultural and group variations in political socialization may have the same value as cross-cultural research. One good example of this type of research is a 1968 study by Dean Jaros and others: Through a study of a specific American subculture, in this case the "Appalachian personality," Jaros attempted to theorize not only about the effectiveness of certain agents of socialization in Appalachia as compared with an earlier and comparable study in New Haven, Connecticut,[24] but also attempted to make several theoretical suggestions pertaining to the effects of socialization on the development of political cynicism, and thereby its relevance for system maintenance. Similar studies have been undertaken investigating other subcultural or group characteristics, including race, sex, ethnic group membership, and social class.[25]

The actual question of how learning takes place, the "how" of the socialization question that asks "who learns what from whom, how, and when," is certainly no less important than any other aspect of socialization that we have already mentioned. This "how" question encompasses several components, and can be seen to often include both the "when" and the "from whom" aspects of socialization theory.

When many people ask how political learning takes place, what they are *in fact* asking is what the agents are that are active in the political learning process, rather than really inquiring about learning theory:

Q. "How did Alden come to believe that?"
A. "Oh, it was a book she read."

In many cases this "from whom or what" response to our "how" question is the only response possible. That is, the questioner in this case is not *really* looking for an answer couched in terms of learning theory; the individual is interested in the active elements involved in the process of Johnny coming to believe something that he does. In other instances, the "how" is answered in termporal terms, employing such implicit concepts as maturation, for example:

Q. "How did Darcy come to believe that?"
A. "She is at an age when she rebels against us."

Or an answer in terms of both the "when" and the "from whom":

Q. "How did Alden come to believe that?"
A. "Now that she is 15, she and Darcy talk about politics a great deal."

Thus we can see that often in political socialization research the question being answered, which is ostensibly our "how" question, often is not answered in "how" (learning theory) terms at all, but rather is answered in terms of either the agents of socialization involved, or temporal-chronological factors, or both.[26]

By far the most attention in political socialization research has been given to the "by whom or what" question: the examination of those agents and factors that are most influential in the socialization process. Many different factors have been suggested by political scientists as being the most influential in the socialization process, including among the most visible sources of political socialization parents, teachers, neighbors, peers, the media, and members of the extended family.[27]

It has been almost traditionally accepted that the family is foremost among the many agents of socialization influential during childhood. Aristotle wrote of the overriding importance of the family in socialization. A more contemporary author suggests that "the most important source of children's conceptions of authority undoubtedly is the civic instruction which goes on incidental to normal activities in the family."[28]

The literature also shows us that one by-product of the impressionability of the socialization process is that the child is likely to form political impressions, images, and even opinions before he or she has any real political knowledge upon which to base those feelings. The child's first conception of political authority seems to have "more affective than cognitive content... the prevailing adult theme of cynicism toward politics and politicians evidently develops at adolescence or later."[29] There is a tendency for children to develop political party identification early, with no cognitive reason for preferring one party over another. Greenstein writes that by the fourth grade, more than 60 percent of the children in one study[30] could give a party identification, even if they could not give a satisfactory reason for why they had chosen that party.

The ninth general set of issues suggested by Jack Dennis concerns the "extent" of political socialization, that is, to what degree one is politicized when one is socialized to politics. Does political socialization merely involve imparting a sensitivity or awareness of issues upon an individual, or does it imply a true politicization of the individual: Not only is the individual aware of issues but he or she also has opinions on all the issues involved.

This has severe consequences for the political system— in a truly participatory democracy in which a characteristic of the system is the encouragement of citizen participation in the governmental process, it is important to know those factors that are more and less influential in politicizing the electorate. This is yet another aspect of political socialization research that has received relatively little attention, but which certainly merits a great deal of investigation.

A final area of political socialization research involves specialized political socialization. This has especially focused upon elite socialization, specifically upon those who are politically active, including legislators. In many ways this area of political socialization research has claimed to be the most relevant for the political system, generally, by arguing that *"who the legislators are* affects the product generated by the systems of which they are a part."[31] By studying the socialization of legislators or other political elites we know better what *kind* of individual attains formal office, for example, and thereby we have some basis for predicting *how* political elites will perform. As political socialization theory becomes more developed, we should better be able to predict how those political elites will behave once they are in office.

The Study of Political Recruitment

The study of political recruitment has not been subjected to the same questions of "relevance for the political system" as has political socialization research. Potential critics and challengers have been satisfied with observations that the channels which are open for people to enter the political elite level, and subsequently to become officeholders, influence to a large extent *which* people become political elites and subsequent officeholders. This has *de facto* significance for the political system, and therefore is relevant for study, since potential critics accept the argument that who the political elite are makes a difference in terms of policy and action in the political system.[32]

Political recruitment research, however, suffers from several of the same theoretical problems as does political socialization research, significant among which is that theorists are not in agreement as to exactly *what* political recruitment is. Although, as with socialization literature, theorists agree that political recruitment is a *process*, definitions suggested in the literature differ, and these differences are not always of an insignificant nature. One author, for example, suggests that:

> political recruitment refers to the processes that select from among the several million socially favored and politically motivated citizens comprising the political stratum those several thousand who reach positions of significant national influence.[33]

The definitional problem is not an insignificant one. Moshe Czudnowski clearly recognized this problem when he asked:

> Should [political recruitment] be defined with reference to a point of destination, a state of affairs which indicates the completion of the process and if so, what is this terminal point? Or should it be defined with reference to motivations or behavioral characteristics, and the conditions under which they occur?[34]

It seems that perhaps the definition of Gabriel Almond may be more broadly applicable, in which he defines recruitment as the function of the political system which draws upon members of the society, inducts them "into the specialized roles of the political system, trains them with political cognitive maps, values, expectations, and affects." Thereby, he writes, the recruitment function "takes up where the general political socialization function leaves off."[35]

Part of the definition problem is that the term "recruitment" is used to cover two actual processes, *initial recruitment* to politics, and *promotion* within the political infrastructure. Lester Milbrath breaks down the overall recruitment process into several levels of participation.[36] He argues that there is a hierarchy of political involvement and participation in the United States, ranging from the individual who is merely a "spectator" to a "gladiator" who is actively involved in the political arena, with "transitionals" in the middle. The advantage of this type of approach is that it allows us to break down the general process into its component parts, and thereby allows us to examine more closely each distinct segment of the overall recruitment process.

Although a number of studies of political recruitment have been undertaken, with a wide diversity of foci, several central areas of research can be singled out as a basis for an examination of this area, much as we did with the political socialization question. To take one example, Moshe Czudnowski suggests a sixfold framework for the study of political recruitment, including (1) social background characteristics; (2) political socialization and recruitment factors; (3) initial activity and apprenticeship, (4) occupations; (5) motivations; and (6) the selection process itself.[37]

Although this particular framework is made up of several components, a broader examination of the literature seems to indicate the existence of two *major* foci of study: (1) studies examining the characteristics or background of those who are recruited, and (2) studies focusing upon the recruitment process itself. It is interesting to note at this point that while most theorists do recognize political recruitment as a process, similar to political socialization, the bulk of the attention in the literature is not focused upon the process—the "how" aspect—of the question, but rather upon the "who" of the question, the social background studies as they have been called.

The rationale for gathering social background data, and therefore for this type of study, is based upon two assumptions. The first assumption is that "relationships exist between social background characteristics and opportunities to gain access to political offices"; the second assumption is that "the social background characteristics are related to variations in the attitudes and behavior of political elites."[38] Available data to support the latter hypothesis, that there is a link between social background characteristics and attitudes and behavior of political elites, do not appear consistent. Rather, the degree of association appears to vary from one political system to another.[39]

Generally speaking, the literature has tended to substantiate the first assumption underlying the study of social background data; there *does* appears to be a relationship between social background characteristics and the opportunity to gain access to political office. It *does* appear to be the case that individuals from the middle and upper classes of some societies tend to be disproportionately recruited in relation to their size in populations as a whole. This bias appears to exist not only in national political office but also in *all* aspects of the political system, including party work and local level offices.[40]

One interesting finding of the social background research has been the discovery of the strong association between certain occupations and subsequent elective office. The relationship between legislators and the practice of law prior to election has frequently been cited; in the United States "it is proverbial that U.S. Congressmen are lawyers."[41] While the relationship may be "proverbial" in the United States, studies show that this American affinity is not as universal as many believe. It has been demonstrated that whereas 58 percent of American legislators are lawyers, only about 2 percent of Swedish legislators are lawyers. In fact, of twenty-two nations examined in one study, the average percentage of legislators who previously were lawyers was 16 percent, a far cry from a universally "proverbial" relationship.[42]

In addition to the "who" of recruitment, considerable attention has been paid to the questions of how and why individuals are recruited; this attention is directed toward an examination of the recruitment process itself. A number of studies have focused on the role that parties and other groups play in the recruitment process. Still others are oriented toward psychological factors involved in the recruitment process, and the roles that the electoral system and opportunity in general play in the process. This focus upon the *process* of political recruitment, the channels of the selection process and gates and gatekeepers involved, has not received the same amount of attention as have studies of social background variables, although it has become a more popular area of research in recent years.

Studies focusing on the role played by parties in the recruitment process have shown that the significance of parties in recruitment varies on a country-by-country basis. In the United States, for example, political parties have lost much of the influence that they once controlled over the recruitment process, and they are currently struggling to maintain control over candidate selection. The loss of their influence can primarily be attributed to changes in the primary system and the increased openness of party conventions, and as such the loss of influence varies on a state-by-state basis, depending upon electoral laws in force.[43] Outside of the United States, one need not look too far to see evidence of the importance of the party in the recruitment process, although it too varies on a country-by-country basis.[44] To take one example, it has been suggested that one of the more striking features of the preparliamentary political careers of legislators in the Canadian Parliament is the "large proportion of

MPs, regardless of party, who had been party activists."[45] In Israel, to take another example, it would be almost unheard of for anyone to attain a political office *without* being a strong party worker.[46]

Other groups have been shown to have an impact on the recruitment process, sometimes through the political party itself. In two studies Czudnowski[47] demonstrated the conditions under which political parties may become very group-oriented in their selection procedures for candidates for the national legislature, to the extent of permitting groups to dictate who "their" representatives on the party electoral list will be. It was suggested that group- oriented recruitment is positively associated with a proportional representation electoral system. If this is correct, then groups other than political parties in a political system may take on explicitly political recruitment roles.

Yet another important factor that can influence the recruitment process is opportunity. Regardless of the size of the political strata, or the number of "self-starters" ready to run for office, recruitment cannot take place if vacancies in office are not present.[48] Moreover, different recruitment rates exist for different offices; in the United States, recruitment to the presidency is more difficult than is recruitment to the Senate, because turnover in the Senate is greater, and there are more opportunities there. Similarly, recruitment will be greater for the House of Representatives than for the Senate, and greater for state legislative offices than for national legislative office.

The Role of the Political Elite

Now that we have briefly examined *how* the political elite become the elite, it is important to understand the *role* of the political elite in the polity. Is "elitism" compatible with democratic government? How should the elite behave, and how should the masses relate to the elite? The use of the word "should" here warns us that we are leaving the empirical world and entering the normative world, more the realm of philosophers than most questions we have addressed thus far in this volume. However, because these are important questions we will endeavor to highlight some of the most important issues raised by them. The concept of a political elite is, like several we have met in this text, a problematic one:

It means different things to different people. On one hand, "elite" simply means "best," and there is very little that is objectionable in that. On the other hand, "elite" is sometimes interpreted more broadly to refer to "the power holders of a body politic."[49] In this sense:

> The concept of the elite is classificatory and descriptive, designating the holders of high positions in a given society. There are as many elites as there are values. Besides an elite of power (the political elite) there are elites of wealth, respect, and knowledge (to name but a few).[50]

The question is: How does the existence of a political elite fit in with the idea of democratic government? We know that the requirements of democracy place many demands on citizens, including that they be informed, knowledgeable, have principles, and be rational, and we know that not all voters are like that. Fortunately, we have been told that not *all* voters need to have these characteristics for a system to survive.[51] If enough individuals are adquately motivated and informed, the system can continue to operate.

The key ingredient here is what are called "elite-mass linkages," the pattern of relationships existing between the elite and the masses that allow the elite to govern on behalf of the masses. The elite can govern by force, through coercion such as we find in military regimes (which we shall discuss in just a moment); in the contemporary world, military regimes are more and more common. The political system will be more stable, however, and will have to expend less of its resources on coercive measures if it can govern through a sense of legitimacy on the part of the mass public, not through a sense of coercion. This will be based upon the degree to which the mass public shares the views of the political and socioeconomic elite.[52]

The existence of elites *can* be compatible with democratic government under some circumstances.[53] The most important single characteristic appears to be that an *open elite* exist: that it is possible for the masses to become part of the elite.[54] Again, this ties in with our earlier discussion of recruitment processes in a regime, because where there are effective recruitment structures a relatively open elite can exist. Where sufficient opportunities do not exist, and where we find a relatively "closed" elite, we will invaribly find a system of lower legitimacy and less stability.[55]

The Military

The military is another societal structure that is significant in both the socialization and recruitment processes, sometimes regarded as *the* elite in developing nations, and *also* a structure that can be significant on its own in shaping the type and style of political participation permitted in the political arena. Although the military is not perceived as a politically significant actor in most stable Western democracies, we should not let a pervasive Western ethnocentrism (and here we really mean an Anglo-American ethnocentrism, since the military has clearly played significant political roles in modern French and German history) blind us to the fact that the military, as an institution, *is* a *highly significant* political actor in many developing regimes.

One need only look at military or military-support coups or attempted coups in very recent history in Spain, Nigeria, Bolivia, the Philippines, Fiji, and Sri Lanka to see that in many instances political leaders are more concerned with what the military reaction will be to their decisions than they are with what the reactions of their respective legislatures or courts will be to their decisions. In fact, even in countries such as India or Guatemala, where civilian governments "are clearly in control," the armed forces have been shown to exert considerable political influence.

> They are symbols of state sovereignty and the primary defenders against possible external or internal attack against the government. Given their prestige, responsibilities, and the material resources needed to fulfill these responsibilities, all military establishments exercise a significant degree of political influence. . . .[56]

The study of what has been called "praetorianism," or military coups, has been justified on many counts, including the fact that such events happen frequently; as Chairman Mao said in China, political power "grows out of the barrel of a gun." Among twenty Latin American nations, only two—Costa Rica and Mexico—have not experienced at least an attempted coup since 1945. In one recent study it was estimated that 57 percent of the Third World states examined had been under military rule for half or more than half of their respective periods of independence.[57] According to one observer, "Between 1945 and 1976, soldiers carried out successful coups in half of the eighteen Asian states." and, more generally, "it turns out that the military have intervened in approximately two-thirds of the more than one hundred non-Western states since 1945."[58]

Although coups may be ostensibly motivated "for public-spirited reasons on behalf of constitution and nation," research has shown that "almost all coups are at least partly, and usually primarily, inspired by the military's own interests."[59] One result of a military takeover is almost invariably a significant increase in the defense budget of the regime.[60] Examined more broadly, the result of recent research shows that "military rule was found to have negative or zero-order correlations with economic development." Moreover, "'politicians in uniform' invariably caused political decay."[61]

The issue of civilian control of the military is a very important one, especially so in developing societies in which (civilian) governments may not yet have acquired the same degree of legitimacy and stability that one finds in the older Western democracies. The key issue involved in the maintenance of civilian control involves finding ways to set limits within which military leaders, and all members of the armed forces, "accept the government's definition of appropriate areas of responsibility."[62] This does not mean in the final analysis that the military is prohibited from lobbying for policies it supports, but it does mean that the military agrees to do this in acceptable ways, and that the military agrees to accept the consequences of the policy-making process. Thus, the military accepts a subordinate role in the political system. Ironically, in military regimes the leaders face the same problems as previous civilian governments did: how to keep their military underlings loyal and prevent an overthrow of the (military) forces in power at the time.[63]

It must be remembered that the military *is* a political institution in most countries. The role of the military in a political system is also significantly affected by that country's political culture, history, and tradition: In some Latin American systems the idea of a military coup, if not desirable, is certainly recognized as a statistical possibility—in fact, probability—over the course of time.

Political Participation and Political Violence

The discussion of the role of the military in democratic politics shows that it is not only *participation* that is crucial for regimes but also the *type* of participation that takes place. There is one type of participation that we should mention briefly here that can be of great significance in the political arena and that we have not yet discussed: political violence.

"Violence" is one of those terms that we encounter so often that it means different things to different people. We all might agree that throwing a brick through a window—or shooting someone—is an act of violence, but there are also other types of violence, as well, that we should keep in mind. Some would argue that there are certain social patterns of behavior—such as racism, for example—that can be referred to as "institutional violence," although others specifically reject "unjust social or political policies" as long as they do not involve physical force.[64] If we define violence as the use or threat of violence against persons or objects, we can see that a *very* wide range of behavior can be included in our discussion.

The range of actions that might be classified as political violence is so broad that systematic theory construction is terribly difficult. One recent attempt began with a framework focusing upon *"Who"* did *"What"* to *"Whom,"* and subsequently tried to study the "symbolic addressee" of the violence, the claimed "social basis" of the act of violence, the size of the organization undertaking the violence, and *"Why"* the action took place.[65]

Among the many types of behavior that we can consider to be examples of political violence might be a riot or a demonstration that turns violent, an assassination, a kidnapping, a mass revolution, a coup d'état, guerrilla warfare, terrorism, and, of course, conventional war. Motivations for these actions might be ideological (e.g., a Marxist revolution or Marxist-inspired coup), religious (the Islamic revolution in Iran, or the Sikh separatist battles in the Punjab in India), nationalistic (resistance of the Afghan guerrillas against Soviet military forces), or personal (an assassination ordered by a leader to remove a potential political competitor), or the motivation could come from some combination of these and other reasons.

Consistent with other warnings about ethnocentrism in this text, it is important to remember that American politics in recent years has not been completely confined to peaceful constitutional discourse. Political assassinations, such as the shootings of President John F. Kennedy, or the Rev. Martin Luthor King, Jr., are acts of political violence. Ku Klux Klan violence in the American South is political violence. Illegal activities by the Federal Bureau of Investigation in the 1960s and 1970s caused "violence" against American citizens. The Ohio National Guard *did* fire on college students at Kent State University who were participating in a demonstration against the Vietnam War, resulting in the death of four students. That was political violence. This is not meant to suggest that all American politics is violent, but it should serve as a reminder that political violence can exist even in stable, democratic societies.

Because our space is limited here, we shall confine our discussion to a limited number of types of violence. We shall briefly discuss two types of revolution, revolution from "above," the *coup d'état*, and revolution from "below," otherwise known as the *jacquerie*. We shall also briefly discuss guerrilla movements and terrorism, and attempt to point out similarities and differences between the two.

Most simply, a revolution can involve changing one government, or type of government, for another. One relatively rigid definition that has been offered argues that a revolution involves a "relatively sudden violent and illegal attempt to change the regime of a state or other political organisation, in which large sections of the population are involved as participants."[66] Others might disagree with this view, however, claiming that revolutions often seek to restore legality against a regime that has voided the country's law, and thus cannot be "illegal" actions. In brief, although there may not be universal agreement over exactly how we define "revolution," there is a general consensus that it involves a change of regimes.

A mass revolution is sometimes referred to as a *jacquerie*, and involves significant and radical changes in the ruling class. Four "great" revolutions of modern times are the American Revolution (1776), the French Revolution (1789), the Russian Revolution (1917–1921), and the Chinese Revolution (1927–1949).

Another type of revolutionary change, although not one directly involving "large sections of the population," is the *coup d'état*, a sudden seizure of power from above instead of using the masses from below. A coup "does not call on mass support to effect [leadership] changes, though it may seek legitimation of the changes by a plebiscite or mass demonstration."[67] Coups are usually carried out by individuals near to the center of power who have access to resources and political support. The most common type of coup is called a *military coup*. The military coup, sometimes dubbed a "colonel's" or a "general's coup," involves military leaders taking over a polity because of their dissatisfaction with civilian control, as has happened recently in Bolivia, Fiji, and Nigeria. A coup may also be led by nonmilitary individuals outside of the leadership structure assassinating or deposing the incumbent ruler to substitute themselves as rulers, such as took place in Afghanistan several years ago when the Soviet-supported regime was established.

The distinction between *terrorism* and a *guerrilla* action can sometimes become unclear. Generally, we can define terrorism as "the use of violence or the threat of violence, to coerce governments, authorities, or populations by inducing fear."[68] There is often a symbolic dimension to the terrorist act, as well. The terrorist seeks to influence political behavior of a government through extranormal means, usually having tried and exhausted all conventional political options. "Terrorism" is a relatively recent political label in its common usage, although phrases such as "Reign of Terror" (in the French Revolution in 1794) demonstrate that the concept certainly existed long ago.[69]

If we look at groups generally labelled as "terrorists" today, we often find self-ascribed "national liberation" groups (such as the Irish Republican Army fighting for independence against the British, or the Palestine Liberation Organization fighting for independence against the Israelis). This highlights one very problematic characteristic of the label "terrorist"; it is strongly influenced by perspective, as the following example shows.

When Menachem Begin, the prime minister of Israel from 1977 to 1984, was asked how he responded to charges that there was really no difference between his actions against the British in Palestine preceding Israeli independence in 1948—the British referred to him at the time as a "terrorist" and offered a reward of £10,000, dead or alive, for his capture—and the actions of Yassir

Arafat and the Palestine Liberation Organization against Israel in recent years, Begin's response illustrated this point perfectly. He said, "Of course there is a difference. He is a terrorist. I was a freedom fighter."[70]

"Terrorist" is also used as a label for more random acts of violence, such as one finds in the case of the Japanese Red Army, the Italian Red Brigade, the West German Bader-Meinhof Gang, Saddam Hussein's act of "environmental terrorism"in dumping oil in the Persian Gulf as part of Iraq's war effort, and in the yet unused but often discussed context of "nuclear terrorism". In these cases, the terrorist motive is not nationalism, but is instead directed at some policy-related goal, such as the presence of foreign multinationals, environmental concerns, foreign policy issues, the release of "political prisoners," and the like.

Guerrilla action, on the other hand, tends to be a bit different in terms of the targets sought by the participants. The usual distinction drawn suggests that guerrillas tend to focus their attention on *government* targets, usually military targets, rather than the often random *civilian* targets used by terrorists. Using this distinction, the Afghan "freedom fighters" might be classified as guerrilla fighters because their targets were Soviet Army tanks, barracks, and supply depots; what distinguished them from a "conventional" army was that they weren't representing a conventional government, and they would strike and then retreat into the mountains to avoid Soviet retribution and subsequently re- group. By contrast, an incident in which the Irish Republican Army left a bomb in front of Harrods department store in London, killing and injuring innocent passersby, would be called an act of terrorism because the target was "random" and in no way strategic.

These and other types of political violence are of significance for the political system because they offer fundamental challenges to the institutions of the regime. They operate *outside* the system, as it were, simply rejecting the ability of the institutions and behaviors of the political system to handle their demands.

The Political Environment in Perspective

We have, in this chapter, briefly looked at a number of what might be called *environmental* characteristics of political regimes, in addition to the structural characteristics that we have been examining until this time. Although our discussion here has not been comprehensive, we have undertaken to introduce the student to many of the concepts currently discussed by comparativists engaged in cross-national research.

It is clear that political structures, just as with constitutions, cannot be examined in a vacuum. While constitutions might do a great deal to inform us about the behavior of a political regime and the relationships between and among the various actors and structures within that regime, we know from what we have already seen that there may well be a number of *very significant* details of the political regime that are *not* included in the constitution (such as customs, traditions, political culture, political parties, and the like). Similarly, just studying the constitutional structures of a regime may omit a number of significant political details, and to this extent other variables must be included in area studies to make them complete.

In some political regimes, an understanding of the political party system is absolutely essential for an accurate understanding of the way the regime operates. In other systems, ideology is more important than political parties. Elsewhere the political culture may be terribly significant, and so on. The fact of the matter is that the political environments within which we must study political regimes vary widely, and significant structures in one environment will not necessarily be significant in another environment.

The remainder of this book focuses on our area studies or "portraits." These are not full-scale studies of the political systems concerned; obviously such an undertaking could not be expected in the amount of space allocated here. What these "portraits" *do* attempt is to provide the student with an *introduction* to the political structures and processes *of major significance* in that particular regime. Federalism is a major variable in the German political system; thus it is discussed; it is not relevant (except insofar as it does not exist) in Japan. The upper house of the legislature is significant in Germany and relatively insignificant in Great Britain; accordingly, it receives more attention in our discussion in relation to the former than to the latter.

The comparative study of politics can be a fascinating and highly informative undertaking. In these days of a constantly shrinking world, where a "spaceship earth" conception of international relations is becoming more common, it is to be hoped that the student will take more of an interest in the political world outside of our national borders. It is hoped that the following mini-studies will encourage interested students to go further, to undertake more cross-national study, and to use a comparative approach in future activities of inquiry.

Notes

1. An example of the latter is G. Almond and G. Bingham Powell, eds., *Comparative Politics Today: A World View* (Boston: Little, Brown, 1980).
2. Allan Kornberg, *Canadian Legislative Behavior* (New York: Holt, Rinehart & Winston, 1967), p. 42.
3. Jean Blondel, *Comparative Legislatures* (Englewood Cliffs, N.J.: Prentice Hall, 1973), p. 76.
4. David Easton and Jack Dennis, *Children in the Political System* (New York: McGraw Hill, 1969), p. 76. For other discussions of the classical heritage of the debate over socialization, see the following: Kenneth Langton, *Political Socialization* (New York: Oxford University Press, 1969), p. 3; Richard Dawson and Kenneth Prewitt, *Political Socialization* (Boston: Little, Brown, 1969), p. 6; Fred Greenstein, *Children and Politics* (New Haven: Yale University Press, 1965), pp. 2–3; and Roberta Sigel, "Assumptions About the Learning of Political Values," *The Annals of the American Academy of Political and Social Science* 361 (1965): 1–9.
5. Edward Greenberg, *Political Socialization* (New York: Atherton, 1970), p. 3. See also Herbert Hyman, *Political Socialization* (Glencoe, Ill.: The Free Press, 1959), p. 18.
6. Easton and Dennis, *Children*, p. 7.
7. Greenstein, *Children and Politics*, p. 5.
8. Jack Dennis, ed., *Socialization to Politics* (New York: Wiley, 1973), p. 4.
9. Ibid., p. 5.
10. See David Easton, *A Framework for Political Analysis* (Englewood Cliffs, N.J.: Prentice Hall, 1965), pp. 124–125.
11. Dean Jaros and others, "The Malevolent Leader: Political Socialization in an American Subculture," *American Political Science Review* 62 (1968): 564–575; see also David Easton and Jack Dennis, "The Child's Image of Government," *The Annals* 361 (1965): 40–57; Robert Hess and David Easton, "The Child's Changing Image of the President," *Public Opinion Quarterly* 24 (1960): 632–644; David Easton and Robert Hess, "The Child's Political World," *Midwest Journal of Political Science* 6 (1962): 229–246; and Fred Greenstein, "The Benevolent Leader: Children's Images of Political Authority," *American Political Science Review* 54 (1960): 934–943.
12. Gabriel Almond and Sidney Verba, *The Civic Culture* (Boston: Little, Brown, 1965), p. 14.
13. Gabriel Almond, "Introduction," in Gabriel Almond and James Coleman *The Politics of the Developing Areas* (Princeton: Princeton University Press, 1960), p. 27.
14. Raymond Hopkins, "The Role of the MP in Tanzania," *American Political Science Review* 64 (1970): 754–771.

15. Kenneth Prewitt, Heinz Eulau, and Betty Zisk, "Political Socialization and Political Roles," *Public Opinion Quarterly* 30 (1966–1967): 569–583.
16. Lewis Froman and James Skipper, "An Approach to the Learning of Party Identification," *Public Opinion Quarterly* 27 (1963): 473–480.
17. Norman Nie, G. Bingham Powell, and Kenneth Prewitt, "Social Structure and Political Participation," *American Political Science Review* 63 (1969): 361–378; and Lester Milbrath, *Political Participation* (Chicago: Rand McNally, 1965).
18. Allan Kornberg and Norman Thomas, "The Political Socialization of National Legislative Elites in the United States and Canada," *Journal of Politics* 27 (1965): 761–775.
19. See, for example, Greenstein, *Children and Politics*, pp. 60–61.
20. Jean Piaget and Anne-Marie Weil, "The Development in Children of the Idea of the Homeland," *International Social Science Bulletin* 3 (1951): 561–578.
21. John Crittendon, "Aging and Political Participation," *Western Political Quarterly* 16 (1962): 648–657.
22. Dennis, *Socialization*, p. 16.
23. An example of such a study would be Allan Kornberg and Joel Smith, "Self Concepts of American and Canadian Party Officials," *Polity* (1970): 70–99.
24. Jaros and others, "The Malevolent Leader," pp. 564–575; and Greenstein, "The Benevolent Leader," pp. 934–943.
25. Other studies would include Dwayne Marvick, "Political Socialization of the American Negro," *The Annals* 361 (1965): 112–127; Michael Parenti, "Ethnic Politics and the Persistence of Ethnic Identification," *American Political Science Review* 61 (1967): 717–726; and Martin Levin, "Social Climates and Political Socialization," *Public Opinion Quarterly* 25 (1961): 596–606.
26. Lewis Froman, "Learning Political Attitudes," *Western Political Quarterly* 15 (1962): 304–313.
27. Greenstein, *Children and Politics*, p. 12.
28. Ibid., p. 44.
29. Ibid, p. 154.
30. Ibid., p. 71.
31. See Kornberg, *Canadian Legislative Behavior*, p. 42, for an example.
32. See Jean Blondel, *World Leaders: Heads of Government in the Postwar Period* (Beverly Hills, Calif.: Sage Publications, 1980), p. 115.
33. Robert Putnam, *The Comparative Study of Political Elites* (New York, Prentice Hall, 1976), p. 46.
34. Moshe Czudnowski, "Political Recruitment," in Fred Greenstein and Nelson Polsby, eds., *Handbook of Political Science* (Reading, Mass.: Addison-Wesley, 1975), p. 159.
35. Almond, "Introduction," p. 31.
36. Milbrath, *Political Participation*.
37. Czudnowski, "Political Recruitment," pp. 178–229.
38. Harold Clarke and Richard Price, "Political Recruitment: Theoretical Overview and Review of the Literature," in Harold Clarke and Richard Price, eds., *Recruitment and Leadership Selection in Canada* (Toronto: Holt, Rinehart, & Winston, 1976), p. 7.
39. As reported in Louis Edinger and Donald Searing, "Social Background in Elite Analysis: A Methodological Inquiry," *American Political Science Review* 59 (1967): 428–445.
40. See, for examples of such studies, the following: Donald Matthews, *U.S.*

Senators and Their World (New York: Vintage Books, 1960); or Frederick Frey, *The Turkish Political Elite* (Cambridge: M.I.T. Press, 1965).
41. M. Pederson, "Lawyers in Politics: The Danish Folketing and United States Legislatures," in Samuel Patterson and John Wahlke, eds., *Comparative Legislative Behavior: Frontiers of Research* (New York: Wiley, 1972), p. 25.
42. Ibid., p. 25.
43. See Leo Snowiss, "Congressional Recruitment and Representation," *American Political Science Review* 60 (1966): 627–639.
44. A very good review of the literature on political parties can be found in Frank Belloni and Dennis Beller, eds., *Faction Politics: Political Parties and Factionalism in Comparative Perspective* (Santa Barbara, Calif.: A.B.C.-Clio, 1987).
45. Kornberg, *Canadian Legislative Behavior*, p. 54.
46. Gregory Mahler, *The Knesset: Parliament in the Israeli Political System* (Rutherford, N.J.: Fairleigh-Dickinson University Press, 1981), especially chap. 6.
47. Moshe Czudnowski, "Sociocultural Variables and Legislative Recruitment," *Comparative Politics* 4 (1972): 561–587; and Moshe Czudnowski, "Legislative Recruitment Under Proportional Representation in Israel: A Model and a Case Study," *Midwest Journal of Political Science* 14 (1970): 216–248.
48. Malcolm Jewell and Samuel Patterson, *The Legislative Process in the United States* (New York: Random House, 1973), p. 88.
49. Harold Lasswell, Daniel Lerner, and C. Easton Rothwell, *The Comparative Study of Elites* (Cambridge: M.I.T Press, 1965), p. 13.
50. Ibid., p. 4.
51. Bernard Berelson, Paul Lazarsfeld, and William McPhee, *Voting* (Chicago: University of Chicago Press, 1954), pp. 305–323.
52. Putnam, *Political Elites*, p. 138–139.
53. A very good discussion of these issues can be found in Peter Bachrach, ed., *Political Elites in a Democracy* (New York: Atherton, 1973).
54. Peter Y. Medding, "Patterns of Elite Consensus and Elite Competition: A Model and a Case Study," in *Political Elites in Anglo-American Democracies*, ed. Harold Clarke and Moshe Czudnowski (DeKalb: Northern Illinois University Press, 1987), pp. 17–43.
55. See Peter McDonough, " 'Let Us Make the Revolution, Before the People Do': Elite-Mass Relations in Brazil," in *Political Elites and Social Change: Studies of Elite Roles and Attitudes*, ed. Moshe Czudnowski (DeKalb: Northern Illinois University Press, 1983), pp. 188–218.
56. Eric Nordlinger, *Soldiers in Politics: Military Coups and Governments* (Englewood Cliffs, N.J.: Prentice Hall, 1977), p. 3.
57. Talukder Maniruzzaman, *Military Withdrawal from Politics: A Comparative Study* (Cambridge, Mass.: Ballinger Publishing, 1987), p. 18.
58. Nordlinger, *Soldiers*, pp. 5–6. For examples of this type of literature see the following: William Gutteridge, *The Military in African Politics* (London: Methuen, 1969); J. Stephen Hoadley, *Soldiers and Politics in Southeast Asia: Civil-Military Relations in Comparative Perspective* (Cambridge, Mass.: Schenkman, 1975); John J. Johnson, *The Military and Society in Latin America* (Stanford, Calif.: Stanford University Press, 1964); Claude E. Welch, ed., *Soldier and State in Africa* (Evanston, Ill.: Northwestern University Press, 1970).
59. Nordlinger, *Soldiers*, p. 192.
60. Maniruzzaman, *Military Withdrawal from Politics*, p. 3.

61. Ibid., p. 205.
62. Claude E. Welch, Jr., *Civilian Control of the Military: Theory and Cases from Developing Countries* (Albany: State University of New York Press, 1976), p. 2.
63. Christopher Clapham and George Philip, *The Political Dilemmas of Military Regimes* (Totowa, N.J.: Barnes and Noble Books, 1985).
64. Peter Merkl, ed., *Political Violence and Terror: Motifs and Motivations* (Berkeley: University of California Press, 1986), p. 20.
65. Ibid., pp. 32–33.
66. John R. Thackrah, *Encyclopedia of Terrorism and Political Violence* (London: Routledge and Kegan Paul, 1987), p. 215.
67. Ibid., p. 42.
68. Richard Clutterbuck, *Guerrillas and Terrorists* (London: Faber and Faber, 1977), p. 21.
69. Edgar O'Ballance, *Language of Violence: The Blood Politics of Terrorism* (San Rafael, Calif.: Presidio Press, 1979), pp. 1–8.
70. Interview with the author in the Knesset, April 3, 1975.

9

The British Political System

The British political system is regarded by many as the "mother" of modern democratic political systems. The institution of Parliament developed in Great Britain, and the role of the monarchy in Britain devolved to a point at which it could exist in harmony with democratic political norms. The Westminster model of parliamentary government to which we have referred again and again in this book is derived, of course, from the parliamentary system which evolved in Britain at Westminster. It seems logical, therefore, that the subject of our first area studies chapter should be Great Britain.

Many students are confused as to the distinctions that should be drawn between the names England, (Great) Britain, and the United Kingdom. These three names are, strictly speaking, not interchangeable; they refer to different political systems. The United Kingdom is a country in Western Europe with a population of nearly 60 million people and a national capital in London. The formal name of the United Kingdom (usually abbreviated U.K.) is the United Kingdom of Great Britain and Northern

Ireland. (Prior to 1922, when Ireland was divided into Northern Ireland and the Republic of Ireland, it was called the United Kingdom of Great Britain and Ireland.) Great Britain is the principal island of the United Kingdom, including England, Scotland, and Wales. England is an administrative unit of the United Kingdom of Great Britain and Northern Ireland occupying most of the southern half of the island of Great Britain. Having said all of this we should note that today the term Britain is generally used interchangeably with United Kingdom or England, even though they do not refer to precisely the same thing.

The British Constitution

In Chapter 2 of this book we discussed the distinction between governments with written constitutions and "constitutional government," and pointed out that a political system need not have a written document entitled "Ye Olde Constitution" in order to be referred to as a constitutional regime. Indeed, the example that we used at that time was the case of Great Britain. Students of British politics agree that for all intents and purposes, there is a British Constitution, in the sense that there is a body of fundamental precepts underlying the British political regime. The fact that Britain does not have a specific document called a constitution has led some to say that Britain has no constitution. This error "confuses the constitution with what is usually only one of its sources."[1]

The lack of a written constitution for Britain is certainly not a result of British inexperience with constitution writing. The British Parliament has written constitutions for a number of former territories and possessions that are today independent nations, most in the Commonwealth of Nations. In 1867 the British North America Act was passed by Parliament, uniting Canada (today Ontario and Quebec) with Nova Scotia and New Brunswick to form the Dominion of Canada. Australia received its constitution in 1901. The Union of South Africa Constitution was passed in 1909. New Zealand was granted responsible government in 1852.[2]

Constitutions of political regimes can frequently be said to have several components: (1) written charters or collections of historic documents, (2) legislative statutes of "constitutional" significance, (3) judicial interpretation, and (4) customs and precedents.

> If the core of the constitution consists of a written document adopted or promulgated at a particular time, the state is said to have a written constitution. If, on the other hand, there is no such single document, the state is usually considered to possess an unwritten constitution. The importance of such a classification may be easily exaggerated. The "written" constitutions acquire many unwritten parts and through the years they become overlaid with legislative amplifications, judicial interpretations, and customary provisions. The "unwritten" ones usually have important parts committed to paper as charters or broad constitutional statues. In the course of time the two types come more and more to resemble one another.[3]

One scholar of the British constitutional system suggests that there are essentially three sources from which the British Constitution emanates: statutory law (Acts of Parliament), common law and judicial decisions, and "the customs of the Constitution."[4] Although there is no single document that can be called "the" British Constitution, scholars agree that fundamentally this is not significant; whether there is a single document or not, Britain "has" a constitution.

Statutory law is law that derives from Acts of Parliament. These acts result from a prescribed legislative process in the British Parliament—the House of Commons and the House of Lords. We should note that while not all Acts of Parliament can or should be regarded as constitutional acts, "there is scarcely a session of Parliament that does not contribute to the constitutional structure statutes that add to or alter the basic law of the land."[5] As indicated above, constitutional acts are those that address broad or fundamental questions of major significance to the regime, questions relating to the monarchy, the Parliament, rights and freedoms of citizens, elections, and the like. Acts that are usually considered to be part of the "unwritten" British Constitution are the Magna Carta (1215), the Petition of Right (1626), the Habeas Corpus Act (1679), the Bill of Rights (1689), the Act of Settlement (1701), the Acts of Union with Scotland (1707) and Ireland (1800), the Great Reform Act (1832), the

Parliament Act (1911), and the Statute of Westminster (1931), among many others.[6]

Common-law sources of constitutional doctrines are a bit harder to pin down, for they are less precise. Common law, by definition, is concerned with customs, according to Blackstone "not set down in any written statute or ordinance, but depending on immemorial usage for their support."[7] Many judicial decisions eventually become part of the body of common law in a political system and acquire "constitutional" status over time. Generally speaking, judicial interpretation is of less significance in the British Constitution than in the American Constitution. Because Britain operates under a system of legislative supremacy, with no judicial review of legislative statutes, the British judiciary has a lower profile than its American counterpart. As one observer has noted: "The British courts, however, in interpreting and clarifying the law frequently declare what the constitution is. The civil liberties of British subjects are largely embedded in the common law and thus have been defined and protected by the courts."[8]

The third source of British constitutional doctrine has been referred to as "customs of the Constitution." A number of these customs are highlighted here:

1. The Cabinet consists of members of, and is responsible to, Parliament.
2. The Sovereign does not attend Cabinet meetings.
3. The Sovereign does not withhold assent from (veto) Bills which have passed the two Houses of Parliament.
4. The Speaker (presiding officer) of the House of Commons takes no part in political controversy.[9]

These four points are illustrative of the many customs of behavior that have evolved over the years in the British political system to the point at which they can be referred to as being "constitutional" in nature. Although the monarch today may *legally* retain the right to veto or withhold assent from an act of the British Parliament, it would be regarded as *unconstitutional* for her to do so.[10] The distinction may strike many students as being quite curious, that an action may be at the same time both *legal* and *unconstitutional*. The law may permit an action that has, through custom over time, become impermissible. This is a valid distinction, and an important one to recall.

It has been suggested that it is important to distinguish "between the Constitution and the principles which underlie it. The Principles are in one sense more important that the Constitution itself." Constitutions may change, through statutory acts, common law, judicial decisions, or custom—but principles remain.[11] Two fundamental principles underly the British Constitution. The first principle involves the *rule of law*. Citizens are entitled to the protection of law, and both individuals and the government of the state are to be limited in what they can do by the law of the regime. The second principle is that *Parliament is sovereign*. This point can be further stated to mean that (1) there is no law of an earlier Parliament that the current Parliament cannot change if it wishes to do so, (2) there is no clear distinction between "constitutional" Acts of Parliament and Acts of Parliament that are not "constitutional," and (3) no person or body (e.g., the courts) can nullify an Act of Parliament on the grounds that the act is opposed to the Constitution.[12] Anything the British Parliament does, by definition then, is constitutional.

A number of structural characteristics of the British political system can be regarded as almost "constitutional" in their significance for, and centrality in, the regime.[13] First, the United Kingdom is a unitary political system, not a federal system. There is no "sharing" of power between the national government and some intermediate level of government; there is no intermediate level of government in the United Kingdom to correspond to states in the United States or provinces in Canada or Länder in Germany. This is significant in that Parliament thereby becomes more relevant to the daily routine of life in Britain by virtue of the fact that it influences many aspects of life affected by intermediate levels of government in other political systems.

Second, the Westminster model generally is composed of four parts. First, the chief executive is not the same as the head of state. Second, the executive powers of government are exercised by the chief executive and his or her cabinet. Third, the chief executive and the cabinet all come from and are part of the legislature. Fourth, the chief executive and the cabinet are responsible to, and can be fired by, the legislature. This Westminster model differs significantly from the American system in that there is no clear separation of powers that is so important to the American political culture. The concern of the American Founding Fathers over "checks and balances" simply is not to be found in the Westminster political structure. The political executive is actually part of the legislature, and the courts do not have the power to limit what the legislature does.

A third political structure identified with the British constitutional regime, and which was implied in the preceding paragraph, is that the prime minister and cabinet are drawn from, and are responsible to, the national legislature. Although occasionally some cabinet members may not be from the legislature, the prime minister and the bulk of the cabinet will invariably be from the House of Commons. They will remain in office only as long as they continue to be supported by a majority of the lower house of the national legislature.

A fourth major significant political structure in the British system is that of political parties. Political parties are so much a part of the British political system that it is almost impossible to imagine British politics operating in their absence.

The British Executive

The British case, as we have made clear, is the model for the "split executive" parliamentary model that we described and discussed earlier in this text. The role of the monarch is one that has evolved over a long period of time; its function is one of both substance and style. George Orwell, the noted English author, observed in 1944 that:

> in a dictatorship the power and the glory belong to the same person. In England the real power belongs to unprepossessing men in bowler hats: the creature who rides in a gilded coach behind soldiers in steel breast—plates is really a waxwork. It is at any rate possible that while this division of functions exists a Hitler or a Stalin cannot come to power.[14]

The Monarch

In our discussion of the political executive earlier, a brief outline of the evolution—and perhaps devolution is a more appropriate term—of the power of the British monarchy was presented, tracing the many stages of change in the influence of the British monarch in the British political system. We saw at that time that while at one point in time the monarch had absolute power to promulgate laws, fire the legislature, and imprison political opponents, the situation changed radically but gradually over time. As democratic institutions became more popular they also became more powerful, and the ability of the monarch (who happened to be in power at the time) to resist reform became less and less effective. Monarchs more sympathetic to liberal ideas, such as William and Mary (who were proclaimed king and queen by Parliament in 1688), helped the process to maintain, and in fact increase, its momentum.

Over the last three centuries, the relationship between the monarch and the Parliament has evolved to a point that not even William and Mary would recognize. *De jure*, under law, most powers of British government are still exercised in the name of the king or queen, but today they are exercised "on the advice" of the chief executive. In the eighteenth and nineteenth centuries, the king relied more and more on his cabinet—a group of advisors—for guidance. In the early eighteenth century, the role of the Cabinet was *only* that of providing *advice*; the king still did as he pleased.

As ideas of democratic and republican government grew over the next two centuries, the power relationship had changed so that the king was now *obligated* (although not *legally* required) to accept the advice of his cabinet, who now were exclusively drawn from the House of Parliament that was chosen by the public, namely the House of Commons. Now the cabinet was in reality governing in the name of the king without consulting him.

> The monarch has the constitutional right, as Bagehot put it, to be consulted, to advise, and to warn. When Anthony Eden resigned as Foreign Secretary in 1938, King George VI protested to Neville Chamberlain, the Prime Minister, that he had not been kept properly informed. It is clearly a valuable safeguard that Prime Ministers should be under such an obligation, and should have to bear it in mind when they may be tempted to arbitrary action. Cabinet papers, Foreign Office dispatches from overseas posts, and major departmental memoranda are sent to the Monarch.[15]

"The elaborate pretense that the Queen is still the real ruler of Britain still decorates the machinery of British government," notes one observer. Two examples of this pretense can be offered here by way of illustration. All Royal Commissions begin with a message from the monarch: "Greeting! Now Know Ye That We, reposing great trust and confidence in your knowledge and ability. . . ." Legislative acts begin with the words "Be it enacted by the Queen most Excellent Majesty, by and with the advice and consent of the Lords Spiritual and Temporal, and Commons, in this present Parliament assembled. . . ."[16]

The most visible example of the "Royal Pretence," though, occurs on an annual basis when the queen opens the session of Parliament, seated on her throne in the House of Lords. She "summons the Commons" to the chamber of the House of Lords and reads her speech from the throne, in which she outlines the plans she has for "her" government. The fraud here, of course, is that the speech that she reads is written by the prime minister and cabinet; like a puppet, she says whatever she is told to say.[17]

The Selection of the Chief Executive

Among the most striking characteristics of British parliamentary government today is the duality of its executive leadership that we referred to earlier. The monarch is the official (*de jure*) head of state, but the active (*de facto*) head of government is the prime minister. Appointments are made, acts of Parliament are proclaimed, and all government is carried on in the name of the monarch, although it is the prime minister and his or her cabinet who make all the selections for appointments, who author or sponsor legislative proposals, and who make the administrative decisions that keep government running. The legal claim to power of the cabinet rests in the fact that, ever since the seventeenth century, the monarch has had a Privy Council to advise him or her—a kind of present-day cabinet. Today, although the Privy Council is no longer active, cabinet members must *first* be made members of the Privy Council, and *then* are appointed to the cabinet.[18] The cabinet meets as a subcommittee of the (inactive) Privy Council and acts in the name of the Privy Council.

> The Privy Council has survived as the formal machinery through which the monarch exercises her prerogative powers when necessary. Although membership of the Privy Council is extensive, comprising all past and present cabinet ministers and a number of other public figures to a total of about three hundred in all, its working character is that of a small number of ministers who are called together to witness the signature by the monarch of some formal document.[19]

Although the British monarch was free to choose whomever he or she wanted as advisors in the seventeenth and eighteenth centuries, such is no longer the case today. As soon as election returns are in, if an incumbent prime minister's party has lost its majority, this person submits his or her resignation to the queen, and subsequently the new majority leader in the House of Commons is "invited" to form a government. Symbolically the act is described as "the queen has invited Mrs. Thatcher to form a Government," or "the queen has invited Mr. Major to form a Government," but this is not a realistic description of the process today; there really is no alternative to the invitation that is issued.

"In theory, the Queen has the right both to dissolve parliament and to choose the prime minister"; the first power has not really been exercised in the past hundred years; the second power "only recently has become a fiction."[20] This lack of real power in the selection of a prime minister is, to a very large degree, the result of clear majorities existing in the House of Commons with "obvious" prime ministerial choices. Should some future election produce an inconclusive result, with no clear majority present in the House of Commons, the monarch may again be called upon to take part in the selection process.

The Cabinet and the Prime Minister

In his classic work on the British cabinet, Sir Ivor Jennings wrote in 1951 that "it is a peculiarity of our Constitution that the principles governing the formation and working of the Cabinet and its relations with Parliament can be stated with hardly any reference to the law."[21] In 1937 the British Parliament finally took statutory notice of the cabinet when it passed the Ministers of the Crown Act (1937) naming a number of "cabinet rank" positions and fixing appropriate salaries for the positions.[22]

The development of the position of prime minister is generally regarded as following the evolution of the cabinet itself. The earliest of cabinets, it will be recalled, were simply collections of advisors to powerful monarchs. Cabinet members held little power, and none was first among the group of equals. George I (who ruled from 1714–1727) started the practice of having his cabinet meet in his absence. The result of this:

was to transform what had been a mere inner group of royal advisors into a board of government with an independent existence of its own. Having lost its natural president, it was inevitable that it should find one of its own, a "prime minister" in fact, upon whom would fall the task of coordinating policy, which before had been the King's.[23]

The first "modern" prime minister is usually cited as being Sir Robert Walpole (held office 1721–1742).

Ever since World War II the style and power of prime ministers have varied, and the range of roles played by the prime minister "has prompted a long-running debate about the power of the Prime Minister between 'the presidential school' and 'the chairmanship school.' "[24] One student of the office has observed that "prime ministers do not have to be exceptional individuals in order to dominate their ministries." There are devices by which even less exceptional individuals can keep their colleagues under control, such as assignments to cabinet committees, the frequency with which cabinet meetings are held, and even periodic reconstruction of the cabinet.[25]

The prime minister is first minister of the cabinet, but the power exercised by the incumbent of that position varies widely depending upon the political environment of the time. Some British prime ministers have had a tremendous amount of power, others have simply been in the role of "chairman of the board." "Viewed from the top, British government looks more like a mountain range than a single pyramid of power. The Prime Minister is preeminent among these peaks, but the political significance of this preeminence is ambiguous."[26]

Although the prime minister has traditionally received the bulk of the attention of scholarship related to the executive branch of government in Britain, there has been some scholarship in recent years that focuses upon the cabinet itself and upon individual ministers. As one scholar has noted, it is ministries that "are responsible for converting public resources into the programme outputs of the mixed economy welfare state, such as defence, health, agriculture, and education."[27] It is the ministers after all, who are responsible for maintaining some degree of continuity in the various ministries, and who are responsible for gathering resources for public programs. It is the ministers who are in a position to oversee and—to some degree—direct the vast civil service, a subject to which we shall return momentarily.

The individual ministries are also important to some degree because they may serve as a step on the way to the prime ministership for a given individual. Some ministries have more status—such as Treasury or Defense—than others—such as Agriculture, or the Welsh Office.[28]

Individual ministers have several different constituencies that must be kept in mind, simultaneously, as they perform their jobs. First, they must direct their own ministries, thus being in a position of responsibility for a vast network of civil service employees. Second, they must be aware of and responsible to Parliament, for the Government as a whole is responsible to Parliament for what it does. Third, they must respond to the needs and desires of the public outside of Westminster, including their own political parties, trade unions, chambers of commerce, professional organizations and interest groups, as well as international factors.[29]

The cabinet has varied in size in this century, ranging from 16 to 23 members. This size is a function of both the preferences of the prime minister and of the political situation of the time. Although the prime minister may have a free hand in the selection of his or her cabinet—in that the monarch will appoint whomever the prime minister requests to the cabinet—this "free hand" is not *totally* free. The prime minister is guided by a number of factors:

> by the need to include as many of the leading members of his party as possible and to represent the various groups and shades of opinion; by the convenience of having a reasonable number of reliable friends and close supporters; by the need to achieve adequate co-ordination between departments; and by the desirability of avoiding friction and jealousy between the "ins" and the "outs" as well as to silence potential critics.[30]

The role of the prime minister in the British political system can be analytically broken down into seven different components.[31] First, the prime minister is concerned with *party management*. The prime minister is prime minister precisely because the individual is head of his or her party in the House of Commons, and prime ministers must be careful during their tenure in office as prime minister to maintain party support. Certainly one way to do this is through party patronage; much of the prime minister's influence is said to stem from the exercise of patronage, appointments to either cabinet level or subcabinet level positions. This patronage assures a good deal of the necessary support for a prime minister. A majority of the 635 members of the House of Commons is 318; by the time a prime minister appoints about 20 MPs to cabinet positions, and another 60 to subcabinet rank positions, and yet another two to three dozen to positions of parliamentary private secretary, this individual has a block of almost one-third of the votes necessary for remaining in office.

The Government exists strictly because it controls a majority in the House of Commons. "In theory, the House of Commons controls the Government, the latter is responsible to the former. . . . In practice, through the party system the Government controls the House." The ultimate weapon of the Government to keep its party members in control is the power of dissolution, but this is too severe a threat to banty about lightly. "The majority must be treated with respect and given reasonably full information in response to questions. . . . Even the strongest Governments have been known to bow to 'the sense of the House.' "[32] The relationship between the House of Commons and the prime minister and cabinet is one that has traditionally received a good deal of attention. A modern classic in this area is Bernard Crick's *The Reform of Parliament*,[33] which argues that there has been a decline in the power of Parliament to the extent that British government is no longer really parliamentary government, but really is simply cabinet government.

> Experience between 1976 and 1979 showed that it is for the Government itself to decide when its majority must be considered as lost. So long as the [Labour] Callaghan Government could rely on the Liberal Party's support in any vote of confidence, it was prepared to accept a number of defeats which might have prompted another Government to dissolve Parliament. In other words, the vital votes, other than those of no confidence, are those the Government chooses to regard as such; then the possibility of calling a second vote normally allows any intra-party rebellions to be contained by permitting the rebels to return to the party fold on the crucial question of confidence after voting against the leadership on the substantive issue.[34]

The second major job of a prime minister involves the *timing and winning of a general election*. Although six of the ten individuals who became prime minister since World War II assumed their office in the middle of a Parliament, including the incumbent prime minister, John Major, "winning" a national election is necessary for a prime minister to retain his or her power. Assuming that a Parliament does not die simply by the "efflux of time," only the prime minister has the power to choose a date for a national election (and to advise the queen to dissolve Parliament and call for an election on the given day). Prime ministers want to set election dates such that balloting day corresponds to their parties' popular periods, not with inevitable slippages in popularity.

A third dimension of activity for the prime minister involves his or her *image in Parliament*. Contacts in both the majority and opposition parties must be nurtured. Until World War II, the prime minister was personally "Leader of the House of Commons." Since that time other requirements have prevented the prime minister from holding this position personally, but the prime minister must still be aware of, and concerned with, happenings in the House of Commons.

Related to this is a fourth facet of the prime minister's role, participating in *parliamentary question time*. Twice a week the prime minister appears in the House of Commons to answer parliamentary questions, primarily from the members of the Opposition. Prime ministers take this activity seriously, as a poor performance can affect both their image in Parliament and their image with the public. Accordingly, prime ministers devote a significant amount of time to preparation for this encounter. One student of this phenomenon indicates that "on two nights a week the Prime Minister receives up to three boxes of files in preparation for the next day's ordeal, reading these ahead of Cabinet papers or Foreign Office telegrams."[35]

Yet another dimension of the prime minister's activity involves *debating policy*. The prime minister does not devote a great deal of his or her time to general debate; this individual's energies are focused elsewhere. Research has shown that in a typical year the prime minister will participate in only six debates, which are usually on only three issues: international affairs, the economy, and the business of the Government.[36] As far as general debate is concerned, the prime minister usually has ministers in charge of relevant departments articulate the Government's position in a debate.

Prime ministers are also concerned with *press publicity*. The prime minister, after all, must worry about the general image of his or her Government, and there is a continuous activity on the part of prime ministers to convince the public that their party merits public support. Generally speaking, the press is happy to oblige the prime minister with media attention; this is an example of a symbiotic relationship in which both the prime minister and the press profit from media coverage of the prime minister.

The seventh and final component of behavior of the prime minister is one to which we have already alluded: *chairing the cabinet*. The once or twice a week that the prime minister sits down with the heads of the various departments of government allows for crucial policy discussion to take place, as well as for communication of problems from ministers to the prime minister. All cabinet members are affected by the principle of "collective responsibility." This means that the cabinet as a whole is responsible for acts of the Government, and no member of cabinet may attack or criticize actions of the Government.

The cabinet meeting provides an opportunity for recalcitrant ministers to air their views; beyond this their only recourse is to resign from the cabinet. The rule of collective responsibility applies to both the prime minister and departmental ministers, so it is important for the prime minister to use the cabinet meeting to find out what his or her Government is doing. "Constitutionally, a Cabinet decision takes precedence over the wishes of an individual Minister, including the Prime Minister."[37] Because a prime minister does not want to be in a position in which he or she is fighting with a majority of his or her own party leaders, the prime minister will often lead by following the decisions of the cabinet.

Margaret Thatcher and "Thatcherism"

The arrival of Margaret Thatcher as prime minister in May 1979 affected British politics significantly and "changed the nature of contemporary Conservatism,"[38] notwithstanding her sudden and unexpected departure from the public arena in 1990. Mrs. Thatcher's strong anti-socialist and anti-union style was not an example of a consensual style of leadership: She knew what she wanted to accomplish, and she worked in a determined manner to accomplish it, introducing a style to contemporary British politics that came to be known as "conviction politics," and subsequently "Thatcherism."

> "Thatcherism" is more usefully regarded as a style than as an ideology: an ideology is a consistent system of ideas whereas what she called her conviction politics were largely instinctive and very much the product of her own experience. These instincts were narrow in range, dogmatically voiced; that she came to be credited with an "ism," a most un-Tory achievement, is a tribute to the force of her beliefs rather than to their coherence.[39]

If this meant engaging in an ideological battle within her own party, she was quite willing to do so.[40] Indeed, many observers of British politics have indicated that "the main feature of the first Thatcher administration was the Prime Minister's near total dominance over economic policy formation."[41]

When Mrs. Thatcher moved into 10 Downing Street the British economy was weak and she had a goal of "reshaping the public sector,"[42] seeking to turn the economy around, to a substantial degree through legislation nullifying many of the socialist policies that had been directing the economy for years, and engaging in direct conflict with the powerful labor unions.[43] In the 1979 campaign, Mrs. Thatcher had called for "a radical 'counter revolution' to set the people free," declaring that:

> the last two decades had seen an inexorable rise in government spending, accounting for 33% of the nation's GDP in 1959 and 41% in 1978; a dangerous growth in trade union power; a diminution in freedom of choice; and a decline in moral standards and law and order. [She] saw the ratchet shifting slowly but surely leftwards, with the country on the verge of becoming an Eastern European-style socialist state. The 1979 election was thus depicted as the "last chance" to halt this movement and to restore the proper balance between the individual and the state.[44]

The Thatcher Government "privatized" a number of government-owned industries, for instance overseeing the conversion of British Telecom from a government-run business to being a private corporation with stockholders. The government cut subsidies, reduced services, and fought with local governments, which—often still controlled by the Labour opposition party—sought to move into policy areas vacated by the central government. After her 1983 reelection, Margaret Thatcher continued in the same directions: "Inflation would be brought lower, public expenditure and borrowing firmly controlled, taxes cut. This time there was a list of industries to be privatised. . . ."[45]

Ultimately, Thatcher's "conviction style" of politics—specifically her insistence on new taxes and her opposition to further integrating Britain into the European economy—alienated even most of her supporters in the Conservative party. In November of 1990 Margaret Thatcher's leadership of the Conservative party was challenged by former (Conservative) defense minister Michael Heseltine. Heseltine received enough votes on the first ballot of the party leadership vote to convince Thatcher that she would not win, and she indicated that she would resign as leader and prime minister once the party selected a new leader. On the next ballot it was not Heseltine, but Thatcher's hand-picked successor, John Major, who was elected leader of the Conservative party. The day after that vote Margaret Thatcher visited the Queen to submit her resignation, and the Queen "invited" John Major to form a Government.

The Civil Service

It was suggested above that the civil service is an integral part of British government and politics.[46] When cabinet ministers seek to have policy put into operation, it is through the civil service that they operate. The civil service is, ostensibly, nonpolitical, and its function is to administer the policies of the government of the day.

The issue of the political role of the civil service came to the fore on several highly visible and political controversial issues in the 1980s. One case involved the Official Secrets Act (1911) and the leaking of certain documents to the House of Commons, documents critical of government policy in the 1982 Falklands war against Argentina. Another case involved whether the testimony of civil servants could be required by the Defense Committee of the House of Commons in its investigation into a scandal involving military contracts to manufacture helicopters. Still another case involved a former intelligence agent and dealt with the degree to which he was free to publish his memoirs.[47]

All of these cases were significant in helping to define the role of the civil servant as an apolitical servant of the government. Today nearly 600,000 civil servants work for the British government (down from a high of 732,000 in 1979), about one-sixth of them working in the Inner London area.[48] Only a very small proportion of the civil servants are high-ranking policymakers; the vast majority are individuals working in offices of the many government agencies around the nation. The Thatcher Government has been concerned with the higher ranks of the civil service because "civil service and administrative reforms have been seen as intimately linked to the 'sharp end' of the Government's policy outputs."[49]

The high-ranking civil servants, sometimes referred to as "Mandarins," play an important role in government. The Permanent Secretaries, the highest nonpolitical appointments in the civil service, provide the continuity and expertise that links one government to the next. "The relationship between ministers and permanent secretaries has been described as 'the vital joint in Whitehall—the elbow of government, between decision and execution.'"[50] One study of this relationship has concluded that "civil servants have more influence, and ministers less, than constitutional theory suggests."[51]

The British civil service has been modified in several ways ever since the arrival of Margaret Thatcher as prime minister. Management structures, financial organization, privatization, and reorganization have all contributed to a decrease in the cost of running the central government bureaucracy. Some observers have noted, however, that most of these modifications have been at the edges of the bureaucracy, in one case "concentrated on the 2 percent of the Department's budget which it spends on running itself," and that essentially little of substance has been accomplished in the way of reform.[52]

Local Government

Another level of government in Great Britain that cannot be ignored here is the local level. Although we earlier referred to Britain as a unitary, and not a federal, government because all sovereignty was based at Westminster, it is the case that although ultimate sovereignty resides at Westminster, the central government has decentralized many governmental functions, and local government is often significant in Britain.

This became especially true after the arrival of Margaret Thatcher as prime minister when Thatcherism was reshaping many fundamental domestic policies of the central government. In many regions of Britain, where Thatcher's Conservative party was very unpopular, local governments sought to continue many of the programs that Thatcher was discontinuing, or on which she was cutting back, at the national level.[53] This resulted, ultimately, in Thatcher pushing a bill through Parliament doing away with some local governments (such as the Greater London Council, for example), and putting a number of different systems into operation that sought to establish limits on the financial resources of the local governments.[54] Similarly, the Thatcher Government sought to regulate and limit the powers of the QUANGOs (Quasi-Autonomous Non-Government Organizations), which were so much a part of the British state that had developed through the late 1970s.

The theme that permeated the Thatcher years more than any other, according to one student of the period, was the search by the central government "for more effective instruments of control (not influence) over the expenditures of subcentral government. . . . The government has also sought to restrict the size of the public sector by privatization."[55]

The British Parliament

We have already discussed the manner in which the British political system came to be bicameral: The House of Lords evolved as a political structure prior to the creation of the House of Commons. In the British case, a bicameral national legislature is not a function of a federal regime as is the case in the United States, Germany, or Canada. Instead, it is a result of a class-conscious society and political evolution.

For a brief period of time, 1649 to 1660, the House of Commons declared that the House of Lords "was useless and dangerous" and was accordingly "wholly abolished and taken away."[56] The House of Lords was revived in 1660, and since that time the relationship between the two houses has passed through three distinct phases. The first phase, from 1660 to 1810, saw a period of general predominance of the House of Lords, although the House of Commons was not without influence.

Between 1811 and 1911 a number of changes took place that affected the relationship between the two houses. The Reform Acts of 1832, 1867, and 1884 strengthened the House of Commons in relation to the House of Lords. The increased acceptance of the idea that the cabinet should be responsible to the House of Commons (and should, therefore, resign if the House of Commons should fail to support its policies) clearly limited the future role of the House of Lords. When the House of Lords rejected a number of Government bills that had passed the House of Commons in 1910, the Government pushed through The Parliament Act (1911), which limited the power of the Lords in two aspects: (1) money bills could only be delayed for one month after being approved by the House of Commons, and then they became law even without the approval of the Lords; and (2) other public bills could be delayed for up to two years, after that time they would become law with only the approval of the Commons. (This period was shortened to one year by The Parliament Act of 1949.) The Parliament Act of 1911, which institutionalized these two radical limitations on the power of the House of Lords, was passed by the Lords only after it became clear that if they failed to do so the king was prepared to appoint enough new peers sympathetic to the bill to guarantee its passage.[57]

The third phase, from 1911 to the present time, has seen the House of Commons as the clearly dominant power in the relationship. The House of Lords no longer challenges major legislative policy of the Government. It occasionally revises or amend bills, and has been known to oppose outright acts of the Commons, but under the Parliament Act of 1911 its power to influence policy of the Government is severely limited.[58]

The House of Lords

One of the major roles of the House of Lords is not legislative at all, but judicial. The House of Lords inherited a number of judicial functions from the Curia Regis, and is now the supreme judicial tribunal of Britain. Originally, the entire House of Lords acted as an appeals court; in 1876 an act was passed allowing for the appointment to the House of Lords of "Lords of Appeal in Ordinary," holding peerage for life. (That is, their membership in the House of Lords was only for those individuals, and would not be hereditary and thereby passed to their children.) Today there is an Appellate Committee of the House of Lords, specially appointed Lords who act an an Appellate Court for Britain.

The House of Lords may not act as a "constitutional court" as is the case with the Supreme Court in the United States, though. Since there is no single "written" British Constitution, all legislation in Britain that is properly passed is constitutional and cannot be voided.

The nonjudicial function of the House of Lords has been said to have four components:

1. The examination and revision of Bills brought from the House of Commons. . . .
2. The initiation of Bills dealing with subjects of a comparatively non-controversial character. . . .
3. The interposition of so much delay (and no more) in the passing of a Bill into law as may be needed to enable the opinion of the nation to be adequately expressed upon it. . . .
4. Full and free discussion of large and important questions. . . .[59]

Early in its existence, prior to the seventeenth century, "there were usually between seventy and one hundred persons who sat in the House of Lords in response to the King's writ of summons."[60] Today there are almost 800 hereditary peers and peeresses and 350 life peers and peeresses. Additionally, membership of the House of Lords includes 20 Law Lords and 26 Lords Spiritual (bishops and archbishops in the Church of England). One source has calculated that among the regular attendees in the House of Lords, 49 percent support the Conservative party, 16 percent support the Labour party, 10 percent support the Liberal- Social Democratic Alliance, and 25 percent are "independent 'crossbenchers.'" Average daily attendance in the House of Lords has increased from 142 in 1960 to 322 in 1984.[61]

A number of efforts have been undertaken to "reform" the House of Lords, but none has been effective. Some argue that the House of Lords should be replaced by an elected second chamber. Others have argued that the second chamber should simply be abolished. Still others have argued that if the House of Lords is retained, at least its members should be elected, and not appointed, with their positions not to be inherited by their children.

One response to the demand for reform has been the introduction of Life Peerages. Since the late nineteenth century, more and more members of the House of Lords have been appointed as Life Peers, to serve as members of the House of Lords as long as they live, but their titles would not be passed to their heirs as is the case with normal peerages. The Life Peerages Act (1958) has resulted in a great increase in the number of Life Peers in the House of Lords, and since 1964 few new hereditary peerages have been created.[62]

One idea proposed in 1948 was that women should be permitted to serve in the House of Lords, but the tradition-conscious House of Lords opposed the idea. Peeresses, women who inherited a seat in the House of Lords from their fathers in the absence of a male heir, were forbidden from sitting and voting in the House of Lords. This policy has since been changed, and today there are a few Peeresses in the Lords.[63]

Only since 1963 has it been possible for individuals to resign from the House of Lords, to renounce their peerages. Traditionally, one could not renounced one's title, and since the law forbade individuals from serving in both Houses of Parliament, if a member of the House of Commons had a father who was a Peer in the House of Lords, and his father died, that Commons member had to resign his seat in the Commons and take his father's seat in the Lords; he could not simply renounce his new peerage and stay in the Commons. In 1948, party leaders in Parliament agreed to allow Peers to renounce their positions, thus allowing members of the House of Commons who "accidentally" became Peers to retain their elected positions.[64]

Levels of activity in the House of Lords have varied widely over the years. In the mid-1950s, daily attendance in the House of Lords was below 100 on the average; today the average attendance is about 280 members. "Among those who take an active part in the work of the House of Lords, over 400 take the Conservative whip. About 150 take the Labour whip and about 40 the Liberal whip."[65]

The House of Commons

We saw earlier that the original *raison d'étre* of the House of Commons was a fund-raising one; the king needed to raise more money than the House of Lords could provide, and politically he could do so only by summoning representatives of the public. Early Parliaments were primarily concerned with two tasks: First, they agreed to requests from the king for money, and second, as a *quid pro quo* for giving the king money, they presented the king with petitions of grievances.

The nineteenth century was a century of reform for the House of Commons, during which time the franchise was expanded and direct representation was improved. The Reform Act of 1867 allowed all householders to vote, as well as all persons occupying lodgings of an annual value of £10 or more. Similar measures were enacted for Scotland and Ireland in 1868. The Ballot Act of 1872 brought secret voting and a Reform Act of 1884 further expanded suffrage. (Women over 30 were first allowed to vote in 1918; in 1928 requirements for women to vote were made the same as those for men.)[66]

The development of the cabinet in the eighteenth century greatly changed the role of the House of Commons.[67] The position of the Speaker became very important for the behavior of the House. The Speaker was originally perceived as the king's representative in the House; by 1640 the Speaker was the representative of the House of Commons to the king. Today, the Speaker has great power to control debate and legislation. Speakers are elected by a new House of Commons immediately after a general election. The majority party nominates a candidate who invariably wins on a party-line vote. The Speaker will maintain his position for the life of the Parliament. He can suspend a member from the House should the member's behavior be perceived as sufficiently disruptive to merit such a punishment.

Although it was not always thus, a filibuster—unlimited debate to block legislative action—is no longer possible in the House of Commons. Members of Parliament whose speech is repetitious or irrelevant, or who are clearly attempting to be procrastinating, can be ruled out of order by the Speaker. Debate can be limited by the Speaker, and ever since 1968 the Speaker has not even been required to give his reasons for not accepting motion for debate.[68] Moreover, debate can be controlled by the Government through use of a number of technical devices so as to have its legislative program passed.

One of the most important functions of the House is to serve as a link between the people and the government. There is a wide range of pressure groups in Britain, and these groups regularly focus their efforts upon the House of Commons, although in the Thatcher era the pressure groups were not as successful as they were in earlier years.[69] "The experience of the first two years of the 1979 Conservative government shows that Governments can, in the medium term at any rate, ignore a wide range of political pressures if they want to."[70]

Legislation

There are a number of different *types* of legislation in the British House of Commons. We can initially distinguish between *Government bills* and *private members' bills*. Government bills are bills that are introduced and sponsored by the cabinet, and to which strong party discipline is applied. These bills are virtually assured of passage and account for an overwhelming share of the legislation of the House of Commons. Private members' bills are proposals for legislation that are introduced by noncabinet members (including members of the majority party who are not in the cabinet, as well as members of the opposition party).

When the Parliament that had been elected in October 1974 adjourned in August 1978, in its almost four-year session it had passed 48 private members' bills into law, only 11.5 percent of the 417 private members' bills that had been introduced over that period of time. As a measure of comparison, nearly 93 percent of the Government bills introduced during the same period of time were passed into law.[71] Private members' bills are legally restricted in only one way; they may not deal with money, either raising money or spending money. Moreover, private members' bills are placed on a separate calendar, usually handled only on Friday afternoons, and few members of Parliament have the opportunity to introduce their own proposals over the course of a legislative session due to the limitation of time.[72]

Since there would not be time in a legislative session for all members of Parliament who wanted to submit private members' bills of their own to do so, a "ballot," or drawing, is held at the beginning of each new legislative session in the fall to determine which members of Parliament will have the opportunity to introduce their own pieces of legislation. One recent recommendation made by members of Parliament for a change in House rules involves this "ballot":

the ballot for private members' bills should be held before the summer adjournment of the House instead of the autumn at the beginning of the new session. This would give the lucky members who come high in the ballot much more time to decide their topic of legislation and to prepare the content of the bill.[73]

Besides distinguishing between bills on the basis of who introduces them in the House of Commons, we can also distinguish between bills in terms of their scope: What do the proposed pieces of legislation intend to do? *Public bills* are drafts of new laws that would affect the country as a whole, such as tax law, criminal law, and so on. *Private bills* have individual application only, such as a special act of citizenship, for instance.[74]

The legislative process in the House of Commons involves the "standard" parliamentary procedure that we covered earlier in this text.

> When a Bill, thrashed out in the Cabinet or in its Legislation Committee and drawn up by the parliamentary counsel in due legal form . . . is presented to the Commons (or in some cases first to the Lords) its First Reading is generally formal. Second Reading Debate, normally in the full House (though in 1965 it was agreed that certain Second Readings of "uncontroversial Bills" might go to Committee) provides an opportunity for the discussion of general principles but it also lays down the basic framework of the Bill which cannot be altered at the Committee stage. This stage is concerned with the details of the Bill and amendments are confined within the aforementioned principles. . . . It is usually taken "upstairs" in one of the Standing Committees of about fifty members unless the Bill is of great constitutional significance, is likely to go through quickly, or a Government with a small majority fears too frequent defeat. There follows the Report Stage, usually brief, and a final Third Reading at which the major parties once more deploy their general arguments of principle, though the result, with the Whips on, is normally a foregone conclusion. Governments, of course, during all this process, may accept amendments which do not go to the heart of the Bill. Any other proposed change is discussed as a matter of "confidence" and defeat would normally lead to the Government's resignation or, more usually now to a dissolution and a General election.[75]

After bills are passed in the House of Commons they are sent to the House of Lords where they follow a similar three-reading procedure prior to passage. As was indicated above, if the House of Lords does not approve a bill, it no longer can kill the bill, but can only delay its eventual passage.

A final, special, procedure should be mentioned here that relates again to the "royal pretense" that was mentioned earlier. Bills approved by both Houses of Parliament must be given the Royal Assent, approval by the queen, before they become law. Ever since 1707 this Royal Assent has not been refused to a bill that has passed both Houses of Parliament. The monarch has not given the Royal Assent in person since 1854; today it is done by a Commission.

> For the giving of the Royal Assent, the Commons are summoned to the Lords' Chamber by the Gentlemen Usher of the Black Rod. Three Commissioners are seated between the Woolsack and the Throne. The title of each Bill which is to receive the Assent is read, and the Assent is signified by the Clerk of the Parliaments. The assenting formula is still given in Norman French. For Public Bills, and Private Bills of a local character, it is "La reine le veult" (the Queen wishes it). For Private Bills of a personal character the formula is "Soit fait comme il est desire" (let what is desired be done). The formula for Bills granting supply or imposing taxation is "La reine remercie ses bons sujets, accepte leur benevolence, et ainsi le veult" (the Queen thanks her good subjects, accepts their benevolence, and so wishes it). The formula for refusing the assent was formerly "La reine s'avisera" (the Queen will consider the matter).[76]

Political Parties and Voting

It has been suggested by a noted scholar that "British government is party government."[77] Parties organize electoral activity, including the selection of candidates in elections, the construction of programs, and the operation of election campaigns. In the general elections, citizens vote not so much for the individual candidates whose names appear on the ballot papers, but rather for the party team with which the candidate is affiliated.

Politics in Britain has often been referred to as "the politics of class,"[78] so it should come as no surprise that support for political parties in Britain has frequently been explained in terms of class allegiances. Today the allegiances have been described as "Labour, representing the working community, versus the Conservatives, representing capital."[79]

An interesting aspect of the ubiquity of parties in the British political system, though, is that they are "unknown to the constitutional law."[80] Parties originally developed in Britain over the issue of royal power, with the Tories (later to be called the Conservatives) favoring the royalty, and the Whigs (later to become the Liberals) opposing the royalists. Around the time of their development, in 1688 or so, neither the Tories nor the Whigs could have been called political parties in the contemporary sense of the word.[81] Neither group was mass-based nor electoral in nature; both were groups of elite politicians acting as factions.

One of the early developmental problems of political parties involved the question of opposition to the monarch.[82] The concept of a "loyal opposition" developed slowly, and not without a great deal of friction, because early on it was difficult for many to accept the notion that it was possible to be *against* a government in power without being against the regime *itself*.

> So long as government was the task of the King and his friends at court, to be opposed to the acts of the government was to be opposed to the King, and it was no doubt difficult to distinguish between the King as a person and the monarchy as an institution. This attitude reached its logical conclusion in the Civil War. The majority of parliamentary leaders did not see how they could oppose Charles I without opposing the monarchial system; so having beheaded Charles, they abolished Kingship.[83]

By the middle of the eighteenth century the concept of a "loyal opposition" was accepted. Edmund Burke, a great British politician of the time, argued that to combine to oppose or topple the government was not treason: "when bad men combine, the good must associate; else they will fall, one by one. . . ."[84]

Generally, the British party system is an integral part of the British political system. "The most obvious virtue of the party system," one student of British politics has written, "is that it ensures stable government and that it always presents the possibility of an alternative government." Parties contribute a great deal of stability to the political system by providing the basis for the formation of Governments, by "enabling the Government, as leaders of the most powerful party in the House of Commons, to secure the passage of their programme of legislation."[85]

Britain is usually regarded as a two-party political system. Strictly speaking, this is not true. Britain can be said to have a two-party system by one measure only: The number of political parties that have formed a Government since 1945 are two—Conservative and Labour. By any other measure, however, Britain has a multiparty system. (See Table 9.1.)

> FACT: In 1987, on the average, there were 3.6 candidates contesting each seat in the British House of Commons, not two as we would expect in a two-party system.
>
> FACT: The two major parties—Labour and Conservative—have together received *at most* 75 percent of the vote in national elections since 1974; put another way, at least one voter in four has voted for a party other than the "big two" in all recent elections.
>
> FACT: Outside of England (in Northern Ireland, Scotland, and Wales), the "minor" parties win significant proportions of votes in electoral competitions.
>
> FACT: The two major parties do not control all of the seats in the House of Commons today.[86]

The major part of the cause of this misperception about the British party system is due to the relationship between electoral systems and party systems that we discussed earlier. Britain has a single-member-district, plurality voting electoral system—what has been called a "first past the post" system. It doesn't matter whether a given candidate receives a *majority* of votes in a constitutency as long as he or she has a *plurality*—more votes than any other candidate. From 1945 through 1970, about three-fourths of the members of Parliament were elected with more than one-half of the votes of their constituencies. "But the proportion of MPs elected with an absolute majority fell to 36 percent elected in February, 1974, rising again to 40 percent in October, 1974."[87]

Table 9.1
The 1987 British General Election

Party	No. Seats	Percent of Seats	Percent of Vote
Conservative	375	57.7	42.2
Labour	229	35.2	30.8
Liberal/Social Democratic	22	3.4	22.6
Other	2	3.7	4.4

Source: *The Guardian*, June 15, 1987, p. 1.

One development in the political system in recent years which has proven to be significant was the appearance of the Alliance, a partnership of the Liberal party with the new Social Democratic Party.[88] The Liberals, led by David Steel, and the Social Democrats, led by David Owen, garnered over 25 percent of the vote in 1983 and approximately 23 percent of the vote in 1987.[89]

Just as we indicated was the general case earlier, in the British political system one consequence of the single-member-district, plurality voting system is that the nonmajor parties are systematically and continuously underrepresented in the House of Commons. As one scholar has noted, "there is probably no facet of British government more in need of reform than the electoral system by which the nation chooses its representatives at Westminster."[90] If the (today very tiny) Liberal party were contesting elections in a system of proportional representation, "it would be a major party with approximately 100 seats or more."[91]

The fact is that the British electoral system usually "manufactures a majority party in Parliament from a minority of votes."[92] There has not been a single political party that has won over half of the votes in a parliamentary election since 1935. The closest that any party has come to a majority of the votes was in 1955 when the Conservatives won 49.7 percent of the vote. The extreme bias of the single-member-district, plurality system can be found in the October 1974 election in which the Labour party won a bare majority in the House of Commons of 319 seats (out of 635, a *bare* majority) with 39.2 percent of the vote, while the Liberal party had 18.3 percent of the vote (almost half of the Labour vote), and yet received only 13 seats in the House of Commons (4 percent of the Labour total).[93]

This situation was repeated, only more vividly, in the elections of 1983. The Conservative Government of Margaret Thatcher was returned to power, winning 397 of 650 seats in the House of Commons (61 percent of the seats) in return for 42 percent of the votes. The Labour Party won 209 seats (32 percent of the seats) in return for 28 percent of the votes. The Liberal-Social Democratic Alliance won 23 seats (3.5 percent of the seats) in return for 25 percent of the total vote. Labour got 3 percent more votes than did the Liberal-Social Democratic Alliance, and won 186 more seats. Post-election analysis suggested that:

A lasting controversy is expected to arise because of the failure of the Alliance to win anything approaching the number of seats that their share of the vote would seem to have justified, and which they would have received under the proportional representation system used in most European countries. The British winner-take-all system, on which the American system is based, has survived unchanged for 700 years of parliamentary history.[94]

Although Britain is erroneously referred to as a two-party system, it traditionally has been dominated by three parties—the Conservative, the Labour, and the Liberal parties. The traditional competition for power through the early twentieth century took place between the Liberals and the Conservatives, which evolved from the Whigs and the Tories, respectively. During the latter part of the nineteenth century, the rivalry between these two parties increased as electoral reforms were undertaken and more people began to participate in politics.

The Labour party came on the political scene around the time of the turn of the century. Toward the end of the nineteenth century in Britain there were several movements mobilizing for working-class representation in the House of Commons. In 1900 they met in London and formed the Labour Representation Committee.[95] Two candidates from this group were elected to the House of Commons in 1900, and twenty-seven were elected in 1906. In 1918 the Labour party was formally organized.

The decline of the Liberals and the ascent of Labour as the second of two "major" parties took place in relatively rapid order.

In 1906 the Liberals dominated the political scene. They had won the largest majority in the House of Commons since the Reform Bill, even without their parliamentary allies, the new Labour Party, they secured over 50 percent of the popular vote. Less than two decades later, although they were still getting 30 percent of the vote, they were struggling desperately for survival. In 1929, their last serious challenge for governmental power won them 23 percent of the vote. Until 1974 they never again rose above 12 percent, and in 1951 and 1955, when they contested barely a sixth of the seats in Commons, they sank to a mere 2.5 percent of the vote.[96]

Constitutionally, elections for the House of Commons must be held at least every five years. As we have seen, however, because the British Constitution is "unwritten," the constitutional parameters relating to elections are whatever the House of Commons says they should be. In 1694, the Commons passed the Triennial Act, setting the maximum term of the House at three years; in 1716 the maximum term was extended to seven years by the Septennial Act. It wasn't until 1911 that the present five year constitutional limitation was set. Since 1911 it has usually been the case that elections have been called before the five-year limit on the life of a Parliament. There have been two noteworthy exceptions to this, however. During both World War I and World War II, Parliament decided, and legislated accordingly, to postpone elections because of the feeling that electoral uncertainty would not help the war effort. Consequently, "the Parliament chosen in 1910 was not dissolved until the end of 1918, and there was no general election in Britain between 1935 and 1945."[97]

Essentially it can be argued that one person, the prime minister, decides when a national election will take place. Although since 1911 the British Constitution has required (with the two exceptions noted) that elections be held at least every five years, in point of fact the prime minister has felt free over the years to request that the monarch dissolve Parliament and call for new elections at a time earlier than required that is an advantage to the Government in power. Tradition requires (although technically the law does not) that the monarch grant a dissolution when one is requested by the prime minister.

One of the most remarkable differences between the British electoral process and many other electoral processes is the relative brevity of the campaign period in Britain. In the American system, for example, primaries sometimes start as much as eleven months before elections, and informal campaigning often begins before that. In Britain, the Government's ability to call a "surprise" election can be a real strategic advantage; "approximately three weeks after a dissolution, the entire electorate of Britain goes to the polls."[98]

One of the reasons that such a short campaign period is possible is that there are no required party primaries to select nominees to stand for election. Party candidates are selected by local party organizations (although the precise method of the selection process differs among the parties). Nomination to run for office requires only ten signatures on a petition, in addition to a deposit of £150, which is forfeited if a candidate does not receive at least one-eighth of the vote in a constituency.[99] This is intended to discourage "frivolous" candidacies, although with the decline of the value of the pound it is less and less effective today.

Summary

There are few major deviations presented here from what we learned in earlier chapters. The British political system is the "Westminister Model" that we met earlier. Albeit brief, in this presentation of major structures in the British political system we have shown the manner in which it is possible to look at a political system using the general approach we introduced at the beginning of this book.

We have seen in this chapter that custom and tradition may be just as important, if not more so, in a nation's constitutional makeup as are written statues. The fact that it is even possible to imagine actions in the British political system that might be *legal* yet *unconstitutional* attests to the relative importance of the unwritten law of tradition. The British case is a clear example of a political system in which one must be familiar with the political environment and political history of a nation before one can seriously attempt to understand how public policy is made there.

Notes

1. Max Beloff and Gillian Peele, *The Government of the United Kingdom* (New York: W.W. Norton & Co., 1980), p. 10.
2. George W. Keeton, *Government in Action in the United Kingdom* (London: Ernest Benn Ltd., 1970), pp. 29–30.
3. Hiram Stout, *British Government* (New York: Oxford University Press, 1953), p. 19.
4. Sydney D. Bailey, *British Parliamentary Democracy* (Boston: Houghton Mifflin, 1958), p. 2.
5. Stout, *British Government*, pp. 20–21.
6. Ibid., p. 20. See also Bailey, *British Parliamentary Democracy*, p. 3.
7. Beloff and Peele, *Government*, pp. 10-11; Bailey, *British Parliamentary Democracy*, p. 3.
8. Stout, *British Government*, p. 21.
9. Bailey, *British Parliamentary Democracy*, p. 4.
10. See *The Monarchy in Britain* (London: Her Majesty's Stationery Office, 1981), pp. 8–11.
11. Bailey, *British Parliamentary Democracy*, p. 5.
12. Ibid., p. 6.

13. Stout, *British Government*, pp. 26–27.
14. Anthony Sampson, *The New Anatomy of Britain* (New York: Stein and Day, 1972), p. 215.
15. Max Nicholson, *The System* (New York: McGraw Hill, 1967), p. 158.
16. Sampson, *New Anatomy*, p. 215.
17. Ibid., p. 215.
18. Stout, *British Government*, pp. 70–71.
19. Beloff and Peele, *Government*, p. 67.
20. Sampson, *New Anatomy*, pp. 217–18.
21. Sir Ivor Jennings, *Cabinet Government* (Cambridge: Cambridge University Press, 1951), p. 79.
22. Stout, *British Government*, p. 77.
23. K. R. MacKenzie, *The English Parliament* (New York: Penguin Books, 1950), p. 81.
24. James Barber, "The Power of the Prime Minister," in R. L. Borthwick and J.E. Spence, *British Politics in Perspective* (New York: St. Martin's Press, 1984), p. 73.
25. John P. Mackintosh, "The Position of the Prime Minister," in Anthony King, ed., *The British Prime Minister* (London: Macmillan, 1969), p. 33. See also Martin Burch, "The Demise of Cabinet Government?" in Lynton Robins, ed., *Political Institutions in Britain: Development and Change* (New York: Longman, 1987), pp. 19–37.
26. Richard Rose, "British Government: The Job at the Top," in Richard Rose and Ezra Suleiman, eds., *Presidents and Prime Ministers* (Washington, D.C.: American Enterprise Institute, 1980), p. 1.
27. Richard Rose, *Ministers and Ministries: A Functional Analysis* (Oxford: Clarendon Press, 1987), p. 4.
28. A table ranking the political status of the many cabinet portfolios can be found in Rose, ibid., p. 86.
29. Peter Hennessy, *Cabinet* (Oxford: Basil Blackwell, 1986), pp. 1–15.
30. H. Victor Wiseman, *Politics in Everyday Life* (Oxford: Basil Blackwell, 1966), pp. 167–169.
31. Rose, "The Job at the Top," pp. 3-26.
32. Wiseman, *Politics in Everyday Life* , p. 159.
33. Bernard Crick, *The Reform of Parliament* (New York: Anchor Books, 1964).
34. Beloff and Peele, *Government*, p. 102.
35. Rose, "The Job at the Top," pp. 12-13.
36. Ibid., p. 16.
37. Ibid., p. 25.
38. Martin Holmes, *The First Thatcher Government, 1979–1983: Contemporary Conservatism and Economic Change* (Boulder, Col.: Westview Press, 1985), p. 1.
39. Peter Jenkins, *Mrs. Thatcher's Revolution: The Ending of the Socialist Era* (Cambridge: Harvard University Press, 1988), p. 81. See also Dennis Kavanagh, "Margaret Thatcher: A Case of Prime Ministerial Power?" in Lynton Robins, ed., *Political Institutions in Britain: Development and Change* (New York: Longman, 1987), p. 9–18.
40. Indeed, the Thatcher government's goal of lowering inflation at almost any cost "brought about a fundamenal division of opinion within the Conservative Cabinet, backbench MPs and the party itself. The conflict between the political monetarists, or dries, and the leftwing Conservatives, or wets, was a marked feature of the whole of the period from 1979 to 1983." Holmes, *Thatcher Government*, p. 74.

41. Holmes, *Thatcher Government*, p. 199.
42. Anthony Harrison and John Gretton, eds., *Reshaping Central Government* (New Brunswick, N.J.: Transaction Books, 1987), p. 1.
43. A good description of this relationship is in Dave Marsh and Jeff King, "The Unions Under Thatcher," in Robins, *Political Institutions in Britain*, pp. 213–229.
44. Ian Derbyshire, *Politics in Britain* (Oxford: W & R Chambers, 1988), p. 73.
45. Jenkins, *Mrs. Thatcher's Revolution*, pp. 173–74. See also a description of her goals and plans in Derbyshire, *Politics in Britain*, pp. 109-113.
46. A good general treatment of this is in the volume by Andrew Gray and William Jenkins, *Administrative Politics in British Government* (New York: St. Martin's Press, 1985).
47. See the discussion of the cases of Clive Ponting, Westland Helicopters, and Peter Wright in Gavin Drewry and Tony Butcher, *The Civil Service Today* (Oxford: Basil Blackwell, 1988), pp. 1-8.
48. Harrison and Gretton, *Reshaping Central Government*, p. 2. See also Drewry and Butcher, *The Civil Service Today*, p. 10.
49. John R. Greenaway, "The Higher Civil Service at the Crossroads: The Impact of the Thatcher Government," in Robins, *Political Institutions in Britain*, p. 49.
50. Anthony Sampson as quoted in Drewry and Butcher, *The Civil Service Today*, p. 151.
51. John Greenwood and David Wilson, *Public Administration in Britain* (London: Allen and Unwin, 1984), p. 84.
52. Harrison and Gretton, *Reshaping Central Government*, pp. 192–193.
53. A very good essay discussing this problem is that by Mike Goldsmith and Ken Newton, "Central-Local Government Relations: The Irresistible Rise of Centralised Power," in Hugh Berrington, ed. *Change in British Politics* (London: Frank Cass, 1984), pp. 216–233. See also R. A. W. Rhodes, "Mrs. Thatcher and Local Government: Intentions and Achievements," in Robins, *Political Institutions in Britain*, pp. 98–120.
54. A good discussion of this problem can be found in George Jones and John Stewart, *The Case for Local Government* (London: Allen and Unwin, 1985).
55. R. A. W. Rhodes, *Beyond Westminster and Whitehall: The Sub-Central Governments of Britain* (London: Allen and Unwin, 1988), p. 381.
56. Bailey, *British Parliamentary Democracy*, p. 35. See also Stout, *British Government*, pp. 89–92.
57. Frank Stacey, *British Government* (London: Oxford University Press, 1975), p. 72.
58. Bailey, *British Parliamentary Democracy*, pp. 36–37, 41.
59. Ibid., p. 38.
60. Ibid., p. 42.
61. Derbyshire, *Politics in Britain*, p. 4.
62. Nicholson, *The System*, p. 153.
63. Keeton, *Government in Action*, p. 63.
64. Nicholson, *The System*, p. 153.
65. Beloff and Peele, *Government*, p. 99.
66. Bailey, *British Parliamentary Democracy*, pp. 65–69.
67. A very good description of the development of parliamentary government and the role of the Parliament can be found in Michael Rush, *Parliamentary Government in Britain* (New York: Holmes and Meier, 1981), pp. 19–47.
68. Stacey, *British Government*, pp. 38–39.

69. See Michael Moran, "The Changing World of British Pressure Groups," in Robins, *Political Institutions in Britain*, pp. 179–187.
70. Wyn Grant, "The Role and Power of Pressure Groups," in Borthwick and Spence, *British Politics in Perspective*, p. 142.
71. Beloff and Peele, *Government*, p. 107.
72. Wiseman, *Politics in Everyday Life*, p. 147.
73. Stacey, *British Government*, p. 56.
74. Stout, *British Government*, pp. 128–137.
75. Wiseman, *Politics in Everyday Life,* p. 148. See also, for a very good cross-national treatment of this subject, David Olson, *The Legislative Process: A Comparative Approach* (New York: Harper & Row, 1980), p. 346.
76. Bailey, *British Parliamentary Democracy*, p. 108.
77. Richard Rose, *Politics in England* (Boston: Little, Brown, 1980), p. 249. (Hereafter *Politics in England*)
78. Derbyshire, *Politics in Britain*, p. 5.
79. Ibid. There is a much longer discussion of the nature of the interparty differences in economic and social policy here, pp. 6–14.
80. Keeton, *Government in Action*, p. 90.
81. Stout, *British Government*, p. 163.
82. A very good discussion of the evolution of British parties can be found in H.M. Crucker, "The Evolution of the Political Parties," in Borthwick and Spence, *British Politics in Perspective*, pp. 104–121.
83. Bailey, *British Parliamentary Democracy*, p. 138.
84. Ibid., p. 138.
85. Keeton, *Government in Action*, p. 93.
86. Richard Rose, *Politics in England: Change and Persistence*, 5th ed. (Glenview, Ill.: Scott, Foresman and Co., 1989) pp. 251–253. (Hereafter *Change and Persistence.)*
87. Rose, *Politics in England*, p. 255.
88. A discussion of the creation of the Alliance can be found in David Denver, "The S.D.P.–Liberal Alliance: The End of the Two-Party System?" in Hugh Berrington, ed., *Change in British Politics* (London: Frank Cass, 1984), pp. 75-102. A very good description of recent Alliance strategy can be found in David Butler and Paul Jowett, *Party Strategies in Britain: A Study of the 1984 European Elections* (New York: St. Martin's Press, 1985), Chap. 8, "The Alliance and Others."
89. Derbyshire, *Politics in Britain*, pp. 146-7.
90. Geoffrey Alderman, "The Electoral System," in Borthwick and Spence, *British Politics in Perspective*, p. 19.
91. Rose, *Politics in England*, p. 258.
92. Ibid., p. 256.
93. Ibid.
94. See *The New York Times*, June 10, 1983, p. 14; June 11, 1983, p. 4.
95. Stout, *British Government*, p. 200.
96. David Butler and Donald Stokes, *Political Change in Britain* (New York: St. Martin's Press, 1976), p. 117.
97. Stout, *British Government*, p. 200.
98. Ibid., p. 211.
99. Rose, *Politics in England*, p. 251.

10

The French Political System

We saw in the last chapter that the constitutional system of Great Britain is the product of a gradual evolutionary process that has taken place over a period of several hundred years; the same thing cannot be said of the constitutional system of France. In the British case, to be sure, we can point to specific dates of constitutional significance—for instance, the signing of the Magna Carta in 1215—but the general constitutional *system*, broadly interpreted, has remained intact and has changed only slowly over a long period of time. The French system is more properly characterized as experiencing a number of (more or less) sudden and severe alterations of the entire political regime, not merely evolutionary modifications of aspects of the system.

A Constitutional History of France

The fact that we refer to the current system of government in France as the Fifth Republic suggests, and properly so, that earlier republics have come and gone. Many of these arrivals and departures have not been slow and moderate, but have been abrupt and violent substitutions of one system of government for another—revolutions in fact if not in name.

It behooves us at this point to examine briefly the constitutional history of France that has led to the establishment of the Fifth Republic. This is an appropriate inquiry for us to undertake because it will become clear, as we continue our examination of significant French political structures later in this chapter, that many contemporary political institutions in the French system were designed as they are precisely because of experiences earlier in France's political and constitutional history.

The Early Years

Since 1789, the year of the demise of the Old Regime, political leaders in France have proven unable for long periods of time to reach a general consensus as to the type of political institutions most appropriate for France. "No single regime has ever enjoyed the kind of legitimacy which the English constitutional monarchy has enjoyed since the late seventeenth century. . . ." Moreover, ever since the end of the French Revolution in 1793, "France has lived under two monarchies, two empires, five republics, the Vichy regime . . . not to mention several short-lived variants."[1]

The decade from 1789 to 1799 was one of great turmoil in France. The forces of the Revolution threw out the old order but found that it was not so easy to install a new regime and establish peace. As Table 10.1 (on page 254) illustrates, the decade was characterized by changes in leadership, moving from radical liberal leadership to conservative leadership and back again.

In 1795, as part of the cycle of revolution and counterrevolution that had begun earlier, a five-man Directory was given power. The Directory proved to be no more effective or stable a government than its predecessors, however, and:

> there was little popular desire to defend so uninspiring a regime when Napoleon Bonaparte, one of the distinguished generals of the Revolutionary armies, attacked it, proclaimed the [regime that was called the] Consulate (with himself as First Consul) in 1799, made himself Consul for life in 1802, and established an empire (with himself as Emperor) in 1804.[2]

The Napoleonic Empire was short-lived, certainly in compar-

Table 10.1
French Regimes in Modern Times

Date	Regime
Before 1789	Old Regime
1789–1792	Revolutionary and counterrevolutionary struggles
1792–1799	First Republic
	1792–1795: Convention
	1792–1794: Radical Republican rule
	1794–1795: Conservative reaction
	1795–1799: Directory: moderate Republican rule
1799–1814	Age of Napoleon
	1799–1802: First Consul
	1802–1804: Life Consul
	1804–1814: The First Empire
1814–1830	Bourbon Restoration: constitutional monarchy, traditional authoritarianism
1830–1848	July Monarchy: Orleanist constitutionalism, emerging business interests
1848–1852	Second Republic
1852–1870	Second Empire: Louis Napoleon
1870–1940	Third Republic
1940–1944	Vichy regime
1944–1946	Provisional government of Charles de Gaulle
1947–1958	Fourth Republic
1958–	Fifth Republic
	1958–1969: Charles de Gaulle, president
	1969–1973: Georges Pompidou, president
	1973–1980: Valery Giscard d'Estaing, president
	1980– : François Mitterrand, president

Source: Adapted from Roy Pierce, *French Politics and Political Institutions* (New York: Harper & Row, 1968), p. 3; and Roy C. Macridis, *French Politics in Transition: The Years After DeGaulle* (Cambridge, Mass.: Winthrop, 1975), p. 101.

ison with the British monarchies that were contemporary to it. During the fifteen years that Napoleon ruled France, several legal and administrative reforms were enacted throughout the empire that proved to be long-lasting.

> The Napoleonic Code, the centralized prefecture system, the Council of State—survived him to become permanent features of the French state, whether organized as a monarchy, empire, or republic. When Louis XVIII was maneuvered onto the throne in 1814 with the assent of France's conquerors, it was not a question of turning the clock back to 1789. Rather, it was announced that

although the King was to exercise all executive power, his legislative proposals would become law only with the approval of the Chamber of Peers and the Chamber of Deputies. . . . Such gifts of the Revolution as abolition of feudal privileges, equality before the law, and religious freedom, were to be preserved in a *constitutional monarchy*.[3]

Between 1814 and 1848, a number of monarchs succeeded to the throne, including Louis XVIII (1814–1824), Charles X (1824–1830), and Louis Philippe (1830–1848). The riots of 1848 that deposed Louis Philippe led to the creation of the Second Republic, and in the presidential election of December 1848 (France's only experiment with a president prior to 1958), Louis Napoleon, the nephew of Napoleon, was elected president.

There was some hope for political stability in 1848 and 1849, with the ascendancy of Louis Napoleon and the subsequent election of a monarchist majority in the legislative elections of 1849. The honeymoon did not last, however; Louis Napoleon and the National Assembly were soon involved in a number of disputes, primary among which was the question of whether the president could run for a second term. In December 1851 a coup led by Louis Napoleon himself ended the short life of the Second Republic. Louis Napoleon subsequently became emperor, and the Second Empire came into being, lasting for almost twenty years.

Like his uncle, Louis Napoleon made a number of contributions to the French political arena. He reintroduced, and often used, the *plebiscite* (referring political questions directly to voters) as a means of claiming popular support for his policies. Moreover, he decreed that the legislature had the capacity to fire any cabinet that it did not support (although there were no false ideas about legislative supremacy in relation to the monarch!). The empire of Louis Napoleon was defeated by the Prussians in the Franco-Prussian War of 1870, bringing about the creation of the Third Republic, which lasted from 1870 until the time of the Nazi conquest of France in 1940.

The Third Republic

The Third Republic has been referred to as a "republic by default."

The National Assembly that was hurriedly elected in 1871 to provide a government capable of negotiating peace with Bismarck's Germany did not want a republic at all: more than 400 of its 650 deputies were monarchists. But since the Assembly could not agree on which of the three dynasties (Bourbon, Orleans, Bonaparte) should be called upon to provide a King, the precise nature of the regime was left unsettled.[4]

Although the Third Republic dates from 1870, its constitution was not assembled until 1875. The political structures of the Third Republic were fairly basic: The bicameral parliament was composed of a Chamber of Deputies and a Senate, the deputies elected by the people and the senators elected indirectly and overrepresenting rural areas.[5] The combined legislature, called the National Assembly, elected a president for a seven year term. Ministers were responsible to the legislature, and with the consent of the Senate the president could dissolve the Chamber of Deputies before its four year term expired.

The fact that the Third Republic lasted as long as it did—seventy years, from 1870 until 1940—is an anomaly of French political history. One should not deduce from the relative longevity of the Republic that its life was placid and stable, for such was clearly not the case. A number of crises arose during the life of the Republic caused many people to fear that the Republic was in danger of extinction.

The "Sixteenth of May" (1877) episode involved a conflict between a strongly church-oriented President Comte de Mac-Mahon and an anticlerical Chamber of Deputies. The Chamber of Deputies passed an anticlerical resolution and was promptly rebuked by the president. This caused the premier, Jules Simon, to resign in protest of the president's action. The president then appointed a proclerical premier and cabinet that did not have the confidence of the Chamber of Deputies and dissolved the Chamber of Deputies, with a bare majority of support in the Senate.[6]

When the subsequent election was held in 1879, the proclerical candidates supporting President MacMahon were defeated, and the president resigned. One of the lasting implications of this chain of events, for the Third Republic at least, was that dissolution was perceived as such a drastic political weapon that it was never used again.

As the President of France came to resemble the King of England more than the President of the United States, executive leadership was left to a series of coalition cabinets with a life expectancy of little over six months.[7]

In 1892 the Dreyfus affair captured the world's attention. Alfred Dreyfus was a young Jewish army captain who was tried and found guilty of selling military information to Germany. It later became public knowledge that Dreyfus was not guilty, but instead had been falsely accused by a number of officers to cover the actions of a certain Major Charles Esterhazy, who was a nephew of an important general. The charges of conspiracy against the army caused a national crisis; many people believed that it was far better to imprison an innocent Jew on Devil's Island than to impugn the dignity of the army, which was seen as the same as an attack on the nation. Eventually Esterhazy and his co-conspirators confessed and Dreyfus was freed, but the government was embarrassed by the event.[8]

Interestingly, World War I did not appear to have a deleterious effect upon the regime. Rather, the economic depression that rampaged through Europe after the war damaged the Government. In 1935 a temporary electoral alliance of a number of political parties helped elect Leon Blum—both a Socialist and a Jew—premier. The Spanish Civil War in 1936 affected the stability of the Blum regime, as did a number of other social issues, and the Blum Government resigned after a year.

From 1936 through 1940 several governments were created and dissolved. The Spanish Civil War, the Munich Agreement of 1938 between Neville Chamberlain (the British prime minister) and Adolf Hitler over the annexation of Czechoslovakia by Germany, the Nazi-Soviet Nonaggression Pact of 1939, and the German invasion of Norway and the Low Countries, left French governments powerless to act.

The phenomenon that most people associate with French politics under the Third and Fourth Republics is no doubt ministerial instability, the frequent turnovers of cabinets. The phenomenon can be illustrated by comparing the number of French and British cabinets and premiers (or prime ministers) during similar periods, as indicated in Table 10.2 (on page 258).

The major explanation for the frequency of new cabinets in France during the Third Republic can be found in the popularly elected Chamber of Deputies. There were usually eight to ten parties to be found in the legislature, which invariably meant that coalitions were necessary to form government majorities. These coalitions, as is often the case with coalitions, were not durable enough to withstand the short-term pressures brought about by

Table 10.2
Ministerial Instability in France: A Comparative Perspective

	3rd Rep. France, 1879– 1940	Britain, 1880– 1940	4th Rep. France, 1947– 1958	Britain, 1945– 1963
Number of cabinets	94	21	18	5
Average cabinet life	8 mos.	36 mos.	8 mos.	43 mos.
Number of premiers	44	11	15	4
Average tenure of premier	16 mos.	60 mos.	9 mos.	54 mos.

Source: Adapted from material in Roy Pierce, *French Politics and Political Institutions* (New York: Harper & Row, 1968), pp. 19–21.

rapidly evolving political events, which resulted in the collapse of government after government.

In June 1940 a new cabinet was formed that was led by the World War I hero Marshal Henri Pétain. The hope was that Pétain, as a military hero, would be able to provide strong leadership in the face of powerful external pressure from Hitler's Nazi Germany. He *did* provide leadership, but in an unexpected direction. Immediately after taking power on June 16, 1940, Pétain opened negotiations with the Nazis, and less than a week later (on June 22, 1940) he signed an armistice with Germany dividing France into an occupied northern half, and an unoccupied southern half, governed from the city of Vichy. From this time until November 1942, when Germany occupied all of France, the Vichy regime governed the southern half of France without a constitution, a legislature, or presidential elections. The Third Republic was dead.[9]

The Fourth Republic

When France was liberated in 1944, General Charles de Gaulle, who had led a National Council of Resistance from London during the war, became head of the new Government.

An assembly existed, but it was purely consultative. The cabinet was chosen by de Gaulle and was responsible to him alone. Thus the regime in the first fourteen months following the Liberation was rightly called a "dictatorship by consent." This situation was probably inevitable, for the political balance at the time of liberation was seriously distorted, as future instability and uncertainty were to demonstrate.[10]

In October 1945, "French voters by an overwhelming majority of 18,600,000 to 700,777 decided to leave the Third Republic in its grave."[11] The first postwar legislature was subsequently elected, and one of its first tasks was to construct a new constitution; this combination legislature-constitutional convention was called the Constituent Assembly. There was no agreement, however, on the direction that should be followed in France's constitutional future.[12]

The first draft constitution was presented to the voters in May 1946 for ratification and was rejected by a narrow margin: 10,584,539 to 9,454,034. This plan proposed abolition of the Senate as an essentially "undemocratic" institution (since it was not directly elected by the public), and proposed a weak executive, with virtually all powers vested in a unicameral National Assembly. The draft had the support of the left parties, the Communists and the Socialists, but was opposed by moderate parties and a new political organization, the Popular Republican Movement (MRP).

The second Constituent Assembly, which was elected in June 1946, produced a modified draft constitution that resembled the first proposal in many respects, placing almost complete authority in the elected National Assembly, with a weak Council of the Republic as a second legislative house.

> Recalling the Senate's frequent obstruction of reform measures under the Third Republic, however, the drafters deprived it of the right of legislative initiative, and empowered the lower house to override Senate amendments. The lower house was purposefully renamed the National Assembly, a term previously used to designate the entire two-house parliament."[13]

Members of the National Assembly were to be elected from multimember districts, averaging five deputies per district, by proportional representation. The executive was to remain weak.

In October 1946 this plan was presented to the French public, and it received a singularly unenthusiastic approval: 9,297,470 votes in favor, 8,165,459 against, and 7,775,893 eligible voters not voting. General de Gaulle and his supporters, who had argued for a stronger executive and opposed the plan, claimed that the new constitution would never last since it was supported by only slightly more than a third of the electorate.[14]

A number of constitutional devices were included in the constitution to promote governmental stability, such as the constitutional change of 1954 making the investiture of a prime minister easier by requiring that this individual have a relative, or simple, majority (a majority of those present and voting) rather than an absolute majority (a majority of all members of the legislature) in order to become prime minister. Despite this, however, the multiparty system encouraged by the proportional representation electoral framework led to an *absence* of stable parliamentary majorities, producing a change in cabinets averaging one every six months.

Although domestic issues were the primary source of political conflict in the early postwar years, by the mid-1950s it was international events that consumed governmental attention. The Government was able to handle almost all of the crises it faced. The War in Indochina (Vietnam) was ended in 1954. France accepted West Germany into the North Atlantic Treaty Organization (NATO) in 1957, and it joined the European Economic Community (the Common Market). Both Morocco and Tunisia were granted independence in 1956. Also in 1956 the French Government passed legislation to "set France's African colonies south of the Sahara on the road to real, and not sham, self-government."[15] The question of Algeria, however, proved to be too much for the Government to resolve.

In April 1958 the French army stationed in Algeria supported a revolt launched by European settlers in Algiers and called for the formation of a "Government of Public Safety" in Paris, demanding that the present Government resign, and that General de Gaulle be called out of political retirement to take power.[16] The Government in power proved to be unequal to the challenge and accepted General de Gaulle as "the only possible savior-assassin of the regime. On June 1, 1958, by a vote of 329 to 224, the Assembly accepted de Gaulle as Prime Minister, and the next day empowered him to supervise the drafting of a new constitution."[17] The Fourth Republic was dead.

The Constitutional System of the Fifth Republic

When on June 1, 1958, the National Assembly invested de Gaulle as prime minister, there were many deputies in the Assembly who were suspicious of de Gaulle and feared that his selection would lead to the creation of another Napoleon-like empire. De Gaulle had done a good deal himself to foster this kind of fear during the years he was out of government, calling for strong executive leadership and a new constitutional regime. In June 1946 de Gaulle had delivered in the town of Bayeux what would prove to be one of his most famous speeches. He set forth his notion of the type of strong, vigorous executive leadership that he thought France needed.[18]

In spite of de Gaulle's protestations that at the age of 67 he did not pose a Napoleon-like threat to French liberty, when the legislature authorized him to draft a new constitution it attached two highly significant conditions: First, the constitution of the new Fifth Republic had to retain the president and the premier. Second, the new constitution would have to retain the characteristic of having the premier "responsible to" the legislature. The latter requirement was included on the (understandable) assumption that de Gaulle himself would seek the premier's office, and thus the legislature would still have some degree of control over any future acts of de Gaulle.[19]

It should be noted, interestingly, that although de Gaulle was given authority by the legislature of the Fourth Republic to draft a new constitution that he would subsequently submit to the public in a referendum for approval, many have argued since 1958 that this grant of power was illegal. The constitution of the Fourth Republic, still in effect when de Gaulle was working on his draft, provided that constitutional amendments could be initiated *only* in parliament. Thus it has been argued by anti-Gaullists that the de Gaulle constitution of the Fifth Republic was simply a "coup d'état that had only a thin veneer of legality."[20]

The de Gaulle constitution does not fit neatly into one or the other of the two major models of executive leadership (presidential or parliamentary) that we introduced earlier in this book. The presidential model has a single individual playing both the head of state and chief executive roles, elected independently of the legislature, and having a base of power independent of the legislature as well. The parliamentary model separates the two executive roles, with the weak figurehead chosen by one of a number of different mechanisms (heredity, election, or some other), and with the powerful chief executive coming from, being a part of, and being responsible to, the legislature. The de Gaulle constitution bridges the two systems, and it is accordingly sometimes referred to as either a "quasi-presidential" or a "quasi-parliamentary" system.

The de Gaulle constitution of 1958 brought together elements of both the Bonaparte era and the Republican era. "The Constitution established a strong Executive in the form of a President with independent power to govern and a cabinet headed by a Prime Minister responsible to a popularly elected assembly."[21] To put the institution of the French president in a comparative perspective, the president of France has both in theory and in practice the power that the British prime minister has in practice but not in theory. The French model, unlike the standard Westminster-model power relationship, gives us a politically significant head of state and a weak chief executive. This is a significant departure from other parliamentary regimes that we have met and will meet later, and it warrants more attention here.

The so-called de Gaulle constitution of 1958 was drafted by a small group of individuals, led by Michel Debré, the future prime minister[22]; no person, other than de Gaulle, had more influence on the 1958 constitution than did Debré. The new constitution was submitted to a Constitutional Advisory Committee, primarily made up of legislators, and subsequently presented to the public for approval in a national referendum.

A strong presidency, coupled with some structural changes in the powers of the legislature, was the major thrust of changes that the Fifth Republic would make to the political system of the Fourth Republic. This was clearly in response to what was seen as the fundamental weakness of the Fourth Republic: a lack of leadership and parliamentary instability. We now turn our attention to an examination of the organization of the Fifth Republic, and to some of the prominent political structures to be found therein.

Unitary Government in France

"The political framework within which French cities deal with the changing needs and demands of their populations is built on three levels of government: the commune, the department, and the national government."[23] Just as French parliamentary government is a variation of the "normal" parliamentary model, so too the French style of unitary government appears to be different from other unitary governments.

It will be recalled that while unitary governments and federal governments both have local as well as national levels of government, they differ in the existence of an intermediate level of government. The United States, Canada, and Germany are examples of federal governments in which power is shared (to different degrees) between the "central" or "national" governments and the intermediate governments—states, provinces, or Länder. The primary alternative to the federal system is the unitary regime, in which there is no intermediate level of government. The "typical" unitary government (if such can be said to exist) is found in Great Britain, in which a national level of government and a local level of government divide functions that would be of concern to the intermediate level of government in a federal regime.

The French system is an odd form of unitary government, because although there is much sharing of power between the national and local levels of government, there are intermediate levels of government designed to assist in the administration of policy. Locally, the mayor and municipal council deal with two types of decisions: how to carry out and finance state-mandated services, and priority-setting decisions in areas not controlled by the state. The *commune*, the lowest-level political organization of the state, is the central administrative unit of the nation.

The second level of French government is the *department*. The *prefect* is the representative of national government in the department. This individual has "wide-ranging powers over local government, . . . control of the legality of local governmental decisions and review of the substance of the commune's decisions in policy areas where the commune is not bound by national legislation."[24] A good deal of the commune's legislation cannot go into effect without the prefect's approval. There are ninety-five departments in France, most of which today have the same borders they did at the time of the French Revolution in 1789.

Departments are governed by a departmental council (*conseil général*); for purposes of administration, departments are divided into subunits called *cantons*, and each canton elects one member to the departmental council. Like the commune, the department "is both a self-governing body and an administrative level of the state."[25] The chief executive of government at the departmental level is not an elected official at all, but is the prefect who is appointed.

It can be seen, then, that although France is invariably classified as a unitary regime, it is a unitary regime with many characteristics that might be thought to be more appropriate for a federal system than a unitary system. Departments and cantons both exist above the local (commune) level, and as we shall see later, particularly in regard to the Senate, they play a significant role in the French political system.

The Executive Structure

The Presidency

"When General de Gaulle returned to power in 1958, it was generally expected that the presidency of the Republic would be invested with a novel significance in the policy processes of the new Republic."[26] The "keystone" of the Fifth Republic's constitutional makeup is the presidency.[27] It was by making the president (usually the weak figurehead actor in split-executive parliamentary systems) the keystone of the system, rather than the prime minister, that de Gaulle and his coauthors of the new constitution were able to put so much power in the hands of a single political actor and yet were still able to stay within the conditions set down by the Fourth Republic legislators permitting a new constitution to be written and submitted to the public for approval.

The system of executive power in the Fifth Republic is similar in many respects to those found today in Austria, Finland, Ireland, and Iceland, in which the president is popularly elected. In those systems, however, the president is significantly weaker than in the French system, "because his role is circumscribed by his being subject to ouster by Parliament (as in Iceland), by strong legislative powers that Parliament possesses (as in Finland), or by the role of strong, disciplined parties (as in Austria). The French president, in contrast, suffers from none of these limitations."[28]

"The Constitution of the Fifth Republic was written in reaction against the constitutional pattern of the parliamentary system,"[29] and the new institution of the French president was a reaction against the weak, impotent prime ministers of the Fourth Republic. The president has powers that can be exercised without the consent of either the Government (the prime minister and the cabinet) or the legislature, and it is these powers that place the president in the paramount position of leadership in the French political system.

De Gaulle's goal in designing the constitution the way he did was "to free the executive from legislative domination and so to make possible greater governmental stability."[30] Article 5 of the French Constitution presents the broad perception of the president's powers:

> The President of the Republic shall see that the Constitution is respected. He shall ensure, by his arbitration, the regular functioning of the governmental authorities, as well as the continuance of the State. He shall be the guarantor of national independence, of the integrity of the territory, and of respect for Community agreements and treaties.

The president is given absolute power, without the consent of either the Government or the legislature, to:

1. Appoint the Prime Minister;
2. Dissolve Parliament;
3. Assume Emergency Powers under Article 16;
4. Ask Parliament to reconsider a law just passed;
5. Refer a law to the Constitutional Council for judgment on its constitutionality;
6. Preside over the Council of Ministers (the Cabinet);
7. Serve as Commander in Chief;
8. Exercise the right of Pardon;
9. Decide whether or not to submit a bill to popular referendum when the Parliament or the Prime Minister suggest it.[31]

The presidential power to dissolve the National Assembly

(the lower house of the bicameral legislature) at any time the president wishes, except while exercising emergency powers under Article 16 (see below) or if the National Assembly has already been dissolved once within a year, is worth note. It is not unusual to find this power in the hands of the head of state in a given political system; the queen of England has the same power.

The difference, and a significant difference, is that although *de jure* (in law) the queen of England may use this power at any time, *de facto* (in fact) she will use it *only* "on the advice" of the prime minister. The French president possesses this power both *de jure* and *de facto*, and French presidents since the time of de Gaulle have used the power on their own initiative, without consulting, or seeking approval of, or acting on request of, the prime minister and cabinet.

To take one example, in October 1962, angered by de Gaulle's use of the referendum to secure an amendment to the constitution providing for direct popular election of the president, the National Assembly took its anger out on de Gaulle's prime minister, Georges Pompidou, and voted to censure the Government. De Gaulle responded to this action by activating Article 12 of the constitution and dissolving the National Assembly, and elections took place the following month.[32] The act of dissolution worked to the advantage of both de Gaulle and Pompidou, because the newly elected National Assembly had significantly more Gaullists than had the legislature that was dissolved.

A major set of presidential powers included in the de Gaulle constitution of the Fifth Republic deals with emergency powers of the president. Article 16 of the constitution states that "when the institutions of the Republic, national independence, the integrity of national territory, or the application of international commitments are threatened in a serious and immediate fashion, and the normal functioning of public institutions is interrupted," the president is authorized to "take the measures required by these circumstances."[33]

The measures that the president can take are virtually unlimited. The only checks on his (or her) power (and they are really not checks at all) are that (1) the president must consult with the prime minister, the presidents of the two houses of the legislature, and the Constitutional Council, and (2) the legislature must remain in session during the period of the declared emergency. It should be noted that the first item requires the president only to *consult* with others, not seek their approval or permission, so these "checks" really do nothing to limit what the president does.

Article 16 has been used only once during the Fifth Republic. In April 1961 a group of French generals who opposed governmental policy leading to Algerian independence from France threatened to invade the French mainland and take over the Government. De Gaulle acted under Article 16, announced that "the institutions of the Republic" were threatened, and declared a state of emergency. The attempted coup was put down within a very few days, but de Gaulle let his Article 16 powers remain in force for over five more months; only the president decides when to deactivate the Article 16 powers.[34]

It can clearly be seen, then, that there really are no "checks and balances" in the traditional sense over the president's use of the broad emergency powers given this individual in Article 16. The president needs no countersignature, no "advice and consent," no one's permission to declare the state of emergency, and the state of emergency remains until the president, and only the president, decides to declare the emergency over. A president who wished to assume dictatorial powers could constitutionally do so.

Yet another set of powers exclusively reserved for the president has to do with justice-related issues. Again, without the permission or countersignature of either the Government or the legislature, the president has the power to appoint three of the nine members of the Constitutional Council, which will be further discussed later. Moreover, the president has the right of pardon.

Beyond these powers, anything the president wants to do in the French political system can only be done in collaboration with others. For example, only the president has the power to call for a referendum, to submit a political issue to the voters, but theoretically the president can call a referendum only if asked to do so by either the Government or the legislature.

In practice, however, the president, and not the Government or the legislature, has decided whether or not to hold a referendum. A communiqué issued by the Council of Ministers on November 16, 1960, stated: "General de Gaulle indicated his intention of submitting . . . by means of the referendum, a Government bill relating to the organization of the public powers in Algeria, pending self-determination." The president has usually made known his desire for a referendum, and the prime minister has accordingly requested the referendum, thus observing the constitutional requirements. The French legislature has never to date used its constitutional right to request the president to submit a question to referendum.[35]

This theoretical control over the referendum was in direct response to the history of its (ab)use in French politics. Napoleon frequently resorted to the referendum, often as a means of achieving a goal that the legislature would not permit, and the public at the time did not prove to be terribly discriminating in its approval of Napoleon's ideas. The founders of the Fifth Republic, while giving the president great emergency powers, did not want to give a charismatic president license to regularly go around the duly elected legislators in the policy-making process.

> The device of the referendum allows the President to present an issue to the public in terms that often simplify complex matters by demanding a yes or no answer from the voter. By [threatening to resign if he lost and] staking his office on the outcome of the referendum and threatening the public that without him the political system would return to the disorders of the Fourth Republic, de Gaulle was able to win massive public approvals in the referendum.[36]

The idea of the referendum was "essential" to de Gaulle's constitutional scheme because it provided "an alternative to Parliament as the agency for legitimizing public policy." De Gaulle perceived that in the French political system the political parties were a "screen rather than a transmission belt" between the government and the public, and "as parliament is the arena of partisan representation, it was important that the executive be able to bypass Parliament in the policy-making process in cases where it believed that it could win popular, but not parliamentary, support."[37]

Given that the president has only the above-mentioned powers that he can perform independently of all others, even though they *are* significant powers, what has caused the French political leadership system to evolve to a point at which it has been argued that it resembles the American presidency as much as, if not more than, the Westminster model of parliamentary government?

The answer can only partially be attributed to the constitutional grant of special powers to the president. There is in French politics a "fundamental difference between the role which the constitution and those who actually drafted it assigned to the presidency and the actual significance which the office has taken on in the process of decision making." This divergence of reality from intent demonstrates how a "conjunction of circumstances of personality can thoroughly transform constitutional institutions and their underlying ideas."[38]

Certainly a major reason for the evolution of the presidency as a significant political institution must be indicated as being the result of acts of the first holder of the office, Charles de Gaulle.[39] De Gaulle was a charismatic leader who favored strong executive leadership, and in the same way that initial incumbents of many political offices leave lasting impressions on the institutions they helped to create, de Gaulle's role in the development of the French presidency cannot be overstated. Charles de Gaulle was a hero of World War II, leader of the Resistance, and leader of the transition team of 1958 that guided the Fourth Republic into the Fifth Republic. His perception of the presidency, which we have seen he first expressed in 1946 in his Bayeux speech, was almost bound to become embedded in the political system.

A second reason for the growth of the relative power of the French presidency can be found in the constitutional amendment of October 1962, which established the direct popular election of the president for a seven-year term of office.[40] In the 1958 constitution the president was to be elected by an electoral college made up of local and provincial officials and national legislators. By having the president directly elected by the people, and therefore responsible to them and not to the legislators, de Gaulle gave the presidency a tremendous infusion of power and legitimacy.

Direct popular election "endowed the presidency with the legitimacy of a direct popular vote which, it was hoped, would accrue to the office when it was occupied by a less charismatic personality than General de Gaulle."[41] The result of this is "a mixed system of authority in which, as long as the President and government are of the same party, the presidential elements are likely to dominate." As Pompidou described the system in 1964:

> France has now chosen a system midway between the American presidential regime and the British parliamentary regime, where the chief of state, who formulates general policy, has the basis of his authority in universal suffrage but can only exercise his func-

tions with a government that he may have chosen and named, but which in order to survive must maintain the confidence of the Assembly.[42]

The similarity to the American system can be overstated, however. Apart from the strong head of state, which is a single deviation from "normal" parliamentary systems, the French system is still much closer to the parliamentary model than to the American presidential model. This is so for a number of reasons:

1. By holding the power of dissolution (Article 12) over parliament, the French President can "interfere directly" with parliamentary organization and activity. The American President, of course, cannot.
2. By dissolving parliament the French President can, like the British Prime Minister, create a plebiscitory situation to receive popular support for his actions. The American President, of course, cannot dissolve the legislature.
3. The President has vast emergency powers under Article 16, with no judicial oversight as exists in the United States with the judicial review of the Supreme Court.[43]

The Prime Minister

Given the dominant role of the president in the French political system, it should be fairly clear that the role of the prime minister in the Fifth Republic will be of considerably *less* significance than it is in most parliamentary systems. (It should be noted that the formal title of the chief executive in France is "prime minister," not "premier." "Premier" was used in the Third and Fourth Republics, and is still often used today as an incorrect holdover from former regimes.)

In the French system the role of the prime minister "has been limited to a joint formulation of policy with the President (in which the premier has played an increasingly subordinate role), and to manage the legislature so that it will accept the government's program."[44] One student of the French political system has suggested that in the Fifth Republic the prime minister is "merely the 'head of government,' while the president is the actual decision-maker. He leaves to the premier the role of being a link between the president and Parliament, particularly on matters the president is not interested in."[45]

Having said that the prime minister is the very junior partner of the "dual executive," in terms of the division of executive power, it should be pointed out that:

> the premier and his government have become a great deal stronger than ever before in their relations with the Assembly.
>   Among the new rights accorded to the government by the Fifth Republic . . . are the right to the priority of government bills in the parliamentary timetable, the right to propose amendments to bills, and the right to open a general debate on a measure in either chamber. Thus deputies now hear the government's case on a bill before the *rapporteur* of the relevant committee can present his criticisms, and the debate takes place on the government's text, not the text that emerges from committee. Moreover, the government has the right to reject amendments proposed from the floor after the committee stage and also to force the chamber to vote either on particular clauses of the bill or on the bill as a whole. The government can also spur a decision on a bill over which there is disagreement between the Senate and the Assembly. What the government cannot do, however, is to secure the passage of a bill (unless it is on finance) that the Assembly refuses to approve.[46]

The President, Prime Minister, and Cohabitation

The model of French politics described above seemed to operate reasonably well until the election of 1986. In April and May of 1981 François Mitterrand was elected president, the first time a Socialist had been elected president of France. One of his first actions was to dissolve the (conservative-dominated) National Assembly and call for new elections, producing a Socialist-dominated legislature. At that point he appointed a Socialist prime minister, Pierre Mauroy, and everything continued normally until the next elections.

However, by the time elections for the National Assembly arrived—something we shall discuss in more detail later—the Socialists had lost much of their glamour and captured only 216 out of 577 seats in the Assembly. President Mitterrand invited Jacques Chirac, leader of the largest party within the majority (conservative) coalition, to become prime minister, and he and Chirac agreed to a new power-sharing arrangement between the (Socialist) president and the (conservative) prime minister, something that came to be called *cohabitation*.[47] For the duration of

Mitterrand's term, his powers were considerably reduced from their pre-1986 level, and the powers of the prime minister were considerably greater than they had been previously.[48]

The Legislature

The Legislature and the Government

The executive branch dominates the legislative process in a number of ways in the Fifth Republic. Two of these forms of domination are functions of direct limitation on the power of the legislature. First, the legislature cannot propose "increasing expenditures or lowering revenue in relation to the details of and total range of government budgetary proposals."[49] Second, the legislature can only pass laws dealing with matters that are specifically delegated to it in the constitution. Each of these points is of sufficient significance to warrant further discussion.

The budgetary process in any political system is a point of vulnerability for the Government. Governments that are unable to have their budgets passed may find themselves at the mercy of their respective legislatures, literally unable to carry on the business of governing. The Fifth Republic's constitution places strong restrictions on the legislature's ability to obstruct or delay the Government in the budgetary arena.

> The Fifth Republic has streamlined budgetary procedures by giving the Assembly only forty days in which to vote on the government's proposals, thereafter the budget goes automatically to the Senate for two weeks. Differences are debated in conference committee. But if parliament does not vote the budget within seventy days, the government may bring it into effect by ordinance. Under any circumstances, the six-sevenths of the budget for "continuing services" must become law without change, and under Article 40 no deputy can propose increasing expenditures or lowering revenue in relation to the details of and total range of government budgetary proposals.[50]

The knowledge that the essence of the Government's budget will become law in any case, and the limitations imposed upon the legislature in terms of changes it can and cannot propose to the Government's budget, place the legislature at a severe disadvantage in relation to the Government.

In addition, the 1958 constitution departed from "the traditional French republican principle of unrestricted parliamentary sovereignty" by specifically listing the legislative powers of parliament (Article 34), indicating those areas in which parliament could legislate; fields not specifically reserved for the legislature were left to the Government "to decide by decree."

> This arrangement, which might seem like a serious encroachment on the power of Parliament, is not highly restrictive for two reasons. First, no subject of central importance is omitted from the list. Second, the list can be extended by Parliament through the adoption of an organic law (a law implementing provisions of the Constitution). The procedure for the adoption of an organic law is different from that required for ordinary laws, but a determined Parliament could easily extend its legislative jurisdiction. The main difference between organic laws and ordinary laws is that in the absence of agreement between the two chambers after a joint conference committee has met, the National Assembly must make the final decision by a majority of all its legal members in the case of an organic law, while a majority only of those voting is sufficient for an ordinary law. Organic laws affecting the Senate must be agreed to by the Senate, while the approval of the Senate can be dispensed with for ordinary legislation if the Government can secure the approval of the National Assembly.[51]

In addition to the two aspects of executive dominance indicated above, there are a number of other ways in which the executive is able to influence the legislative process. First, the Government controls the agenda of the National Assembly, and "by means of its power to determine the agenda the government can insure that its bills have priority over 'private members'." The Government has the power to stipulate which portions of its legislative proposals can be amended, and how much time can be spent on each section of the bill.

Moreover, the Government can call for a "blocked vote" requiring the legislative chambers to vote on a bill in its original text "incorporating only those amendments proposed or accepted by the government."[52] As a more severe action, the Government can announce that it is making the passage of a bill into a question of confidence. If it does this, the bill automatically passes "unless a censure motion is filed by one-tenth of the deputies within 24 hours and an absolute majority of the deputies vote in support of censure."[53]

The question of the relation between the Government and the National Assembly over the concept of "censure" or "confidence" is interesting, because it is another area in which the usual vulnerability of the executive branch to the will of the legislature has been modified from the "standard" model. Although some texts declare that "if a motion of censure is adopted by the National Assembly, the Government must resign,"[54] this rule of thumb has not always been followed.

The French president has the right to dissolve the National Assembly virtually at will, and Charles de Gaulle on more than one occasion dissolved the National Assembly when it censured his prime minister and Government. He then immediately reappointed the same prime minister and cabinet without their having resigned.

The censure process is more difficult to operate in France than it is in many parliamentary systems, although it is not as difficult as we shall see to be the case with the German "positive vote of no confidence." Opposition members can introduce motions of censure if the motion is signed by one-tenth of the deputies of the National Assembly (totalling 491). After the motion is introduced, 48 hours must pass before it can be debated and voted on; in order for it to pass, the motion must receive an absolute majority of deputies' support (half plus one of the 491 deputies), not just a majority of deputies present and voting. Opposition members who sign a motion of censure are enjoined from being cosignatories of another such motion during the same legislative session; this is designed to prevent a constant stream of motions that are sure to be defeated.[55]

Although the National Assembly may pass motions censuring the Government, or withdrawing its support from the Government, it may not "pass resolutions or otherwise express its views on policy unless the government asks it to do so." The reason for this is that "the framers of the constitution of the Fifth Republic wanted to maintain the ultimate control of the National Assembly over the Government without permitting either the National Assembly or the Senate to become policymaking agencies."[56]

The Senate

In 1947 the founders of the Fourth Republic decided to do away with the Senate as the second half of the legislative body in the (then) new regime. Their argument was that the Senate was (1) undemocratically selected, since it was not directly elected by the people; (2) overrepresentative of rural areas; and (3) either redundant or antidemocratic; if it agreed with the lower house it was redundant and therefore unnecessary, and if it disagreed with the popularly elected lower house it was antidemocratic, since the lower house *was* popularly elected and the Senate was not. After some discussion, a weak "Council of the Republic" was substituted for the Senate in the Fourth Republic.

In 1958 Charles de Gaulle brought back the second house to the French legislative system.

> During the Third Republic, the Senate was a very powerful legislative chamber. It was virtually equal to the Assembly in the sense that the Senate could render an absolute veto over an Assembly bill. . . . In the Fourth Republic the Senate was abolished. . . . The founding fathers of the Fifth Republic, among them notably Michel Debré, wished to restore the Senate to the position it had occupied in the Third Republic. . . .[57]

The Senate is sometimes referred to as the "agricultural" chamber of the legislature, because it tends to overrepresent rural areas of France. The unit of representation in the Senate is the *department*; the number of senators representing a given department varies from one or two to over five, depending upon the size and population of the department. The precise manner by which senators are selected will be discussed further; here we are interested in the Senate's role in the French legislative system.

Generally speaking, the Senate is the inferior of the two legislative bodies in France today. Although the founding fathers sought to restore the Senate to the position of legislative equality it had enjoyed in the Third Republic, today its position actually falls far short of that target. This inferior position can be measured in a number of ways. For instance, the Senate meets less frequently than does the Assembly. Between 1959 and 1974, the Senate met an average of 66 times a year, while the National Assembly met an average of 91 times a year in the same period—almost 50 percent more frequently. As another indicator, in the

1959–1977 period only 245 bills introduced by legislators became laws (as compared with 1,617 bills introduced by the Government); of these only 23 percent originated in the Senate.[58]

We do not want to *over*state the argument for the Senate's inferior position.[59] The Senate sometimes can be an effective legislative body in terms of its ability to provide a "sober second thought" to legislative proposals, especially to Government proposals. This is true for very much the same reason as it is for the House of Lords in Britain. Because the Government is responsible to the lower house, and can be fired by the lower house, party discipline will keep criticism in that body to a minimum. The upper house, to which the Government is *not* responsible, often has more freedom to inquire and criticize than does the lower house. An additional basis of power for the Senate in France is more parallel to the upper house in Germany (the Bundesrat) than to the House of Lords in Britain; although France is not a federal regime, senators represent geographical districts, or departments, and when Government bills deal with regional issues, agriculture, or similar questions, the Senate is likely to play a more significant role in the legislative process than it otherwise would.

The Legislative Process

This having been said, it must be noted again that the Senate of the Fifth Republic is not an equal partner in the legislative process, regardless of the desires of Michel Debré and others of the founding fathers in 1958. The legislative process in the Fifth Republic is clearly dominated by the Government in the National Assembly, with the Senate often not much more than an afterthought in the process.

> As in the Fourth Republic, and in Britain, West Germany, and Italy, a distinction is made between government bills (*projets de loi*) and private members' bills (*propositions de loi*), with the former accounting for most of the bills introduced in the Assembly. When a bill is introduced, it is sent first to the *bureau*; and the speaker, who heads that unit, transmits the bill directly to a legislative committee. When the committee has done its work, the *rapporteur* formally reports the bill to the floor for what is technically the initial "reading" of it. The ensuing debate, which provides an opportunity for the introduction of amendments, is followed by a

vote. After its passage by the Assembly, the bill is transmitted to the Senate. If that chamber accepts the original version of the bill, it is sent to the government for signature. If the Senate rejects the bill, the subsequent procedure varies. There can be a resort to the shuttle (*navette*)—the sending of a bill back and forth between the two chambers until a common version is achieved; second, the government may request the establishment of a conference committee (*commission mixte paritaire*); third, the government may ask each chamber for a "second reading" (i.e., a reconsideration and new vote on the original bill); and fourth, if disagreement persists, the government may ask the Assembly to determine the final version of the bill by simple majority vote.[60]

The Government's ability to select among these several options when interchamber disagreement arises in the legislative process gives it a great deal of power. Ultimately, the Government can choose to simply ignore the Senate and ask the National Assembly to determine the final version of a bill. If the National Assembly wants to pass a bill that the Government does not want, it can simply let the *navette* go on endlessly, or keep the bill off the agenda. Finally, of course, if the Government finds both chambers noncompliant, it has the ultimate power to couple a "blocked vote" with a question of confidence to force its proposals through the legislative process.

The Constitutional Council

"France has no tradition of judicial review. . . . The sovereignty of parliament means that the legislature has the last word and that a law enacted in constitutionally prescribed form is not subject to further scrutiny."[61] In spite of this, the Constitutional Council of the Fifth Republic was designed (Articles 56–63 of the Constitution) "to ensure that constitutional provisions would possess a certain superiority over ordinary laws." Its function is to rule on the standing orders of the legislature and, on request of the Government majority (but not a legislative minority), to determine the boundaries of executive and legislative competence and "whether laws . . . or treaties are in conformity with the constitution."[62] It also is required to supervise presidential and parliamentary elections, as well as referenda.

Many people in 1958 feared the creation of a Constitutional Council as it was described at the time because it sounded very much like the U.S. Supreme Court; the powers of the U.S. Supreme Court were thought to be too sweeping to transplant to the French system. The fears of an activist judiciary have not been realized, however, primarily because members of the Constitutional Council were generally sympathetic to Government policy. Three of the nine regular judges are appointed by the president, three by the president of the National Assembly, and three by the president of the Senate. The nine judges serve nine-year terms. Former presidents of the Republic are on the Constitutional Council for life terms.

The bulk of the Constitutional Council's work has been in adjudicating jurisdictional disputes between the presidency and the legislature "over boundaries of law and regulation." The Constitutional Council so consistently ruled on behalf of the president's point of view that it became perceived as an "auxiliary of executive authority."[63]

> By the end of 1963, the Constitutional Council had decided 31 disputes over the respective rule-making powers of the Parliament and the Government. In 22 cases it decided that the rule-making power in question was properly the Government's; in four it decided that the proper jurisdiction was parliamentary, and in the others there was either no decision or a decision dividing the rule-making power between the Government and Parliament.[64]

Party Politics and the Electoral Process

There have traditionally been a number of political parties active in the French political system. In modern times, it was not until "the Fifth Republic that France possessed a majority party," the UNR-UDR (Union for a New Republic–Democratic Union for the Republic).[65] Throughout French history, the political party systems that existed failed to provide a basis for stable elections; the parties failed to govern. "In a fragmented multiparty system elections never conferred the right to govern upon a majority, no party saw as its role support for the government of the day and the defense of its record before the electorate."[66] Henry Ehrmann has written:

> The inconveniences of the French multiparty system were compounded by the constitutional arrangements and parliamentary

practices of the Third and Fourth Republics. To survive and to govern effectively, a government needed more than just the absence of a majority willing to overthrow it; it needed a positive majority in favor of the government's policy and its legislative proposals. This, however, was difficult to obtain where majorities consisted not of disciplined parties or of parliamentary groups kept in line by an effective whip, but to a large extent of ephemeral coalitions. Their cohesion or disruption depended on whatever problem was under consideration. As different problems came up, governments toppled or were condemned to immobility."[67]

General Charles de Gaulle, in his criticisms of the Government in the Fourth Republic, described this anarchic situation of no responsible government and no responsible opposition as *"le régime des partis."*[68] It was strictly speaking, a regime *with* parties, not a regime of parties. Party *control* (in the sense of stable party government) of the regime did not come until de Gaulle's supporters won parliamentary majorities in the Fifth Republic.

Gaullism and Presidential Leadership

Certainly among the most significant modern phenomena in the French party system must be considered to be the rise of the Gaullist "nonparty" that became institutionalized as the significant political organization of the regime. Originally, Gaullism was a movement of support for Charles de Gaulle that claimed to be an alternative to divisive political parties; both organizationally and ideologically it insisted upon being regarded simply as a following for de Gaulle. Its ideology was the ideology of de Gaulle; its organization was designed to further the interests and goals of de Gaulle. It "pretended not to be a party at all, but rather a national *movement*, an alternative to parties."[69]

We can see the roots of the Gaullist movement as having developed prior to the creation of the Fifth Republic. De Gaulle's speeches attacking the weakness of the Fourth Republic led to the creation of the RPF, the Rally of the French People, in the mid-1940s. In 1947 the RPF won more than a third of the votes cast in municipal elections nationwide. The party continued to grow, and in the 1951 parliamentary elections it captured slightly more than 20 percent of the popular vote.[70] In 1958 when de Gaulle was called to power by the National Assembly, a new group was organized to serve as an organizational base upon which his leadership could be founded. The Union for a New Republic (UNR) was established in October 1958 as a point around which groups supporting de Gaulle could rally.

The Gaullist ideology was perceived as a rightist ideology because of de Gaulle's pro-business attitudes and his frequent indifference to socioeconomic political issues. However, the Gaullist party was able to draw from the political left as well as the political right because of de Gaulle's antiparliamentary attitudes, shared with the Communist party (the PCF), his positive view of the Church, which was shared with the Popular Republican Movement (MRP), and his commitment to plebiscitary democracy and frequent referenda, generally a left-wing attitude. In 1962 the UNR combined with a generally conservative working-class party called the Democratic Union of Labor to form the Democratic Union for the Republic (UDR).

When de Gaulle left the political scene and Georges Pompidou, his former prime minister, became president, the Gaullist movement weakened somewhat, but not as much or as rapidly as many had predicted it would. Pompidou's presidency "was no period of dramatic social and economic change. By now the broad lines of French development were clearly fixed and Pompidou continued the course set in the 1960s."[71] Many had claimed that the UDR, and Gaullism in general, were simply personalistic followings for de Gaulle; as soon as de Gaulle left politics, the critics said, the Gaullists as a political bloc would fall apart.

Pompidou reigned over the demise of the UDR between 1970 and 1974. By the time of the parliamentary elections in 1973, the UDR had so weakened that it joined with the Independent Republicans and the Center of Democracy and Progress (CDP) in an electoral alliance called the Union of Republicans for Progress (URP), but even with that its parliamentary representation fell from 273 seats in 1968 to 185 in 1973.

With the election of Valéry Giscard d'Estaing as president in 1974, the UDR became an "also-ran." Giscard, an Independent Republican, drew a good deal of what was left in the UDR to the Independent Republican party. The Giscard years were associated with economic liberalism, a theme of national unity, and a "more liberal functioning of institutions,"[72] the latter including a slight increase of the power of the legislature compared to earlier regimes.

The year 1981 saw the rise to prominence of the Socialist party under President François Mitterrand. In the 1981 campaign many of the principal issues were economic, and Mitterrand was able to convince a majority of the French voters that they should give the political left a chance to lead France. Mitterrand became the first Socialist to be elected president, and he immediately dissolved the National Assembly and called for new elections so that he could have a Socialist-dominated Assembly to help enact his program. The Socialists, riding on the coattails of the newly elected president, won a clear majority (262 of the 491 seats), and with their non-Communist allies controlled 285 seats in the National Assembly. With a clear majority in the legislature, Mitterrand was able to implement a number of Socialist policies.[73]

The perception at the time was that the "intention of the French Socialist administration, presided over by Mitterrand, was 'to give the state back to the people.' "[74] Mitterrand believed that centralization had been necessary in the creation of France, but at the time of his election decentralization was necessary for the future of France. Mitterrand was a political realist, recognizing that the forces which elected him were as much a response to the economic climate of the time as they were indications of fundamental agreement with his ideology.[75] However:

> the euphoria which surrounded the Socialists' victory became short-lived. Despite commitments to a substantially higher rate of economic growth and to a sharp decline in unemployment, the reality of their first years in government proved very different. Stimulating demand failed to revive a sluggish economy and unemployment continued its inexorable rise.[76]

Public reaction against the Mitterrand Government and some of its policies led to a decline in public support for the Socialists. In local elections in 1982 and 1983 many of the supporters who had worked so hard for Mitterrand in 1981 supported conservative candidates, and the conservative parties made great progress. In the long view, "the years of socialist government did not produce the revolution of which many of its supporters dreamed." Social inequality and injustice did not disappear; the economy did not expand as promised. "Instead economic growth proved sluggish and many of the basic divisive features of society showed themselves highly resilient to change."[77]

In March 1986 the "French socialist experience"[78] came to an end with a conservative victory in the elections for the National Assembly, resulting in the *cohabitation* arrangement between Socialist President Mitterrand and conservative Prime Minister Chirac discussed earlier. The conservatives thought that this was a foreshadowing of a presidential victory in 1988, but such was not the case and President Mitterrand, with a much more economically moderate and ideologically toned-down campaign than he had run in 1981, defeated Prime Minister Chirac and won reelection to the presidency.

French Political Parties

The political party system of contemporary France presents a broad spectrum of ideologies to the observer, with parties in existence representing a variety of shades of public opinion from the far left to the far right. Most contemporary texts dealing with French politics[79] discuss the party system in terms of component parties, and move from left to right (or right to left) along the political spectrum describing the respective ideologies and policy positions of the many contemporary French parties.[80]

The number of political parties has varied over the years, with various temporary and permanent alliances and coalitions affecting the number and structures of political organizations active at any given time. Moreover, a number of political parties have changed their names over the years, so at first glance it is often difficult to follow the evolution of the parties over time.

This point of temporary electoral alliances between parties is worth noting. Because of the nature of the electoral system—a point to which we shall turn shortly—many parties have decided that although they are not going to *merge* permanently with one another, their views are sufficiently similar so that they should not compete *against* each other in elections. This type of attitude gave rise to the Union of Republicans for Progress (URP) in 1973, leading to a coordination of candidacies around France among the Independent Republican Party, the Democratic Union for the Republic (UDR), and the Center for Democracy and Progress. The same thing happened in the elections of 1978 and 1981 with the French Democratic Union (UDF) resulting from coordination among the Republican Party (PR, formed by Giscard from the Independent Republican Party in 1977), the Center for Social

Democrats (CDS, a new party organized from the earlier CDP), and some others.

Elections to the National Assembly

If France were a "typical" parliamentary system, we would have only elections to the national legislature to study at this point. However, because of de Gaulle's 1962 referendum—to have the president directly elected by the citizenry rather than indirectly elected by a complex electoral college as had been the case previously—any discussion of French elections must include both presidential and parliamentary elections. We will begin our brief discussion with the National Assembly, move to the presidency, and conclude with a discussion of selection of the senators.

French elections for the National Assembly are for terms of five years (or less if the Assembly is dissolved early) and for the most part have been based upon a *majority* approach to voting rather than a *plurality* approach, as is the case in Britain (or the United States). That is, in electoral contests for the National Assembly the initial question that is asked on election day after the polls close is *not* "Who received the most votes?" The reader will recall that in single-member district, plurality voting systems, the candidate who receives the most votes is the winner; if there are six candidates and the candidate with the most votes receives only 25 percent of the total vote, that candidate is elected even though 75 percent of the electorate did not vote for him or her. In majority-based elections, unlike the plurality-based elections, to win a race on the first ballot one must receive a majority of the vote.

We said earlier that French elections for the National Assembly have "for the most part been based upon a majority approach" because for about one year—from March 1986 until June 1987—the electoral system was changed from universal direct election as described below to a proportional representation electoral system. (That is, proportional representation within departments, not nationally, with a 5 percent threshold necessary for election.)[81] Proportional representation replaced the single-member-district model when it became clear to President Mitterrand that his Socialist party faced an overwhelming rejection by the voters in the election of March 1986.

With the majority voting system and only a 30 percent level

of public opinion support, the Socialists would very likely have become a tiny minority in the Assembly. With proportional representation voting, the Socialists won 206 out of 577 seats in the National Assembly, but the parties of the right controlled a majority in the Assembly and a conservative government was formed. This was the period of *cohabitation* we referred to earlier. The system of proportional representation elections "generated a storm from political elites, indifference from the public, and a commitment by the new government to get rid of it again."[82] Within a year of the election the new conservative-dominated government restored the former electoral system.[83]

When the presidential elections were held in April-May 1988 and President Mitterrand was reelected, he again—much as he did immediately after his first electoral victory seven years earlier—dissolved the National Assembly and called for new elections. Again, as in 1981, the French public gave the left a majority in the Assembly, although the Socialist party alone did not receive the outright majority in 1988 that it did in 1981, and it had to make arrangements with the Communists to maintain a majority.

Given the number of political parties in the French electoral system, it is clear that few candidates will win majorities outright. This has led to France's unique two-ballot "simple majority" system of voting.[84] To be a candidate for the National Assembly, an individual must post a deposit of 1,000 francs (about $200), which is refunded if the candidate receives at least 5 percent of the vote. The first election is held on a Sunday, and a candidate who receives an absolute majority (50 percent of the vote plus one vote) of the total votes cast in his or her district is elected on the first round of balloting.[85] If no candidate wins a majority on the first ballot, a second ballot is held on the following Sunday. At that time, whichever candidate receives a *plurality* of the votes is declared the winner. (See Table 10.3.)

Elections to the National Assembly on the first ballot are the exception rather than the rule. In the June 1988 parliamentary elections only 122 of 577 races (21.1 percent) were decided on the first ballot.[86]

When the second round of elections are held, no new candidate for office may register. In order to contest the second ballot, a candidate must have received 12.5 percent of the vote on the first round. (This was 10 percent in the 1978 election). Although this means that technically several candidates could compete in the second round of voting (since more than two candidates could receive 12.5 percent of the vote on the first round), most second ballots turn out to be duels between two parties because of the alliances that we mentioned earlier.

For example, the Republican party and the Center of Social Democrats may sign a preelection agreement within the framework of the UDF that they would both compete in the first round, but that the second place party of the two would bow out in the second round and throw its support to the other in order to help defeat the Socialist party or Communist party candidate in the district.

This type of preelectoral alliance/agreement has had the effect in many cases of turning the first ballot into a kind of primary election, in which a number of candidates from the left may compete, and a number of candidates from the right may compete, with the understanding that the top vote-getter from the left will "represent" the left, and the top vote-getter from the right will "represent" the right. "The parties of the left have agreed at every election since 1962 . . . that only one candidate of the left shall remain at the second ballot and that it shall be he who scored most votes at the first."[87]

Presidential Elections

The electoral system for the presidency is essentially the same. Anyone can be a candidate for president, providing he or she puts up 10,000 francs ($2,000, which is forfeited if the candidate fails to receive at least 5 percent of the vote), as well as nominating petitions signed by 100 "notables" (National Assembly deputies,

Table 10.3
The Parliamentary Election of 1988

Left		Right		Other	
Socialists + allies	276	URC + allies	271	Independents	2
Communists	27	National Front	1		
Total	303		272		

Total members in National Assembly: 577
Absolute majority in National Assembly: 289

Source: *The Times* (London), June 14, 1988, p. 1.

senators, mayors, or departmental councillors). Candidates are given free TV and radio time by the state.

A candidate must receive an absolute majority of the public votes in order to win on the first ballot. This has never happened in Fifth Republic France; the most votes that Charles de Gaulle ever received on the first ballot was 44 percent of the total votes cast. The second ballot is limited to the top two vote-getters from the first round, and takes place two weeks after the first round of voting.

As the data in Table 10.4 show, it is possible to win (receive a plurality) on the first ballot and lose on the second ballot. In the April 26, 1981, first-round voting for the presidency, the incumbent, Valéry Giscard d'Estaing, won a plurality with 28.3 percent of the vote, with François Mitterrand coming in second place with 25.9 percent of the vote. On the second ballot, Republican Giscard received the votes of the rightist voters, and Socialist Mitterrand received the support of the leftist voters. The combined leftist vote defeated the combined rightist vote. On the other hand, in the 1988 presidential election (Table 10.5) President Mitterrand re-

Table 10.4
The French Presidential Election of 1981

Candidate	No. Votes	Percentage of Vote
First Round: April 26, 1981		
V. Giscard d'Estaing[a]	8,222,432	28.3
F. Mitterrand	7,505,960	25.9
J. Chirac	5,225,848	18.0
G. Marchais	4,456,922	15.3
B. LaLonde	1,126,254	3.9
A. LaGuiller	668,057	2.3
M. Crepeau	642,847	2.2
M. Debré	481,821	1.7
M.-F. Garaud	386,623	1.3
H. Bouchardeau	321,353	1.1
Second Round: May 10, 1981		
F. Mitterrand	15,708,262	51.75
V. Giscard d'Estaing	14,642,306	48.24

[a]Incumbent.

Source: Dominique and Michele Fremy, eds., *Quid* (Paris: Éditions Robert Laffont, 1981), p. 755.

Table 10.5
The FrenchPresidential Election of 1988

Candidate	No. Votes	Percentage of Vote
First Round: April 24, 1988		
F. Mitterrand[a]	10,381,332	34.1
J. Chirac	6,075,160	20.0
R. Barre	5,035,144	16.5
J.-M. Le Pen	4,376,742	14.4
A. LaJoinie	2,056,261	6.8
A. Waechter	1,149,897	3.8
P. Juquin	639,133	2.1
A. LaGuiller	606,201	2.0
P. Boussel	116,874	0.4
Second Round: May 8, 1988		
F. Mitterrand	16,704,279	54.02
J. Chirac	14,218,970	45.98

[a]Incumbent.

Source: Dominique and Michele Fremy, eds., *Quid* (Paris: Éditions Robert Laffont, 1989), p. 727.

ceived a plurality on the first ballot with 34.1 percent of the vote, and went on to win on the second ballot with 54 percent of the vote.[88]

Election of Senators

The selection of senators differs from the single-member-district, majority voting selection of deputies to the National Assembly. Senators are intended to represent the administrative/territorial units of France, and the method of their selection reflects this.

Senators are elected for terms of nine years by "indirect universal suffrage."[89] The department is the unit of representation; senators are elected from departments by departmental electoral colleges. These electoral colleges range from 270 electors in smaller departments, to over 6,000 electors in the larger departments, depending on the population of the department.[90] Deputies in the National Assembly from districts in a given department, departmental councillors, and delegates chosen by municipal councils—all comprise these electoral colleges. Thus

Table 10.6
The 1986–1989 French Senate

Party	Number of Members
UDF, Centrist, other right	154
RPR and allies	77
Socialists	64
PCF	15
MRG	9
Total	319

Abbreviations:
  UDF: Union pour la Démocratie Française: center-right
  RPR: Rassemblement pour la Republique: neo-Gaullist
  PCF: Parti Communiste Français: Communist
  MRG: Mouvement des Radicaux de Gauche: center-left

Source: Adapted from Ian Derbyshire, *Politics in France: From Giscard to Mitterrand* (London: W & R Chambers, 1987), p. 131.

the Senate is elected by the 577 National Assembly deputies, about 3,000 *conseillers généraux*, and about 100,000 delegates from the municipal councils.[91] (See Table 10.6.)

The larger departments (seven in all) elect five or more senators; smaller departments will choose fewer. In the departments that choose five or more senators, senators are chosen by PR (proportional representation) voting, electors vote for a party list, and parties receive a number of senatorial positions corresponding to the proportion of the vote they received. In the smaller departments, senators are elected on a two-ballot system very similar to elections for the National Assembly, a majority is required on the first ballot, and a plurality is required on the second ballot.

The Senate is often referred to as an "agricultural chamber" because of its malrepresentation of the French population. "Rural France is overrepresented and urban France is underrepresented in the Senate." For example, "the eight departments of the Paris Region, plus five other departments which each had more than one million inhabitants . . . contain one-third of the French population, and while they have 32 percent of the . . . seats in the

National Assembly, they have only 26 percent of such seats in the Senate."[92]

Although senators serve nine-year terms, Senate elections are held every three years. The Senate is divided into three equal groups, referred to as Series A (102 seats), Series B (102 seats), and Series C (117 seats, of which 115 are elected), determined by an alphabetical list of departments.[93] One group is elected each three years.

Summary

We have seen in this chapter that the French political system can almost be seen as a variation of the Westminster model of government in several respects, many of them quite significant. The dual executive, although resembling the British model on paper, is quite different in its actual day-to-day behavior and power structure. The French president is virtually one of a kind (except for political systems modelled after France) in the parliamentary world, having both in theory and in practice all of the power that the British monarchy has only in theory.

The French Constitution is partially responsible for this. When Charles de Gaulle and his colleagues designed the constitutional structures in the Fifth Republic, they took pains to provide for strong executive leadership, to a large extent to compensate for years of weak executives and strong, and uncontrollable, legislatures. The fact that the legislatures in both the Third and Fourth Republics were unstable foundations upon which to base a government was not lost on the founders of the Fifth Republic.

The legislative bodies of the Fifth Republic are typical of other parliamentary legislatures in a number of respects. First, of course, they are inferior to the executive branch of government. The legislature is *not* expected to be a major policy-making body in the political system. Its function is to approve the policies of the executive, and, if the executive becomes too unpopular, to replace the Government. Second, the upper house of the legislature is inferior to the lower house of the legislature. Ultimately, the Senate can have only a suspensory veto over the actions of the National Assembly; it can slow down the actions of that house, but it cannot prevent National Assembly legislation from becoming law.

French elections differ from elections in other political systems because of the single-member-district, majority voting system used for the National Assembly, and the two-wave voting for the presidency, and again we see that the structure of the electoral system can have an impact on the political party system in a country. France has a number of political parties, not just one or two, and these parties do their best to operate within the rules of the Fifth Republic's electoral system.

In the French case, then, we have been able to see a number of applications of the material we described in the first part of this book. Constitutions, executives, legislatures, electoral systems, and political parties all matter in the day-to-day operation of a political regime. We will continue to see in the chapters that follow that some of the idiosyncratic features of political regimes are of tremendous significance in the daily operation of government.

Notes

1. Roy Pierce, *French Politics and Political Institutions* (New York: Harper & Row, 1968), p. 2.
2. Gwendolen Carter, *The Government of France* (New York: Harcourt Brace Jovanovich, 1972), p. 20. See also William Safran, *The French Polity* (New York: David McKay, 1977), p. 6.
3. John Ambler, *The Government and Politics of France* (Boston: Houghton Mifflin, 1971), pp. 3–4.
4. William Safran, *The French Polity*, 2nd ed. (New York: Longman, 1985), p. 5.
5. Ambler, *Government and Politics of France*, p. 7.
6. Carter, *Government of France*, p. 22.
7. Ambler, *Government and Politics of France*, p. 7.
8. Carter, *Government of France*, p. 23.
9. See Stanley Hoffman, "Aspects du Régime de Vichy," *Revue Français de Science Politique* 6 (1956): 44–69.
10. Carter, *Government of France*, p. 25.
11. Ambler, *Government and Politics of France*, p. 10.
12. The best general discussions of problems and performances of the Fourth Republic are to be found in three sources: Philip Williams, *Crisis and Compromise: Politics in the Fourth Republic* (New York: Doubleday, 1966); Duncan MacRae, *Parliament, Parties, and Society in France: 1946–1958* (New York: St. Martin's Press, 1967); and François Goguel, *France Under the Fourth Republic* (Ithaca, N.Y.: Cornell University Press, 1952).
13. Ambler, *Government and Politics of France*, p. 11.
14. Ibid., p. 11.
15. Pierce, *French Politics and Political Institutions*, p. 44.

16. Safran, *The French Polity*, 2nd ed., p. 11.

17. Ambler, *Government and Politics of France*, p. 13.

18. See the text of de Gaulle's Bayeux speech in Martin Harrison, ed., *French Politics* (Lexington, Mass.: D.C. Heath, 1969), pp. 24–28.

19. Safran, *The French Polity*, 2nd ed., pp. 127–28.

20. Ibid., p. 59.

21. Roy C. Macridis, *French Politics in Transition* (Cambridge, Mass.: Winthrop, 1975), p. 6.

22. On the origins and drafting of the new constitution, see Nicholas Wahl and Stanley Hoffman, "The French Constitution of 1958," *American Political Science Review* 53 (1959): 332–382. See Michel Debré's essay "The New Constitution" in Harrison, *French Politics*, pp. 31–33.

23. Suzanne Berger, *The French Political System* (New York: Random House, 1974), p. 126. Much of the material in this section, and all quotes unless otherwise noted, derive from Berger, pp. 126–131.

24. Ibid., p. 127.

25. Ibid., p. 131.

26. Henry Ehrmann, *Politics in France* (Boston: Little, Brown, 1976), p. 267.

27. Ambler, *Government and Politics of France*, p. 125.

28. Safran, *The French Polity*, p. 128.

29. Berger, *The French Political System*, p. 40.

30. Leslie Derfler, *President and Parliament: A Short History of the French Presidency* (Boca Raton: University Presses of Florida, 1983), p. 169.

31. Ambler, *Government and Politics of France*, p. 126.

32. Pierce, *French Politics and Political Institutions*, pp. 62–63.

33. For the full text of the constitution, see Pierce, *French Politics and Political Institutions*, pp. 227–254, or Ambler, *Government and Politics of France*, pp. 237–248.

34. Berger, *The French Political System*, pp. 52–53.

35. Pierce, *French Politics and Political Institutions*, pp. 54–55.

36. Berger, *The French Political System*, p. 54.

37. Pierce, *French Politics and Political Institutions*, p. 54.

38. Ehrmann, *Politics in France*, p. 268.

39. See de Gaulle's essay "Charles de Gaulle and the Presidency," in Harrison, *French Politics*, pp. 48–54.

40. See Henry Ehrmann, "Direct Democracy in France," *American Political Science Review* 57 (1963): 883–901.

41. Ehrmann, *Politics in France*, p. 269.

42. Berger, *The French Political System*, p. 56.

43. Ehrmann, *Politics in France*, pp. 270–272.

44. Carter, *Government of France*, p. 81. See also Michel Debré's essay "The Need for a Prime Minister," and Merry Bromberger's essays "Georges Pompidou Becomes Prime Minister," and "President and Prime Minister: Two Conflicting Analyses," in Harrison, *French Politics*, pp. 65–78.

45. Safran, *The French Polity*, p. 130.

46. Carter, *The Government of France*, p. 83.

47. See John Frears, "Cohabitation," in Howard Penniman, *France at the Polls, 1981 and 1986: Three National Elections* (Durham, N.C.: Duke University Press, 1988) pp. 228–236.

48. A good description of this period can be found in Ian Derbyshire, *Politics in France: From Giscard to Mitterand* (London: W & R Chambers, 1987), pp. 105–114.

49. Carter, *Government of France*, p. 75.

50. Ibid., p. 75. See also Pierce, *French Politics and Political Institutions*, p. 87.
51. Pierce, *French Politics and Political Institutions*, pp. 78–79.
52. Philip E. Converse and Roy Pierce, *Political Representation in France* (Cambridge: Harvard University Press, 1986), p. 533.
53. Carter, *Government of France*, p. 72.
54. Pierce, *French Politics and Political Institutions*, p. 91.
55. Carter, *Government of France*, p. 72.
56. Pierce, *French Politics and Political Institutions*, p. 91.
57. Safran, *The French Polity*, p. 169.
58. Ibid., pp. 171–172.
59. See the essays by François Goguel, "The Role of the Senate," and Michel Debré, "The Future of the Senate," in Harrison, *French Politics*, pp. 114–118.
60. Safran, *The French Polity*, p. 165.
61. Carter, *Government of France,* p. 324.
62. Ibid., p. 323.
63. Berger, *The French Political System*, p. 57.
64. Pierce, *French Politics and Political Institutions*, p. 80.
65. Carter, *Government of France*, p. 39.
66. J. R. Frears, *Political Parties and Elections in the French Fifth Republic* (New York: St. Martin's Press, 1977), p. 12.
67. Ehrmann, *Politics in France*, pp. 223–224.
68. Frears, *Political Parties*, p. 12.
69. Safran, *The French Polity*, p. 68.
70. Dominique and Michele Fremy, eds., *Quid* (Paris: Éditions Robert Laffont, 1981), p. 747. This will henceforth be cited as *Quid.*
71. D. L. Hanley, A. P. Kerr, and N. H. Waites, *Contemporary France: Politics and Society Since 1945* (Boston: Routledge and Kegan Paul, 1979), p. 41.
72. J. R. Frears, *France in the Giscard Presidency* (London: Allen and Unwin, 1981), p. 162. See also the volume edited by Vincent Wright, *Continuity and Change in France* (London: Allen and Unwin, 1984), for a collection of essays offering a general description of the Giscard years.
73. A very good book about François Mitterand written before his candidacy is that by C. L. Manceron and B. Pingaud, *François Mitterand: L'Homme, Les Idées, Le Programme* (Paris: Flammarion, 1981).
74. Michael Keating and Paul Hainsworth, *Decentralisation and Change in Contemporary France* (Brookfield, Vt.: Gower, 1986), p. 15.
75. Maurice Larkin, *France Since the Popular Front: Government and People, 1936–1986* (Oxford: Clarendon Press, 1988), p. 356.
76. John Tuppen, *France Under Recession: 1981–1986* (Albany: State University of New York Press, 1988), p. 1.
77. Ibid., p. 257.
78. Sonia Mazey and Michael Newman, eds., *Mitterand's France* (London: Croom Helm, 1987), p. 4. A very good analysis of Mitterand's success/failure in the first years can be found in the chapter by Michael Newman, "Conclusion: The Balance Sheet," pp. 218–234.
79. See Berger, *The French Political System*, pp. 78–97; Ehrmann, *Politics in France*, pp. 226–262; Pierce, *French Politics and Political Institutions*, pp. 100–128; Carter, *Government of France*, pp. 40–49; Safran, *The French Polity*, pp. 74–97.
80. A very good survey of French parties is that edited by David S. Bell, *Contemporary French Political Parties* (New York: St. Martin's Press, 1981).

81. The exact operation of this proportional representation system can be found in John Frears, "The 1986 Parliamentary Elections," in Penniman, *France at the Polls*, pp. 211–214.
82. Ibid., p. 211.
83. See Dominique and Michele Fremy, *Quid 1989* (Paris: Éditions Robert Laffont, 1989), pp. 686, 732.
84. J. R. Frears and Jean-Luc Parodi, *War Will Not Take Place: The French Parliamentary Elections of March 1978* (New York: Holmes and Meier, 1979), p. 11. Much within the paragraphs that follow is based upon material from this source.
85. Unless turnout is very small and the candidate has received the votes of less than one-quarter of all of the registered electors.
86. *Quid, 1989*, p. 732–733.
87. Frears and Parodi, *War Will Not Take Place*, p. 12.
88. *Quid, 1989*, p. 727.
89. *Quid*, p. 705.
90. Pierce, *French Politics and Political Institutions*, p. 75.
91. Frears, *Political Parties*, p. 224. Each department has a council, called the *conseil général*, which consists of from about twenty to seventy members who are elected from subdivisions of the department, called *cantons*. Elections of departmental councillors (*conseillers généraux*) are called *elections cantonales*. Each city and town in France has a municipal council. Elections of municipal councillors are called *elections municipales*. See Pierce, *French Politics and Political Institutions*, p. 75.
92. Pierce, *French Politics and Political Institutions*, p. 75.
93. Dominique and Michele Fremy, *Quid, 1989*, p. 685.

11

The German Political System

The German Constitutional Framework

When World War II ended in 1945, the four Occupying Powers (the United States, the United Kingdom, France, and the Soviet Union) agreed to work toward an eventual reunification of the occupied German territories. By December 1947, however, at the London Conference of the Council of Foreign Ministers of the four Occupying Powers, it was becoming clear to the British, French, and American representatives that the Soviet Union was not prepared to move speedily to a "normalization" and reunification of Germany. Accordingly, the three Western powers decided to move forward and attempt to restore normal civilian government on their own.

Many of the German political leaders were concerned about this decision; they believed that such an action would result in a permanent division of Germany, with the Soviet Union controlling the eastern half of the country. On this ground, many West German leaders opposed the creation of a West German constitution until such time as Germany was reunified. After some discussion, a compromise was reached: The West Germans agreed to construct a "temporary" constitution that would serve as the basis of the political system until such time as Germany was reunified.

In September 1948 the Parliamentary Council met in Bonn and drafted a document called the *Basic Law* for the three Western Occupied Zones. According to its preamble, the Basic Law was designed to "give a new order to political life for a transitional period," and was constructed not only for the West Germans but also "on behalf of those Germans to whom participation was denied." Article 146 stated that the Basic Law "shall cease to be in force on the day on which a constitution adopted by a free decision of the German people comes into force."[1] The document was drafted by representatives of the three Western Occupying Powers and West German leaders acceptable to the Occupying Powers.

The construction of the Basic Law was finally completed in May 1949. To avoid the appearance of establishing a permanent political system, the Basic Law was never submitted to the West German people for ratification by popular approval. Rather, the Basic Law was submitted to the legislatures of the West German states, the Länder, and approved by that mechanism, winning the endorsement of all of the West German Länder except Bavaria.[2] The West German Basic Law was finally approved on May 23, 1949. And, just as so many West German leaders had feared, the German Democratic Republic (East Germany) came into existence less than a month later.

Just over forty-one years later, on October 2, 1990, East and West Germany reunited after four decades of partition and tension. The early years of the separation included a blockade of West Berlin; the most dramatic sign of the partition was a wall dividing the East and West parts of the city of Berlin. The reunited Germany, now the most populous and economically powerful nation in the European Community, adopted West Germany's constitutional system; the highly centralized political structures of communist East Germany disappeared. The period of reunification was a difficult one, with many Germans excited about the prospect of reuniting East and West Germany but at the same time concerned about the costs of reunification and the fear that their reunification and their new role as the largest and most economically powerful European nation might engender among other European nations.

Many details can be pointed out that distinguish the 1949 Basic Law from the Weimar Constitution of 1919 that preceded it. One of the major perceived shortcomings of the Weimar Constitution was that it actually promoted internal discord through a number of supposedly democratic structures, especially the power of the presidency and the mass plebiscites that were so frequently utilized. The Basic Law sought, through a number of political structures, to remedy the defect of "too much democracy"[3] in the earlier regime.

Essentially, the Basic Law sought to modify many of the structures of direct democracy that had existed earlier. Except in extraordinary circumstances, elections would be held every four years. Moreover, the public would vote *only* for representatives to the lower house of the legislature. The president, the chancellor, and members of the upper legislative house would all be chosen by indirect means. Additionally, structures were established to make it more difficult to overthrow chancellors with votes of no confidence, something to which we shall return later in this chapter.

Although the Basic Law sought to "dampen" or "modify" many of the (perceived) "overly democratic" structures of the Weimar regime, it did *not* intend correspondingly to restrict individual freedoms or rights. To the contrary: Articles of the Basic Law that deal with civil and political rights (Articles 1–19) are given a "preferred position" in the Basic Law; as one scholar has noted, "for the first time in German history, there were no loopholes left in the protection of individual rights."[4] Both Article 1, which focuses on human dignity, and Article 20, which guarantees Germans the "right to resist any person or persons seeking to abolish [the German] constitutional order," *cannot* be amended. Other articles dealing with civil and political rights cannot be suspended except after a ruling by the Federal Constitutional Court (Article 18).[5] The Basic Law can be amended by a two-thirds majority vote of each house of the federal legislature (subject to the limitations mentioned above), and "has been altered more often in twenty-five years than the American in two hundred."[6]

Federalism In Germany

Germany is the only major state of Western Europe that has a federal rather than a unitary political structure, and some have regarded this as "an unexpected state of affairs":

> The Federal Republic is no larger than Britain and more or less as densely populated. Socially the country is more homogeneous than at any time in the past. The economy is highly integrated on a nation-wide basis, and communications are very well developed. Culturally there are provincial variations, but these are probably less marked than in a number of other European countries of comparable size.[7]

After some reflection, however, German federalism should not be such a surprise. This is so for several reasons, including (1) a general fear of centralized government that developed during the Nazi period; (2) a history of federal and confederal relations in Germany, with the exception of the centralized Nazi era, going back to 1871 when the German Reich was formed and "composed of twenty-five 'historic' German states that 'voluntarily' entered into a federation"[8]; and (3) the pattern of administration of the Occupying Powers from 1945–1949 that led to the creation of seven of today's sixteen states or Länder (the singular of *Länder* is *Land*). Three of today's Länder existed as separate political entities prior to 1945.[9] Thus German federalism was "a device which perpetuated into the era of a single national state the particularist habits and traditions of the dynasties and estates which were dominant in the separate states of Germany."[10]

The federal nature of the German political system has resulted in wide disparities between and among the intermediate levels of political organization. The Länder vary greatly in size and in population, as illustrated in Table 11.1, on page 298.

The German federal system, often referred to as "cooperative federalism,"[11] gives the intermediate level components of the regime, the Länder, a great deal of political power, far more than is found in American states. There are a number of formal, constitutional mechanisms that help to institutionalize the power bases of the Länder. Article 28 of the Basic Law requires that the Länder "conform to the principles of republican, democratic, and social government based on the rule of law," but leaves questions of specific governmental structure, on the Länder level, up to the state governments. The state of Bavaria has a bicameral legislature; all others have unicameral legislatures. States are allowed to determine their own electoral structures.

It can be suggested that a major reason that the Länder are as powerful as they are in the German political system is due to the several different types of legislation discussed in the Basic Law. The Basic Law essentially balances centralized and decentralized powers by distinguishing among three different types of legislation.

Article 73 gives exclusive *federal jurisdiction* over legislation involving foreign affairs, citizenship, money, customs, immigration, federal railroads, post and telecommunications services, federal employees, copyrights, and cooperation of the central

Table 11.1
Länder in the German Federal System

Land	Area (in sq. mi.)	Population (in millions)	Bundesrat Seats
Baden-Württemberg	13,739	9.35	6
Bavaria	27,114	11.04	6
Berlin[a]	184	1.88	4
Brandenburg[a]	10,036	2.70	4
Bremen	155	0.65	3
Hamburg	287	1.57	3
Hesse	8,113	5.55	4
Lower Saxony	18,127	7.19	6
Mecklenburg-Vorpommern[a]	8,685	2.10	4
N. Rhine-Westphalia	13,084	16.67	6
Rhineland-Palatinate	7,621	3.61	4
Saarland	987	1.04	3
Saxony[a]	6,562	4.90	4
Saxony-Anhalt[a]	9,650	3.00	4
Schleswig-Holstein	6,018	2.61	4
Thuringia[a]	5,983	2.50	4

[a]Formerly part of the German Democratic Republic.

Source: Adapted from Guido Goldman, *The German Political System* (New York: Random House, 1974), pp. 155–156; M. Donald Hancock, *West Germany: The Politics of Democratic Corporatism* (Chatham, N.J.: Chatham House, 1989), p. 74; "Update Germany," Inter-Nationes Press, Bonn, Report SO–7–1990, p. 2.

government and Länder in criminal matters. The Länder are given *residual* powers in Article 70: "The Länder shall have the right to legislate insofar as this Basic Law does not confer legislative power on the Federation." Finally, Articles 72 and 74 list twenty-three specific areas in which *jurisdiction is concurrent*: The Länder may legislate in these areas "as long as, and to the extent that, the Federation does not exercise its right to legislate." Among these areas of concurrent jurisdiction would be included civil and criminal law; registration of births, deaths, marriages; issues related to public welfare; labor laws; regulation of education; road traffic and highways; and some health-related matters.

The Länder have maintained a great deal of influence in the German political system for several reasons. One is that there are many legislative powers left residually to them. Another is the constitutional provision that stimulates the "cooperative federalism" by requiring that the states administer most national policy, although this does not include foreign affairs and defense matters.[12]

Certainly another factor that must be considered is the role of the upper house of the federal parliament, the Bundesrat, in the political process. This is a structure that we will discuss further later in this chapter, but at this point we need to mention that all deputies in the upper house are chosen by the Länder governments, not the people, and are correspondingly perceived to represent the Länder governments.

Legislation within the federal jurisdiction that affects the Länder, even if the Länder themselves cannot legislate on the issue, must be approved by a majority of the Länder's representatives in the Bundesrat, or it does not become law. The Länder, therefore, have *sole* jurisdiction through the residual clause of Article 70 over any subject matter not given to the federal government. They have *concurrent* (shared) jurisdiction over a number of subject matters in areas specified by the Basic Law. Even in the areas that are described in the Basic Law as exclusively federal jurisdiction, the Länder are not without influence, because issues that might affect them must be approved by their representatives in the Bundesrat.

The Constitutional Court. Yet another structure in Germany that reinforces the federal nature of the polity is the Constitutional Court. Unlike the Supreme Court of the United

States, the Constitutional Court of Germany is not a court of appeal for either criminal or civil cases. Rather, the Constitutional Court:

> is a watchdog for the Basic Law. Its mission is not only to defend individual liberty and civil rights but to protect the legislature from the courts applying laws incorrectly. The Court is the final arbiter of disputes between the federal executive and the Bundestag, between the federal government and the states, between the different states, and between other courts.[13]

Like the U.S. Supreme Court, the Constitutional Court is autonomous and has an extremely broad jurisdiction. On a number of occasions over the years the Constitutional Court has ruled against the federal government, supporting an interpretation of the Basic Law favoring expansion of the powers of the Länder.

Executive Structures

We indicated earlier that the office of the president was seen by many in Germany to be one of the structural weaknesses of the Weimar regime. The Parliamentary Council that drafted the Basic Law in 1948 felt that the institution of the presidency in the Weimar period was, to some degree, responsible for the weakness of the chancellor at that time, and consequently responsible for the use of "emergency rule" that led to the rise of Hitler and the corresponding abuse of law.

Consequently, when members of the Parliamentary Council met in 1948 to construct a new set of political structures, there was little sense that a strong head of state was necessary for the political regime. Their primary goals with respect to executive powers were straightforward, and dealt with a "neutralized" Presidency, a strengthened Chancellorship, and controls on Parliament.[14]

First, members of the Parliamentary Council believed that the president should be "neutralized," which meant that (s)he should have few, if any, significant political powers, and should play the figurehead role in office that the constitutional monarchs of Britain or Scandinavia play. This also meant that the presidency should be an explicitly nonpolitical office.

Second, members felt that the position of the head of the

government, the chancellor, should be strengthened. The chancellor should not be as vulnerable to short-term political pressures as he had been in the Weimar regime, and his base of power should be more secure.[15]

Third, members of the council wanted to design a structure in which there would be "penalties" imposed on the legislature if it started to use its power in relation to the chancellor "irresponsibly." "Irresponsibly" in this case refers to the type of behavior observed in the Weimar regime in which several small parties would get together to vote no confidence in a chancellor and subsequently not be able to agree on a replacement. The "penalty" structure designed was part of a "constructive" vote of no confidence, something that we shall describe below.

The Federal President

Articles 54 through 61 of the Basic Law deal with the office of the federal president. The president is to be elected, without debate, by a special Federal Convention made up of members of the Bundestag and an equal number of members elected by the legislative assemblies of the states. The vote in the special convention must be by a majority of the delegates, on the first two ballots; if no one wins a majority on either of the first two ballots, the candidate receiving a plurality on the third ballot is elected.

The federal president has very few real powers. All orders and decrees of the federal president *must* be countersigned by the federal chancellor or an appropriate federal minister. This is significantly different from the relationship between most heads of state and their chief executives and cabinets: In most systems, legally (*de jure*) the head of state has a great deal of political power, although actually (*de facto*) it is recognized that the head of state will only act "on the advice" of his or her chief executive. In Germany, the head of state is *legally* restricted to the passive role. The fact that the head of state must have all orders and decrees countersigned is a legal acknowledgment of this individual's lack of power in the political system. The two exceptions to the countersignature rule are (1) the appointment and dismissal of the federal chancellor, and (2) the dissolution of the Bundestag (lower house of the legislature), both of which we will address later.

The president appoints and dismisses ministers, federal

judges, and federal civil servants; promulgates laws, represents the federation in its international relations, and concludes treaties, all "on the advice," of course, of the federal chancellor. Above all, the federal president is expected to be "above politics," to be nonpartisan, and to represent Germany to the world.

The Chancellor and the Cabinet

What is officially referred to as "the Federal Government" in Germany refers to the federal chancellor and his or her cabinet.[16] The chief executive in Germany is the chancellor, and as is usually the case with parliamentary systems of government, it is the chief executive, not the head of state, to whom we must turn to see the real locus of power in the German political arena. The chancellor "has been seen as the keystone of the political system, the guarantee of stability and coherence in the democratic structure of German politics."[17] The chancellor is more powerful than most parliamentary chief executives, primarily because the chancellor has greater job security than most. This is, in fact, the single most significant difference between the German chief executive and chief executives in other political regimes, and it has led the German system to be referred to as "Chancellor Democracy."[18]

Elections are held for the Bundestag (lower house) at least every four years. According to Article 39, "The Bundestag . . . term shall end four years after its first meeting or on its dissolution. The new election shall be held during the last three months of the term or within sixty days after dissolution." The Bundestag must assemble within thirty days after the election. The Bundestag determines the termination and resumption of its meetings, but may be called into special session by the federal president, the federal chancellor, or one-third of the Bundestag members.

After the elections of the members of the Bundestag, the president proposes a chancellor-designate, which in the German case has either been the leader of the majority party in the Bundestag (in 1957) or has been the leader of the apparent majority coalition. Article 63 of the Basic Law stipulates the procedure of the election of the federal chancellor, and states that "the Federal Chancellor shall be elected, without debate, by the Bundestag upon the proposal of the Federal President." If the federal president makes a designation that is not supported by a majority in the Bundestag, the Bundestag has the power to reject his candidate: If the person proposed by the president is not supported by a majority, "the Bundestag may elect within fourteen days of the ballot a Federal Chancellor by more than one-half of its members."

If the Bundestag rejects the federal president's nominee, and cannot agree on majority support for its *own* candidate within fourteen days, a new vote in the Bundestag must be taken "without delay, in which the person obtaining the largest number of votes shall be elected." If this person has been elected by a majority of Bundestag members, the federal president *must* appoint him (or her) within seven days. If this newly elected individual has *not* been elected by a majority, but only by a plurality, the federal president must *either* appoint him (or her) within seven days, or else dissolve the Bundestag and call for new elections within sixty days. (To date, all chancellors have been those approved as initial presidential designations, indicating the degree to which federal presidents make only "realistic" nominations.)

Once a chancellor has been confirmed by the Bundestag, it is *extremely* hard to fire that individual. One of the major distinctions between presidential and parliamentary systems that we observed earlier in this text was in respect to tenure: Presidents generally have fixed terms of office, whereas prime ministers can lose their positions at any time through votes of no confidence by the legislature. The Parliamentary Council of 1948 did not want the chancellor to be in an overly vulnerable position and, accordingly, developed a new political structure to help protect the chancellor's job security: the *positive* or *constructive vote of no confidence*.

The positive vote of no confidence is described in Article 67 of the Basic Law:

> The Bundestag can express its lack of confidence in the Federal Chancellor only by electing a successor with the majority of its members and by requesting the Federal President to dismiss the Federal Chancellor. The Federal President must comply with this request and appoint the person elected. . . . Forty-eight hours must elapse between the motion and the vote thereon.

In short, having a majority of members of the Bundestag express their lack of confidence in a chancellor is *not* sufficient to dismiss that chancellor; they must at the same time (actually, prior to that time) agree on a successor that a majority of the Bundestag can support. This is, as might be guessed, a very difficult task, and has helped the federal chancellor to weather strife and complaints that might have much more serious consequences—such as causing the Government to fall—in other political systems.

This positive vote of no confidence has led some to refer to the German political system as a "semiparliamentary system" rather than a parliamentary system, arguing that a "genuine parliamentary system, in the sense of enforceable responsibility of the executive to parliament, existed in Germany only as long as the Weimar Constitution functioned."[19] The difficulty of obtaining a positive vote of no confidence is so great that the Government is virtually no longer responsible to the Bundestag, except in truly extraordinary instances.

In September 1982, for the first time, just such an unusual incident did arise. After constant feuding within the Social Democratic/Free Democratic party coalition, the Free Democratic party (FDP) minor partner decided to withdraw its support for the Government of Helmut Schmidt.[20] In itself this guaranteed only a simple vote of no confidence, and not a positive, or constructive, vote of no confidence. After consultation, however, it became clear that the leader of the more conservative Christian Democratic/Christian Socialist Union (CDU/CSU) bloc was willing to make policy concessions to the Free Democrats that convinced the FDP deputies to join with the CDU/CSU deputies in a positive vote of no confidence, voting Helmut Schmidt out and Helmut Kohl in. This was, for reasons we have suggested above, an extremely rare occurrence in German politics.[21]

In addition to the unlikelihood that the chancellor will be thrown out of office, the chancellor has the added leverage of being able to *use* a vote of confidence as a weapon. Article 68 states that if the chancellor *asks* for a vote of confidence, and does not receive it, he or she can ask for a dissolution of the Bundestag and call for new elections. This has been used in the past by chancellors either to (1) push a piece of legislation through the Bundestag that might have difficulty otherwise by referring to the vote on the bill as a question of confidence; or (2) bring about an early dissolution for electoral gain; newly selected chancellor Kohl used this vehicle after his accession to the chancellorship in September

1982, to seek a popular mandate from the German people, since his party had not won a majority with him as leader. He received the mandate he sought in the March 1983 elections.

Unlike other political systems, in Germany the head of state does not possess the legal power to dissolve the Bundestag anytime he or she wants to do so. (We did point out, of course, that although most heads of state have this power legally, they really only exercise it "on the advice" of their chief executives. In Germany the head of state does not even possess the power legally.) The federal president can dissolve the Bundestag *only* under one of two circumstances: first, if his nominee for chancellor is not approved by the Bundestag, and the chancellor eventually chosen by the Bundestag does not have majority support and is not acceptable to the president; and second, if the chancellor requests a vote of confidence in the Bundestag, and the Bundestag fails to give him one, *and* the chancellor subsequently requests a dissolution.

Chancellors who know that elections must be held within the next year or so, and who see their popularity as being very high, have been known to use the "confidence mechanism" to secure an early dissolution. They do this by asking for a vote of confidence *and instructing their own party supporters to vote against them*, thereby ensuring that they will lose the vote of confidence. (Note, however, that this is not the same as a positive vote of no confidence; the Bundestag has not agreed on a replacement for the chancellor.) The chancellor's supporters will go along with this, of course, since it is in their own interest to have elections held at a time when their party and their leader are both popular.

We can see, then, that the German chancellor is stronger in his political system than virtually any other parliamentary chief executive we can think of. The chancellor not only has the usual tool of party discipline at his disposal, but *also* has the resources of (1) being extraordinarily difficult to dismiss, and (2) being able to threaten the legislature with dissolution if it is not cooperative.

Ministers in the Federal Republic share in collective responsibility, as do ministers in other parliamentary regimes, but they have more individual authority than do ministers in many other parliamentary systems because they tend to manage their individual departments "on their own responsibility," with less collective input than in many other parliamentary systems. The cabinet, as well, tends to be smaller than in many other nations, with recent cabinets consisting of fifteen or sixteen members. The major limitation on the cabinet as a collective policymaker has been the fact that governments have involved coalitions, and in many instances the coalition partners represented in the cabinet have not been able to agree in cabinet meetings on which policy option to adopt, and "many policy issues have to be prepared outside the Government."[22]

The Legislative Structures

The Bundestag

Several aspects of the federal legislature have already been introduced. We have already seen how the members of the Bundestag (the "federal diet," the lower house of the legislature) are elected. We have seen the relationship between the Bundestag and the federal chancellor; the chancellor is dominant and is beyond the normal reach of the legislature in terms of the usual meaning of "responsible government." We saw in a very introductory manner that the Bundesrat (the "federal council," the upper house of the legislature) is important in the federal structure of the regime. Some of these items deserve further consideration at this point.

The Bundestag is clearly perceived in the Basic Law to be the center of legislative activity in the German political regime. To this should be added the qualification, however, that the German political system is essentially designed to be managed by the chancellor and his cabinet. The job of the Bundestag is to choose its leader; once this is accomplished, it is expected that the Bundestag will sit back and let itself be led by the Government. The degree of difficulty of the positive vote of no confidence is an indication that the framers of the Basic Law did not *intend* for the Bundestag to exercise its role as the ultimate authority in the regime very often. This scenario, in fact, has been the case.

The Bundesrat

Article 50 of the Basic Law indicates that "the Länder shall participate through the Bundesrat in the legislation and administration of the Federation." The Bundesrat, the upper house in the political regime, is primarily important insofar as the federal distribution of powers is concerned. As was seen in Table 11.1, the Länder each have either three, four, five, or six deputies in the Bundesrat, depending upon their size. Article 51 of the Basic Law indicates that every Land shall have at least three seats in the Bundesrat; Länder with more than 2 million inhabitants shall have four, Länder with more than 6 million inhabitants shall have five, and Länder with more than 7 million inhabitants shall have six votes.[23]

This difference in the size of Bundesrat delegations, however, does not alleviate disproportionate representation. To take two examples, the city-state of Bremen (with three delegates) has one Bundesrat representative for each 266,666 people, and the state of North Rhine–Westphalia (with six delegates) has one Bundesrat representative for each 2.8 million people.

The Land governments (the legislative assemblies of the Länder) choose their three, four, five, or six delegates to the Bundesrat. Since the Bundesrat delegates are chosen by the Land governments, they will all be of the political party that controls the majority in the Land legislature. Bundesrat delegates from a Land *must* cast their votes as a bloc; they may not divide their three, four, five, or six votes.

The role of the Bundesrat in the German legislative process varies, depending upon the specific piece of legislation involved. According to the Basic Law (Articles 77 and 78), bills intended to become federal law require adoption by the Bundestag. Bills can be introduced in the Bundestag by either the Bundesrat, the Bundestag, or the federal Government (the chancellor and the cabinet).

The Legislative Process

The legislative process is relatively complex: All bills begin their legislative journey in the Bundestag. Bills introduced by the Bundesrat (a small number) go first to the Government for comment before being introduced in the Bundestag.[24] Bills being introduced by the Government (more than half of the total)[25] go first to the Bundesrat for comment before being introduced in the Bundestag. In each of these cases, *scrutiny* is implied, not *veto* power; the goal is for government actors to let other government actors know what is happening. Bills starting in the Bundestag (almost half) are simply introduced there, and they do not go to either the Bundesrat or the Government for advance scrutiny and comment.

Once bills are introduced, they first go through the "Bundestag phase" of the legislative process, including a first reading, a vote in the Bundestag, assignment to committee followed by a committee report, a second reading and vote in the Bundestag covering specific details of the proposed legislation, followed by a third reading and vote.

If a bill passes the Bundestag phase of the legislative process—and it is possible it might not—it goes to the Bundesrat. This is the first opportunity for the Bundesrat to see bills that were initiated in the Bundestag (other bills either were initiated in the Bundesrat, or were initiated in the Government and were first sent to the Bundesrat for review and comment prior to going to the Bundestag). The Bundesrat can either approve the bill, in which case it is sent on to the federal president to sign and to the chancellor or appropriate minister to countersign, or within two weeks the Bundesrat may ask for a meeting of the Bundestag-Bundesrat Mediation Committee to try to find a compromise.

At this point an important distinction must be made. Bills that "affect the Länder" *require the approval* of the Bundesrat: It has an *absolute veto* over this kind of legislation.[26] Bills that do not directly affect the Länder—for example, questions dealing with foreign policy—do not require Bundesrat approval; over these bills the Bundesrat has only a *suspensory veto*.

In cases over which the Bundesrat has an absolute veto, and in which it does not approve of the Bundestag bill, a compromise must be reached by the Mediation Committee and must be subsequently approved by both houses before it can be promulgated, handed down as law. Failing this, the bill does not become law. In cases over which the Bundesrat does not have an absolute veto, and in which the Bundesrat does not approve of the Bundestag bill,

> it may enter a suspensive veto, but only after an effort at compromise through the Mediation Committee has been made. In that case, it must act within one week of Bundestag action on the compromise, or, if no new compromise is proposed by the committee, within one week of the completion of its work. If the Bundesrat enters its objection by a vote of a majority of its members, then the Bundestag can override it by the same majority; if the Bundesrat

has entered its objections by a vote of two-thirds of its members, it can only be overriden in the Bundestag by a vote of two-thirds of the Members present, but these two-thirds must also constitute at least a majority of the total membership. If the Bundesrat fails to act within the prescribed time limits, bills which do not specifically require its approval are ready for promulgation.[27]

The structure of the Mediation Committee is modelled after the conference committee of the U.S. Congress. Members are appointed from *each* house of the legislature. Unlike the American conference committee, however, which is only a temporary political structure and which is created *de novo* for each bill over which a compromise is necessary, the Mediation Committee is a standing committee—permanent for the life of the legislature. It is composed of Bundesrat members (one from each Land) and Bundestag members, divided proportionally to reflect party distribution in that house (see Table 11.2).

The Bundesrat, then, while not having an absolute veto in all cases as is the situation in the United States Senate, is a

Table 11.2
Legislative Productivity, 1983–1987

Productivity Measure	Number
Bills initiated by:	
Federal government	280
Bundestag	183
Bundesrat	59
Total	522
Origins of ratified bills:	
Federal government	273
Bundestag	42
Bundesrat	32
Joint	9
Total	356
Mediation committees created:	6

Source: *Statistisches Jahrbuch für die Bundesrepublik Deutschland 1988*, p. 91, as cited in M. Donald Hancock, *West Germany: The Politics of Democratic Corporatism* (Chatham, N.J.: Chatham House, 1989), p. 60.

reasonably powerful upper house. Over the years its veto power has expanded to include a substantial proportion of all federal legislation. To some degree this expansion occured through judicial decisions. Article 84 of the Basic Law gave the states the task of administering much federal legislation; the states argued before the courts—successfully—that since they had to *administer* the law, they were *affected by* the law, and accordingly the Bundesrat should have absolute veto power. Accordingly, today, states argue that even if a law affects them only because they must administer it, the entire law can be vetoed by the Bundesrat in the legislative process.

Political Parties and the Electoral Process

The Electoral Process

Germany is a political system with many political parties, but one which has been dominated by just a few parties over the last thirty years; the system has evolved since the 1949 election to become a two-coalition, if not a two-party, system. In the elections of October 5, 1980, although twenty political parties appeared on West German ballots, the five major parties (CDU, CSU, FDP, SPD, Greens) won 99.5 percent of the votes; in the March 6, 1983 elections, the five major parties again won 99.5 percent of the votes; in the January 1987 elections, the five major parties won 98.7 percent of the votes; in the December 1990 election—the first election after unification—these five parties won 92.2 percent of the votes.[28] The reasons for this are complex, and to explain the pattern of the parties' election returns over the years we must know something of the manner in which the German electoral system operates.

In 1949, at the time of the creation of the Federal Republic, each citizen voted only once in each election. This system was changed in 1953 when a second vote for each citizen in each election was added.[29] When Germans go to the polls they receive a ballot with two columns, as illustrated on the following page. In the left-hand column, the citizen votes directly for a candidate that has been nominated by a local political party organization (there are no primary elections in Germany), in a single-member-district, plurality voting electoral framework. Germany is now

Stimmzettel

für die Wahl zum Deutschen Bundestag im Wahlkreis 63 Bonn am 6. März 1983

Sie haben 2 Stimmen

Ⓧ   Ⓧ

hier 1 Stimme
für die Wahl
eines Wahlkreisabgeordneten
(Erststimme)

hier 1 Stimme
für die Wahl
einer Landesliste (Partei)
(Zweitstimme)

1	Prof. Dr. Ehmke, Horst		
	Professor für öffentliches Recht Bonn Am Römerlager 4	**SPD**	Sozialdemokratische Partei Deutschlands	○

| ○ | **SPD** | Sozialdemokratische
Partei Deutschlands

Brandt, Wischnewski, Frau Huber, Schmidt,
Frau Renger | 1 |

2	Dr. Daniels, Hans		
	Notar Bonn Schmidtbonnstr. 7	**CDU**	Christlich Demokratische Union Deutschlands	○

| ○ | **CDU** | Christlich Demokratische
Union Deutschlands

Dr. Barzel, Dr. Blüm, Frau Dr. Wilms, Vogel,
Frau Hürland | 2 |

3	Rentrop, Franz Friedhelm		
	Steuerberater u. Wirtschaftsprüfer Bonn-Bad Godesberg Langenbergsweg 72	**F.D.P.**	Freie Demokratische Partei	○

| ○ | **F.D.P.** | Freie Demokratische
Partei

Genscher, Dr. Graf Lambsdorff, Frau Dr.
Adam-Schwaetzer, Dr. Hirsch, Möllemann | 3 |

4	Rohde, Volker August Wilhelm Fritz		
	Journalist Bonn-Beuel Stroofstr. 15	**DKP**	Deutsche Kommunistische Partei	○

| ○ | **DKP** | Deutsche Kommunistische
Partei

Mies, Frau Nieth, Frau Bobrzik, Bublitz,
Frau Buschmann | 4 |

5	Dr. Skupnik, Wilfried Bruno		
	Beamter Bonn Clausiusstr. 21	**GRÜNE**	DIE GRÜNEN	○

| ○ | **GRÜNE** | DIE GRÜNEN

Vogel, Frau Dr. Vollmer, Stratmann,
Frau Nickels, Schily | 5 |

| ○ | **EAP** | Europäische
Arbeiterpartei

Frau Zepp-La Rouche, Cramer, Frau Cramer,
Schiele, Vitt | 6 |

| ○ | **KPD** | Kommunistische Partei
Deutschlands
(Marxisten-Leninisten)
Brand, Detjen, Frau Schnoor, Voß
Frau Lenger-Koloska | 7 |

| ○ | **NPD** | Nationaldemokratische
Partei Deutschlands

Schultz, Gerlach, Frau Krüger, Siepmann,
Aengenvoort | 8 |

| ○ | **USD** | Unabhängige
Soziale Demokraten

Bönnemann, Vorhagen, Thränhardt, Bartz,
Stahlschmidt | 9 |

A Sample Ballot. Source: *"Procedures, Programmes, Profiles: The Federal Republic of Germany Elects the German Bundestag on 25 January, 1987" (Bonn: Inter-Nationes, 1987), p. 7.*

divided into 328 single-member districts[30] from which deputies are selected by simple plurality margins: Whichever candidate in a district receives the most votes wins. Interestingly, if two or more candidates receive the same number of votes, the returning officer (the official in charge of administering the election) for the electoral district draws lots to decide the winner.

In the right-hand column the citizen casts a "second vote" for a political party, not a candidate, in a proportional respresentation electoral competition. Parties receive seats on the basis of the percentage of votes they receive in the election. Another 328 deputies are elected to the Bundestag through this electoral route, bringing the total number of seats in the Bundestag to 656.

Some argue that the second ballot is in many ways more important than the first, "direct," ballot, because it is the second ballot that determines the final proportion of parliamentary seats that each party will receive in the Bundestag. The number of "district" seats is subtracted from the total number of seats due to the party on the basis of its performance in the proportional representation elections, determining the number of "at large" seats the party will receive. For example, if a party wins 25 percent of the vote on the proportional ballot—thus earning a total of 164 seats in the new Bundestag (25 percent of 656 total seats available yields 164 seats)—and it wins 80 district seats, it will be awarded 84 at large seats to bring its total to the percentage it earned in the election. Individual candidates will be selected, in order, from party lists that have already been filed with the government.

> The second ballot provision made the system basically proportional, with two important exceptions. A party had to secure at least five percent of the second ballot vote, or win three "direct" district (first ballot) contests in order to share in the proportional distribution of parliamentary seats. Secondly, if a party won more district contests (first ballot) than it was entitled to according to its totals on the second ballot, it was allowed to keep the extra seats and the parliament was enlarged accordingly. In the last West German parliament, for example, there was one of these "excess mandates" and the Bundestag had 497 members in addition to 22 from West Berlin.[31]

Table 11.3 indicates the distribution of seats in the Bundestag among the several states in the single-member-district races.

The rationale behind the two-vote electoral system is that it allows for the accuracy of proportional representation, while still

Table 11.3
Bundestag District Representation of German Länder

District	No. Seats[a]
Bavaria	44
Baden-Württemberg	36
Berlin	13[b]
Brandenburg	12[b]
Bremen	3
Hamburg	8
Hesse	22
Lower Saxony	30
Mecklenburg-West Pomerania	9[b]
N. Rhine-Westphalia	73
Rhineland-Palatinate	16
Saarland	5
Saxony	21[b]
Saxony-Anhalt	13[b]
Schleswig-Holstein	11
Thüringia	12[b]
Total district seats	328

[a]Unless otherwise noted, number of seats won in the 1987 federal election.
[b]Number of districts created in the former regions of East Germany and reunified Berlin for the 1990 elections.

Source: Adapted from Helmut Goebel and Herbert Blondiau, eds., *Procedures, Programmes, Profiles: The Federal Republic of Germany Elects the German Bundestag* (Bonn: Inter-Nationes, 1980), p. 31; and "Bulletin: Vertrag zur Vorbereitung und Durchführung der ersten gesamtdeutschen Wahl des Deutschen Bundestages," *Presse- und Informationsamt der Bundesregierung*, Nr. 97/S, Bonn, den 7. August, 1990 pp. 831–832.

allowing for the "personal representation" of the single-member-district electoral structure. Another function of the system has to do with interest groups and interest group representation. One study has suggested that for individual candidates who seek to enter the parliament from outside of political party organizations, it is "virtually impossible to gain nomination as a party candidate for a direct seat,"[32] that is, for a seat for which voters ballot directly for an individual candidate. However, significant interest groups may have sufficient influence at the Länder level to be able to influence the Länder political parties to include "their" candidates on the party's "proportional representation" part of the ballot.

Voting turnout is regularly high; 89 percent of the electorate voted in 1983; 84.3 percent voted in 1987; and in the first election after unification 77.8 percent of the eligible voters participated.[33] Every citizen over the age of 18 years has a vote, and eligibility certificates are mailed by the Federal Board of Elections to lists of eligible voters prepared by the local census bureau. Overall, the German electorate "is both *stable* in the sense of supporting prosystem parties over time, and *in transition* in the sense of becoming more sophisticated about issues and policies and more willing to use the ballot to effect political change and secure the desired policy outputs."[34]

We might think that the proportional representation component of the electoral system would encourage a large number of political parties to flourish in the Federal Republic of Germany, as was the case in Weimar Germany. There was much discussion about this possible consequence when the authors of the Basic Law met in 1948; the structure that has evolved over the years to prevent the proliferation of minor parties in Germany is called the Five Percent Clause.

Proportional representation electoral systems, as we saw earlier in this text, can have the negative effect in a political system of providing *too much* representation. If every party that receives, say, 1 percent of the vote is given representation in the legislature, we may find a legislature with so many political parties that coalition governments are necessary, leading to what we saw can be less stable governments. Under the Weimar Constitution, which preceded World War II, a proportional representation system existed in Germany, which resulted in a large number of political parties. In fact, fourteen different parties successfully competed for the Reichstag election of September 14, 1930, and nine of them received between three and thirty seats. Many Germans thought that it was wrong that "although none of these nine parties had even five percent of the total vote, they still took part in deciding who was to form the government."[35]

There is a difficult trade-off involved in this policy, one that we discussed earlier. On one hand, single-member districts fail to represent minority blocs in electoral districts; on the other hand, proportional representation systems can result in unreasonable influence for minor parties and consequent system instability. To limit the danger of tiny parliamentary blocs gaining a disproportionate amount of political influence and resulting in political instability through resultant coalition governments, the Federal Election Law introduced the *Five Percent Clause*.[36]

The Five Percent Clause indicates that parties can win seats from the proportional representation "second votes" *only* if they poll at least 5 percent of the second votes, or (1) if they have won at least three constituency seats, or (2) if they represent an officially registered "national minority" (such as the party of the Danish minority in Schleswig-Holstein).[37]

The Five Percent Clause has been of tremendous significance for the political parties in Germany. In the first Bundestag in 1949 there were ten parties represented, but ever since the Five Percent Clause was introduced, there have been only four parties until the 1983 election added a fifth. The 1990 post-unification election expanded this slightly. The Five Percent Clause serves as a real psychological barrier for new parties, as well as a legal or structural barrier; many voters feel that voting for a minor party is "throwing away" their votes, since the minor parties will probably *not* win 5 percent of the vote. The major parties usually can be counted upon to remind the voters of this principle. This is undoubtedly why only one new party has emerged in the Bundestag since the Five Percent Clause came into force.

When East and West Germany were reunified in 1990, there was serious concern expressed on the part of many political parties in (what had been) East Germany that they would not be able to compete with the larger, better organized parties in (what had been) West Germany in the 1990 elections. The Supreme Court, in fact, threw out the Five Percent Clause as unconstitutionally discriminating against the smaller (formerly) East German parties. On the advice of the Supreme Court the law was amended so that political parties in the former German Democratic Republic (East Germany) could form alliances and run on joint tickets, and so that votes for the proportional seats would be counted separately in the what was once East Germany and West Germany,[38] thereby allowing smaller East German parties to compete against smaller East German parties, and not have to compete against the larger, better-organized West German parties.

Political Parties

As is the case in most democratic systems, it is impossible to discuss the German political system without an explicit discussion of political parties. Unlike many democracies, however, in Germany political parties are constitutionally included in the political system: The Basic Law specifically refers to political parties, and in Article 21 "guarantees the legitimacy of parties and their right to exist—if they accept the principles of democratic government."[39] The Federal Republic has thoroughly institutionalized the structure of political parties, and we describe the working of the German politics as "party government," as we do in other parliamentary democracies.

Although a large number of political parties have consistently competed in German elections, various structures in the political system—most notably the Five Percent Clause we just discussed—have made it extremely difficult for minority or splinter parties to form and flourish. The Five Percent Clause "was designed to prevent a recurrence of the splintering of the parliament into numerous parties which drastically weakened the Weimar Republic."[40]

It has been successful in this goal, and in the elections in West Germany since the Five Percent Clause came into effect, support for political parties other than the five large parties has decreased markedly, as indicated in Table 11.4. In the election of October 1980, twenty parties appeared on the ballot; only four parties won seats. The Greens, the newest small party, which was supported by a coalition of "environmentalists, nuclear energy opponents, and people reacting against an industrial society,"[41] received only 1.5 percent of the vote. Two other extremist parties of the left and right, the (left wing) German Communist Party (DKP) and the (right wing) National Democratic Party (NPD) each won less than 0.3 percent of the vote. In the March 1983 elections the Greens finally broke the Five Percent Clause barrier (with 5.6 percent of the vote) and won 27 seats in the Bundestag[42]; they won 42 seats in the Bundestag in 1987.[43]

Four political parties have proven over time to play a significant political role in the German political system, all participating in government coalitions at one point or another in time. From 1949 through 1956, and from 1961 through 1965, West Germany was governed by a coalition of the Christian Democratic Union

Table 11.4
Federal Election Results in Germany (in Percent of Votes Cast)

				Party					
Year	CDU/ CSU	SPD	FDP	Green	PDS	DSU	Alliance 90/ Greens	Other	Turnout
1949	31.6	29.2	11.9					27.8	78.5
1953	45.2	28.8	9.5					16.5	86.0
1957	50.2	31.8	7.7					10.3	87.8
1961	45.3	36.2	12.8					5.7	87.7
1965	47.6	39.3	9.5					3.6	86.8
1969	46.1	42.7	5.8					5.4	86.7
1972	44.9	45.8	8.4					0.9	91.2
1976	48.6	42.6	7.9					0.9	91.0
1980	44.5	42.9	10.6	1.5				0.5	88.7
1983	48.8	38.2	6.9	5.6				0.5	89.1
1987	44.3	37.0	9.1	8.4				1.2	84.3
1990	43.8	33.5	11.0	3.9	2.4	0.2	1.2	4.0	77.8

Former West German parties:
  CDU   Christian Democratic Union
  CSU   Christian Socialist Union
  SPD   Social Democratic Party
  FDP   Free Democratic Party
  Green   Green-Environmental Party
Former East German parties:
  PDS   Party of Democratic Socialism
  DSU   German Social Union
  Alliance 90/Greens   East German Green Party

Source: Adapted from *The Week in Germany*, October 10, 1980, p. 2, and December 7, 1990, p. 1 (New York: German Information Center); and M. Donald Hancock, *West Germany: The Politics of Democratic Corporatism* (Chatham, N.J.: Chatham House, 1989), p. 79.

(CDU) and Christian Socialist Union (CSU) parties (the CSU is the CDU in the state of Bavaria—they act as one party in the government), and the Free Democratic party (FDP). In 1957 the CDU/CSU had an outright majority in the Bundestag, the only time a majority has been obtained by a political party, and formed a government without a coalition, which lasted until elections in 1961. From 1965 through 1969 a "grand coalition" existed, in which all the major parties including the Social Democrats (SPD) participated in the Government. From 1969 until 1982, all governments were SPD and FDP coalitions.[44]

In September 1982, as we have already discussed, as a result primarily of economic pressure exerted on the Government, the FDP/SPD coalition came apart, and the FDP gave its support instead to the CDU/CSU bloc. Accordingly, Chancellor Schmidt of the Social Democratic party resigned, and Helmut Kohl of the Christian Democratic Union/Christian Socialist Union bloc became chancellor. This coalition has stayed in power since that time.

The CDU is essentially a conservative party, and was founded in 1945 based upon Christian, conservative, social principles.[45] The CSU was also founded in 1945 and appears on the ballot only in Bavaria, while the CDU is a more national party, appearing on *all* ballots *except* in Bavaria. The CDU and CSU are almost always in agreement on major issues, and are considered as one party in the Bundestag. From 1949 through the 1969 election the CDU/CSU pair dominated West German elections, and it has continued to do so since the March 1983 election.[46] In its early years the CDU had very little in the way of internal party organization, but this changed following its loss of power in 1969, and the CDU party made a number of changes in its internal organization and party machinery to help mobilize and control its members and supporters.[47]

The Free Democratic party (FDP) is the liberal-center party in Germany, and has proven to be much more active in the German political system than its relatively small size might suggest. It has been referred to as the "party of coalition,"[48] having served as a coalition partner with both the CDU/CSU and the SPD. The FDP is generally perceived as a centrist party, and thus has been the only acceptable partner for the more conservative CDU/CSU and for the more liberal SPD.[49]

Although the results of the elections shown in Table 11.4 do not demonstrate it, many supporters of the FDP were seriously concerned at the time of the 1987 election campaign that the FDP might not meet the 5 percent threshold for the legislature, given the gradual decline in the public level of support for the party and the increase in support for the Greens. Indeed, as one scholar has written, the FDP is "a part of electoral instability. Less than half its voters are loyal regulars,"[50] and that means that its electoral strength is seriously vulnerable to short-term political issues.

The Social Democratic party (SPD) dates back to the 1860s, and was a traditional social democratic party, oriented to the working class.

> By 1912 it had become the strongest political party in Germany. After the First World War, during the Weimar period, it worked toward securing an orderly transition from the imperial state to the newly-formed republic. During the Nazi period, many SPD leaders fled into exile, or were imprisoned in concentration camps. At the end of World War II, the SPD reemerged as a major political party.[51]

The SPD is a left-of-center political party, although not perceived as a radically left organization. Its economic policies are a very moderate version of socialist thought, much more sympathetic to free-market economic policies than to Marxist thought. The SPD first participated in a cabinet in the Grand Coalition of 1965; in 1969 the SPD led the cabinet formation process for the first time, joining in a coalition with the FDP. This alliance continued through the elections of 1972, 1976, and 1980, dissolving in October 1982, as indicated above.[52]

As already stated, the Green Movement in Germany became a parliamentary political party only in recent years.[53] The Green Movement emerged in Germany in 1975, and for many years existed as a lobby in West Germany, applying pressure for changes in society that "did not pose an immediate threat to the established 'people's' or 'catch-all' parties."[54] Membership in the Greens rose from 3,000 in October 1979, to over 10,000 in January 1980; in March 1980 the Greens met to formulate a formal political party program.[55]

The Greens were especially important as a demonstration that views that were outside the mainstream of West German political thought could win representation in government. As some scholars have noted, "the acid test of any truly democratic legitimation of protest movements, however large their following, is their ability to achieve representation of their interests in parliament."[56] Although there had been several protest movements with various degrees of popular support in West Germany between the formation of the Federal Republic and 1983,[57] the

Table 11.5
West German Party Organization and Voter Support, 1983

Party	Voters	Members	Ratio
Greens	2,167,431	25,000	87:1
SPD	14,865,807	950,000	16:1
CDU	14,857,680	734,082	20:1
CSU	4,140,865	182,665	23:1
FDP	2,706,942	78,763	34:1

Source: Adapted from Werner Hulsberg, *The German Greens: A Social and Political Profile*, trans. Gus Fagan (London: Verso, 1988), p. 108.

Greens' victory in 1983 offered the first instance of parliamentary political victory for an organization that could be called a "protest movement."

The Greens have not been a typical German party, and their parliamentarians have not been typical legislators, in either behavior or demeanor.[58] The average Green legislator was almost ten years younger than other legislators, and "six of the ten youngest deputies in Parliament were Greens."[59] The Green party also has the lowest degree of organization of the major German parties. That is, the ratio of its voters to its formal members is higher than the other parties, as indicated in Table 11.5.

In the 1980 federal elections the Greens did not cross the threshold required for representation. In the 1983 federal election the Greens received 5.6 percent of the vote, and entered the federal Parliament for the first time.[60] They increased this margin of voter support in 1987 with 8.4 percent of the vote.[61] The (former West German) Greens did not get enough votes in the 1990 election to win any seats in the new legislature. The (former East German) Alliance 90/Greens, however, did win sufficient votes to be represented, so the Green movement will continue to be represented in the federal legislature.

The reunification of Germany introduced several new political parties to the democratic arena. The largest of these, the former communist East German party—the Socialist Unity party—changed its name to the Party of Democratic Socialism in preparation for the first national elections, which were held in 1990.[62]

The German Political System

We see in Germany, then, a political system that is *similar to* others that we have already seen, and others that we will yet see, but one that differs in a number of important aspects from those other systems. Although many idiosyncratic structural and procedural differences exist between Germany and other nations, the most significant differences that we have highlighted in this chapter number four.

First, Germany is federal, and the role of the states (Länder) in the German political system is quite significant. Through the veto power of the Bundesrat, the Länder exercise a great influence in the policy-making process generally, and in the legislative process specifically. The federal distribution of power in Germany makes Germany unlike any other political system we will see here.

Second, the "normal" responsibility of the chief executive to the (lower house of the) legislature is different in the German political system. The political structure of the "positive vote of no confidence" has many implications for the degree to which the chancellor must worry about the likelihood that he will be dismissed by the Bundestag.

Third, the German electoral structure offers a unique blend of methods of selection for a national legislature. By combining single-member-district with proportional-representation selection, the Germans have attempted to blend the advantages of each: the minority representation of proportional representation with the stability and orientation of district-based representation. Moreover, by establishing the "Five Percent Clause" the Germans have attempted to resolve the major drawback of proportional representation—namely a proliferation of political parties and the ensuing political instability of the regime. By all appearances, they have succeeded.

Fourth, from a legislative point of view the German case is quite interesting. In some political systems (such as that of the

United States, for example) the upper house has, both in law *(de jure)* and in fact *(de facto)* an absolute veto. Laws cannot be made without the approval of the upper house, and the legislative process operates accordingly. In other political systems (such as those of Britain and France, for example) the upper house has only a suspensory veto, in both law and in fact. If both the Government and the lower house want a piece of proposed legislation passed, it will become law, and the most that the upper chamber can do is to slow down the process (of course, the technical details of how this is accomplished vary from country to country). In Germany, on the other hand, in both law and in fact, the upper house sometimes has an *absolute veto*, and sometimes has a *suspensory veto*, depending on the focus of legislation under consideration.

This brief discussion of the German political system, then, although only covering a very small portion of all of the significant structures of the political regime, points out some of the interesting, significant, and, in some cases, unique characteristics of the German polity. We will see in the several chapters that follow that many of these political structures that are so appropriate to the German political culture would *not* work elsewhere. Other regimes have developed their own mechanisms and structures for processing political demands and supports.

Notes

1. Guido Goldman, *The German Political System* (New York: Random House, 1974), pp. 157, 214. The full text of the Basic Law can be found here.
2. See M. Donald Hancock, *West Germany: The Politics of Democratic Corporatism* (Chatham, N.J.: Chatham House, 1989), pp. 29–30. According to Hancock, a majority of the members of Bavaria's parliament opposed the Basic Law "because it provided for a more centralized form of government than they would have wished. Nonetheless, the Bavarian Landtag endorsed the Basic Law as binding on the state."
3. On this note, an interesting study was published in 1966 by Karl Jasper, a well-known German philosopher who argued that "the Federal Republic of Germany is well on its way to abolishing parliamentary democracy and may be drifting toward some kind of dictatorship. . . ." See Karl Jaspers, *The Future of Germany*, trans. E. B. Ashton (Chicago: University of Chicago Press, 1967), p. v.
4. Klaus von Beyme, *The Political System of the Federal Republic of Germany*, (New York: St. Martin's Press, 1983), p. 12.
5. See Goldman, *The German Political System*, pp. 157–164. All quotes from

the Basic Law are taken from the text in Goldman and will not be given individual citations.

6. Lewis Edinger, *Politics in West Germany* (Boston: Little, Brown, 1977), p. 11.

7. Nevil Johnson, *State and Government in the Federal Republic of Germany: The Executive at Work* (New York: Pergamon, 1983), p. 3.

8. David Conradt, *The German Polity*, 3rd ed. (New York: Longman, 1986), p. 210.

9. The three were Bavaria, Hamburg, and Bremen. Ibid., p. 212.

10. Johnson, *State and Government*, p. 7.

11. Hancock, *West Germany*, p. 49.

12. Ibid., p. 49.

13. Peter Katzenstein, *Policy and Politics in West Germany: The Growth of a Semisovereign State* (Philadelphia: Temple University Press, 1987), pp. 17–18.

14. Johnson, *State and Government*, pp. 49–50.

15. See the discussion of "The Elevation of the Chancellor," in Gordon Smith, *Democracy in Western Germany: Parties and Politics in the Federal Republic* (New York: Holmes and Meier, 1986), p. 56.

16. Johnson, *State and Government*, p. 50.

17. Ibid., p. 54.

18. For example, see Conradt, *The German Polity*, p. 162.

19. John Herz, *The Government of Germany* (New York: Harcourt Brace Jovanovich, 1972), p. 123.

20. A good analysis of this period can be found in Ian Derbyshire, *Politics in West Germany: From Schmidt to Kohl* (London: W & R Chambers, 1987), pp. 35–39.

21. This is discussed in some detail in Hancock, *West Germany*, pp. 121–124.

22. Johnson, *State and Government*, pp. 68–69.

23. This was a change in the law approved in 1990 prior to reunification. "Focus on the German Unification Process," German Information Center, New York, 1990, p. 9.

24. See Gerhardt Loewenberg, *Parliament in the German Political System* (Ithaca, N.Y.: Cornell University Press, 1967), p. 269.

25. Ibid., p. 270.

26. Loewenberg writes that about 60 percent of important measures require Bundesrat approval. The Basic Law sections that determine which subjects are subject to Bundesrat approval are "scattered over many sections of the document." Loewenberg, *Parliament*, pp. 365–366, note 214.

27. Ibid., p. 366.

28. "Germany: Elections, Parliament, and Political Parties" (New York: German Information Center, 1990), pp. 20–21. Results of the December 1990 election were published in *The Week in Germany*, December 7, 1990, p. 1 (New York: German Information Center).

29. Von Beyme, *The Political System of the Federal Republic of Germany*, p. 26.

30. A list of the new districts was published in a bulletin released by the German Information Office: "Bulletin: Vertrag zur Vorbereitung und Durchführung der ersten gesamtdeutschen Wahl des Deutschen Bundestages," Presse- und Informationsamt der Bundesregierung, Nr. 97/S, Bonn, den 7. August, 1990," pp. 831–832.

31. David P. Conradt, *Unified Germany at the Polls: Political Parties and the*

1990 Federal Election (Baltimore: Johns Hopkins University Press, 1990), pp. 23–24.

32. Eva Kolinsky, _Parties, Opposition, and Society in West Germany_ (New York: St. Martin's Press, 1984), p. 40.
33. "Germany: Elections, Parliament, and Political Parties," p. 21. The 1990 turnout data come from _The Week in Germany_, December 7, 1990, p. 1.
34. Conradt, _The German Polity_, p. 140.
35. Helmut Gobel and Herbert Blondiau, eds., _Procedures, Programmes, Profiles: The Federal Republic of Germany Elects the German Bundestag on 5 October, 1980_ (Bonn: Inter-Nationes, 1980), p. 13.
36. For a discussion of the evolution of this point, see Karl H. Cerny, ed., _Germany at the Polls: The Bundestag Election of 1976_ (Washington, D.C.: American Enterprise Institute, 1978), pp. 3–17.
37. Gobel and Blondiau, _Procedures_, p. 13.
38. "Germany: Elections, Parliament, and Political Parties," p. 8.
39. Russell J. Dalton, _Politics: West Germany_ (Boston: Little, Brown, 1989), p. 246.
40. G. Merten, ed., _The Week in Germany_ 11:35 (September 19, 1980) (New York: German Information Center, 1980), p. 2.
41. Ibid., p. 2.
42. For 1980 election results see Merten, _The Week in Germany_ 11:38 (October 10, 1980), p. 2.
43. "Procedures, Programs, Profiles: First All-German Election" (Bonn: Inter-Nationes, 1990), p. 11.
44. There is much good discussion of the evolution of the party system in the chapter by Gerhard Loewenberg, "The Remaking of the German Party System," in _Germany at the Polls_.
45. See Geoffrey Pridham, _Christian Democracy in Western Germany_ (New York: St. Martin's Press, 1977).
46. A good description of West German politics under the CDU/CSU/FDP coalition can be found in Derbyshire, _Politics in West Germany_, pp. 46–56.
47. See Kolinsky, _Parties, Opposition, and Society_, pp. 122–149.
48. Merten, _The Week in Germany_ 11:35, p. 3.
49. See Christian Soe, "The Free Democratic Party," in _West German Politics in the Mid-Eighties_, ed. H. Peter Wallach and George Romoser (New York: Praeger, 1985).
50. Kolinsky, _Parties, Opposition, and Society_, p. 101.
51. Merten, _The Week in Germany_ 11:35, p. 3.
52. A very good study of the role of the Social Democrats while in power can be found in the work by Gerard Braunthal, _The West German Social Democrats, 1969–1982: Profile of a Party in Power_ (Boulder, Col.: Westview Press, 1983). He specifically discusses the series of coalition governments on pp. 224–232. See also Douglas Chalmers, _The Social Democratic Party of Germany_ (New Haven: Yale University Press, 1966).
53. See Gerd Langguth, _The Green Factor in German Politics: From Protest Movement to Political Party_ (Boulder, Col.: Westview Press, 1986).
54. Elim Papadakis, _The Green Movement in West Germany_ (New York: St. Martin's Press, 1984), p. 13.
55. Ibid., pp. 159, 161.
56. Rob Burns and Wilfried van der Will, _Protest and Democracy in West Germany: Extra-Parliamentary Opposition and the Democratic Agenda_ (New York: St. Martin's Press, 1988), p. 230.
57. Among these might be included the opposition to remilitarization and

nuclear weapons (1950–1969), the movement of students against authoritarianism (1965–1969), the women's movement (1968–1985), environmentalism (1970s and 1980s), and mass opposition to nuclear arms (1980–1986). See Burns and van der Will, *Protest and Democracy*, who have chapters on each of these protest movements.

58. A good analysis of the Greens can be found in Werner Hulsberg, *The German Greens: A Social and Political Profile*, trans. Gus Fagan (London: Verso, 1988), especially Chap. 7, "The Greens: A Preliminary Assessment," and chap. 8, "The Crisis of Orientation."

59. Dalton, *Politics: West Germany*, p. 293 note 15.

60. Papadakis, *The Green Movement*, p. 196.

61. Hulsberg, *German Greens*, p. 247. In Appendix I of his study Hulsberg provides election results for the Greens in Land and federal elections between 1978 and 1987.

62. "Germany: Elections, Parliament, and Political Parties," p. 19.

12

The Japanese Political System

The Japanese Political Heritage

Modern Japanese political history usually is said to have begun with a series of events in 1867–1868 known as the *Meiji Restoration.* That period signifies the time at which the emperor Meiji ended the history of rule of the Tokugawa Shogunate, which had lasted since 1603, and took power.[1] Between 1603 and 1867 the political regime of the Tokugawa Shogunate had "coordinated" Japanese government; the Shogunate system "was far from being a centralized government; some three-fourths of the national territory and considerable political power were still held by more than two hundred fifty feudal lords."[2]

The Meiji Restoration changed this and centralized Japanese politics considerably. This "restoration" in 1867 did not entail directly substituting a Meiji emperor for the Tokugawa rulers; the leaders of the movement to abolish the Tokugawa power system did not intend to support the 15-year-old Meiji in his claim to be heir to powers of his eighth-century ancestors "who were vested by right of divine descent with absolute power over the state."[3] The Meiji claim, though, was a focal point for the various forces supporting the overthrow of the Tokugawa regime.

During the period beginning in 1868, by which time Tokugawa rule was finished, until the establishment of the Meiji Constitution in 1889, a number of significant experiments in social and political thought were undertaken; some were successful, and some were not. Many social innovations were undertaken successfully, such as the abolition of the traditional land-tenure system and the rigid four-class system of merchant, artisan, peasant, and samurai. In the place of these archaic social institutions were substituted mass public education, equal protection under law, a merchant marine, modern industrial and technological development, and modern armed forces.

Politically, the interregnum was uncertain; leaders could agree on a dislike for the old Shogunate, but could not agree on what they wanted in its place. Some leaders favored bringing Western ideas to Japan and studied Western political philosophers such as Rousseau, Montesquieu, Locke, and others. Finally, however, the traditional power bases were victorious; the Constitution of 1889 "reflected the natural desire of the oligarchs to perpetuate their own authority" under the Meiji emperor.

> Although scarcely ideal as a foundation for a liberal political system . . . it should not be forgotten that the Meiji Constitution and governmental system were not notably illiberal in terms of prevailing European practice in 1890. They did mark a major departure from earlier Japanese political institutions and processes.[4]

Constitutions

Modern Japanese politics has taken place in two significantly different constitutional regimes. The Meiji Constitution was drawn up in 1889 and put into effect in the name of Emperor Meiji. The present-day constitution of Japan, sometimes referred to as the "MacArthur Constitution," was primarily authored by Americans operating out of the office of the Supreme Commander for the Allied Powers (SCAP) occupying Japan at the end of World War II, and it was put into effect by Emperor Hirohito in the name of the Japanese people.

As late as January 30, 1946, General Douglas MacArthur assured visiting Allied representatives that constitutional reform was not within his powers. One month later, however, he had decided the best way to prod reform was to prepare a model constitution for the Japanese. Within another three weeks, an entirely new constitution was drafted by SCAP officials. Symbolically, on Washington's birthday, Japan accepted the basic principles of the constitution. By March 5, the Emperor had approved the "drastic revision." By late June, the Japanese had writhed through four drafts, which were but slight revisions of the original document. By October 7, the new constitution had passed both houses of the Diet, under tremendous pressure from SCAP, and had been approved by the defunct Privy Council. On November 3, 1946, the Emperor promulgated the new constitution of Japan, which went into effect May 3, 1947.[5]

The Meiji Constitution was based upon the emperor, granted by the emperor, and amendable only by the emperor. Its basic philosophy was that "the Emperor is sacred and inviolable." Although others acted in the name of the emperor, his ultimate authority was never questioned in theory. The MacArthur Constitution was "revolutionary" to the extent that its preamble began with the (American style) phrase "We, the Japanese people, acting through our duly elected representatives . . . do proclaim that sovereign power resides with the people and do firmly establish this Constitution." One student of this subject concluded that "these are most explicit expressions of the doctrine of popular sovereignty, *a doctrine completely alien to Japanese thoughts*"[6] (emphasis added).

The new constitution also redirected the basic distribution of powers of the state. The Meiji Constitution had placed the bulk of power in the hands of the emperor's ministers, responsible to the emperor. Over time, through World War II, this power was gradually eroded as the consent of the Imperial Diet (parliament) became necessary for the passage of laws. "Thus the Diet could deliberate on laws; it could not determine them." Under the MacArthur Constitution, the Diet is "the highest organ of state power, and shall be the lawmaking organ of the state (Chapter 4, Article 41)."[7] This formula redistributed power away from the emperor and his ministers and directed it to the legislature. The MacArthur Constitution drafted by the Americans in 1946:

patched together an almost ideally democratic constitution, one that could scarcely have gained serious consideration if advocated for adoption in the United States. It had even less relevance to the traditional and dominant political aspirations of practices of Japan.[8]

Certainly among the most interesting and unique features of the MacArthur Constitution was the "renunciation of war" clause (Article 9). In this clause of the constitution the Japanese "forever renounce war as a sovereign right of the nation and the threat or use of force as a means of settling international disputes." To achieve this goal, "land, sea, and air forces, as well as other war potential, *will never be maintained*"[9] (emphasis added). This last part of Article 9 has not survived, in practice, since 1946. Today, Japan does have an army and a navy, and is (ironically) encouraged by the United States to further develop these forces as a strategic balance to Soviet and Chinese military forces in that part of the world.

Many critics of the Japanese Constitution argued that not only was it literally "imposed" on Japan by the Occupation forces, but that it was *conceptually* alien to Japan's political culture, that it had "foreign ideas which did not accord with Japanese character and tradition." It is worth noting, however, that in the almost forty years since the constitution was promulgated, "there has yet to be a formal motion in the Diet to amend the Constitution."[10]

The Executive Structures

The executive structure of the Japanese political system bears some resemblance to a Westminster-model executive, at least superficially. Upon initial inspection we can see a prime minister and an emperor, with the former apparently actively involved in the day-to-day operations of the Government, and the latter evidently held in great esteem by the public, with primarily symbolic functions.

This first impression does not tell the full story, however. The assumption that the emperor plays a role in Japanese politics corresponding to the role of the queen in British politics is an overstatement of the emperor's position. Similarly, because of some idiosyncratic characteristics of the Japanese political world that we will discuss below, the position of the prime minister in Tokyo is different from that of the prime minister in London.

The Emperor

The royal family in Japan has an impressive lineage. The late Emperor Hirohito was "officially held to be the 124th monarch of Japan descended in a direct line from the legendary Emperor Jimmu, who supposedly founded the dynasty in 660 B.C."[11] This date, traditionally ascribed as the founding date of the empire, is regarded by students of Japanese politics as being "mythological," but "there is reliable evidence that [the dynasty] existed by at least the early sixth century, A.D., and has been continuous since then."[12]

The name of the former emperor, Hirohito, was given to him by his grandfather, the Emperor Meiji. The current emperor, Akihito, was given his name by his father. In present-day Japan it is not considered proper to use the emperor's name in public; it almost never appears in print nor is it heard in conversation. Hirohito chose the name Showa as the name of his regime. "He will be known posthumously as the Emperor Showa; meanwhile he is referred to politely as *Tenno* (Emperor) or *Heika* (His Majesty), or as *Tenno Heika*. There is no dynastic or family name."[13]

The difference in the role of the emperor in the two modern Japanese constitutions cannot be overstated. The Meiji Constitution stated that "the Empire of Japan shall be reigned over and governed by a line of Emperors unbroken for ages eternal," and that "the Emperor is sacred and inviolable . . . the head of the Empire, combining in Himself the rights of sovereignty."[14] Even though the power of the emperor vis-à-vis the military eroded after 1932, allowing the military leaders to force the emperor into a war with the United States, the emperor remained a dominant figure in the constitutional system.

In the MacArthur Constitution, the status of the emperor was *radically* altered; "perhaps the most profound change brought about by the new constitution was the change in the status of the emperor."[15] The authors of the new constitution knew that the Japanese would strenuously object to their doing away with the institution of the imperial family, so they kept the institution but stripped it of all power. The emperor today has only a symbolic role in the political system. Not only does he not have any political or executive functions, but he is specifically enjoined, prohibited, from such tasks. Article 1 of the constitution states that "the Emperor shall be the symbol of the state and of the unity of the people, deriving his position from the will of the people with whom resides sovereign power." Article 1 goes on to be quite explicit: "the Emperor shall perform only such acts in matters of state as are provided for in this Constitution, and *he shall not have powers related to government*"[16] (emphasis added).

Under the constitution of his grandfather, Meiji, the emperor was supreme; today, the emperor "is no longer absolute monarch, and his activities in matters of state are strictly ceremonial; . . . in both theory and practice he is powerless." To put his role in a comparative perspective, "he does not even have the traditional 'right to be consulted, the right to encourage, the right to warn' which Bagehot ascribed to British monarchs."

> In attending to ceremonial state functions, he acts under the direction of the Cabinet, and he does not have "powers related to government." He appoints the Prime Minister as designated by the Diet—in this act he does not retain even the theoretical discretion that the Queen of England still enjoys—and the Chief Justice of the Supreme Court as recommended by the Cabinet. Under instruction from the Cabinet, he promulgates all laws, convokes the Diet, dissolves the House of Representatives, proclaims elections, attests the appointment and dismissal of state ministers, awards honors, receives foreign ambassadors and dignitaries, and performs other ceremonial functions. In short, the constitutional role of the Emperor is to clothe the every day acts of the government with the dignity and majesty of the throne.[17]

None of the many tasks of the emperor involve initiative, decisions, or choice by him; he acts "on the advice" of government leaders. On rare occasions it is possible that the emperor may exert some influence, primarily in areas concerning the Imperial family, or in a moment of grave national crisis. One such instance occurred at the end of World War II, in August 1945, when the cabinet was unable to reach a decision on whether to surrender or not; the emperor apparently played a pivotal role in convincing the cabinet to accept Allied surrender terms. When the emperor does exert influence today, it is usually based purely upon his "personal and institutional prestige. He has no legal or theoretical right to do so, and thus his official position is far weaker than the British monarch."[18]

Technically, it is worth noting (and is not merely an exercise in semantics to do so) that the emperor is not even a "chief of state" or "head of state," but is only the "symbol of the state." He does not possess powers that most chiefs of state or heads of state, such as the British monarch or the German president, possess, even only in theory. Thus, while the Meiji emperor was among the most powerful individuals in the world by virtue of his position in the Japanese political system, the Japanese emperor today has extremely little political significance, and comparatively speaking is less powerful than most comparable political figures in other political systems.

The Prime Minister

As we would predict from our basic Westminster-model format, the real power in Japan lies in the hands of the Government, namely the prime minister and the cabinet, and not the emperor. Because the emperor is explicitly prohibited from *all* political action, however, the Japanese Government in many respects has *more* power than the British Government.

In Britain, and British-model countries, although the head of state acts "on the advice of the Government" when he or she dissolves the legislature and calls for new elections, for example, it is *still* the head of state who has the power of dissolution. Under extraordinary circumstances the head of state may choose *not* to follow the advice of his or her Government. In Japan, those powers usually held by the head of state (even only formally) to be exercised "on the advice of the Government" are *not* held by the emperor; they are simply held by the Government both *de jure* (in law) and *de facto* (in fact).

As in many other parliamentary systems, the Japanese legislature, the Diet, is bicameral: It has two chambers, and as is usually the case in bicameral parliamentary systems, the Government is "responsible," or answerable, only to the lower house, the House of Representatives.

> The Constitution does not require that the Prime Minister be a Representative (merely that he be a member of the Diet), but as in

England constitutional practice demands that he be nominated from the lower house. The reason is that in the event of a disagreement between Representatives and Councillors on the choice of a Prime Minister, the decision of the House of Representatives is final (Article 67 of the Constitution).[19]

To date, all of Japan's postwar prime ministers have been members of the House of Representatives.[20] In practice, virtually all members of the cabinet come from the House of Representatives, with perhaps two or three members coming from the upper house, the House of Councillors.

Also typical of other parliamentary nations, cabinet members wear a number of different hats—they play several roles at the same time. They are members of the legislative branch of government, they are members of the cabinet and thereby the executive branch of government, and they are each responsible for vast government bureaucracies and thereby play administrative roles. In addition to these three roles that are typical of all parliamentary systems, cabinet members in Japan may be said to "wear a fourth hat" characteristic of those countries in which cabinets are based upon coalitions of several political parties: Cabinet members in Japan are either leaders of political parties or leaders of factions of political parties.

"While the Emperor is the symbol of the state under the new Constitution, the Prime Minister is the head of the Government. Since World War Two the roles of the Prime Minister and Cabinet have grown vastly more important than they formerly were." Under the Meiji regime the executive power *de jure* belonged to the emperor, who was advised by his ministers. Article 65 of the 1947 constitution "provides that 'Executive power shall be vested in the Cabinet' so that the Cabinet exercises executive authority in its own right."[21]

The Japanese cabinet is specifically given a large number of powers in the constitution. "It administers the affairs of state through a vast bureaucracy . . . in 53 primary ministries and agencies. . . . Above all, the Cabinet has the right to initiate both ordinary legislation and amendments to the Constitution."[22] Powers of the cabinet can be broken down into several categories—executive, legislative, and judicial—and are illustrated in Table 12.1, on the following page.

Coalition Governments

Because Japan has a multiparty system, it would be predictable that coalition government would form there. What makes the Japanese political system especially interesting is that for the most part all of the coalitions that have formed have been coalitions *within* one massive party, the Liberal-Democratic party (LDP). In 1955 the nonsocialist parties in Japan combined to form the LDP, which has always had a majority in the House of Representatives in combination with a number of smaller conservative offshoot parties. The components of the LDP coalition, however, have not completely disappeared, and the leader of the LDP must always be cognizant of the need to keep leaders of the party's various factions happy if he or she wants to stay in power.

In fact, some have suggested that the real core of Japanese party politics cannot be described by interparty competition. Rather, they argue, the most important single characteristic of Japanese politics is the elaborate factional infighting within the LDP, as well as the interaction between various interest groups and the LDP leadership, some of it clearly corrupt. In the past

Table 12.1
Powers of the Japanese Cabinet As Found in the Constitution

Executive Powers:
1. Supervise the administration of the state (Section 72)
2. Manage foreign affairs and treaties (Section 73)
3. Control financial policy (Sections 83, 87)
4. Enact cabinet orders (Section 73)

Legislative Powers:
1. Submit bills to the Diet (Section 72)
2. Prepare the national budget (Sections 73, 86)
3. Report to the Diet on state expenses (Section 90)
4. "Advise" the emperor as to when to call sessions of the Diet (Section 7)
5. Sign laws (Section 74)

Judicial Powers:
1. Name the chief justice of the Supreme Court (Section 6)
2. Appoint justices to courts (Sections 79, 80)

Source: Based on text in Warren Tsuneishi, *Japanese Political Style* (New York: Harper & Row, 1966), pp. 42–43.

several years, as we shall describe later in this chapter, we have seen a number of political crises brought about by charges of corruption within the LDP.

In a groundbreaking study over twenty years ago, Michael Leiserson was able to identify six levels of cabinet positions in Japan. He suggested that for the LDP leader to stay in power, the party needed to distribute enough "valuable" cabinet positions to each party faction to retain their support. Factions more valuable to the coalition would receive more valuable cabinet positions. Leiserson ranked the cabinet positions as follows:

A. Prime Minister
B. Finance Minister, Party Secretary-General
C. Trade and Industry Minister, Agriculture Minister, Transportation Minister, Construction Minister, Party Executive Board Chairman, Party Policy Board Chairman
D. Foreign Minister, Deputy Prime Minister, Party Vice President, Cabinet Minister without Portfolio
E. Education Minister, Welfare Minister, Labor Minister, Defense Minister, Justice Minister, Post Office Minister, Interior Minister
F. Administrative Management Agency Director, Science and Technology Minister.[23]

Ever since the establishment of the cabinet system in Japan in 1885, nearly seventy cabinets have come into existence under both the Meiji and the 1947 constitutions. Thus the average Japanese cabinet has lasted for about fourteen months.[24] In recent years the cabinet has usually had about twelve members, far smaller than many of its European counterparts.

The prime minister is head of the cabinet, and for reasons that we indicated earlier—because the emperor is unusually weak—the prime minister is unusually strong. This individual's powers include the following:

1. Power to appoint and dismiss other Cabinet members without consulting the Diet;
2. Control over branches of administration;
3. Countersignature power on *all* laws and cabinet orders; they must be signed by the prime minister *as well as* the relevant minister;
4. Power to preside at cabinet meetings;
5. Power to decide jurisdictional disputes between cabinet officers;
6. Power to cause resignation of the entire cabinet by his own resignation.[25]

Under the Meiji Constitution, through 1932, the prime minister was chosen by the emperor from among leaders in the Diet (as is the case in most parliamentary systems); from 1932 until the end of World War II, prime ministers were not party leaders, but instead were generals. Under the 1947 constitution, it is not the emperor who selects the prime minister, even on a *pro forma* basis, but the Diet itself. At its first meeting after a new election, the Diet selects a prime minister from its own membership. If the House of Councillors does not concur with the House of Representatives within a ten-day period, the House of Representatives' choice becomes prime minister anyway. The emperor is then required to ratify the choice of the Diet (which he always has done).[26]

The prime minister has the right to choose his own cabinet, and will do so, as we indicated above, in a manner so as to strengthen his coalition and therefore his political power. As more than one scholar has noted, "The first job of the new prime minister is to distribute Diet, cabinet, and party positions, and finalize the line-up."[27] Unlike other parliamentary systems in which a vote of confidence is needed before the prime minister and cabinet officially take office, the Japanese prime minister (since he is *chosen* by the legislature and not by the head of state) needs no subsequent vote of confidence. What is more, the Japanese prime minister may change the composition of the cabinet at any time he wishes to do so; he does not need to go back to the legislature for a subsequent vote of confidence.[28]

The Cabinet

The cabinet is responsible to the House of Representatives in the same manner that we have seen in other nations. If the House of Representatives (the Government is responsible only to the lower house, not the upper house) passes a resolution of no confidence or fails to pass a resolution of confidence in the cabinet (and this is quite rare in Japanese politics), Article 69 of the constitution requires that "the Cabinet shall resign en masse, unless the House of Representatives is dissolved within ten days."[29]

Thus, the cabinet has a choice to make if it receives a vote of no confidence: It can either resign immediately, or it can dissolve the House of Representatives and call for new elections. If it chooses the latter route, dissolution, it *still* must resign en masse (under Article 70) "upon the first convocation of the Diet after a general election of members of the lower house"—that is, as soon as the House of Representatives meets after the election—even if the party of the Government wins the election. This required resignation does not, of course, prevent the same prime minister from being renamed prime minister in the new Government.[30]

The cabinet is also constitutionally mandated to resign upon the resignation (or death) of the prime minister. Dissolution, of course, affects only the House of Representatives. "The House of Councillors, having a fixed term, cannot be dissolved. Its sessions are, however, suspended when the lower house has been dissolved and resume only with the convocation of the postelection Diet."[31]

Administrative Structures

The number of public employees in Japan increased dramatically between the end of World War II and the mid-1960s. In fact, there was such a growth of the governmental bureaucracy that a "capping" law was passed in 1969 limiting the growth of civil servants in the regular ministries and national government agencies. There is in effect a "zero-sum game" in government personnel: Any increase in one division must be matched by a comparable decrease in another.[32] In fact, a government task force recommended a 5 percent cut in the number of national employees between 1982 and 1986 in an attempt to reduce government expenditures.[33]

The administrative branch of Japanese government "plays an important role in the ongoing process of making decisions and setting national goals, as well as in the implementation of policies."[34] Cabinet officials oversee huge bureaucratic structures; the Japanese administrative bureaucracy contains a vast civil service, with a very small number of political appointments. The bureaucracy plays an active role in the "drafting and implementation of laws and the issuance of ministerial rules,"[35] which are often regarded as being just as important as laws passed by the Diet.

The Diet

The Japanese Diet is the oldest parliamentary body in Asia, having been in continuous existence since 1890.[36] Today, power in the Japanese political system, as we have seen, is not

> vested in the crown to be exercised by the cabinet, as in England. Nor has the power of the cabinet grown in an entirely extra-constitutional fashion, as in the United States. Indeed, in Japanese constitutional theory, the cabinet holds an inferior status, as compared with the Diet, the highest organ of state power.[37]

The constitution describes the Diet as "the highest organ of state power,"[38] and it sets forth in some detail the structure and power of the Diet in relation to other political bodies in the political system. The significance of this is most obvious:

> when compared with comparable clauses of the Meiji Constitution. Under the terms of that document, the emperor was more than the highest organ of state power; in a mystical way, he embodied the state and wielded its sovereign powers. Although laws were formally the product of the Imperial Diet, both the emperor and the Cabinet had the power to issue decrees that had the force of law. The present Constitution vests sovereignty in the people and makes the Diet both the highest organ of the people's sovereignty and the sole source of law. These changes are basic to both the legal and the power structure of the Japanese state. The government has thus been technically transformed from an emperor-centered to a parliament-centered system, and the elected representatives of the people have, in theory at least, become vastly more powerful.[39]

In the new constitution, then, "the Diet was transformed from an instrument for endorsing the Emperor's legislative authority to the highest organ of state power and the sole law-making organ of the state."[40] The Japanese legislature is called the Diet in English because it was modelled upon the German Diet existing when the first Japanese Constitution was drawn up in the late 1880s. The British, French, and American systems were all used as models, in different eras, for Japanese political evolution.[41]

That the Japanese Diet today is a bicameral legislative body is a result of the insistence of the Japanese leaders during the time of MacArthur's governance of Japan. The American constitutional authorities on MacArthur's staff wanted to abolish the House of Peers (the upper house in Japan during the Meiji era), and they argued that Japan did not need a second house in its new constitutional structure, since Japan had a unitary, not a federal, political system. The American authors of the "new" Japanese constitution, in fact, deleted the upper house from the first drafts of their proposed Japanese constitution.

Japanese officials insisted on the inclusion of a second house, however, not because it was justified by a federal political system (which Japan was clearly not), but primarily because it was necessary for a "sober second thought," a "check against hasty, ill-considered measures supported by a majority party in the lower house."[42] The American concession in this regard, "allowing" the Japanese to have a bicameral legislature, was "the only major concession to Japanese opinion made by MacArthur's staff in the new Japanese constitution."[43]

The Diet performs a number of significant political functions in the Japanese system today. First, as with all parliamentary bodies we must identify its primary function not as passing legislation, but as the selection of a Government, the "designation of a cabinet." Second, to a lesser degree that we will discuss below, the Diet does play a role in the making of governmental policy, primarily responding to proposals from the Government. Third, the Diet initiates constitutional amendments, "ratifies treaties, and oversees administration, all powers that previously belonged to the Emperor." Fourth, the Diet participates in the process of making foreign policy, by holding hearings and ratifying treaties undertaken by the Government. Fifth, the Diet participates in the normal operation of Government operations by virtue of its "power to investigate government operations." Finally, and most important to many, the Diet "functions as a public forum where the great issues of the day are publicized, analyzed, debated, and then acted upon."[44]

Bicameralism

The upper house of the bicameral legislature—the House of Councillors—is the less important of the two. It was designed "to attract well-known people who were not necessarily professional politicians."[45] To help distinguish the role of the House of Councillors—supposedly existing to provide stability and a "sober second thought" to actions of the House of Representatives—from the role of the lower house, councillors were given six-year terms of office, with half of the 252 members being elected every three years. Members of the House of Representatives serve up to four-year terms, subject to early dissolution.

The two houses of the Diet do not have equal power. The constitution notes that the lower house is superior to the upper house in several specific areas, including (1) the enactment of laws, (2) the passage of the budget, (3) approving treaties, and (4) the selection of the prime minister.[46]

The relationship is not the same between the Government and each of the two houses of the Diet. The Government is responsible to the House of Representatives, and must maintain the "confidence" of the House of Representatives. In a manner similar to that which we have noted elsewhere, although the Government is vulnerable to the House of Representatives, in that the House of Representatives can pass a motion of no confidence and in effect fire the Government, the House of Representatives is correspondingly vulnerable to the Government, since the Government has the power of dissolution, in effect the power to fire the lower house of the Diet.

The Government is *not* correspondingly responsible to the House of Councillors, and in this respect it is very similar to the relationship between the British cabinet and the House of Commons and the British cabinet and the House of Lords. Accordingly, since the Government is not vulnerable to the councillors, the councillors are not vulnerable to the Government: "The House of Councillors may not be dissolved."[47]

The Legislative Process

The legislative powers of the House of Councillors appear to be very similar to those of the House of Representatives, with the three exceptions noted above: in the area of treaties, budget bills, and the selection of the prime minister. If the two houses cannot agree, the will of a majority of the lower house prevails over the will of the upper house. In all other matters the approval of both houses is necessary, although the lower house can override the upper house with a two-thirds majority if the two houses cannot agree on a compromise over disputed legislation. This has not happened very frequently: Since the end of World War II this has occurred only 29 times.[48]

Although the influence of the House of Councillors in the legislative process may thus be only that of a suspensory veto (since the lower house has the power to override the upper house), in specific political eras when the Government's majority in the House of Representatives does not approach a two-thirds share of the membership, and when the Government knows it does not have the votes to override the upper house, the House of Councillors' veto may in fact be more than merely suspensory. A Government that can count on only 55 or 60 percent of the House of Representatives membership may feel compelled to reach a compromise with the House of Councillors rather than try to override the House of Councillors with a two-thirds vote that it knows it cannot obtain.

Most bills originate somewhere in the ministries, and after working their way through the bureaucratic network the bills appear in the cabinet for its approval for submission in the Diet as a Government bill. Not all ministry proposals are endorsed by the cabinet, but those that are endorsed are submitted by the prime minister to the Diet. "Budget bills must go to the lower house first. Five days after submission of a bill to one house, the other must receive a copy for preliminary study."[49]

When a bill is submitted to either house of the Diet, either the Speaker of the House of Representatives or the President of the House of Councillors immediately channels the bill to the appropriate standing committee. There are sixteen standing committees in each house, and committees are the same in both houses. The committees are:

1. Foreign Affairs
2. Finance
3. Education
4. Welfare and Labor
5. Agriculture, Forestry, and Fisheries
6. Commerce and Industry
7. Transport
8. Communications
9. Construction
10. Local Administration
11. Budget
12. Accounting

13. House Management
14. Discipline
15. Cabinet
16. Judicial Affairs[50]

The committee stage in the House of Representatives may be bypassed if a majority of the House concurs. This does not apply to the House of Councillors. Committees hold hearings on bills, calling as witnesses cabinet members, ministerial officials, concerned bureaucrats, interest group representatives, and members of the public. After the committee has finished its hearings, it reports to the full House. Unlike other parliamentary bodies that employ variations of the "three-reading" model in their legislative process, the houses of the Japanese Diet have only a single reading and vote following the committee stage. Voting in the House of Representatives, as one might guess, "runs strictly along party lines."[51] If a bill passes, it goes to the other house of the Diet where the same procedure is followed.

> If the other house makes changes, the bill goes back to the first house. If there is still disagreement, then a conference committee tries to resolve it, or the lower house can try to override the upper by a two-thirds vote for passage. In the case of disagreement between the houses on budget bills or treaties, or in the absence of upper house action in thirty days, the lower house decision by ordinary majority is sufficient to pass the bill. The bill is signed into law by the sponsoring minister, the Emperor, and the Prime Minister: they do not possess a veto after Diet passage.[52]

The cabinet is not the only source of legislation in the Diet, although it is the largest source. Bills in both houses also originate in committees and from private members; regular private members' bills must have at least twenty co-sponsors, and bills dealing with budgetary matters need fifty co-sponsors.[53] One long-term study found that between 1947 and 1975 approximately 85 percent of all bills passed were bills introduced by the Government, whereas about 15 percent were introduced by private members.

Many of these private members' bills, of course, *really* originated in the bureaucracy and were introduced as private members' bills because of the unwillingness of the cabinet, or the relevant minister, or some bureaucrat in the chain of command below that, to approve the proposal as an official Government idea.

> The scheduling and flow of legislative business is controlled by the Committee on House Management, composed of senior and experienced representatives of each political party in numbers proportional to that party's strength in the lower house. Under normal circumstances—a term that applies to a large majority of the bills coming before the house—this system works quite effectively. On noncontroversial matters, the members of the Committee on House Management are briefed in advance by their parties' Diet Strategy Committee and are able to calendar bills and assign time quotas to each party for speaking on the issue involved. On controversial matters, however, the system sometimes breaks down completely, and the committee is unable to agree. In such cases the matter is usually referred to the secretaries-general of all the parties for negotiation and settlement. Protracted negotiations can ensue during which the normal functioning of the house may come to a complete halt.[54]

Political Parties and Elections

The Japanese political party system has been variously described as a multiparty system,[55] a "one and one-half party system,"[56] and a "six quarter-parties system."[57] Japan has actually had a large number of political parties since the advent of the MacArthur Constitution; at one point immediately after the war there were apparently in excess of 1,000 "registered groups" active in politics.

This fact notwithstanding, however, Japan has had a paucity of truly ideological political parties. "Even the three or four major ones offered a bewildering shift of names, symptomatic of the bland transfer of members' allegiance, and an almost total lack of true political principles."[58] Essentially, in modern times Japan has been led by a single party, the Liberal Democratic party (LDP), with opposition parties rising and falling in popularity while the LDP ruled.

In November 1955 Japan's two major (ideologically) conservative parties, the (inappropriately named) Liberal party and the Democratic party, combined to offer a significant opposition force to the Socialist party, which was a major force in Japan at the time. This new party was called the Liberal-Democratic party.[59] For a brief period of time thereafter, a two-party system prevailed in Japan. Soon, however, intraparty factionalism and competition led to splintering of the parties and Japan reverted to a multiparty system.[60]

The System of Political Parties

The current party structure of Japanese politics is dominated by two major parties, the Liberal Democratic party and the Japan Socialist party. The party system has been characterized as "a dominant party that monopolizes power and alone knows how to govern, while opposed by a permanent minority group that at times seems 'positively afraid of power.' "[61]

The Japan Socialist party (JSP) dates from November 1945, and has been characterized as a party "of permanent opposition."[62] For many years the Socialist party strongly advocated unarmed neutrality in foreign policy, and loudly criticized Japan's Self-Defense Forces as violating the "constitutional renunciation of 'land, sea, and air forces, as well as other war potential' (Article 9)."[63] In recent years the JSP has moderated its view and softened its traditional anti-American positions.

A third significant party, the "Komeito," or Clean Government party, has sought to control the political center in electoral competitions. Komeito was originally created to be the political arm of a major Buddhist sect with over 16 million members.[64] Komeito's philosophy suggests that "centrism is a position in which it should be possible to overcome the confrontation between the left and the right and to create a third solution that can be a national consensus."[65]

> Considering the weakness of the Socialist Party and the fierce hostilities, suspicions, and rivalry that beset the five opposition parties collectively, some understanding of the basic immobilism of Japanese party politics begins to emerge. [The LDP survives as the basis of government] partly because of a lack of any credible alternative.[66]

As can be seen in the results of the 1990 elections for the House of Representatives (summarized in Table 12.2), there are currently a number of parties active in Japanese politics. Many of these parties are the results of a number of evolutionary changes in party names, organizations, and ideology. Some of the contemporary political parties have very clearly delineated policy platforms differentiating them from other parties. Others of the several parties have a number of policy positions in common, and differ on minor points.[67] This situation of uncertainty about party ideology and behavior has led one student of Japanese politics to posit two general characteristics of the political party situation in Japan today:

> First, none of the parties—except perhaps the Clean Government and Communist parties—are truly mass membership organizations. They notably lack solid bases in popular involvement and support. They normally operate in Tokyo and among circles limited almost exclusively to professional politicians and administrators.

Table 12.2
Results of 1990 Elections for the Japanese House of Representatives

Party	No. Seats Won		Percent of Seats	Seats in Last Diet	No. Candi- dates	No. Votes Won	Percent of Votes Won
LDP	275	(0)[a]	53.7	300	337	30,315,410	46.14
JSP	136	(7)	26.6	85	149	13,025,468	19.82
Komeito	45	(1)	8.8	56	58	5,242,674	7.98
JCP	16	(2)	3.1	26	131	5,226,985	7.96
DSP	14	(0)	2.7	26	44	3,178,949	4.84
USD	4	(0)	0.8	4	6	566,957	0.86
Shimpoto	1	(0)	0.2	0	7	281,793	0.43
Minor parties	0	(0)	—	6	64	58,534	0.09
Independent	21	(2)	4.1	9	157	4,807,520	7.32
Missing data						3,000,000	4.56
Total	512	(12)	100.0	512	953	65,704,290	100.0

Abbreviations:
LDP	Liberal Democratic Party
JSP	Japan Socialist Party
JCP	Japan Communist Party
DSP	Democratic Socialist Party
USD	United Socialist Democratic Party

[a]Figures in parentheses are number of women.

Source: Japan Information and Culture Center, Embassy of Japan, Washington, D.C.; Government of Japan, Ministry of Home Affairs.

They are essentially parliamentary parties. Their prime focus of interest is the lower house of the National Diet and what goes on there. Only during election campaigns do they engage in massive and sustained contact with the people.

Second, the two largest parties are internally disunited. . . . The results of such a situation are constant instability and strife within each party.[68]

Electoral Activity

The primary focus of all political parties in Japan, as indicated in the above quote, is the lower house of the Diet, the House of Representatives, and, accordingly, elections to the House of Representatives. Japan has a history of national elections dating back to 1889, although early elections had very small electorates due to rigid restrictions based upon tax and residency qualifications.[69] Today, elections are highly visible, and the public participation rate is correspondingly high, as indicated in Table 12.2.

Japan is a unitary, not a federal, state, and is divided into 47 administrative regions called *prefectures*, which themselves include 655 cities, 2,000 towns, and 591 villages.[70] Each of these bodies has its own autonomous government with an elected assembly.[71]

Elections for both the lower house, the House of Representatives, and for part of the upper house, the House of Councillors, are based upon electoral districts that to varying degrees are themselves based upon these prefectural units. We will discuss each of the electoral frameworks separately here.

Elections for the House of Representatives are based upon multiple-member districts such as those we described earlier in this volume. Currently, there are 130 "medium-sized" districts that elect 512 members to the House of Representatives. The electoral districts are constructed "by dividing up the forty-six [now that Okinawa has been returned to Japanese jurisdiction there are forty-seven] prefectures in such a way that the districts do not cross prefectural boundaries."[72]

Lightly populated prefectures such as Saga and Kochi are single constituencies in themselves; more heavily populated prefectures such as Tokyo may be divided into as many as seven constituencies.[73] The system "has no multiple voting or proportional representation. It is technically a multimember constituency, single-vote system."[74] The 130 districts each send from three to five members to the House of Representatives (with one exception of a single one-member district). Each voter votes once, and the top three or four or five vote-getters (whichever is appropriate to the district in question) are elected. Obviously no majority is required. "Thus, for example, in the Shizuoka Prefecture third district, which is entitled to four seats in the House of Representatives, the four candidates receiving the highest number of votes win the four seats."[75]

How do would-be representatives become candidates for the House of Representatives election? It is done on a flexible basis; there are no nominating conventions or public primary elections. Hopefuls simply notify the chairmen of local election boards and pay deposits that are returned if the candidate wins a minimal percentage of the vote. (This is designed to discourage frivolous candidacies.) Nomination by parties is done by party election committees that are established for that purpose by the party organization.[76]

In the multiple-member-district races, each party can obviously have several candidates competing for seats. This explains how the Liberal Democratic party was able to control 53.7 percent of the seats in the House of Representatives following the 1990 election, although it won only 46.1 percent of the vote. It is worth noting that the Democratic Socialist party won 14 seats (2.7 percent of the total) with 4.8 percent of the vote, wheras the Japan Communist party won almost the same number or seats—16 seats, or 3.1 percent of the total—with 8 percent of the votes. More dramatically, while 7.96 percent of the vote earned the Japan Communist party 16 seats in the House of Representatives, 7.98 percent of the votes earned the Komeito party 45 seats in the House of Representatives! This shows that there is a great value to effective candidacy planning.[77] "The secret of success lies in achieving an optimal relationship between the number of candidates a party runs in a given election district and the number of votes it controls in that area."[78]

These electoral competitions, it has been argued, "exacerbate intraparty factional rivalry" for the simple reason that:

> the candidate's most formidable rivals quite often are members of his own party and not of the opposition. Consider as an extreme case the sad fate of Representative Ozawa Taro, Liberal-Democratic incumbent who in 1963 faced the formidable task of running not only against his Socialist opponents but against two of the

best-known politicians in the country, former Prime Minister Kishi Nobusuke and future Prime Minister Sato Eisaku. Seven candidates contested the five seats allotted to the First District of Yamaguchi Prefecture: 3 Liberal-Democrats, 2 Socialists, a Democratic Socialist, and a Communist. Altogether the conservatives polled 188,583 votes which, if distributed evenly among the three, would have ensured reelection for all. But Sato gained 94,785 votes, Kishi 49,877, and Ozawa only 43,841. Sato's great pulling power reduced Ozawa's total, with the result that his Socialist and Democratic Socialist opponents with 50,000–66,000 votes took the other three seats.[79]

Elections, as in many parliamentary systems, are required at least every four-years, but usually are held more frequently than that for political reasons. In fact, until very recently it was true that no Diet in the postwar period had lasted its full four-year term of office. When the House of Representatives is dissolved, "the Government must call a general election within 60 days. The actual date of the election must be announced at least 25 days in advance."[80]

The upper house of the Diet, the House of Councillors, is not terribly significant in the operation of the Government, as we indicated earlier. Members of the House of Councillors are elected for six-year terms, half of the membership being elected every three years. Like many other parliamentary upper houses, because the Government is not responsible to the House of Councillors, the House of Councillors cannot be dissolved by the Government. Councillors all serve their full six-year terms.

The House of Councillors in Japan has two separate constituencies, like the lower house of the German legislature. Japanese voters each have two votes in elections for the upper house, the House of Councillors. The 252 members of the House of Councillors are divided into two groups, the "prefectural" or "local" representatives, and the national "proportional representation" representatives. Of the 252 members, 152 represent prefectural constituencies, and 100 represent the proportional representation, national constituency. Since half of the House of Councillors is elected every three years, this means that at each House of Councillors election 76 "prefectural" or "local" representatives will be elected and 50 "national" representatives will be elected.

The prefectural or local representatives are elected from

multiple-member districts. "Each of the 47 prefectures is entitled to from two to eight seats in the House of Councillors, the more populous prefectures having more seats than the less populous."[81] Only the prefectures of Tokyo and Hokkaido are large enough to have eight seats in the House of Councillors.[82] Since 76 of the 152 prefectural representatives are elected every three years, half of each prefecture's seats are contested at every election. Much as with the elections for the Japanese House of Representatives, there will be many candidates competing for the one-to-four seats in each prefecture, and each voter casts one vote with the top one-to-four (as appropriate) vote-getters being elected.

The 50 members of the national constituency of the House of Councillors elected every three years were elected until 1980 from a single national multiple-member district (in this case, 50 members) in which there might have been as many as 200 to 250 candidates competing for the 50 seats; the top 50 vote-getters were the winners. In 1980 this system was changed so that the 50 "national" representatives would be elected by a system of proportional representation.

Recent Elections

In all Japanese elections in the last two decades the Liberal Democratic party has dominated seats in the Diet.[83] The December 1972 election for the House of Representatives had been relatively close for the LDP, but the election of the House of Councillors in July 1974 was especially alarming. In this election the LDP faced its most severe challenge to date, controlling 129 seats (along with its conservative allies) against 122 seats for the opposition, a majority of only seven seats.[84]

One of the major issues in the election was the close relationship between the LDP and what was called "big business," and many voters were concerned with what was referred to as the "money-dominated election"[85] in which many candidates spent fortunes (provided by business supporters) on their campaigns. The charge that the interest group exerts a disproportionate influence in Japanese politics (for example, in the legislative process) has frequently—too frequently, many Japanese feel—been a major issue in elections; accusations of corruption, bribery, or some other type of undue influence have figured prominently as campaign issues in recent years.[86]

The next election, in 1976, was the only time in postwar history that the House of Representatives served its full four-year term. The election was held as late as possible because of the massive political scandal at the time dealing with payoffs to politicians by the Lockheed Aircraft Co., thus dubbing the election the "Lockheed election." In that election the LDP won only 249 seats; by co-opting a number of conservative independents after the election the party was able to raise its results to 257, one seat above the "minimum majority" of 256, a figure that was subsequently raised to 260.[87]

The election of October 1979 was called over a year before it was necessary, because Prime Minister Ohira felt that his party was increasing its strength and would do well; the media were predicting an LDP landslide. However, the LDP performed very poorly, winning only 248 seats, far less than a majority. With some postelection co-optation of other conservative independents, the LDP was able to assemble a majority again, but the Ohira Government was weakened by the election results.

Japan had the first simultaneous election for both houses of the Diet in its history scheduled for June 22, 1980. Although the opposition parties had hopes of significant gains, their plans were frustrated by the sudden death of Prime Minister Ohira ten days before the election; the major target of the opposition parties disappeared. It was ironic—although perhaps predictable—that after the prime minister's death his party's performance in the election improved remarkably from the preceding election, to a substantial degree because of a "sympathy vote." The LDP won a landslide victory, winning 286 seats in the House of Representatives, its largest majority since 1969, and maintaining a solid majority in the House of Councillors.

Scandal again was the theme of the 1983 election; this time the general topic was the "Tanaka problem"—referring to the scandal involving former Prime Minister Tanaka, who had been found guilty of accepting bribes offered by Lockheed Aircraft in return for a Japan Airlines purchase of its airplanes—as well as the issue of political ethics in the LDP. Prime Minister Yasuhiro Nakasone sought to distance himself from the guilty verdict, but he was not completely successful; the LDP's majority fell from 286 seats to 250 seats, a much smaller majority.

In June 1986 Prime Minister Nakasone dissolved the House of Representatives eighteen months before elections were re-

quired so that there could be another election of both houses of
the Diet at the same time; it was believed that a double election
encourages greater voter turnout, and would thereby favor the
party that was in power. The election, held July 6, gave the Liberal
Democratic party "its most resounding election victory since it
was formed" in 1955.[88]

Nakasone stepped down as prime minister and president of
the Liberal Democratic party in October 1987, as required by the
constitution of the LDP,[89] and his place was taken by Noboru
Takeshita. Takeshita, as did some of his predecessors, suffered
the effects of a variety of political scandals. His party's candidate
lost in a by-election race in February 1989 as a result "of public
anger about a widening stock scandal and a recently enacted sales
tax."[90] Takeshita resigned as a result of the scandal in the early
summer, and was replaced by Soucuke Uno, who was forced to
resign in less than a month as a result of a sex scandal, leaving
Toshiki Kaifu as prime minister trying to rebuild the reeling
Liberal Democratic party top leadership.

The February 1990 election for the House of Representatives
returned the Liberal Democratic party to power, although with a
smaller majority (275) than it had enjoyed following the 1986
election (300). Prime Minister Kaifu expressed satisfaction at his
party's retaining control of the House of Representatives, and
vowed to restore the credibility of the Liberal Democrats. The big
winners in the 1990 election were the supporters of the Japan
Socialist Party, whose representation in the House increased from
85 seats to 136 seats; the Komeito, Democratic Socialist party, and
United Socialist Democratic party all declined in strength in the
new legislature.

Summary

The Japanese political system is a hybrid one. The modern political structure of Japan is a result of a highly artificial combination
of Western constitutional ideas and Japanese political and cultural history. The authors of the MacArthur Constitution gave
Japan a constitutional framework, which they thought would
lead to stable and democratic government. So far, to the surprise
of some, they appear to have succeeded.

Japan has taken a number of political cues from Western

Europe and the United States, and, as we have seen in this chapter, has adapted many of these cues to be appropriate to the Japanese culture. The Imperial family, although *de jure* of little significance, is still quite important in Japan. The legislature is typical of many of the Westminster-model bodies we have already met, with some extra authority given to the Government as a result of the emperor's unique lack of power. The electoral system is different from any we have met thus far, yet it seems to be consistent with ideas we have met dealing with democratic elections and popular representation.

The Japanese political system, then, is yet another in the series of political portraits we have met in this book. It presents some very interesting variations on the several themes common to the many political systems we have already encountered, and it provides illustrations of the ways in which political structures may alter in order to be appropriate to the political culture in which they are to be found.

Notes

1. A good history of Japanese political institutions can be found in Ryosuke Ishii, *A History of Political Institutions in Japan* (Tokyo: University of Tokyo Press, 1980).
2. Robert E. Ward, *Japan's Political System* (Englewood Cliffs, N.J.: Prentice Hall, 1978), p. 8.
3. Ibid., p. 9.
4. Ibid. p. 11.
5. Ardath Burks, *The Government of Japan* (New York: Crowell, 1964), p. 25.
6. See Kazuo Kawai, "Sovereignty and Democracy in the Japanese Constitution," *American Political Science Review* 49 (1955): 663.
7. Burks, *The Government of Japan*, p. 19.
8. Robert E. Ward, "The Origins of the Present Japanese Constitution," *American Political Science Review* 50 (1956): 1001. All future references to Ward are to his 1978 book, not this article.
9. Burks, *The Government of Japan*, p. 21.
10. Charles F. Bingman, *Japanese Government Leadership and Management* (New York: St. Martin's Press, 1989), p. 5.
11. Warren Tsuneishi, *Japanese Political Style* (New York: Harper & Row, 1966), p. 55.
12. Ward, *Japan's Political System*, p. 147.
13. Tsuneishi, *Japanese Political Style*, p. 56.
14. Theodore McNelly, *Politics and Government in Japan* (Boston: Houghton Mifflin, 1972), p. 181.
15. Bradley Richardson and Scott Flanagan, *Politics: Japan* (Boston: Little, Brown, 1984), p. 36. When the current emperor, Akihito, was enthroned in November 1990, spectators were able to see both the secular and

symbolic importance of his position. See Steven Weisman, "Japan En-thrones Emperor Today in Old Rite with New Twist," *The New York Times*, November 12, 1990, p. A4; Steven Weisman, "The Struggle to Make a Monarchy Fit in Modern-Day Japan," *The New York Times*, November 18, 1990, p. E3.

16. McNelly, *Politics and Government in Japan*, p. 181.
17. Tsuneishi, *Japanese Political Style*, p. 58.
18. Ward, *Japan's Political System*, p. 157.
19. Tsuneishi, *Japanese Political Style*, p. 87.
20. *The Diet, Elections, and Political Parties* (Tokyo: Foreign Press Center, 1985), p. 17.
21. McNelly, *Politics and Government in Japan*, p. 156.
22. Tsuneishi, *Japanese Political Style*, p. 43.
23. Michael Leiserson, "Factions and Coalitions in One-Party Japan," *American Political Science Review* 62 (1968): 778.
24. McNelly, *Politics and Government in Japan*, p. 166.
25. Ibid., p. 159.
26. It is worth noting that the constitution *requires* the emperor to ratify the choice of the House, so the fact that the emperor has consistently done so is not remarkable. It is interesting to speculate what the political results might be if the emperor were to *refuse* to ratify the choice of the House.
27. Jun-ichi Kyogoku, *The Political Dynamics of Japan*, trans. Nobutaka Ike (Tokyo: University of Tokyo Press, 1987), p. 193.
28. Tsuneishi, *Japanese Political Style*, p. 48.
29. Ward, *Japan's Political System*, p. 153.
30. McNelly, *Politics and Government in Japan*, p. 165.
31. Ward, *Japan's Political System*, p. 153.
32. Bingman, *Japanese Government*, pp. 26–27.
33. *Administrative Reform in Japan* (Tokyo: Foreign Press Center, 1984), p. 17.
34. Richardson and Flanagan, *Politics: Japan*, p. 48.
35. Ibid.
36. McNelly, *Politics and Government in Japan*, p. 144.
37. Burks, *The Government of Japan*, p. 107. A very interesting *comparative* study of the Japanese Diet and the U.S. Congress can be found in Francis R. Valeo and Charles E. Morrison, eds., *The Japanese Diet and the U.S. Congress* (Boulder, Col.: Westview Press, 1983).
38. See Hans Baerwald, *Japan's Parliament: An Introduction* (Cambridge: Cambridge University Press, 1974), p. 122.
39. Ward, *Japan's Political System*, p. 149.
40. *The Diet, Elections, and Political Parties*, pp. 9–10.
41. Frank Langdon, *Politics in Japan* (Boston: Little, Brown, 1967), p. 163.
42. McNelly, *Politics and Government in Japan*, p. 134.
43. Tsuneishi, *Japanese Political Style*, p. 87.
44. Ibid., p. 89.
45. Langdon, *Politics in Japan*, p. 164.
46. *The Diet, Elections, and Political Parties*, p. 13.
47. McNelly, *Politics and Government in Japan*, p. 136.
48. *The Diet, Elections, and Political Parties*, p. 14.
49. Langdon, *Politics in Japan*, p. 168.
50. Tsuneishi, *Japanese Political Style*, p. 93; McNelly, *Politics and Government in Japan*, p. 137.
51. McNelly, *Politics and Government in Japan*, p. 139.

52. Langdon, *Politics in Japan*, p. 169.
53. Hattie Kawahara Colton, "The Working of the Japanese Diet," *Pacific Affairs* 28 (1955): 372.
54. Ward, *Japan's Political System*, p. 150.
55. Ibid., p. 110.
56. Tsuneishi, *Japanese Political Style*, p. 124.
57. Burks, *The Government of Japan*, p.77.
58. Ibid., p.75.
59. A very good examination of the Liberal Democratic party can be found in the article by Nobuo Tomita, Akira Nakamura, and Ronald Hrebenar, "The Liberal Democratic Party: The Ruling Party of Japan," in Ronald Hrebenar, ed., *The Japanese Party System: From One-Party Rule to Coalition Government* (Boulder, Col.: Westview Press, 1986), pp. 235–282.
60. McNelly, *Politics and Government in Japan*, pp. 90, 120.
61. Tsuneishi, *Japanese Political Style*, p. 124.
62. Ronald Hrebenar, "The Changing Postwar Party System," in Hrebenar, *The Japanese Party System*, p. 7. See also J. A. A. Stockwin, "The Japan Socialist Party: A Politics of Permanent Opposition," in Hrebenar, *The Japanese Party System*, p. 83.
63. *The Diet, Elections, and Political Parties*, p. 98.
64. Bingman, *Japanese Government*, p. 8.
65. *The Diet, Elections, and Political Parties*, p. 94.
66. Ward, *Japan's Political System*, p. 110.
67. For descriptions of the major issue positions of the large parties in Japan today, see Langdon, *Politics in Japan*, pp. 132–142.
68. Ward, *Japan's Political System*, p. 110.
69. Ibid., p. 113.
70. A good discussion of local government in Japan can be found in Bingman, *Japanese Government*, pp. 47–75. See also Ritsuo Akimoto, "Leadership and Power Structure in Local Politics," in Hiroshi Itoh, *Japanese Politics: An Inside View* (Ithaca, N.Y.: Cornell University Press, 1973), pp. 167–180.
71. As of April 1986, local governments had a total of 3,217,000 employees, of which teachers accounted for 31.3 percent and policemen 6.7 percent. See *Statistical Handbook of Japan* (Tokyo: Statistics Bureau, Management and Coordination Agency, 1988), pp. 145–146.
72. McNelly, *Politics and Government in Japan*, p. 131.
73. Tsuneishi, *Japanese Political Style*, p. 153.
74. Ward, *Japan's Political System*, p. 114.
75. McNelly, *Politics and Government in Japan*, p. 131.
76. Ibid., p. 132.
77. See "Ronald Hrebenar, "Rules of the Game: The Impact of the Electoral System on Political Parties," in Hrebenar, *The Japanese Party System*, pp. 32–54.
78. Ward, *Japan's Political System*, p. 126.
79. Tsuneishi, *Japanese Political Style*, p. 154.
80. Ibid., pp. 150–151.
81. McNelly, *Politics and Government in Japan*, p. 135.
82. Tsuneishi, *Japanese Political Style*, p. 156.
83. Much of what follows in this section is based upon much more substantial discussion in *The Diet, Elections, and Political Parties* (Tokyo: Foreign Press Center, 1985), pp. 51–62.

84. A good discussion of changes in party support as a function of economic variables can be found in Nobutaka Ike, *A Theory of Japanese Democracy* (Boulder, Col.: Westview Press, 1978), pp. 115–120.

85. A saying circulating at the time was " 'five you win and three you lose,' with 'five' standing for Y500 million and 'three' for Y300 million in campaign expenditures." *The Diet, Elections, and Political Parties*, p. 53.

86. See the article by Naoki Kobayashi, "Interest Groups in the Legislative Process," in Hiroshi Itoh, ed., *Japanese Politics: An Inside View* (Ithaca, N.Y.: Cornell University Press, 1973), pp. 68–87.

87. *The Diet, Elections, and Political Parties*, p. 53.

88. Takashi Oka, "Nakasone Wins Big, but Faces Party Leadership Struggle," *Christian Science Monitor*, July 8, 1986, p. 1. See also Sam Jameson, "Japanese Ruling Party Wins Vote in Landslide," *Los Angeles Times*, July 7, 1986, p. 9.

89. The LDP limits its leaders to two terms of two years each, and Nakasone's second term ended October 30, 1987. Andrew Horvat, "Nakasone Sets Stage for July 6 Double Election," *Los Angeles Times*, June 3, 1986, p. 4. On the contest for the new leader, see Makashi Oka, "Race to Replace Nakasone in Full Swing; Math Gets Complicated as Japan's Contenders Tally Factions Support," *Christian Science Monitor*, July 20, 1987, p. 3.

90. Susan Chira, "Japanese Ruling Party Suffers Setback in Upper House By-Election," *The New York Times*, February 13, 1989, p. A7.

13

The Soviet Political System

One of the fundamental premises in this book has been that if we study the basic constitutional structures of a political regime we will develop some understanding of how the regime operates. Thus we have paid relatively little attention, comparatively speaking, to social issues, political parties, ideologies, and interest groups in each of our "country portraits." The Soviet case, until recently, was an exception to the patterns we have seen elsewhere: The "legal" and "constitutional" structures were *not* true indicators of how the political system operated.

While we have suggested that we could understand the essential operation of other political systems by confining our examination to what might be called "constitutional political structures," a similar examination of the Soviet political system would have given us a terribly unrealistic image of the pattern of political operations there. An understanding of the role of the Communist Party of the Soviet Union, although not constitutionally highlighted, was *crucial* to an introduction to the operation of the Soviet political system prior to 1991.

Accordingly, after an examination of the Soviet constitution and the system of constitutional political structures in the Soviet Union, we will devote some of our attention in this chapter to a historical overview of the structure and operation of the Communist Party of the Soviet Union (CPSU) as it operated until 1990, arguing that in the Soviet political system the CPSU took on what might be called "quasi-governmental" characteristics.

The Union of Soviet Socialist Republics

Although many use the name "Russia" interchangeably with "Union of Soviet Socialist Republics," the USSR, such a usage is incorrect. Russia is a *part* of the USSR, but not the *same as* the USSR. The USSR is the largest country in the world, making up nearly one-sixth of the earth's land mass, "more than twice the size of the United States, almost as big as the United States, Canada, and Mexico put together . . . only slightly smaller than the whole continent of Africa."[1] This type of comparison can be misleading, however, because a careful study of the Soviet map shows that a significant portion of the USSR "is not conducive to protracted habitation for sizeable populations."

> In certain areas, such as the Ukranian and Moldavian Soviet Republics, the density of population approaches that of parts of Western Europe, but the USSR as a whole has an average population density of only one-ninth of Western Europe's.[2]

The Soviet Political Heritage

Parts of the USSR have existed for more than eleven centuries, under a variety of names and a variety of rulers. Scholars have suggested that a number of historical factors in the Soviet political heritage have proven to be significant in influencing Soviet development in a non-Western direction.[3] Patterns of behavior such as the "persistent tradition of absolutism in government, the recurrent use of revolutionary violence to solve political problems, and the lack of experience with democratic institutions and constitutional procedures"[4] have all contributed to a political tradition in the Soviet Union that is distinctly different from that shared by most Western (democratic) nations.

One major pattern in the Soviet past is the history of revolutions, which led to the Revolution of 1917.[5] Among the earliest acts that can be called revolutions in Soviet history was a shake-up in government led by Ivan the Terrible in 1564. Ivan was rebelling not against the government (he was tsar at the time!) but against the nobles in his regime, claiming that they were evil and traitorous. Ivan agreed to maintain the throne only under the condition that he be given control of a secret police network called the Oprichnina, which he used to destroy the power of the nobles by arresting them, exiling them, and taking over their estates. Ivan's actions served to neutralize any threat that the nobility had posed to the power of the tsar.

The revolt of December 1825, known as the Decembrist Uprising, was an attempt by the tsar's guards to overthrow the tsar (Nicholas I, 1825–1855) and do away with the restrictive, autocratic government of Russia. Partially because of the uncertainty of the revolutionaries, who could not agree on the kind of regime that they wanted to replace the tsar, the revolt was suppressed and an increase in governmental repression took place at the hand of the tsar.

The oppressiveness of the tsar, however, did not check the spread of revolutionary ideas. Although Alexander II freed the serfs in 1861 as a gesture to placate public unrest, revolutionary fervor continued to spread. Political organization was begun by a revolutionary intelligentsia, primarily organized in the Narodnik movement. The Narodniki were originally intellectually based—drawn from student and intellectual groups—but the movement later drew from wider circles. The movement had as its goal the promotion of a socialist society, maintaining that the traditional Russian village was socialist in orientation. The Narodniki did not view Western-style industrialization as a positive goal for Russian society, and they argued that "once the aristocratic system and the feudal order were destroyed, Russia would spontaneously be recognized as a vast association of agrarian cooperative communities."[6]

The first Marxist organization in Russia, called the Emancipation of Labor, was founded in 1883 by a group led by George Plekhanov. Between 1883 and 1894 similar organizations were formed in most major Russian cities, including one in St. Petersburg in 1895, which was led by Lenin. Both Stalin (whose real name was Joseph Dzhugashvili) and Trotsky (whose real name was Leon Bronstein) became active in politics during this period.

In 1898 the first Russian Social Democratic party convention was held in Minsk, its goal being to consolidate various factions of Marxists. (See Table 13.1).

The second Russian Social Democratic party convention was held in 1903, meeting first in Brussels (because it was not permitted in Russia), then moving to London. In London the party divided into two factions over the issue of organization. Some party members wanted a European-style Social Democratic party. Lenin argued against that form of party, saying that the tsar's secret police would not permit such an open party to operate freely. He argued in favor of a restricted, tightly organized party of dedicated revolutionaries. The party, on a 33–18 vote, split into two factions over this question.[7] Lenin was leader of the majority faction, called the Bolsheviks. The labels "Bolshevik" (majority) and "Menshevik" (minority) stuck to the two factions of the party,

Table 13.1
Some Important Dates in Russian History

1237–40	Mongol (Tatar) conquest of Russia begins 200 years of Mongol rule ("The Tatar Yoke")
1480	Ivan III frees Muscovy from Mongol rule
1712	Peter the Great moves capital of Russia to Saint Petersburg (now Leningrad) for a "window to the West"
1861	Emancipation of the serfs by Alexander II
1905	Revolution forces Nicholas II to grant token reform, including establishment of a parliament (the Duma)
1917	March Revolution overthrows monarchy and establishes moderate socialist government
1917	November Revolution brings Lenin's Bolsheviks to power
1917–21	War Communism
1921–28	New Economic Policy
1924–38	Death of Lenin in 1924 leads to a struggle for power; Stalin emerges on top and then ruthlessly consolidates his control
1953	Death of Stalin
1957	Consolidation of power by Khrushchev
1964	Khrushchev ousted; replaced by Brezhnev and Kosygin
1982	Brezhnev dies; succeeded by Andropov
1984	Andropov dies; succeeded by Chernenko
1985	Chernenko dies; succeeded by Gorbachev

Source: Adapted from David Roth and Frank Wilson, *The Comparative Study of Politics* (Englewood Cliffs, N.J.: Prentice Hall, 1980), p. 24.

and these two wings of the Russian Social Democratic party were thereafter known as the Bolsheviks and the Mensheviks.

Lenin at this time presented his proposals, which he had introduced in his earlier publication *What Is to Be Done?* (published in 1902), in which he called for a new type of nonelectoral party organization that was designed not so much to compete for power in elections, but rather:

> to seize power on behalf of the working class and to establish a "dictatorship of the proletariat." The party was to be restricted to a hard-core elite made up of professional revolutionaries, and organized along military lines. Its guiding principle would be "democratic centralism." The authority of the party would be concentrated in the hands of its central committee. . . .[8]

At the turn of the twentieth century, Russia was again near the point of revolution. Strikes and industrial unrest spread throughout the country as a result of yet another economic crisis. On January 9, 1905, termed "Bloody Sunday," soldiers fired on a procession of workers carrying a list of grievances to Tsar Nicholas II, killing hundreds and triggering a revolt. Workers' councils, called soviets, were formed in many cities to direct strike activities. Leon Trotsky, a leader of the St. Petersburg soviet, issued a call for constitutional reforms, free elections, a parliament, and freedom for political parties to form.

Nicholas managed to put down the revolt, but he acceded to many of the requests as an effort to promote the stability of his regime. In the October Manifesto, he promised a national parliament (the Duma), a constitution, free elections, and protection of civil liberties. Russia after 1905 was a much more liberal and less oppressive society than it had been previously, although the tsar was still the most significant political actor because of his power of absolute veto over the Duma and his ability to dismiss the Duma at will.

> The period of 1907 to 1917 was the only period in the history of modern Russia when something resembling constitutionalism and free political life was in existence. The tsarist government did not have the slightest intention of introducing democracy, not even a constitutional and parliamentary system in our own sense of the word. . . . It must be kept in mind that for the first and only time in the twentieth century (excluding the short period between March and November, 1917), political parties could operate in the

open and literature critical of the government could be distributed legally.[9]

The year 1917 saw new revolution in Russia. The nation's participation in World War I, coupled with continued poor economic performance and increased governmental repression, led to more rebellions. Nicholas II was overthrown in March 1917, and the Duma became the Provisional Government. It granted amnesty to most of the Bolshevik leaders who had been exiled (like Lenin) or sent to Siberia (like Stalin) by the tsar, and allowed them to return to the political scene. From the beginning of the Revolution, the workers' councils, the soviets, played central roles in the coordination of revolutionary activity. In fact, the Petrograd Soviet (the new name for St. Petersburg) rivalled the Provisional Government (the Duma) as a source of leadership.

In April 1917, Lenin returned to Russia and issued his "April Theses," calling for the overthrow of the Provisional Government and the transformation of the "bourgeois democratic revolution" into a revolution sponsored by the "proletarian class." The Provisional Government, headed by Alexander Kerensky, opposed Lenin's policies, but in the end could not stand up to the Bolshevik organization. On the night of November 6/7, 1917, all members of the Provisional Government were arrested by the Red Guard, on order of Lenin. Lenin announced that the former government was dissolved, and that the Petrograd Soviet, headed by its Central Executive Committee, was now in control. The new government was headed by a Council of Peoples' Commissars, led by Lenin as Chairman, Stalin as Commissar of Nationalities, and Trotsky as Commissar of Foreign Affairs.

Federalism in the USSR

The USSR today is composed of fifteen union republics—hence the name *Union* of Soviet Socialist Republics—in a highly heterogeneous political system. The Soviet nation

> consists of more than a hundred large and small ethnic groups with their own distinct cultural heritages. Many, but not all, ethnic groups have their own territories within the USSR. These territories are designated, in descending order of importance, as "Union Republics" (15) "autonomous republics" (11), "autonomous regions" (8), and "autonomous areas" (10).[10]

In recent times the heterogeneous nature of the Soviet Union has been the cause of tension—and open violence—in Soviet politics. The "nationality question"[11] was the cause of many deaths in 1989, 1990, and 1991, as various ethnic groups protested that they were not receiving adequate attention from Moscow.[12] The goals of these ethnic groups are often territorial, but occasionally involve unhappiness with religious, political, or economic policies. According to the U.S. State Department, about thirty-five borders within the Soviet Union were being disputed among different national groups in the Soviet Union in 1991, including conflicts in Armenia, Azerbaijan, Kazakhstan, Uzbekistan, Lithuania, and Georgia, to name just a few.[13]

Between 1989 and 1991, the concepts of "ethnic identity" and "nationalism" simply refused to go away, and several different national groups, represented by "independent republic" legislatures, including those of Russia, Lithuania, Latvia, Estonia, Azerbaijan, the Ukraine, and others, passed legislation that moved in the direction of greater "national" sovereignty and less power for the central government in Moscow. Even the Russian Republic, the largest and most powerful of the components of the USSR, passed strong nationalist legislation in 1990, and the interaction between Soviet President Mikhail Gorbachev and Russian President Boris Yeltsin was the subject of much analysis.[14] This is a topic to which we shall return later in this chapter.

The largest single geographic component of the USSR is the Russian Soviet Federative Socialist Republic (RSFSR), making up over three-fourths of the USSR. The fourteen union republics apart from Russia are all called Soviet Socialist Republics (SSRs) and they are: Armenian SSR, Azerbaijan SSR, Byelorussian SSR, Estonian SSR, Georgian SSR, Latvian SSR, Lithuanian SSR, Kazakh SSR, Kirghiz SSR, Moldavian SSR, Tajik SSR, Turkmen SSR, Ukrainian SSR, and Uzbek SSR (see Table 13.2).

The 1936 constitution, and later the 1977 constitution, have both suggested that the USSR is a federal political system. Article 72 of the 1977 constitution states "each union republic retains the right freely to secede from the U.S.S.R."[15] Such a right has proven to be more imaginary than real, however, and it could even be argued that the USSR is not a true federation as we described the concept earlier in this book. In a true federation, such as we have seen in Germany, the levels of government below the national government *actually* have sovereignty in some areas of politics.

Table 13.2
The Composition of the USSR

Name of Union Republic	Date Created	Capital	Area (in sq. mi.)	Population, 1989 Census (in millions)
Russian SFSR	Nov. 1917	Moscow	6,592,800	147.4
Ukrainian SSR	Dec. 1917	Kiev	233,100	51.7
Byelorussian SSR	Jan. 1919	Minsk	80,200	10.2
Uzbek SSR	Oct. 1924	Tashkent	172,700	19.9
Kazakh SSR	Dec. 1936	Alma-Ata	1,049,200	16.5
Georgian SSR	Feb. 1921	Tbilisi	26,911	5.4
Azerbaijan SSR	Apr. 1920	Baku	33,400	7.0
Lithuanian SSR	Jul. 1940	Vilnius	26,173	3.7
Moldavian SSR	Aug. 1940	Kishinev	13,012	4.3
Latvian SSR	Jul. 1940	Riga	24,695	2.7
Kirghiz SSR	Dec. 1936	Frunze	76,642	4.3
Tajik SSR	Oct. 1929	Dushambe	54,019	5.1
Armenian SSR	Nov. 1920	Erevan	11,306	3.3
Turkmen SSR	Oct. 1924	Ashkabad	188,417	3.5
Estonian SSR	Jul. 1940	Tallin	17,413	1.6

Source: *The World Almanac and Book of Facts, 1991* (New York: World Almanac, 1991), p. 760; Vadim Medish, *The Soviet Union*, rev. 4th ed. (Englewood Cliffs, N.J.: Prentice Hall, 1991), p. 32.

There are some powers that the German Länder have that the Berlin government may *not* challenge.

Soviet federalism was developed by Lenin and Stalin as a vehicle for keeping many of the "independent republics" that had been included in the Russian Empire under control. In the Revolution of 1917 the Bolsheviks had promised self-determination to the various national minorities, and military conquest did not appear to them to be a preferential strategy, if they had any choice. By making the new state a "federation" it was possible to at least maintain the impression that the member units retained some autonomy, albeit token autonomy.

Stalin, one of the founders of the Soviet concept of federalism, articulated the federal association in the Soviet Union as requiring a state "proletarian in content and national in form." This meant that in effect "the various 'union' and 'autonomous' republics could not accept *bona fide* political self-determination once they found themselves within the spectrum of Soviet power."[16]

The constitution of 1924 contained a number of clauses reflecting the federal nature of the regime. In addition to the usual powers granted federal governments (found in federal systems such as Canada, Germany, the United States, Australia, etc.), such as the power to coin money, to have an army, and the like, the Soviet constitution gave the federal government a great many economic planning powers, central to Marxist ideology. The constitution had no bill of rights and no electoral laws, leaving these areas of concern, as well as the areas of civil and criminal law, to the member republics.[17]

It is interesting to note that the 1977 constitution, in an early draft, suggested doing away with the Soviet federation and creating a unitary state. The plan was turned down in the Politburo, and deleted from the final draft of the constitution. The 1977 constitution, in its final form in Chapter 8, Article 70, refers to the USSR as a "unitary, federal, and multinational state, formed on the basis of the principle of socialist federalism and as a result of the free self-determination of nations and the voluntary union of equal Soviet Socialist Republics."[18]

In a number of respects the 1977 constitution weakened the status of member republics, since they were denied the right to tax or spend revenues, among other things, except as approved by the federal government. As suggested earlier, and as we will discuss later, recent developments in the Soviet Union have considerably weakened the power of the central government and strengthened the potential power of the national legislatures.

One illustration of the dubious nature of federalism in the USSR may be provided here. We have already pointed out that the union republics have the constitutional right under Article 72 of the constitution to secede from the Union. However, the Presidium of the Supreme Soviet of the USSR has the power to rescind any decision reached by governments of the union republics!

Article 74 of the constitution states, "In the event of a discrepancy between a Union-Republic law and an all-Union law, the USSR law prevails." It has been argued in the past that it was doubtful that even if a union republic *were* to decide to secede, it would be *permitted* to do so. Recent actions have shown this to be true: An independence resolution passed by the legislature of the Baltic republic of Lithuania in 1990 was rejected as "unacceptable" by Moscow; Moscow even imposed an economic embargo upon Lithuania to force a cancellation of the resolution. Eventually, Lithuania and Moscow agreed to negotiate increased power for the Baltic republic, and the resolution was postponed—but not cancelled. The central government is clearly not as able to block nationalist movements as it was ten or fifteen years ago.[19]

The Soviet federal structure is partially reflected in the constitutional structure of the government in one of the two houses of the Soviet legislature, the Supreme Soviet. Under the 1988 amendment to the constitution, which we shall examine further, 750 members of the Congress of Peoples' Deputies are to be elected on the basis of governmental units, with each of the country's republics having the same representation in the legislature; thus Estonia's 1.5 million citizens would have the same number of representatives as the Ukraine's 50 million citizens.[20] This kind of constitutional structure notwithstanding, the debate over the limitation of powers of the central government in the USSR has been virtually nonexistent, especially when compared with other federal systems such as Canada and Germany.

> Thus the American, Swiss, Canadian, and German systems have since their beginnings been characterized by conflicts and debate as to the extent of federal versus state or provincial powers. Within the Soviet Union the secondary character of the constitutional arrangements has prevented any possibility of such conflicts and has rendered almost superfluous a serious discussion of the division of authority between the center and the union republics. . . . The amount of centralization envisaged in the Constitution is so considerable that an argument could be advanced that, even if one takes into account the strict letter of law and disregards everything else, the Soviet Union is more of a unitary than a bona fide federal state.[21]

The fact that the central government has the power to veto acts of the legislatures of the "independent republics" has led some to suggest that the Soviet system should not really be considered to be truly federal at all, but rather should be considered as a somewhat decentralized unitary state, with all important policy decisions being made at the political center of the nation, and less important policy decisions, and much administration, being undertaken at the so-called independent republic level of government. Obviously, this is a dimension of contemporary Soviet politics that has yet to be resolved.

Ideology

The ideological underpinnings of the Soviet regime are officially referred to as "Marxism-Leninism."[22] This Marxism-Leninism:

> is officially regarded in the Soviet Union as an exact science, a "correct grasp" of which makes possible a scientific understanding of the past, present and future of the human race.[23]

Ultimately, Marxism-Leninism is based upon the *Communist Manifesto* (published in 1848) and subsequent writings of Karl Marx and Friedrich Engels. More directly, however, political ideology in the Soviet Union can be explained as Marxism interpreted and applied by Soviet leaders of the day, including Lenin, Stalin, Khrushchev, Brezhnev, and now Gorbachev. Each of these leaders has, in turn, interpreted and revised Marx's ideas so that the particular version of Marxism would support the regime of the day and provide a rationalization for the policies of the government in power. "Marxian ideology has provided the vehicle by which power has been attained and maintained by a small elite. All of this has been done in the name of the people, the proletariat."[24]

The perspectives of Marx were, in fact, different from those of Lenin, Stalin, Khrushchev, Brezhnev, or Gorbachev. Marx was a theorist, dealing with philosophies and ideas. Lenin and his followers were pragmatists, political actors, interested in the philosophy suggested by Marx, but faced with the challenge of putting the theories into concrete form, of operationalizing the ideology.

As the economic, social, and political characteristics of the Soviet Union have changed, this has required revision of Marx's ideas to fit the times. Lenin, for example, revised Marxian theory to justify its relevance to the conditions of the Soviet Union during the period between 1917 and 1924.

Marxism is a highly elaborate theoretical framework, far beyond our level of analysis here in any detail.[25] The Marxist theory of history is based upon *dialectics*, the dynamic quality of history in which the world is perceived as constantly changing and evolving. Marx used the concept of the dialectic, as developed by the German philosopher Hegel (1770-1831), and modified its major focus, directing its content at materialism and economic relations of society.

Marx's *historical materialism* suggested that history moves through cycles that can be defined in terms of class struggle. There are two classes of people in society, those who own land and the means of production (such as factories, for example), and those who are manual laborers and who work in order to live. Marx saw the property-holding classes exploiting the working class, making profits from the labor of others. According to what can be called an *iron law of wages*, members of the working class, the proletariat, are paid as little as possible, and consequently the class called the bourgeoisie becomes richer (a phenomenon termed *the concentration of wealth*), while the class called the proletariat becomes increasingly poor and miserable (termed *the growing misery of the masses*).

> Society advances through stages depending on forms of ownership, from the feudal order ruled by landowners to the capitalist order dominated by the owners of industry. These, in turn, are destined to be overthrown by the workers [the proletariat], who will become the new ruling class. The proletariat, rightfully ruling by virtue of its overwhelming majority, will establish a higher form of society, socialism, which will grow into the perfect condition of communism. This will be a utopian order of free and voluntary labor, with harmony and sharing of material goods, the climax of history and the redemption of humankind.[26]

Marx argued that the poor working class, the proletariat, would become more and more aware of its role in society and would lead a revolution, elevating itself to the position of the ruling class and establishing a *dictatorship of the proletariat*. During the period of its dictatorship, the proletariat would expropriate the property of the capitalists, doing away with the class called the bourgeoisie, and in turn doing away completely with all class struggles and exploitation in society.

The hero of this scenario, according to Marx, is the proletariat—the industrial workers of society who are the agents of change in society. Lenin argued, modifying Marx's theory considerably, that Russian industrial workers were not prepared to play the role of the vanguard of the revolution. Russia in 1917 was primarily an agricultural economy, with few of the industrial workers that Marx had seen in industrialized Europe and had called the proletariat. Marx may have selected the proletariat to be the agents of change in his theory, but they were not trained to know when or how to act politically in Russia.

Accordingly, Lenin said that a party of trained revolutionaries, not just another European-style social democratic party, could play the role of the industrial workers, leading the revolution on behalf of the proletariat. He argued that "on the organizational base that he devised it was not necessary to await the full maturation of capitalism in Russia before taking power. The party could act for the proletariat and thus speed up the inevitable process."[27] The party would not, of course, be composed only of members of the proletariat, but instead would be made up of a few true ideologues who would act on behalf of the proletariat.

The major goal of Leninism was the same as the major goal of Marxism—economic egalitarianism. The poor would cease to be exploited by the rich. Marx's social revolution, which was not likely on a practical level in Russia of the early twentieth century, was now possible with Lenin's modification: The revolution that could not be undertaken by the ignorant and untrained masses could now take place when organized by a tightly controlled, highly ideological revolutionary party, acting in the name of the poor and exploited workers. For Lenin, then, the idea of the dictatorship of the proletariat was functionally equivalent to the dictatorship of the Communist party.

Lenin's major modifications of Marxism were three: First, he insisted upon a militarylike organization of his party, against the trend of social democratic parties in Europe. His argument was that "in a nondemocratic country a Marxist party built on democratic principles was doomed to failure." Second, he advocated an alliance between the weak Russian proletariat (factory and industrial workers) and the poor majority of peasants, partially to help compensate for the fact that the proletariat was not as large as it was envisioned to be in Marx's theory. Third, Lenin justified a "proletarian revolution" in Russia when, in fact, agrarian Russia was hardly the industrialized society that Marx had in mind when he was writing his treatises.[28]

Lenin died in January 1924. Following his death a major power struggle ensued in the Soviet Union to see who would succeed him. The two major contestants were Joseph Stalin and Leon Trotsky. Stalin's position emerged as the mightier of the two, and within a short time it became apparent that Stalin would be the stronger of the two contestants; as secretary-general of the

Communist Party of the Soviet Union he had been able to build a strong base of power.

In 1936 Stalin had a new constitution written that he proclaimed to be the most democratic in the world. He created a new parliament, and a bill of rights, and at the same time centralized power to guarantee that no one would be able to challenge his control. After securing his hold on power, Stalin argued that the Marxist revolution was completed within the USSR. Stalin wrote in 1939 that "We have abolished the exploiting classes; there are no longer any hostile classes in the country; there is nobody to suppress."[29]

Stalin, accordingly, turned his attention away from the revolution within the nation, to revolution in other nations, looking at the concept of world revolution. Stalin believed that the Soviet system could assist Marxist revolutions in other parts of the world once the USSR had developed into a militarily powerful regime.

In terms of major modifications of Marxism (or of Marxism-Leninism-Stalinism, as he preferred to call it), Stalin's contributions were neither as many nor as significant as those of Lenin. However, he did make some contributions to the Soviet polity. Stalin used the structure of the Five-Year Plan to direct the development of the Soviet state. His modernization program was based on three major principles. First, the nation should emphasize construction of heavy industry to enhance its military might. Second, the nation should collectivize and mechanize agriculture to increase production and destroy capitalist farming. Third, the nation should create a centrally planned and directed program of education to develop a cadre of scientific and skilled workers.[30]

Stalin also introduced the concept of "enemy of the people" into Soviet ideology. "Any person so designated was charged with counter-revolutionary and treasonable activities, and then executed, imprisoned, or banished, with or without trial." Nikita Khrushchev, in a speech indicting Stalin's actions (delivered, naturally, after Stalin's death), told the Twentieth Party Congress of the Communist party in 1956):

> Stalin originated the concept "enemy of the people." This term automatically rendered it unnecessary that the ideological errors of a man or men engaged in a controversy be proved; this term made possible the usage of the most cruel repression; violating all norms of revolutionary legality, against anyone who in any way

disagreed with Stalin, against those who were suspected of hostile intent, against those who had bad reputations.[31]

With the death of Stalin, the "enemy of the people" doctrine disappeared from the Soviet political landscape. "The dominance of the secret police was broken, and mass terror was eliminated. Law was gradually liberalized, and a greater emphasis was placed on 'socialist legality.' "[32] While Malenkov and Bulganin struggled to assume leadership, Khrushchev maneuvered for power, supporting both Bulganin and Malenkov as convenient at the time. "While Malenkov and subsequently Bulganin were deeply involved in administering the state, Khrushchev became first secretary of the party and strengthened his position in the Politburo . . ."[33]; he emerged as Soviet leader in 1957 and contributed five major theoretical modifications of Marxism-Leninism-Stalinism:

1. The dictatorship of the proletariat has fulfilled its historic mission and is now being gradually transformed into a "state of the entire people . . . expressing the interests and will of the people as a whole."
2. The dictatorship of the proletariat is withering away, but "the state as an organization of the entire people will survive until the complete victory of Communism."
3. The organs and institutions of the state will be gradually converted into "organs of public self-government" as it embarks upon the road to oblivion.
4. In the meantime, government officials will be systematically rotated out of office at every election and at all levels, so that leading officials as a rule will hold office for not more than three consecutive terms, unless they are unusually gifted.
5. The military power of the Soviet state will continue to be strengthened to fulfill "its international duty to guarantee . . . the reliable defense and security of the entire socialism camp."[34]

While Khrushchev was vacationing in October 1964, he was deposed by a faction headed by Leonid Brezhnev and Aleksei Kosygin. The post-Khrushchev leadership, primarily Brezhnev, undertook somewhat of a retrenchment following Khrushchev's ouster. The liberalization by Khrushchev of restrictions in the area of the arts, literature, and education was again tightened; the Soviet Union's apparent relaxation of its control over its satellites also was reversed with the 1968 crackdown of the Czechoslovakian uprising. Khrushchev's successors:

> sharpened the division between party and state bureaucracies, introduced a limited rehabilitation of Stalin, promoted repressive measures against dissident authors and other intellectuals, and enforced bureaucratic centralization, although in a context of far-reaching economic reform.[35]

Following the death of Brezhnev in November 1982, the future direction of Soviet ideology was uncertain. Yuri Andropov, former head of the KGB (the state security committee) and Politburo member, was selected to take over as secretary-general of the Communist party, but his period of leadership was brief and did not contribute anything in the way of ideological significance, primarily because of his advanced age and illness. When Andropov died in 1984, he was replaced by Konstantin Chernenko, another senior party leader, who also died in office after a very brief period of leadership.

The accession to power of Mikhail Gorbachev in 1985 suggested the promise of significant change, which certainly was fulfilled in a short period of time. Gorbachev introduced a number of radical reforms in the Soviet system, which we will examine shortly, including the extraordinarily profound one of converting the Soviet economy from communism to capitalism! As will be discussed later in this chapter, the outcome of the "Gorbachev era" in Soviet politics is by no means certain.

The Soviet Constitution

For the person studying American politics, the American Constitution is a highly significant document. Indeed, as we noted at the outset of this chapter, this has been one of the fundamental approaches of this text. In the study of the USSR, however, this position of profound significance has not been held by the Soviet constitution; this explains why most studies of Soviet politics do not spend a great deal of time or attention explaining the document. To the contrary, in fact, if a student were to carefully study the Soviet constitution he or she would undoubtedly find that it made an understanding of the Soviet polity more difficult, rather than easier, to grasp.

As one observer has noted: "The constitutional structure of the Soviet Union has always been an elaborate facade behind which one-party rule and totalitarianism have occupied the political scene. . . . The Statute of the Communist party is a more important document than the Constitution of the USSR."[36] Yet it is clear that the *existence* of a constitution must have been important to the Bolsheviks and to their political successors: The Soviet Union has had a number of constitutions, and political leaders would not have undertaken the effort to create the constitutions if they did not feel that the exercise would be worth their while. Indeed, as recently as the fall of 1988 the Soviet government devoted significant time and effort to the process of constitutional reform.

Since the Revolution of 1917 there have been four constitutional eras in the USSR. In 1918 (July 10) a new constitution was put into force in Russia. This was subsequently superseded by the first constitution of the USSR in January 1924. In 1935 a constitutional commission was appointed and instructed to draft a new constitution for the USSR, to replace the original 1924 document. The new constitution was approved in late 1936.

> The "Stalin Constitution" proclaimed that the Soviet Union had become a "socialist state of workers and peasants." It implied that the class war had ended, secured the peasant's garden plot in basic law, and constitutionally mandated the citizen's right to personal property. Although the "great purge" was reaching its crescendo at the same time, and while the new constitution guarantees of personal security were being honored in the breach for millions of Soviet citizens, the personal economic rights granted under the "Stalin Constitution" did extend to the individual some greater degree of certainty in his daily life.[37]

After Stalin's death, movements were launched to create a new constitution, but progress was slow. In 1962 Nikita Khrushchev began efforts to draft a new document, but his ouster in 1964 stalled the project. Although Leonid Brezhnev became Chairman of the Constitutional Commission, the project was not one of high priority for Brezhnev at the time.

At the Twenty-Fifth CPSU Congress in 1976, Brezhnev mentioned the project for a new constitution, but confounding the predictions of many observers who had guessed that he might unveil a new "Brezhnev Constitution" at that time, the Soviet leader simply indicated that "work on the constitution was going forward, although without haste. Then, without the usual advance clues, there came the abrupt announcement in May 1977 that the new Draft Constitution would soon be published for nationwide discussion."[38]

The question can be asked, Why have Soviet leaders continued the "constitutional ruse," as it could be called, having constitutions that are primarily of symbolic significance? The answer appears to be that the Soviets have an ambivalent attitude toward constitutions. On one hand, ideologically, they see both the state and its structures, such as a constitution, as evils. On the other hand, they are (at least for the time being) willing to recognize constitutions as *necessary* evils, necessary for providing external and internal legitimacy, and for helping to run the regime in the "transitional period" during which time the state "evolves" from capitalism to socialism to communism.

Even though Lenin and his fellow revolutionaries were in the middle of a significant domestic battle with other Soviet political leaders, they still believed that it was important to have a constitutional framework for their new government. Lenin admitted, in fact, that his constitution was not written by legal scholars or based on any other constitution. "It proclaimed the 'dictatorship of the proletariat' and claimed to have replaced 'bourgeois democracy' with 'proletarian democracy'; it was said to have been 'based on the experience of a revolutionary struggle.' "[39]

The role of the constitution in the USSR has been explained as giving "legal expression to the basic ideological norms of Soviet doctrine," including:

1. The abolition of private ownership of the means of production in favor of state or public ownership;
2. The collectivization of agriculture;
3. The nationalization of natural resources;
4. A centrally directed, planned economy;
5. Mandatory employment, in accordance with the formulas "He who does not work, neither shall he eat," and "from each according to his ability, to each according to his work";
6. The legal monopoly of the Communist party over political life.[40]

Some of the principles expressed in the Soviet constitution have been realized to a degree, such as rights dealing with education, equal rights for women, racial equality, and the like. Other principles were described in past years by scholars "as transparent propaganda that is essentially meaningless." These would include assertions that power in the USSR "belongs to the working people," that the Soviet Union "is a voluntary union" of equal republics, that the member republics have the right to secede from the USSR, and that the "highest organ" of political power in the USSR is the Supreme Soviet.[41]

It must be observed at this point, as we have already noted elsewhere and as we will note again later in this chapter, that recent political events in the Soviet Union suggest fundamental changes for the Soviet constitutional structure. Mikhail Gorbachev's reforms include an end to collectivization of agriculture, privatization of the economy, and, in short, radical and fundamental reforms to the central tenets of Soviet life. The implications of these proposed changes have yet to be fully appreciated.

Prior to 1990 it was suggested that changes in constitutional systems in the USSR have not caused "any noticeable ramifications in the structure and operation of the Soviet system."

> The reason for this seeming paradox is the fact that the Soviet constitutions are propagandistic self-images, like misleading advertisements with fine-print disclaimers and qualifications that cancel many important promises, rather than supreme legal instruments that are meant to be used.[42]

The impact of the Gorbachev reforms on Soviet constitutionalism is still unclear. Many believe that there will be "noticeable ramifications" of the changes for the system, but only time will tell.

The constitution itself is divided into nine sections and 174 articles; it is approximately fifty pages in length.[43] The 1977 constitution is considerably longer than the 1936 constitution (approximately 13,000 words as against 8,000 words), but the bulk of the changes are more significant for their symbolic nature than for their substance.

The new constitution has a long prologue dealing with ideology, not included in the 1936 document, and a number of changes in organization from the 1936 constitution. The Communist party is mentioned more often and more prominently. The new constitution has a separate chapter on foreign policy, unlike the 1936 constitution. There appears to be greater emphasis on rights and duties of citizens, judging from the fact that the section discussing this is near the beginning of the 1977 constitution, while it was near the end of the 1936 constitution. Moreover, some changes in formal power seem to give the USSR more influence in relation to the various republics than existed in the 1936 document.[44]

Overall, however, the consensus of scholars who have studied Soviet constitutions is that the significance of all of the differences between the 1936 and 1977 documents was one of style, not substance. It will be recalled that early in this text we discussed the distinction between governments with written constitutions and constitutional governments. For all of its written constitutions, through the early 1990s we still would not have referred to the government of the USSR as a constitutional government. The constitutional/legal reforms introduced by Mikhail Gorbachev moved toward the rule of law within the Soviet system. In this respect, the distinction between Western constitutionalism and Soviet constitutionalism was being broken down by Gorbachev's reforms.

A constitutional government, it will be remembered, is a government of limited powers. As can be seen by qualifications found in the Soviet constitution, the constitution does *not* limit powers of the Soviet regime. To take a couple of examples, let us look at Articles 50 and 51 of the new constitution.

> ARTICLE 50: In accordance with the people's interests and for the purpose of strengthening and developing the socialist system, USSR citizens are guaranteed freedom of speech, of the press, of assembly, of mass meetings and of street processions and demonstrations.
>
> The exercise of these political freedoms is ensured by putting public buildings, streets, and squares at the disposal of the working people and their organizations, by the broad dissemination of information, and by the opportunity to use the press, television, and radio.
>
> ARTICLE 51: In accordance with the goals of communist construction, USSR citizens have the right to unite in public organizations that facilitate the development of political activeness and initiative and the satisfaction of their diverse interests.[45]

It is immediately clear from an examination of these "guarantees" that they in no way limit the power of the government. Freedom of speech, press, meetings, and the like are guaranteed, as long as they are undertaken "in accordance with the people's interests and for the purpose of strengthening and developing the socialist system." Who decides whether these criteria are met? The government decides. Citizens have the right to unite in public organizations as long as they do so "in accordance with the goals of communist construction." Who decides whether uniting is undertaken in this accord? The government decides.

This is a radically different kind of guarantee from the direct limitation on governmental power expressed in the First Amendment to the U.S. Constitution, which says, quite simply, "Congress shall make no law. . . ." Thus, the guarantees of the Soviet constitution are not really limits on governmental power at all, and many argue that although we may say that the USSR has a constitution, we should *not* say that it has a constitutional government.

Structures of the Government

The System of Soviets

The term "soviet" means "council," or small legislative body. One of its earliest uses in USSR politics was in the State Council of Alexander I in 1810; additionally, there was a Council of Ministers in the tsar's government. It was after the 1905 Revolution against Nicholas II that the term "soviet" began to take on political connotations. The St. Petersburg Soviet of Workers assumed a revolutionary role, advocating establishment of a parliament, freedom of expression, a limited working day, and other policy concessions.

Again, after the Revolution of 1917 the Petrograd (St. Petersburg) Soviet of Workers played a leading role. The soviet refused to enter the Provisional Government at the time, which contributed to the ultimate paralysis of the government. In 1917 Lenin "declared war on the Provisional Government and advocated the slogan of 'All Power to the Soviets.' "[46] In the system of soviets, Lenin saw communism's response to what he called "bourgeois parliamentarism." The soviets were argued to be the "outstanding achievement" of the 1917 Revolution. Western parliaments were simply "show windows to delude the masses"; Lenin wanted to "draw the whole of the poor into the practical work of administration." The soviets were perceived as being the vehicle by which this representation would take place.[47]

The system of soviets in the USSR today is vast. At every level of government, from the smallest township, through towns, rural districts, provinces, autonomous republics, and union republics, there is an elected soviet to correspond to that government. All of these soviets are arranged in a hierarchical order, in which the lower soviets are inferior to the higher soviets. Recent publications indicate well over 50,000 soviets in the USSR,[48] although present-day efforts on the part of Mikhail Gorbachev to decrease the role of the Communist party in the Soviet Union will undoubtedly have an effect on this figure.

We must note, however, that while lower soviets are inferior to higher soviets, all soviets, including the USSR Supreme Soviet, were perceived in the past as being inferior to the Communist party organization at each level of government. The 1977 constitution states in Article 2 that the system of soviets makes up the "political foundation of the USSR." The Gorbachev reforms have taken much influence away from the Communist party organization in the country, a theme we shall develop later in this chapter, but it is not yet clear whether these reforms will be permanent or not and what the long-term future holds for the party.

The highest legislative body in the USSR today is the Congress of People's Deputies, a new constitutional structure that met for the first time in 1989. It is directly elected by the people, and one of its functions is to elect from among its own membership the members of the Supreme Soviet.

The Congress of People's Deputies

The idea for the Congress of People's Deputies was first suggested by Mikhail Gorbachev in the late fall of 1988 as part of a package of reforms for soviet government. One observer noted that Gorbachev had become:

> increasingly frustrated and angry at the resistance being mounted to his reforms by Party and state bureaucrats. He holds these officials to blame for the economic stagnation and moral decline from which his country suffers, and accuses them of stifling the initiative of the population.[49]

This legislative body, the first elections for which were held in March 1989, was intended to be a more active legislature than had been the case with the Supreme Soviet in the past; its members would be elected in competitive elections, and it would elect from among its 2,250 members 542 members of a new, much more active and more powerful, Supreme Soviet.

The exact role of the new Congress of People's Deputies was still being negotiated at its first meeting in June 1989. Among the agreements reached at that time were: (1) the body would convene twice a year instead of once, as originally proposed by Gorbachev; (2) deputies of the (2,250-member) Congress who were not elected to the (542-member) Supreme Soviet or its commissions or committees could participate in the sessions and have access to the information and documents made available to the Supreme Soviet; and (3) the Congress would retain the "right to cancel or change any document, any legislative act, and any decision taken by the Supreme Soviet."[50]

In the first year of its life the Congress proved to be much more outspoken and active than many had expected, perhaps including Mikhail Gorbachev. The Congress passed resolutions that would have been unheard of from its predecessor parliament, and it engaged in debates over a wide range of issues, many of which involved subjects that would not have been publicly addressed in previous years.

The Supreme Soviet

Prior to the constitutional amendment proposed by Mikhail Gorbachev in late 1988, the Supreme Soviet was described (in Chapter 15 of the Soviet constitution) as "the supreme body of state power in the USSR . . . empowered to resolve all questions placed within the jurisdiction of the USSR by this constitution."[51] The Supreme Soviet was a bicameral legislative body, composed of two "houses"—the Soviet of the Union and the Soviet of Nationalities, members of which were all elected at the same time for four-year terms.

Members of the Soviet of the Union were elected on the basis of population, with one representative being elected for every 300,000 citizens. Members of the Soviet of Nationalities represented the "federal" nature of the political system, with each union republic having 32 seats, each autonomous republic having

11 seats, each autonomous region having 5 seats, and each national area having 1 seat. The two houses of the Supreme Soviet had over 1,500 representatives.

Much of the business of the Supreme Soviet was accomplished in joint session of the two houses. Laws had to be passed in identical form by both houses. The most important job of the legislature was to approve the slates of candidates for office that were prepared by party leaders. Another major function of Supreme Soviet meetings was an educative one. Delegates who attended meetings of the Supreme Soviet in Moscow were addressed by the Soviet leadership. The media devoted a great deal of attention to the Supreme Soviet meetings, and these meetings served as regular opportunities for policymakers to address the nation in some detail.

The Supreme Soviet usually met twice a year for three or four days each session, during which time it ratified actions that had been taken in its name during its absence by its stand-in, the Presidium of the Supreme Soviet. One scholar of the institution observed that:

> the Supreme Soviet is not a deliberative body; the deliberations take place elsewhere. Nor is it a debating assembly; debates, too, are held elsewhere, if at all. Neither does it formulate policy. It functions essentially as a listening assembly, and most of its "working" time is preoccupied with hearing reports from government ministers.[52]

Most of the "people's deputies" combined their public service with their regular jobs. Deputies were not paid salaries, but received certain special payments, such as *per diem* salaries, transportation allowances, and the like.

In 1988 Mikhail Gorbachev proposed fundamental changes in the body, asking the Supreme Soviet to abolish itself"[53] and to create a new institution in its place, the new Congress of People's Deputies. As part of his package of proposals, Gorbachev proposed that the Congress would elect from among its own members a *new* Supreme Soviet, one that would "act as a full-time legislature for the nearly eight months it will be in session,"[54] meeting for two sessions each year, one in the spring and one in the fall, each lasting three or four months.[55] On paper, at least, the new Supreme Soviet was to be much more active, and important, than its predecessor had been.[56]

Gorbachev wants to change the way in which the USSR is ruled in order to diminish the influence of the resistant Party bureaucracy. Since September, 1988, the leading Party and State organs have been undergoing a significant transitional period. The executive powers of the Party apparatus are about to be transferred to the newly created Supreme Soviet, which, according to Gorbachev's plan, will for the first time begin to play a major role in policy-making.[57]

The Presidium and the New Presidency

Until the 1989 changes in the power of the Supreme Soviet, one of its most important structures was the Presidium (its full title was the Presidium of the Supreme Soviet of the USSR), which had thirty-nine members, including a chairman, a first vice-chairman, fifteen vice-chairmen (one from each union republic supreme soviet), a secretary, and twenty-one members. According to Article 119 of the Soviet constitution, members of the Presidium were elected by the USSR Supreme Soviet "at a joint meeting of its chambers," from among its members in both houses. The Presidium was referred to as "the continuously functioning agency of the USSR Supreme Soviet, accountable to the latter for all its activity, and exercising . . . the functions of supreme body of state power of the USSR in intervals between sessions of the Supreme Soviet."[58]

The Presidium performed functions of an executive, legislative, diplomatic, military, and judicial nature and had a number of specific powers ascribed to it in Article 121 of the constitution. These included setting dates for elections to the Supreme Soviet, convening sessions of the Supreme Soviet, interpreting USSR laws, ensuring conformity between the union-republic constitutions and laws and the USSR constitution and laws, ratifying treaties, appointing and recalling diplomats, proclaiming martial law, mobilizing the army and proclaiming war, establishing titles, and so on. The significance of the Presidium was that in acting *in the name of* the Supreme Soviet, it essentially acted *for* the Supreme Soviet. Thus, its thirty-nine members became, in essence, a mini-legislature unto themselves.

Thus, although the legislative function may have rested *de jure* with the 1,517-member Supreme Soviet, it was possible to say that this function was *usually* exercised by the Presidium's chairman and a few assistants in the name of the Presidium, carrying out "most of the legislative functions of the government."[59] The Presidium chairman was most visible of the thirty-nine members, however, and this person usually acted in the name of the complete body. Until 1989 the Presidium chairman was often referred to by Western media as the President of the USSR.

In October 1988 Andrei Gromyko was forced to retire from the position of Presidium chairman, and was replaced by Mikhail Gorbachev.[60] As part of Gorbachev's package of reforms for the Supreme Soviet, he suggested the creation of a new position of an executive president, called the Chairman of the USSR Supreme Soviet, who would be elected by the—at the time, proposed—Congress of People's Deputies.[61] Gorbachev "made no secret of his intention to become the first holder of the new, extremely powerful post of executive president."[62] On May 23, 1989, Gorbachev was nominated in the newly created Congress of People's Deputies for the new position, and on May 26 he was elected President by 96 percent of the deputies voting[63] (Table 13.3, on page 382).

In September 1990, at a time when rioting and demonstrations were spreading across the Soviet Union because of its failing economy, Gorbachev asked the Supreme Soviet to give him broad new powers to guide the economy. He pledged that his government would move the Soviet economy from its communist orientation to a free-market orientation over a 500-day period of time, and he argued that he needed radical powers in order to make the changes necessary to save the economy. The Supreme Soviet gave him those powers.

The Council of Ministers

The executive branch of government in the USSR is called the Council of Ministers. Prior to the 1989 constitutional changes, the Council of Ministers was officially elected by the Supreme Soviet in its first session after being elected (Article 129), but it was clear that the real selection of members of the Council of Ministers was made in the party leadership. The council was led by a chairman, who was often referred to as the premier or prime minister of the USSR, much as the chairman of a Western cabinet is referred to as a premier or prime minister.

Besides the chairman, the Council of Ministers consisted of the deputy chairmen, heads of ministries, chairs of state commit-

Table 13.3
Heads of State in the USSR

Name	Born-Died	Nationality	Years in Office	Ultimate Fate[a]
Leo Kamenev	1883–1936	Jewish	1917	P/E
Yakov Sverdlov	1885–1919	Jewish	1917–1919	DIO
Mikhail Kalinin	1875–1946	Russian	1919–1946	DIO
Nikolai Shvernik	1888–1968	Ukrainian	1946–1953	MO
Klementi Voroshilov	1881–1969	Russian	1953–1960	P/RD
Leonid Brezhnev	1906–1982	Russian	1960–1964	MO
Anastas Mikoyan	1895–1978	Armenian	1964–1965	RH
Nikolai Podgorny	1903–1983	Ukrainian	1965–1977	RD
Leonid Brezhnev	1906–1982	Russian	1977–1982	DIO
Yuri V. Andropov	1914–1984	Russian	1982–1984	DIO
Konstantin Chernenko	1911–1985	Russian	1984–1985	DIO
Andrei Gromyko	1909–	Russian	1985–1988	RH
Mikhail Gorbachev	1931–	Russian	1988–	

[a]Ultimate fate:

DIO	Died in office
MO	Moved to another top office
P/E	Purged/executed
P/RD	Purged/retired in disgrace
RD	Retired in disgrace
RH	Retired with honors

Sources: Adapted from Vadim Medish, *The Soviet Union*, rev. 4th ed. (Englewood Cliffs, N.J.: Prentice Hall, 1991), p. 138; and *The World Book Encyclopedia* (Chicago: World Book Company, 1989).

tees, and a number of ex-officio members. In 1984 the composition of the Council of Ministers was 118, including the chairman, 3 first vice-chairmen, 11 vice-chairmen, 63 ministers, 22 chairmen of state committees, the chairman of the board of the USSR State Bank, the director of the USSR Central Statistical Administration, the chairman of the USSR People's Control Committee, and the chairmen of the Republic Councils of Ministers.[64]

When the Supreme Soviet was reconstructed in the summer of 1989, so too was the Council of Ministers, which was streamlined and, ostensibly, made more efficient. In June 1989 the newly constructed Council of Ministers met for the first time, chaired by Prime Minister Nikolai Ryzhkov, who indicated the broad scope of the reorganization that had taken place in the council:

Ryzhkov characterized the current government as "unwieldy" and "hypertrophied," and, as a result, unable to move forward with economic reforms. The aim [of the reform], he continued, is to make it "impossible" for any of the central administrative bodies to interfere in production. According to Ryzhkov, two basic principles were followed when setting up the new government. The first is the retention of certain executive-management functions for central government. These include "overall economic regulation" and overseeing the development of the social sphere, defense, and ecology. The second is the development of the material and technical base for production . . . the shift is to be away from ministries with a very specific focus to ministries with a more general portfolio. . . . The new ministries will not, Ryzhkov proclaimed, be super-ministries, but "ministries of a new type, stripped of their economic functions."[65]

The size of the Council of Ministers reflected the heavily centralized economy within which it operateed. In addition to the usual ministries that we find in parliamentary cabinets in Europe—defense, foreign affairs, interior, commerce, housing, and the like—the Soviet system has had a large number of very specific economic ministries. These included ministries of the gas industry, food, electricity, and so on. We would expect that in a socialist economy the government would have the major responsibility for controlling major industries, and this was handled in the Soviet Union through the many ministries in the government.

In November 1990, responding to a worsening economic situation, President Gorbachev abolished the position of prime minister and replaced it with the advisory Federation Council made up of the leaders of the 15 republics. This was seen as a move to strengthen Gorbachev's power to respond to the Soviet Union's economic crisis at the time.[66]

The "old" Council of Ministers was the subject of Chapter 16 of the Soviet constitution, Articles 128-136. It was responsible to the Supreme Soviet, and when the Supreme Soviet was not in session (which was most of the time) it was responsible to the Presidium of the Supreme Soviet. The Council of Ministers was required to submit its resignation to a newly elected Supreme Soviet at its first session. The Council of Ministers also had the power to resolve disputes of jurisdiction between different branches of the state administration. (See Table 13.4, on page 384, for heads of government of the USSR.)

Because of its large size, over a hundred members, the Council of Ministers was really quite an unwieldy body. Accordingly, there existed a subgroup of the Council of Ministers referred to as the Presidium of the Council of Ministers (of the Supreme Soviet of the USSR), which was made up of the chairman (the premier), the first vice-chairman, and a dozen vice-chairmen. The reader should take special care here not to confuse the Presidium of the Council of Ministers (of the Supreme Soviet of the USSR) with the Presidium (of the Supreme Soviet of the USSR). In point of fact, the Presidium of the Council of Ministers was the actual, functioning cabinet where political decisions were made. The other eighty to ninety ministers in the Council of Ministers were really full-time bureaucrats, administering governmental bureaucracies.

Table 13.4
Heads of Government in the USSR

Name	Born–Died	Nationality	Years in Office	Ultimate Fate[a]
Vladimir Lenin	1870–1924	Russian	1917–1924	DIO
Rleksei Rykov	1881–1938	Russian	1924–1930	D/P/E
Viacheslav Molotov	1890–1986	Russian	1930–1941	D/RD
Josef Stalin	1879–1953	Georgian	1941–1953	DIO
Georgi Malenkov	1902–1988	Russian	1953–1955	D/RD
Nikolai Bulganin	1905–1975	Russian	1955–1958	D/RD
Nikita Khrushchev	1894–1971	Russian	1958–1964	RD
Aleksei Kosygin	1904–1980	Russian	1964–1980	RRH
Nikolai Tikhonov	1906–	Russian	1980–1985	RH
Nikolai Ryzhkov	1929–	Russian	1985–1990	

[a]Ultimate fate:

D	Demoted
DIO	Died in office
MO	Moved to another top office
P/E	Purged/executed
P/RD	Purged/retired in disgrace
RD	Retired in disgrace
RH	Retired with honors
RRH	Resigned for reasons of health

Sources: Vadim Medish, *The Soviet Union*, rev. 4th ed. (Englewood Cliffs, N.J.: Prentice Hall, 1991), p. 144; *Current Digest of the Soviet Press*, 32:43 (1980), p. 5; *The World Book Encyclopedia* (Chicago: World Book Company, 1989).

Elections in the USSR

Soviet elections are ostensibly direct, equal, and secret, but there traditionally was almost always only one candidate for each contested seat in the Supreme Soviet (or any level soviet, for that matter). Thus the elections were perceived as "not designed to provide the voters with a choice of representatives, but merely a superficial opportunity to ratify and approve the policies of the Communist party."[67] Under the revised 1989 electoral system, elections became far more open and competitive than they had been in the past.

Under the "old" system, elections to the USSR Supreme Soviet took place every four years on even-numbered years; voting for supreme soviets of union and autonomous republics—unchanged in the "new" system—took place every four years on odd-numbered years. Elections for soviets on other levels take place every two years.

Voting was based on single-member districts. "In view of the fact that more than 2.2 million deputies are elected to more than 50,000 soviets ranging from villages to the U.S.S.R. Supreme Soviet, the number of overlapping constituencies is very great."[68] A typical voter would vote for one deputy for each chamber of the USSR Supreme Soviet, a deputy to his or her independent republic's supreme soviet, a deputy to the province soviet, a deputy to the city soviet, and perhaps one for a district soviet as well.

Since there was usually no opposition in elections, nomination was tantamount to being elected. However, not just anyone could nominate a candidate; only "public organizations" were permitted to nominate candidates. The Communist party, of course, was a public organization, as were other Communist party-supervised organizations such as trade unions and other organs. This explains why not *all* deputies to the various levels of soviets were Communist party members; the selection of candidates by the Electoral Commission of the district under examination was coordinated by the Communist party, sometimes selecting Communist party members, sometimes non-Communist party members.[69] A description of the pre-1989 electoral system might have said:

A typical election campaign for the Supreme Soviet of the USSR may run something like this: A few months before election day, three candidates are nominated for the contested seat. A signal to begin the nomination is given by the appropriate party committee responsible for the particular election district. The initial public nominations take place at mass meetings at three local factories or other enterprises. The three proposed names belong to the current General Secretary of the CC [Central Committee], CPSU; the minister of defense of the USSR, and an outstanding worker-innovator at a local factory. The third candidate could also be a milkmaid from a local collective farm who has been exceeding her quota of production, a famous scientist in good standing with the authorities, who was born in this town, or another sort of local hero. The three candidates then receive enthusiastic endorsements from other local groups who obtained their cue through party channels. When the election is still several weeks away, the first two candidates gratefully acknowledge their nomination but request that their names be withdrawn from the slate because they have chosen to run for the same offices elsewhere. Since there are no residence requirements in order to represent various election districts, they had complete freedom of choice from a long list of nominations. Now the slate is down to one name, that of the local talent proposed by the party committee. Since he or she is running unopposed, the results of the forthcoming election are quite predictable.[70]

Even though elections in the USSR might not have been significant in terms of surprise outcomes in the selection of national legislators, the Soviet electoral system provided a number of important functions for the regime. First, the elections provided a "facade of legitimacy and legality" for the regime, since the system claimed to be a democratic one. Second, elections gave the public an opportunity to feel as if they were participating in their political system, even if they were not *really* making decisions. Third, elections served "as barometers of dissatisfaction for the regime" and acted "as warning devices." Very slight variations in the number of blank ballots handed in indicated to officials significant patterns of public dissatisfaction in parts of the country. Fourth, elections provided occasions of ceremony, giving leaders the opportunity to announce new policies. Finally, elections provided "a spectacular occasion for disseminating propaganda abroad."[71]

The "new" (1989) electoral system is complex. Under this system the Congress of People's Deputies is directly elected by the people and consists of three types of deputies, two-thirds to be elected by the public. First, 750 deputies are elected from "territorial election districts" with an equal number of voters in each district. Another 750 deputies are elected on the basis of governmental units, with each of the USSR republics having an equal number of representatives. Still another 750 Deputies—not selected in public elections—were allocated to "public and professional organizations." This was "one of the innovations introduced by Gorbachev at the All-Union Party Conference in June, 1988, in connection with the creation of the Congress."[72] Of these 750 seats, 425 "are reserved for the Communist Party and for a cluster of semi-independent public organizations that are either affiliated with the Party or dominated by it."[73]

There was real competition for the first election for seats for the Congress. By the end of February 1989, some 2,895 candidates had been nominated for the 1,500 seats that were to be elected by the general public, and 880 candidates were nominated for the 750 seats allotted to the "public organizations." In 1,116 (of the 1,500) electoral constituencies, voters had a choice of two or more candidates; in 384 constituencies there was only one candidate.[74] District caucuses met to decide on candidates in the electoral competitions. "Voters caucuses were made up of electors committed to various candidates. . . . Often these meetings were stormy marathons, but in some cases the authorities manipulated them to make sure the local machine candidates ran unopposed."[75]

At the first meeting of the Congress of People's Deputies at the end of May 1989, its members elected from among their numbers a 542-member Supreme Soviet, which held its first meeting in the first week of June. Only time will tell whether the new Supreme Soviet will, in fact, be more powerful and more active than its predecessor.

Soviet Courts and Justice

Justice and equality are two of the major themes of Marxism. Marx argued that law was used in the West as a means by which the ruling class stayed in power.

Judges in capitalist states, according to Marx, because of their training and background would favor the interests of property in their decisions. He felt that even guarantees of equality before the law were of little value to the poor because they could not afford the best lawyers and the high cost of legal proceedings.[76]

The Soviet Union has, obviously, not yet attained that level of pure communism forecast by Marx in which all law and government are no longer necessary. In fact, law is very much a part of the Soviet regime, because so many areas of daily life are regulated by the government.

The procurator-general (attorney-general) of the USSR and all members of the Supreme Court of the USSR are appointed by the Supreme Soviet for seven- and five-year terms, respectively. Below the USSR level, members of courts are appointed by their respective soviets for five-year terms. (That is, the provincial soviet appoints judges for province-level courts.) The bulk of all litigation in the USSR, both civil and criminal cases, begins in town-level courts called "People's Courts," presided over by a professional judge and two citizen-judges. The citizen-judges are prohibited from being full-time jurists; they serve for about two weeks in their judicial positions, then return to their regular jobs. Verdicts in all cases are decided by a majority of the three-judge panel. Appeals courts do not have citizen-judges, but have three full-time jurists hearing cases.[77]

One significant variation of the Soviet legal system from Anglo-American legal systems is the fact that the state has the right to appeal criminal cases it loses; there is no protection against "double jeopardy"—being tried twice for the same crime—in the Soviet system.

The *role* of law in the Soviet system is notably different from the role of law in Western democracies. "According to the ideology of Marxism-Leninism, law and justice are not anterior or superior to politics, but rather are instruments for achieving political-ideological goals. . . . Soviet law is just another instrument for building Communism."[78] Thus it is virtually impossible, almost by definition, for the state to do anything illegal. Law exists as a tool of the state, to help the state achieve its goals. Since all state actions are designed to help accomplish its goals, they must be legal; therefore, anything the state does is legal.

Structures of the Communist Party

The Communist Party of the Soviet Union (hereafter referred to as the CPSU) was, until 1990, *virtually* a governing organization in the USSR, and was "by far the most important political institution in that country."[79] We say "virtually" because the legal, *de jure*, role of the CPSU was very slight. The 1977 constitution indicated that the Soviet system was to be a "party-dominated political system." The CPSU was mentioned in the 1936 constitution only a few times; in the 1977 constitution the CPSU was designated as "the leading and directing force of Soviet society, the nucleus of its political system."[80]

The CPSU, however, was more than generally "a leading and directing force." It "justifies its own existence in terms of its understanding of the ideology" of the Soviet Union.[81] Through the various levels of (legal) governmental structures, the party exercised a control that was so pervasive that we could have said that the Soviet regime was run by the party rather than the government, a point that should be clearly demonstrated by the end of this chapter.

An analysis of the role of the CPSU in the Soviet Union today is made much more difficult, however, by virtue of the Gorbachev reforms of 1989–1991. With the new, "open" elections of 1990, the CPSU was weakened. With the Gorbachev reforms of 1990 reorganizing the executive branch of the government, cutting down the overlap of the party leadership and the government leadership, the Communist party was further weakened. If the Gorbachev reforms endure, the CPSU *could* be reduced to the status of political parties in Western regimes.

The Communist Party

The Party is not bound by any constitutional requirements; for it can change the constitution of the Soviet polity at will, reorganizing the government, replacing or abolishing existing agencies or practices, or even writing a new constitution. The Party retains control of the government and gives direction to its administrative machinery, determining which Party leaders will hold particular governmental positions. . . . It recruits, trains, and advances (or demotes) members of the Soviet political class. The Party develops public policies and defines goals; Party decisions have the force of law. It attempts to resolve the conflicting interests of various subordinate organizations and segments of Soviet society, often counterposing and weakening them to its own advantage.[82]

Through the end of the 1980s, the CPSU could be said to have behaved in a number of characteristic ways, indicated by various behavioral patterns that evolved over the years. First, the party was centralized. The principle of "democratic centralism" in which "the decisions of the higher organs are absolutely binding on the lower organs" illustrated this. Party statutes argued against "localism," allowing local party organizations to make their own decisions "provided they are not contrary to party policy."

Second, the party was antifactional. Party statutes said that "any manifestation of factionalism . . . is incompatible with Marxist-Leninist party principles and party membership." Third, the party made demands of its members. Membership in the party was a privilege, and the party required that applicants undergo a one-year period of candidacy, a probationary period. Applicants needed to be recommended by three party members of at least five years' membership. Members had to pay dues ranging from 0.5 to 3 percent of their income, and had to be schooled in party ideology.[83]

The "Party Rules" was a document somewhat like a constitution of the CPSU, and it set out the requirements for admission to, and continued membership in, the party. Members were expected to "master Marxist-Leninist theory," to "serve as an example of the communist attitude toward labor," to "take an active part in the political affairs of the country," and so on. These exhortations, then, made it clear that party membership was an active role. The party on occasion undertook an "exchange of party cards" to expel nonactive members; "in 1976 some 347,000 people were dropped from the Party."[84]

The CPSU served a great many functions for the Soviet polity. First, the party provided leadership personnel for all governmental structures. (This, of course, is one of the characteristics of the party that has changed most drastically in the last several years.) Second, the party regularly provided guidelines, "giving guiding directions derived from basic party doctrines and

current party priorities on all important matters requiring decision in governmental and nongovernmental bodies." Third, the
party regularly monitored all levels of government to see if guidelines were being followed. Finally, the CPSU served the function
of "mobilizing the masses" for the government. In addition to
these major functions, the Communist party was also concerned
with recruitment, indoctrination, socialization, politicization,
communication, and other important functions.[85]

Party Membership and Organizations

The CPSU had almost 19.5 million members in 1989, including
both full and candidate members, comprising approximately 9
percent of the adult population of the Soviet Union, or about 6.5
percent of the total Soviet population.[86] Although these figures
may seem reasonably small to the Western student who has
assumed that all citizens of the USSR are communists, "were
Lenin alive today he would no doubt be astonished that the party
is so *large*.... Throughout the Lenin period, party members made
up considerably less than 1 percent of the Soviet population."[87]
Since the middle of the 1970s, most scholars have suggested that
the party membership has continued to grow at an overall rate
somewhere between 1.5 and 2.5 percent per year,[88] although
recent reports have indicated that party membership may, in fact,
be starting to decline.[89]

Frequently, individuals are "invited" to join the party, or
"co-opted," rather than simply "signing up" on their own volition.
Party membership entails a number of obligations,[90] including
participation in study groups, political discussions, meetings, and
electoral work, and a number of party activities requiring a great
deal of time. The rewards of party membership can be material
as well as psychological, and may include more rapid promotion
in one's career as well as preferred treatment in housing and other
aspects of daily life.

In addition to direct membership in the party, the CPSU has
a number of auxiliary organizations to help it maintain control of
the political system, although obviously these controls have weakened in the last few years. These organizations include the All
Union Council of Trade Unions; Komsomol, the All-Union Lenin-

ist Communist League of Youth, with almost 35 million members between 14 and 28 years of age; and the Young Pioneers, with more than 20 million members between the ages of 10 and 15.

The CPSU also has directed the Committee of State Security, the KGB.[91] When this body was first created in 1917 it was called CHEKA (an acronym for the Russian words meaning "Extraordinary Commission for the Struggle Against Counter-Revolution, Sabotage, and Breach of Duty by Officials"). When the USSR came into being, CHEKA became the GUP (acronym for "State Political Administration"); in 1934 it was renamed the NKVD (in Russian the "People's Commissariat for Internal Affairs"). In 1943, as a result of extra wartime duties, the NKVD was reorganized as the NKGB, and was again reorganized as the KGB in 1954.

The KGB has a vast amount of power in the USSR. Its personnel number in the hundreds of thousands, and its jurisdiction includes intelligence and counterintelligence, censorship, and a general mandate for national security concerns.

The Primary Party Organizations

The Primary Party Organizations (PPOs) are the lowest level of party organization, and every Communist party member must belong to a PPO. One of the unique characteristics of the PPO is that most of them are located at the members' places of work. Not all PPOs are of equal size; indeed, there is a remarkable range in size in PPOs in the party, ranging from the Moscow University PPO with over 7,000 members to the minimum size of the PPO, which is three members. About 40 percent of the approximately 400,000 PPOs have 15 members or less.

The PPOs are the building blocks of the party organization, formed whenever there are three or more party members in immediate proximity to one another. Above the PPO level the Communist party is organized at a variety of levels, including rural districts, cities, provinces, republics, and, of course, the USSR level. The general pattern is that wherever there is a defined geographical area, it will have a governmental organization as well as a party organization. The local party organizations serve as a communication link between party headquarters in Moscow and local communities, supervising media, arranging for visits of outside speakers, and the like.

The Party Congress

According to CPSU rules, the Party Congress "is the supreme organ of the party." Its functions ostensibly include determining current party policy, changing rules of the party, and electing members of the Central Committee, which is designed to be the body that makes party policy between meetings of the Party Congress. The real relationship between the Central Committee and the Party Congress, however, is different; the Party Congress serves as a legitimating body for the policies of the Central Committee.

It would be wrong, however, to suggest that Party Congresses are completely without significance. Politically, it may be true that congresses are not terribly powerful, but the tremendous visibility of Party Congress meetings has meant that significant political actions have taken place *at* the congress, with the congress acting as a backdrop for policy decisions, leadership selection, and the like (Table 13.5, on page 394).

Party Congresses are supposed to meet every five years. In recent years the 22nd Party Congress met in 1961, the 23rd congress met in 1966, the 24th met in 1971, the 25th in 1976, the 26th in 1981, and the 27th Party Congress convened in 1986.

As for the Central Committee, its role is to administer the CPSU during the five-year interregnum between meetings of the All-Union Party Congress. The Central Committee (CC) in 1986 numbered 477 members, of which 307 were voting members and 107 were nonvoting "candidate" members. As with the Party Congress, however, the importance of the Central Committee is often overstated. The Central Committee is required to meet every six months, and usually meets on the day preceding the meeting of the Supreme Soviet.

There were a number of linkages between the old Supreme Soviet and the Central Committee. The old Supreme Soviet meetings usually took several days and were accompanied by *massive* publicity. The Central Committee meetings were, and still are, generally finished in one day, and press coverage is minimal. A very high percentage of Central Committee members (party officeholders) were *also* members of the old Supreme Soviet (government officeholders). When the Central Committee meeting was over, they simply stayed in Moscow for

Table 13.5
Party Congresses and Membership

Designation	Year	Place	No. Delegates[a]	Membership[b]
1st	1898	Minsk	9	1,000
2	1903	Brussels/London	57	4,000
3	1905	London	38	8,400
4	1906	Stockholm	134	45,000
5	1907	London	342	46,000
6	1917	Petrograd	267	250,000
7	1918	Petrograd	104	390,000
8	1919	Moscow	403	350,000
9	1920	Moscow	716	611,978
10	1921	Moscow	990	732,521
11	1922	Moscow	687	528,354
12	1923	Moscow	825	499,100
13	1924	Moscow	1,164	472,000
14	1925	Moscow	1,306	801,804
15	1927	Moscow	1,669	1,212,505
16	1930	Moscow	2,159	1,677,910
17	1934	Moscow	1,961	2,701,608
18	1939	Moscow	2,035	2,306,973
19	1952	Moscow	1,359	6,707,539
20	1956	Moscow	1,430	7,137,521
21	1959	Moscow	1,367	8,239,131
22	1961	Moscow	4,799	9,275,826
23	1966	Moscow	4,942	12,357,308
24	1971	Moscow	4,949	14,372,563
25	1976	Moscow	4,998	15,694,000
26	1981	Moscow	5,003	17,480,768
27	1986	Moscow	5,000	18,300,000
1989 estimated membership				19,487,822

[a]The figure includes nonvoting delegates (usually about 5 percent of the total).
[b]The figure includes candidate-members. The current membership of about 19.5 million includes 512,000 candidate-members.

Sources: Vadim Medish, *The Soviet Union*, rev. 4th ed. (Englewood Cliffs, N.J.: Prentice Hall, 1991), p. 103; *Current Digest of the Soviet Press*, 33:38 (1981), p. 1; *Radio Liberty: Report on the USSR* 1:15 (April 14, 1989), p. 17.

the Supreme Soviet meeting that followed. This overlapping membership was the primary way the party controlled the government.

This relationship, like so many others we have met, has become much more problematic since the Gorbachev reforms of 1989 and the 1990 elections. While many CPSU leaders engaged in electoral battles so that they (and members of the Central Committee) could be elected to the new Congress of People's Deputies, and subsequently to the Supreme Soviet, they no longer had the monopoly of power following the 1990 election that they had enjoyed prior to that time.

The most important function of the Central Committee was to elect the Politburo and the Secretariat. The Central Committee was important because its membership made up the top 500 individuals in the CPSU. All the members of the Politburo, the Secretariat, and many regional party leaders were to be found at the Central Committee meeting. The Central Committee had great *potential* power in that party decisions were made in its name and it could overrule party leaders, but it did not make a habit of doing so in the past.

The Politburo and the Secretariat

"Technically, the Politburo and the Secretariat are standing subcommittees of the Central Committee. By tradition, rather than by any set rule, their memberships overlap, and both bodies are chaired by the General Secretary."[92] With the Soviet Union being as closed to outside observers as it has been, the Politburo and the Secretariat were not readily available for study by students of politics.

This tendency was exacerbated by the perpetuation of the myth that the real governmental decisions in the USSR were made in the government, and not within the leadership of the CPSU. Accordingly, there was not a tremendous amount of material available on the operation of the two most important political bodies in the USSR, the Politburo (Political Bureau of the Central Committee of the CPSU), and the Secretariat (of the Central Committee of the CPSU).

This observation, too, has become more questionable ever since the Gorbachev reforms of the late 1980s. Until that time scholars felt that:

> The Politburo is the ultimate center of power within the Communist party. It makes the most important decisions on policies and appointments. The greatest freedom of discussion occurs within its ranks, but the greatest secrecy cloaks the number of its meetings and the character of its discussion.[93]

Now that there are leaders in the Soviet Union who are not members of the CPSU, who specifically reject it, the role of the Politburo is less than it was. Again, whether this will be a permanent phenomenon or a temporary phenomenon can only be determined after the passage of some time.

The Secretariat was usually considered as being second only to the Politburo in terms of the significance of its actions for the regime, but it should be noted that the lone individual usually designated as being the single most important person in the USSR was the leader of the Secretariat, namely the general secretary.

Secretaries of the Central Committee were elected by the Central Committee, although this apparently was simply a formal approval of decisions made elsewhere. The number of secretaries in the post-Stalin era has gone from three to ten, most recently standing at ten.

Generally the roles of the two leadership bodies could be distinguished in terms of their activities. Much of the Secretariat's time was devoted to overseeing the functioning of the vast party bureaucracy. The Politburo, on the other hand, spent more of its time formulating policy.

While the Politburo could have been said to be the ultimate center of power in the USSR, very few actions were publicly undertaken in its name. The power of the Politburo, then, was a *potential* power. As one observer has noted:

> The Soviet Politburo probably holds the single most awesome collection of powers of any body of human beings in the world but, like Gulliver, it can be rendered virtually powerless by the Lilliputians of an unresponsive bureaucracy.[94]

Secretariat meetings were as anonymous as Politburo meetings, if not more so. In fact, it was not until about 1971 that it was publicly acknowledged that the Secretariat held regular meetings.

Leadership and Succession

The issue of the succession of leadership in the Soviet Union illustrates the overlapping of both the party and the government hierarchy. It is very clear that, although formal—legal—office in the government comes through formal and legal channels, it is nonetheless the case that until 1990 the *reason* an individual would receive formal and legal office was because he or she had risen to power within the CPSU. This is illustrated by the many changes of leadership that have taken place since the fall of Nikita Khrushchev in October 1964.[95]

Leonid Brezhnev was able to arrange the ouster of Khrushchev through political alliances in the Politburo; in 1977 he expanded his base of power by acquiring the position of chairman of the Presidium of the Supreme Soviet in addition to his position as general secretary of the Communist party. The leaders who followed Brezhnev to the post of party general secretary, Yuri Andropov and Konstantin Chernenko, were both old party functionaries, and because of their ages (79 and 82 years, respectively) and accompanying illness, their opportunities to lead and to suggest significant policy innovations were few.

Many Sovietologists were keenly interested in what would happen in the process of succession of Brezhnev; some thought it would introduce conflict and instability, some thought it would simply maintain the status quo, and some thought that it would open up significant avenues for reform in Soviet politics. In fact, scholars have begun to conclude that the most accurate characterization would be a combination of the second and third outcomes.

> Not only did Brezhnev's death not precipitate a political cataclysm or usurpation of party authority, but equilibrium was preserved through the death and replacement of two short-lived successors, Yuri Andropov and Konstantin Chernenko. The transition has not ground out a replica of the Brezhnev regime, either. Brezhnev's style and important parts of his program have been disowned by new leaders, starting with Andropov and then, after a lull under Chernenko, more forcefully by Mikhail Gorbachev.[96]

Andropov's health made him a weak leader, and he placed a

special emphasis on what was called "collective leadership" during his brief time in office. He was not able to create a new cabinet to reflect his own preferences, but was forced to permit the existing members of the Politburo, the Party Secretariat, and most top government functionaries to retain their positions. This was to no small degree because he "owed his election as general secretary primarily to [Defense Minister Marshal] Ustinov and [Foreign Minister Aleksei] Gromyko.

> Because of the political power situation, he was equally dependent on an alliance with Chernenko, who had been the losing candidate in the election, and with Prime Minister Tikhonov and Grishin, head of the large Moscow party organization. Both were supporters of Chernenko. Andropov also had to show consideration for that part of the "Brezhnev faction" . . . who had voted for him.[97]

When Chernenko succeeded to the general secretary position he was able to arrange for himself to be elected chairman of the Presidium of the Supreme Soviet relatively quickly, in June 1983, but, like Andropov, his health very quickly limited his ability to exercise the potential power of his office. At this time Mikhail Gorbachev rose to the position of second secretary of the Central Committee, and frequently substituted for Chernenko when his health forced him to take lengthy breaks from activity.

When Mikhail Gorbachev assumed the USSR's top position in the spring of 1985, some suggested that his assumption of power "may well prove to be a major turning point in Soviet history"[98]; others wondered aloud whether he would "make a difference" in the way the Soviet regime functioned.[99] As we have already noted, Gorbachev has introduced a number of what undoubtedly will be seen to be significant structural changes in his first few years in office, although he has continued to face strong resistance from the entrenched bureaucracy to his call for "a qualitatively new state of society, and that in the broadest sense of the word."[100]

There were three "environmental situations" with which Gorbachev had to deal when he assumed office: (1) the human environment, including the entrenched bureaucracy, the Communist party leadership, and the Soviet population at large; (2) the system, including "Soviet-style socialism," public ownership, a one-party system, centralized planning of production and distribution, and related features of the society; and (3) the international environment.[101]

"No Soviet leader in his first year of office ever presided over such sweeping changes in the composition of the highest party and state organs as Mikhail Gorbachev,"[102] although he has certainly not been as successful as he would have liked. It is ironic that it is precisely the centralization of power in the Soviet system that explains why Gorbachev has found it so difficult to enact many of the reforms he sought.

> It is the very factors which concentrate so much power in the hands of the Soviet leadership, and potentially in those of the General Secretary himself, that obstruct the speedy implementation of a reform program. One consequence of single-party rule is that when the General Secretary changes, the rest of the ruling oligarchy initially remains; the new chief executive does not *form* a government, he *inherits* one. . . . He must therefore devote much attention to the Byzantine intricacies of bureaucratic politics at the same time as building up his alliances and authority step-by-step within the ruling oligarchy itself.[103]

The Interlocking Directorate

One of the major reasons why it was so hard to precisely delineate positions of power and influence in the Soviet political system through the end of the 1980s was that we found the same few individuals holding several different positions in the political realm. Because this was the case, it was difficult to decide whether a given individual was influential by himself, whether he was influential because he held an important party or government office, or whether the party or government office was perceived as important because of the individual holding that position. An illustration of this structural overlap is the fact that the chairman of the Presidium of the Supreme Soviet was always a member of the party Politburo. This overlap was sometimes referred to as an "interlocking directorate."

The liberalizing of the electoral system in 1989, and the introduction of many outsiders to the political elite in 1990, weakened this interlocking directorate considerably, although as we noted above, one of Gorbachev's major battles has continued to be against the entrenched bureaucracy in government. Whether the CPSU leadership will be able to continue to guide the direction of the government is something that can only be determined after Gorbachev's reforms have been given time to work.

The concept of an interlocking directorate, of course, was not originated in the Soviet context. It also refers to the phenomenon of members of corporate boards of directors in the world of big business being on more than one board. (For example, a board member at ITT might also be associated with IBM, Exxon, and so on.) This interlocking relationship between the CPSU and the state reinforced the party's importance in the government, of course, "by ensuring that those who are involved in adopting the policy are also present in force when it comes to explaining that policy and giving it legal status."[104]

Many possibilities existed for an interlocking directorate to form in the Soviet government. Given the ideas of centralized leadership and Communist party domination of leadership positions, it was inevitable that an interlocking directorate would result. Members of the Politburo appeared in a number of significant offices in the Secretariat, the Presidium, and in other offices. Members of the Council of Ministers were to be found in the Politburo as well. Members of the Presidium were also to be found in local republic party organizations. The relations were truly interlocking. To a significant degree this is still true today, but it is less true than it was a decade ago.

The Soviet System in Perspective

The Soviet system provides an interesting case study, both in its own right and in a comparative perspective. The Soviet system is one that is in a state of flux today, and although we can describe its history, and its present form, it is very difficult to know exactly what the regime will look like in another five or ten years.

In its own right, the USSR shows a political system in which power relationships as described in a constitution may not, in fact, be those that really exist. This certainly was the case in the past. Soviet federalism, if indeed it really is federalism, is unlike federalism in other political systems we have seen. The ruling Soviet ideology is, in many cases, more of an exercise in propaganda than an expression of the apparent philosophy behind the government in power, although contemporary Soviet ideology is changing, as are contemporary Soviet political structures. The Soviet constitution is an exercise in symbolism, not really guaranteeing rights it says it guarantees.

In a comparative perspective the USSR provides us with a number of new twists to our study of political structures. We have already met a parliamentary "dual executive" (a head of state and a chief executive) and we have seen how it differs from the single executive of the presidential model. The USSR shows us an instance of a new type of executive, one that is just beginning to become "institutionalized" and to see exactly how effectively it can govern. We have seen governments that we would refer to as constitutional governments, both with and without written constitutions. The USSR shows us an instance of a government with a written constitution that we would still refer to as an unconstitutional government. We have seen political systems in which parties play greater and lesser roles in politics. The USSR shows us an instance in which the party is—or at least has been until very recently—virtually everything in politics.

In short, the Soviet system is quite different from other political systems we have met over the course of our inquiry. We should look at the variations exhibited by USSR politics as a valuable lesson broadening our horizons. The *single most important* lesson we should draw from our investigation is that we cannot walk into any new political study with the assumption that politics everywhere else operates in the same fashion as it does in the United States. In this manner, we can see the values of cross-national political inquiry. Our new perspective provides us with a better ability to make our own observations in the future and to draw our own conclusions as we continue our studies.

Notes

1. Vadim Medish, *The Soviet Union* (Englewood Cliffs, N.J.: Prentice Hall, 1981), p. 1.
2. John S. Reshetar, *The Soviet Polity* (New York: Harper & Row, 1978), p. 21.
3. Adam Ulam, *A History of Soviet Russia* (New York: Praeger, 1976) is a good reference in this area.
4. Gwendolen M. Carter, *The Government of the Soviet Union* (New York: Harcourt Brace Jovanovich, 1972), p. 14.

5. This section is based upon a much longer section written by Vernon V. Aspaturian, "Soviet Politics," in Roy C. Macridis, *Modern Political Systems: Europe* (Englewood Cliffs, N.J.: Prentice Hall, 1978), pp. 335–340. See also the very good discussion of Russia's revolutionary heritage in Gordon B. Smith, *Soviet Politics: Continuity and Contradiction* (New York: St. Martin's Press, 1988).

6. Aspaturian, "Soviet Politics," p. 336.

7. Michael G. Roskin, *Countries and Concepts* (Englewood Cliffs, N.J.: Prentice Hall, 1982), p. 219.

8. Aspaturian, "Soviet Politics," p. 338.

9. Adam B. Ulam, *The Russian Political System* (New York: Random House, 1974), p. 27.

10. Medish, *The Soviet Union*, pp. 29–30.

11. Ronald Grigor Suny, "The Nationality Question," in Janet Podell and Steven Anzovin, eds., *The Soviet Union* (New York: H. W. Wilson, 1988), p. 136.

12. Indeed, "in his closing speech to the first session of the new Congress of People's Deputies, Mikhail Gorbachev commented that no single issue had been so widely discussed by the Congress as that of interethnic relations." *Radio Liberty: Report on the USSR* 1:24 (June 16, 1989), p. 21.

13. Celestine Bohlen, "The Soviets and the Enmities Within," *The New York Times*, April 16, 1989, Section E, p. 1. Description of the non-Russian nationalities may be found in some detail in Reshetar, *The Soviet Polity*, pp. 10–18.

14. For an example of the kind of discussion taking place, see Daniel Sneider, "Gorbachev and Yeltsin Face Off over Economy, Role of Republics," *The Christian Science Monitor*, Sepbember 13, 1990, p. 3.

15. Robert Sharlet, *The New Soviet Constitution of 1977* (Brunswick, Ohio: King's Court Communications, Inc., 1978), p. 97.

16. Ulam, *The Russian Political System*, p. 69.

17. John N. Hazard, *The Soviet System of Government* (Chicago: University of Chicago Press, 1980), pp. 98–99.

18. Sharlet, *The New Soviet Constitution of 1977*, p. 97.

19. Ibid., p. 9. See also, for examples of reports of these events, Francis Clines, "Byelorussia Calls Itself Sovereign; Parliament Declares Primacy of Laws and Claims Share of All Soviet Resources," *The New York Times*, July 28, 1990, p. A4; or Michael Parks, "Sweeping Sovereignty Declared by Ukraine," *Los Angeles Times*, July 17, 1990, p. A4.

20. Felicity Barringer, "Soviets Draft Plans for Government Change," *The New York Times* October 22, 1988, p. 3.

21. Ulam, *The Russian Political System*, pp. 72–73.

22. A very good collection on ideology in the Soviet Union is in Steven White and Alex Pravda, eds., *Ideology and Soviet Politics* (New York: St. Martin's Press, 1988).

23. Hugh Seton-Watson, "The Historical Roots," in Curtis Keeble, ed., *The Soviet State: The Domestic Roots of Soviet Foreign Policy* (Boulder, Col.: Westview Press, 1985), p. 9.

24. Sam C. Sarkesian and James Buck, *Comparative Politics* (Sherman Oaks, Calif.: Alfred Publishing Co., 1979), pp. 97–98.

25. See Gustav Wetter, *Soviet Ideology* (New York: Praeger, 1962).

26. Robert G. Wesson, *Modern Governments* (Englewood Cliffs, N.J.: Prentice Hall, 1981), p. 308.

27. Donald D. Barry and Carol Barner-Barry, *Contemporary Soviet Politics* (Englewood Cliffs, N.J.: Prentice Hall, 1978), p. 27.
28. Medish, *The Soviet Union*, pp. 67–68.
29. Sarkesian and Buck, *Comparative Politics*, p. 101.
30. Aspaturian, "Soviet Politics," p. 356.
31. Ibid.
32. Carter, *The Government of the Soviet Union*, p. 11.
33. Sarkesian and Buck, *Comparative Politics*, p. 107.
34. Aspaturian, "Soviet Politics," p. 358.
35. Carter, *The Government of the Soviet Union*, p. 13. See also Donald R. Kelley, "Developments in Ideology," in Donald R. Kelley, ed., *Soviet Politics in the Brezhnev Era* (New York: Praeger, 1980), pp. 182–199.
36. Ulam, *The Russian Political System*, p. 59.
37. Sharlet, *The New Soviet Constitution of 1977*, p. 4.
38. Ibid., pp. 4–6.
39. Reshetar, *The Soviet Polity*, p. 172.
40. Aspaturian, "Soviet Politics," p. 401.
41. Ibid.
42. Medish, *The Soviet Union*, p. 116.
43. In the Sharlet volume, the text goes from p. 73 to p. 130.
44. Barry and Barner-Barry, *Contemporary Soviet Politics*, p. 73.
45. Sharlet, *The New Soviet Constitution of 1977*, p. 93.
46. Reshetar, *The Soviet Polity*, p. 169.
47. Carter, *The Government of the Soviet Union*, p. 62.
48. D. Richard Little, *Governing the Soviet Union* (New York: Longman, 1989), p. 172.
49. Elizabeth Teague, "Gorbachev's First Four Years," *Radio Liberty: Report on the USSR* 1:9 (March 3, 1989), pp. 3–4.
50. See Dawn Mann, "The Opening of the Congress," *Radio Liberty: Report on the USSR* 1:23 (June 9, 1989), pp. 1–2.
51. Sharlet, *The New Soviet Constitution of 1977*, p. 108.
52. Aspaturian, "Soviet Politics," p. 409.
53. Paul Quinn-Judge, "Gorbachev Dominance Displayed in Parliament," *Christian Science Monitor*, December 1, 1988, p. 1.
54. David Remnick, "New Soviet Congress Tackles Procedure," *Washington Post*, May 27, 1989, p. A15.
55. Bill Keller, "A Guide to the Election Process," *The New York Times*, March 26, 1989, p. E3.
56. Dawn Mann and Julia Wishnevsky, "Composition of Congress of People's Deputies," *Radio Liberty, Report on the USSR* 1:18 (May 5, 1989), p. 6.
57. Alexander Rahr, "Gorbachev Battles with Opposition," *Radio Liberty: Report on the USSR* 1:5 (February 3, 1989), p. 3.
58. Sharlet, *The New Soviet Constitution of 1977*, p. 112.
59. Little, *Governing the Soviet Union*, p. 157.
60. Paul Quinn-Judge, "New Parliament: How Different?" *The Christian Science Monitor*, March 24, 1989, p. 2.
61. Vera Tolz, "The USSR This Week," *Radio Liberty: Report on the USSR* 1:1 (January 6, 1989), p. 26.
62. Teague, "Gorbachev's First Four Years," p. 4.
63. See Michael Parks, "Party Picks Gorbachev as Nominee for President at People's Congress," *The Los Angeles Times*, May 23, 1989, p. 8; and Michael

Parks, "New Soviet Congress Elects Gorbachev to Presidency," *The Los Angeles Times*, May 26, 1989, p. 1.

64. Little, *Governing the Soviet Union*, p. 131.
65. Vera Tolz, "The USSR This Week," *Radio Liberty: Report on the USSR* 1:25 (June 23, 1989), pp. 26–27.
66. See John Burke, "Soviet Premier May Soon Resign: Ryzhkov Is Left Out on a Limb After Gorbachev Backs a Radical Economic Plan in Parliament," *Christian Science Monitor*, September 13, 1990, p. 3.
67. Aspaturian, "Soviet Politics," p. 406.
68. Reshetar, *The Soviet Polity*, p. 194.
69. Carter, *The Government of the Soviet Union*, p. 65.
70. Medish, *The Soviet Union*, p. 123.
71. Aspaturian, "Soviet Politics," p. 407.
72. There was an official list of "public organizations" published that indicated how many "mandates" (deputies) each of the officially recognized "organizations" could have. Some examples from the list of 36 organizations: The Communist party received 100 seats, Komsomol received 75, the All-Union Central Trade-Union Council received 100, the USSR Union of Architects received 10, the USSR Union of Designers received 5, the Union of Red Cross and Red Crescent Societies received 10, the Soviet Peace Fund received 7, Public Sports Organizations received 3, and the All-Union Voluntary Temperance Society received 1. Dawn Mann, "Elections to the Congress of People's Deputies Nearly Over," *Radio Liberty: Report on the USSR* 1:15 (April 14, 1989), pp. 8–9.
73. Victor Yasmann, "Quotas of Seats in Congress of People's Deputies for Public and Professional Organizations," *Radio Liberty Report on the USSR* 1:4 (January 27, 1989), p. 9.
74. Bill Keller, "Soviets Savor Vote in Freest Election Since '17 Revolution," *The New York Times*, March 27, 1989, p. A1.
75. "A Guide to the Election Process," *The New York Times*, March 26, 1989, p. E3.
76. Herbert Winter and Thomas Bellows, *People and Politics* (New York: Wiley, 1977), p. 317.
77. A good description of the Soviet legal institutions can be found in Smith, *Soviet Politics: Continuity and Contradiction*, pp. 143–146.
78. Medish, *The Soviet Union*, p. 131.
79. Ronald Hill and Peter Frank, *The Soviet Communist Party* (London: Allen and Unwin, 1981), p. 1.
80. Sharlet, *The New Soviet Constitution of 1977*, p. 12.
81. Hill and Frank, *The Soviet Communist Party*, p. 4.
82. Reshetar, *The Soviet Polity*, pp. 133–134.
83. Ibid., pp. 134–137.
84. Barry and Barner-Barry, *Contemporary Soviet Politics*, p. 103–104.
85. Carter, *The Government of the Soviet Union*, p. 42.
86. Philip Handon and Elizabeth Teague, "Has Party Membership Begun to Fall?" *Radio Liberty: Report on the USSR* 1:15 (April 14, 1989), p. 17.
87. Barry and Barner-Barry, *Contemporary Soviet Politics*, p. 102.
88. Smith, *Soviet Politics: Continuity and Contradiction*, p. 57.
89. Handon and Teague, "Has Party Membership Begun to Fall?" p. 17.
90. See Hill and Frank, *The Soviet Communist Party*, pp. 25–28.
91. A recent and impressively well-documented study of the KGB can be found in William R. Corson and Robert T. Crowley, *The New KGB: Engine of Soviet Power* (New York: William Morrow and Co., 1985).

92. Medish, *The Soviet Union*, p. 101.
93. Carter, *The Government of the Soviet Union*, p. 54.
94. Roy D. Laird, *The Politburo: Demographic Trends, Gorbachev, and the Future* (Boulder, Col.: Westview Press, 1986), p. 162.
95. Much of the material in the next few paragraphs is based upon more extensive analysis in Boris Meissner, "Implications of Leadership and Social Change for Soviet Policies," in Kinya Niiseki, ed., *The Soviet Union in Transition* (Boulder, Col.: Westview Press, 1987), pp. 50–56.
96. Timothy Colton, *The Dilemma of Reform in the Soviet Union* (New York: Council on Foreign Relations, 1986), pp. 68–69.
97. Meissner, "Leadership," p. 52.
98. Herbert J. Ellison, "Gorbachev and Reform: An Introduction," in Lawrence W. Lerner and Donald W. Treadgold, eds., *Gorbachev and the Soviet Future* (Boulder, Col.: Westview Press, 1988), p. 1.
99. There is an absolutely massive literature on Gorbachev, only a few years into his occupancy of the leadership position. See, *inter alia*, Ilya Zemtsov and John Farrar, *Gorbachev: The Man and the System* (New Brunswick, N.J.: Transaction Publishers, 1989); Seweryn Bialer, ed., *Politics, Society, and Nationality Inside Gorbachev's Russia* (Boulder, Col.: Westview Press, 1989); or R. F. Miller, J. H. Miller, and T. H. Rigby, eds., *Gorbachev at the Helm: A New Era in Soviet Politics?* (London: Croom Helm, 1987).
100. Robert C. Tucker, *Political Culture and Leadership in Soviet Russia: From Lenin to Gorbachev* (New York: W.W. Norton & Co., 1987), p. 148.
101. Hiroshi Kimura, " 'Gorbachevism'—Simply Old Wine in a New Bottle?" in Niiseki, *The Soviet Union in Transition*, pp. 29–31.
102. Archie Brown, "The Soviet Political Scene: The Era of Gorbachev?" in Lawrence W. Lerner and Donald W. Treadgold, eds., *Gorbachev and the Soviet Future* (Boulder, Col.: Westview Press, 1988), p. 21.
103. T. H. Rigby, "The Gorbachev Era Launched," in Miller, Miller, and Rigby, *Gorbachev at the Helm*, pp. 235–236.
104. Hill and Frank, *The Soviet Communist Party*, p. 116.

14

The Mexican Political System

Mexico represents many different—and interesting and important—variations from other nations we have already examined in this book. It is our first Latin American nation. It is the first nation included in the second part of this text that is presidential, not parliamentary, in its basic political structure. It is also the first nation included in the second part of this book that belongs to the "developing," rather than to the "developed," group of nations as we described them in Chapter 3. These differences—among others—guarantee that in this chapter we shall note several differences in both political structure and political behavior from those we have observed in other chapters.

The Mexican Political Heritage

Although Mexico has not had a revolution since the very early part of this century (1910–1921), this fact alone should not be taken to suggest that there have been no issues of controversy in

Mexican politics since that time, or that there has not been any significant political instability in domestic politics there. Such is not the case. Indeed:

> [T]he Mexican political culture is a fragmented one in which the violence of internecine struggle has appeared again and again in the absence of consensus on fundamentals as to the way government should operate—its relationship to citizens, their relationship to government, and the overall goals toward which policy should be directed, that is, the basic purposes of government. All these matters have been much disputed, leaving in various sectors of society residues of commitment to values regarding proper uses of governmental power and reasons for existence of government which are at variance with major characteristics of the present system.[1]

Mexico has, even in very recent years, experienced some very tense moments in the political arena. In 1968 several hundred students were killed in Mexico City while demonstrating against the government; massive land expropriation was undertaken in 1976; and an economic crisis was encountered in 1982. Indeed, many claimed that the 1988 presidential election was "stolen" by the forces of President Carlos Salinas de Gortari when it was clear that the candidate of the Institutional Revolutionary party (PRI) might actually lose a presidential election for the first time in modern history.[2]

In the early years of the 1970s Mexico seemed to have turned the corner and to have entered an era of rapid development and increasing prosperity. Mexico's oil industry was rapidly expanding and became the fourth largest in the world.[3] Today, however, as we shall learn later in this chapter, primarily as a result of the decline in world oil prices, Mexico's economy is in a shambles, and domestic politics have reflected the economic tensions in society. As one scholar has noted, "Mexico's famed political stability has not been destroyed by the country's current economic crisis. But that stability can no longer be taken for granted."[4]

Mexico's political history falls into several broad eras.[5] Prior to the year 1521 Mexico was ruled by a series of Indian empires. Following that, between 1521 and 1810, Mexico was under Spanish colonial power. Mexico first revolted against the Spanish on September 16, 1810; the struggle took until 1821 before a stable independent government was installed. Between 1821 and 1877 there were a number of emperors, dictators, and presidents in power, and Mexico lost Texas (1836) and later (1846–1848) lost California, Nevada, Utah, most of Arizona and New Mexico, and parts of Wyoming and Colorado, to the United States.

In the year 1855 the Indian leader Benito Juárez began to introduce political reforms in Mexico, but his stay in power was short-lived, and between 1861 and 1867 Mexico fell under the rule of European powers. In 1867 Juárez again took power as president, and he executed Maximilian of Austria, who had become emperor of Mexico in 1864.

From 1877 to 1911 Mexican politics were dominated by the long and dictatorial presidency of Porfirio Díaz (1876–1880, and 1884–1911). The Díaz regime led to the social revolution of 1910–1921,[6] and is regarded by most Mexicans as the beginning of modern Mexican politics.

> The commonly accepted and most convenient symbol for the beginning of Mexico's modernization process is the Mexican Revolution of 1910, although the pressures of both economic and political change had been building up for some time before. Since that date, considering the number and complexity of the problems involved, Mexico has progressed amazingly in its evolution toward modernity.[7]

Political Stability

Mexico's stability has, over the last several decades, been the single most visible characteristic separating it from other Latin American nations. It has continued to operate under the same general political structures for over fifty years, the only major Latin American political system not to have had a military coup since the end of World War II. Additionally, every president elected since the presidential election of 1934 has served out his full six-year term and participated in a peaceful transition of power.

"Stability" as we have used the term here does not mean that Mexican society has not suffered any social tensions, however. Rather, it is used in a more restricted sense to indicate the continuity of major political structures. One important example of this relative stability is the relation between the Mexican military and the civilian government. Where military coups are common in Central and South America, such is not the case in Mexico.

> In the 1980s, the pace of military presence quickened as Mexico faced new experiences and challenges, many of them facilitating the political emergence of men in uniform. . . . Indications pointed to more influence in the future. Conversely, equally convincing indicators argued for the continued superiority of Mexico's civilian authority. In the final analysis, the emerging scenario may produce a change in the degree of military influence, but it is not destined to significantly alter ongoing civil dominance.[8]

Among the many very significant aspects of Mexican culture that have contributed to this pattern of stability is the process of political socialization in Mexico. The socialization process is important "to the reader interested in learning about the complex influences affecting the builders of a nation emerging from a violent twentieth-century revolution."[9]

It has been suggested that Mexico's socialization patterns have been transformed in recent years, resulting in significant changes in the socialization process.[10] These changes include an expansion of mass education—today nearly one-third of Mexicans are in school. Until recently "the elite has generally been able to protect itself in privileged sanctuaries,"[11] but an increasingly educated mass population is beginning to want to change that relationship. In the long run, "the positive impacts of educational changes on political stability are more direct and predictable than the negative consequences."[12] Student groups see increasing educational opportunities not only as avenues for advancement but also as means to further develop governmental expertise and legitimacy.

For those who were adolescents in the early years of the twentieth century, the revolution was an event of overwhelming significance; for the "postrevolutionary generation" the most important characteristic of the environment in which they were reared was "the prevalence of violence and instability."[13] Thus, a stable contemporary regime is an important factor in the lives of most Mexican political elites today.

The Mexican Constitution

Mexico's contemporary political system was born in revolution. The new constitution, amending the constitution of 1857, was announced in February 1917 and has been the constitution of Mexico since then. Three characteristics reflected in the constitution can be identified as being representative of themes running throughout Mexican politics: representative democracy, presidential dictatorship, and corporatism.[14]

Mexico's leadership in 1917 believed in the virtues of classical liberalism and established a constitution based upon *representative democracy*, guaranteeing equal rights for all citizens, providing for separation of powers in the legislative, executive, and judicial branches of government, and establishing representative government based upon the ultimate sovereignty of the people. It also produced a centralized federal government that had significant political powers; for example, permitting the government to nationalize the petroleum industry in 1938 and allowing it to restrict foreign ownership of land in Mexico.[15]

While some aspects of the constitution clearly appear to be based upon fundamental principles of representative democracy, others are much less so, and some observers have suggested that Mexico has virtually a *presidential dictatorship*. The president has the right to issue executive decrees, which have the force of law, and despite the notion of "separation of powers" the president is permitted to introduce proposals in the legislature on his own authority, thus giving him clear legislative power, in addition to his executive power. The president also has the power to appoint and remove judges, giving him clear judicial power as well. Thus the president's power:

> is such that it absorbs and is complementary to the powers of the other two branches of government. In addition, the sovereignty of the states is found to be extremely limited by the Federation and subject to the discretionary powers of the president. The result is the establishment of a constitutional dictatorship of the presidential variety.[16]

The third theme of Mexican politics is that of *corporatism*, which we defined in Chapter 7 as implying a "close interaction of groups and government," where "organizations are integrated in the government decision-making process." As the government's financial planning has come under increased pressures in recent years, tensions have begun to develop in the government-business relationship, and the government has anxiously sought ways to smooth over the sources of tension. Indeed, one recent observation noted that "the period since 1982 has been characterised by the private sector's search for guarantees of its interests within the Mexican political system."[17]

Mexican labor law recognizes classes in society, and the Courts of Conciliation and Arbitration are given authority to resolve conflicts between labor and owners, or, as the law puts it, "to secure the balance of the diverse factors of production, bringing into harmony the labor laws with those of capital." There are many governmental boards and commissions that provide industrial and interest groups with a role in policy making. These commissions can be referred to as "corporate" because through the appointment of leaders of different social and economic groups to membership on the boards, these groups are, indeed, integrated in the government decision-making process.

Mexican Federalism

Mexico is a federal political system, including thirty-one states and one federal district, each of which has some policy jurisdiction, although, as we shall note shortly, the Mexican states do not have the degree of power in relation to Mexico City that the German Länder have in relation to Berlin, for example. Each state has its own constitution and possesses the right to pass its own laws, within some clearly defined parameters. Each state elects its own governor, who holds office for a term of six years. The state legislature has a three-year term of office.

The overwhelming power of the president in the Mexican political system—a subject to which we shall return shortly—has done a great deal to weaken Mexican federalism. The president exercises control over state government, much as he exercises control over other branches of the federal government, through both constitutional and traditional justifications.

> [T]he President is the ultimate power in state politics. He has authority to intervene to replace personnel of state governments

with those who promise greater service in satisfying his policy needs. Under Article 76 of the Constitution, the President, acting through the Senate and the Ministry of Interior, is able to declare that the constitutional powers of a state have disappeared and appoint a provisional governor pending new state elections.[18]

Most frequently, however, the major source of presidential power, rather than coming exclusively from legal or constitutional structures, emanates from practical sources, such as the president's control (through legislation) of grant programs, federal financial aid to the states, and similar sources.

In recent years there has been an increasing policy of administrative decentralization in Mexico. This has been suggested by many to be especially necessary given recent "hyperurbanization" in Mexico—the rush of so many rural residents to the urban area surrounding Mexico City, a topic that we shall examine later in this chapter. The Mexican government has become aware that educational, cultural, and health resources simply must be made available far more broadly geographically in contemporary Mexico; if not, some experts say, the rush to move to urban areas will continue.[19]

Mexico's approach to federalism is, as we noted, far more centralized than that which we observed in Germany. Indeed, "the central government bureaucracy, dominated by the presidency, is the main source of public policy."[20]

The Presidency

Simón Bolivar once observed that the new republics of the Americas needed kings who could be referred to as presidents, and added that, in Mexico at least, these kings were kings for six-year periods.[21] The president is elected by direct popular vote in elections and can hold office for a single six-year term, after which time this individual can never be reelected. He must be at least 35 years of age, and must be a native-born Mexican who is the son of native-born Mexicans.[22] He cannot be a clergyman of a religious group. If he has been in either the military or in the cabinet (which all recent presidents have been), he must have retired from that position at least six months prior to the election.

The president is, very clearly, the single most powerful individual in Mexican politics.

Power

Much of the president's power comes from his constitutional role in government, and students of Mexican politics have suggested that the president "encounters no effective restraint *within* government."[23] In that role he has very wide power to appoint and remove government officials (much broader fiscal powers than, say, the American president), the capacity to initiate and veto legislation, and the power to control the military. (Ever since the revolution, the military has been reorganized, and today it is restricted in its power to influence policy.)[24] Although legislators in Mexico have the power to introduce legislation, legislation is overwhelmingly introduced by the president, not legislators.

> In addition to the President's vast field of action with regard to the initiation of legislation and his work to secure its passage there is also a presidential veto power which never comes into play in practice because the legislature does not amend bills without prior consultation with the executive, thus eliminating the necessity of employing a veto. The veto remains, however, as a legal means at his disposal.[25]

Nomination and Selection

The presidential election of 1988 was the first one in modern history in which the outcome was truly in doubt, although by the time the votes were all counted (and, opposition leaders charged, rigged) the PRI candidate again won.[26] This fact notwithstanding, however, the modern practice of presidential selection in Mexico has more often focused upon *intra*party competition, within the framework of the PRI itself.

The usual practice within the PRI in recent presidential elections has been to have the incumbent president hand-pick his successor, invariably from among those individuals who have been active in his cabinet. The constitution requires that a cabinet officer seeking the presidency must resign from office at least six months before the presidential elections, but this has not provided any difficulties for recent candidates. There are some socio-economic characteristics that are apparently valued by presidents when selecting their successors, including physical appearance, a neutral position in relation to organized religion, a middle-class background, coming from a large state, and having a wife who "has a moderate interest in public affairs."[27] (For a list of recent presidents of Mexico, see Table 14.1.)

When an incumbent president nears the final year of his six-year term of office, pressures begin to be exerted on him to "name" his successor. Incumbents have tried to resist this pressure for as long as possible, however, because once an incumbent names the "heir apparent," he loses much of his own political power and will not be able to accomplish as much as he previously could.[28] One scholar, in fact, has identified nine different stages in the process of the selection of a new president.

1. President consults with advisors and colleagues as to acceptability of possible nominees.
2. The President announces his choice.
3. Power-seekers and political leaders in the PRI praise the candidate-designate.
4. Candidate is officially nominated at the PRI Rally.
5. The Campaign takes place.
6. The Election takes place.
7. The winning candidate officially accepts the election results.
8. The new president selects his advisors.
9. The new president selects an advantageous time to announce his appointments.[29]

Once the outgoing president "nominates" his successor, the nominee of the PRI is expected to travel all over the country campaigning for office, meeting leaders of interest groups, local leaders, business leaders, community politicians, and so on, and

Table 14.1
Some Recent Mexican Presidents

Gustavo Diaz Ordaz	1964–1970
Luis Echeverria Alvarez	1970–1976
José Lopez Portillo	1976–1982
Miguel de la Madrid Hurtado	1982–1988
Carlos Salinas de Gortari	1988–

in fact improving his knowledge of local problems at the same time that he is increasing his own visibility in the eyes of the electorate. Past experience has shown that even the most isolated of Mexican villages will be visited—if not by the candidate himself then by one of his campaign workers—over the course of the campaign.

Some have questioned why Mexico should even go through this ritual if the results of the election are so certain in advance of the process. There are at least two reasons why the national campaign is useful, even if it contains no surprises for political observers. First, the act of campaigning itself helps to create support for the regime, and thereby affords the government greater legitimacy than it might otherwise have without a campaign. Second, the presidential campaign can make a significant difference to candidates for the Senate and the Chamber of Deputies who are running for office, either on the same side as the presidential candidate or on an opposition ticket.

The Congress

The Mexican Congress is bicameral and consists of a Chamber of Deputies and a Senate. The Congress is very clearly inferior to the president in the structures of governmental power, and its consent to presidential legislative proposals can be counted upon.

> As long as the official party carries out its functions of liaison and political communication effectively, and as long as the President successfully balances interest conflicts with regard to special goals of the various organizations, there is every reason to expect that legal approval for the acts of the President can be obtained from the Congress without question.[30]

In fact, recent scholarship has indicated that presidential proposals have been approved unanimously 80 to 95 percent of the time in recent years, and are normally opposed by less than 5 percent of the members.[31]

The Senate

Senators are elected for six-year terms, with two senators elected from each of the thirty-one states and two elected from the federal district. The Senate elected in the elections of July 7, 1988, is made up of sixty senators of the Institutional Revolutionary party (PRI), and four senators of the National Democratic Front. The Senate today is "frankly regarded in Mexico as a rubber stamp for presidential policy."[32] Senators are elected by direct popular vote at the same time as the president (the first Sunday of July in 1976, 1982, and 1988; effective 1994 the election will be held on the first Sunday of September in order to reduce the lame duck period of the outgoing president).

The Chamber of Deputies

The 500 deputies are elected for three-year terms according to a system of single-member-district voting and "partial proportional representation," under which 200 of the 500 seats in the Chamber are elected by proportional representation, while the other 300 seats are elected from single-member districts.

The 300 single-member-district seats are based upon population, but the constitution guarantees each state at least two deputies. Although each state's *number* of seats is based upon the state's total population as a share of the national population, there is no constitutional provision that forces the states to divide their quota of seats into equally populated districts. Indeed, as Table 14.2 shows, there was quite a significant variation in population among the 300 electoral districts in the federal election of 1985.

Table 14.2
Population of Electoral Districts, 1985

No. Voters in District	No. Districts
Over 250,000	1
200,000–249,999	3
150,000–199,999	33
100,000–149,999	186
50,000–99,999	74
Under 50,000	3
Total	300

Source: John Bailey, *Governing Mexico: The State-craft of Crisis Management* (New York: St. Martin's Press, 1988), p. 151.

Comprehensive electoral reform was introduced in 1977, raising the number of deputies from about 200 (the exact number depended upon how many minority party deputies were elected)[33] to 400, and this reform became effective with the 1979–1980 legislative session. For the 1988 election the total number of seats was raised to 500. Of these seats, 300 are elected by a single-member-district, majority-vote system, with those districts based upon population similar to electoral systems we have seen in Britain or Germany (see Table 14.3).

One hundred fifty of these 500 seats are "reserved" for minority parties and are divided among the states to be distributed by a complex proportional representation system. If a party wins fewer than sixty of the district-based seats, and if that party has entered candidates in at least one-third of the 300 district-based electoral contests throughout the entire nation, then it is entitled to a share (determined by a specific formula) of the 200 at-large proportional seats; all of the opposition parties together are guaranteed at least 150 of these 200 at-large proportional seats.

Thus, 25 percent of the seats in the Chamber of Deputies are guaranteed to opposition parties, *as well as* those seats they can win in the 300 district-based electoral races. Although the power of the Chamber of Deputies is limited, the opposition is guaranteed a presence there.[34] The parties that have especially benefitted from the at-large proportional seats are the right-wing National Action party (PAN) and the leftist Unified Socialist Party of Mexico (PSUM).[35]

Table 14.3
The 1988 Election for the Chamber of Deputies

Party	District Seats	Proportional At-Large Seats
Institutional Revolutionary Party (PRI)	234[a]	27
National Action Party (PAN)	38	63
National Democratic Front (FDN)	28	110
Total	300	200

[a]One PRI Deputy changed from the PRI party to the FDN party after the election.

Source: *Keesing's Contemporary Archives* (London: Longman, 1988), vol. 34 (September 1988), p. 36130.

The Bureaucracy

By the middle of the 1970s the Mexican federal public sector included 1,075 agencies with nearly 3.4 million employees, nearly 17 percent of the total work force.[36] The administration of President de la Madrid sought to decentralize some of this bureaucracy, emphasizing regional programs and the increased participation of state and local governments in programs, especially those dealing with health care and education.[37]

We noted in Chapter 3 that there are many quasi-governmental organizations in Mexico that complement the federal and state governments' efforts to enact policy. A recent study listed 123 decentralized agencies, 292 public enterprises, 187 commissions, and 160 development trusts, as well as 18 regular ministries and departments of state making up the federal bureaucratic infrastructure.[38] A critic of the degree of direct government involvement in private business recently wrote that:

> The State participates in, among other things, six firms which manufacture stoves, refrigerators, and other domestic appliances, seven which manufacture cardboard boxes, paper bags, announcement cards, and paper forms; it manufactures, sells, and distributes desk supplies; it owns a soft drink bottling plant, a dish factory, a bicycle manufacturing plant, six textile mills, an airline, fifteen holding companies whose social objectives range from the administration of buildings to the construction of hotels, buildings, homes, warehouses, factories, developments, and urban housing units; it runs a factory which produces balanced animal feed, a television channel, eighteen firms dedicated to theater administration, a casino, three woodworking shops, a firm which makes synthetic rubber, another which makes doorlocks, and a luxury housing development in the Federal District.[39]

As we shall discuss below, one political party—the Institutional Revolutionary party—dominates federal politics, and in a similar way it dominates bureaucratic politics as well. Although the federal government has sought to decentralize the bureaucracy somewhat in recent years, it is still the case that massive bureaucracy affects the ability of the central government to enact policy, especially in central industrial areas such as oil, petroleum exploration, and distribution (PEMEX), steel (SIDERMEX), fertilizers (FERTIMEX), and food purchasing, processing, and distribution (CONASUPO).[40]

Political Parties and Elections

Political Parties

A strong relationship exists between the dominant political party and the state in Mexico, but there remains a clear difference between the two. The primary function of the dominant party is to mobilize support and to legitimize the state. "That is, the party's single most important task is to legitimize and to provide an ideological base of support for the state rather than to press the demands of its formal constituency on the state."[41]

Although Mexico is often thought of as a one-party nation because of the history of the dominance of the PRI, such is not the case; a number of opposition parties operate in the Mexican political arena. Although only three parties won seats to the Chamber of Deputies in 1988, the National Democratic Front took the place of seven smaller parties in the 1985 Congress.[42] There are many opposition groups in society, made up of peasants, students,[43] and workers.[44]

In the state and local elections of 1983 the major opposition party, the National Action party (PAN), won a record number of state capitals and major cities and many were asking what the future held for the dominant party, namely the PRI. To a large degree the problems of the PRI lie in its clear identification with the Mexican status quo, the party that has been in power for literally decades in Mexican politics, and recent leaders have called for significant reform in the PRI.[45]

The PRI has been the major party in Mexico for over fifty years.[46] It is so well entrenched and central to the operation of the government that it "serves as a subordinate extension of the presidency and central government bureaucracy."[47] The PRI has three major factions, an agrarian faction—a labor faction, and a "popular" faction—and is governed by a national party congress called the National Assembly. The National Assembly is directed by the National Executive Committee, selected from among members of the Assembly. Each of the three factions of the PRI vies for power on the Executive Committee, and although these three factions are ostensibly all on the same side in an election, there is often great competition between and among them for formal party leadership positions.

The PRI continues to play a very important role in Mexican politics. It provides a "channel of information to the presidency that complements those of the military and civilian bureaucracies"; it organizes political support for presidential policies; it mobilizes interest groups; it "contributes to socialization of both elite and popular strata"; it controls literally thousands of elective and appointive jobs across the nation and helps to recruit candidates for those positions; it is important in the organization of and participation in elections; and finally, it is crucial in the succession process of the presidency.[48] The PRI has been referred to as a "semi-authoritarian" organization, that is, one that "enjoys genuine popular support, even though it resorts to electoral fraud when such is deemed required."[49]

The National Democratic Front (FDN) was a new competing party in the 1988 election. Its roots, however, were not new, but included the Mexican Communist party (PCM), which changed its name to the Unified Socialist party of Mexico (PSUM) in 1981 when it joined with several smaller parties in a left coalition. The PSUM was able to provide the PRI with some serious competition at the state level of politics, although it was not very effective in federal elections until 1988.[50] The FDN is regarded by many as not really a true party, but rather an electoral coalition whose roots include not only the Communist PCM or PSUM, but also a healthy non-Communist tradition.

The major right-of-center parties include the Mexican Democratic party (PDM) and the National Action party (PAN). Both parties have been more successful in elections since the 1977 reforms, which created the at-large proportional representation in the Chamber of Deputies, and they have offered the PRI some serious competition at the state level of politics. The PDM has been considered "the most conservative party with registration in Mexico,"[51] and has its strongest political support in the countryside.

The PAN is considered the major party of the "political right" in Mexico today.[52] The major difference between the PAN and the PRI included the PAN's greater criticism of the United States, and the PAN's desire to "restore to the church the rights of religious education and political participation which were taken away from it by the Constitution of 1917."[53]

The role of opposition parties has increased in Mexico over time. In recent years:

> Mexico's leadership tinkered with the electoral process as a way of encouraging political opposition and legitimizing their own rule. Their adjustments to the electoral process came about . . . because some government leaders believed the time had arrived for a more pluralistic system.[54]

These changes allowed more members of the opposition parties to win election to the Chamber of Deputies, the lower branch of the legislature, which in Mexico is not a very powerful check on the president's power. Thus, the president and the PRI were able to increase their perceived legitimacy by encouraging the opposition parties, without giving up any real political power at all.[55]

Elections

Despite the fact that the PRI has won nearly every federal election held since 1929, including all presidential races, all state gubernatorial races, and virtually all Senate races, the Mexican electoral arena contains real electoral competition. As we have just indicated, there *are* opposition parties in Mexican politics, and these parties take their roles seriously. Some recent observers have noted that elections in Mexico are not meaningless and have suggested that "the single-party nature of the Mexican regime is passing."[56] The reforms of 1977 and 1988, alluded to earlier, were designed to increase political participation and to stimulate electoral competition. By one measure the reforms were effective; since they were enacted, in fact, opposition to the PRI has increased.

> However, the PRI has mobilized even greater numbers of voters to support the continued rule of the current ruling elite and has shown an ability to still use its old techniques of electoral fraud if necessary to win an important race. Thus, even though the opposition's voice has strengthened, the regime's base has been refortified, at least for now.[57]

Political Development and Economics

Two distinct problem areas confront the Mexican government today. Both of these problems, it can be asserted, are a function of the economic crisis primarily brought about by the fall of the price of oil. One of these concerns urban migration, and the unique set of problems facing Mexico City today. The massive pattern of migration from rural Mexico to the capital city is putting intolerable demands upon the infrastructure of Mexico City and has already had significant effects upon the quality of life there, something to which we shall return momentarily. The second problem has an international dimension and concerns the implications of the (illegal and) massive flow of Mexican population across its northern border with the United States.

Mexico City has suffered the same problems of urban migration as have the major cities of many developing nations. The crises of poverty and high unemployment often serve to push significant populations from rural areas to the urban capital area in search of jobs and better living conditions. In 1910, 28.7 percent of Mexico's population lived in an urban area. This figure increased to 33.5 percent by 1930, 42.6 percent by 1950, 58.6 percent by 1970, and was estimated to be over 65 percent in 1980.[58] Ironically, the migrants usually find neither jobs nor better living conditions; rather, these migrations contribute to greater unemployment and worse living conditions.

> Mexico City has grown faster, and with less coordinated planning, than any other city in the world. After World War II, its population stood at two million; by 1960 it had climbed to five million; and by 1970, nine million. Today [1986] its population exceeds seventeen million, making it the world's second largest city, after Tokyo.[59]

Mexico City is "an environmental disaster" in a variety of respects. Over 2 million of its residents have no running water, sometimes living more than three city blocks from the nearest faucet. Over 3 million of its inhabitants have no sewage facilities. The city produces over 14,000 tons of garbage *every day*, but can process only 8,000 tons. Breathing the polluted air of Mexico City (caused by 3 million cars, 7,000 buses, and over 13,000 factories) has been likened to smoking two packs of cigarettes a day, and the combination of chemical and biological poisons has been estimated to kill over 30,000 children annually through respiratory and gastrointestinal disease. "Overall," one study has noted, "pollution may account for the deaths of nearly 100,000 people a year."[60]

It is this type of situation that has contributed to the desire of many Mexicans to leave their homeland and head north to a country where, they have heard, there are jobs for those who want them and a better life for those who are willing to work for it. About half of Mexico's population of 70 million people are under 21 years of age and have "little or no chance for employment."[61] The Mexican-American border is nearly 2,000 miles long, and issues such as smuggling, illegal immigration,[62] and the border's ecology (including air and water pollution) have proved to be a source of irritation in Mexican-American relations.[63]

Both of these problems are to some degree a function of Mexican economic stagnation; as one scholar has noted, "the causes of Mexico's deepest crisis in modern times are clearly economic."[64] The fall in the price of oil, which contributed to and exacerbated an extremely low economic growth rate (0.2 percent) and a massive foreign debt problem (over $100 billion),[65] and an inflation rate of almost 100 percent,[66] made even worse by natural disasters (an earthquake in September 1985), have left Mexico reeling and Mexicans unsure of the future of their nation.

Mexico's problems became really serious (as we suggested in Chapter 3, this can be the case in countries that base their economic development upon a single "crop") as a result of the fall in the world price of oil.[67] Mexico did a great deal of borrowing through the late 1970s to finance its economic growth, counting upon a continuation of the very high price of oil and agreeing to pay as much as 17 percent interest on its loans. The policy seemed reasonable given the vast expansion of the Mexican petroleum industry, with exports of 200,000 barrels daily in 1977 expanding to 1.5 million barrels in 1982. Because the Mexican government built its budgets on an anticipated price of nearly $36 per barrel, when oil fell to nearly $30 a barrel the country came under tremendous financial stress, and in fact failed to make scheduled payments on its loans in 1982.[68] As the price of oil has fallen lower, Mexico's situation has appeared increasingly grim.

The prognosis for the near future for Mexico—as for many developing nations[69]—does not look good. Mexico today is "a country of poor people living in the midst of an elite becoming rich at their expense. Wherever one turns, there is evidence of official policies and institutions that are heightening the differences among classes." The richest 5 percent of families in 1986 had an average income thirty-six times greater than that of the poorest 10 percent of families; the poorest half of the population receives less than 20 percent of total personal income, while the richest 10 percent of the population receives almost half of Mexico's total income.[70]

> Everywhere urban Mexicans feel they are being strangled as the quality of life worsens. They are extorted by urban transit systems and by the police, medical care is either inadequate or nonexistent, in many proletarian suburbs the running water works only from one to three o'clock in the morning while in the wealthy communities like Pedregal in Mexico City it runs all the time.[71]

The combination of a continued high birth rate, the burden of its external debts, and a continuation of a low world price for oil will not contribute to Mexico rapidly "turning its economy around." In fact, "the country which for so long enjoyed life in the fast lane will have to throttle back its expectations and accustom itself to live in the slow lane instead."[72]

Revolution and Institutionalization

We have seen—albeit briefly—in this chapter that the Mexican case provides us with the opportunity to view a different type of political system from others we have met in this volume, in many respects a significantly different system. Mexico was born in revolution and social upheaval, and for nearly seventy years has been endeavoring to establish the kinds of social and political institutions that would ensure domestic stability and social harmony.

To a substantial degree, especially if we compare Mexico with her neighbors to the south, the endeavors have been successful if for no other reason than Mexico has not experienced either the regular military *coup d'état* experienced so often by so many Latin American nations. Indeed, there has been no revolution in Mexico since the 1910–1921 social dislocation.

However, we must be less laudatory in other respects. The Mexican political system is clearly an authoritarian one, whether we say that the president is an "elective king" or not. Clearly the president dominates the political landscape, essentially preempting the power of the judicial and the legislative branches of government. This is far more than the power given the British prime minister through the convention of party discipline. The vast number of allegations of electoral corruption and voter fraud seem to indicate that although all presidential transitions for the last fifty years have been peaceful ones, there is not a fundamental commitment on the part of political elites to accept the will of the majority.

Moreover, Mexico is still suffering many of the problems faced by other nations in the developing world. Economic problems, distributional problems, and technological problems have meant that the general quality of life in Mexico has not been able to improve as much as Mexico's leaders might have liked. Some of these problems, such as the drop in the price of oil, are beyond the ability of the Mexican government to control. Other problems, such as the birth rate, or the effective distribution of health and education resources, can be influenced by government policy, but only very slowly. Still other problems, such as an effective governmental infrastructure, or a decrease in voter fraud or corruption in government, can be dealt with more quickly, but the government has yet to do so.

Some have argued that it is *the system itself* that is the real problem in Mexico. The relative stability of Mexico until recent times was based upon real reforms, particularly reforms in land ownership, that occurred as a result of the revolution, and that were consolidated during the period from 1934 to 1940 when Lázaro Cárdenas was president. The PRI, it has been argued, dominated the Mexican political arena for so long precisely because it embodied those reforms. As those reforms have begun to become inadequate over the years, problems of stability have resulted.

The PRI system, as with many "corporatist" systems of Latin America, generates greater inequalities as a major output of the system itself. The system is simply not geared to produce more equitable outcomes, nor to produce a more equal and just society. If the system is unable to produce greater equity, it is argued, it is because of the system itself, not solely because of the lack of resources in the society or the general level of development of Mexico.

Notes

1. L. Vincent Padgett, *The Mexican Political System* (Boston: Houghton Mifflin, 1976), p. 10.
2. There was very widespread coverage of these charges in the foreign press. See, to take just a few examples, Marjorie Miller, "Indications of Mexico Election Fraud Mount," *Los Angeles Times*, July 15, 1988, p. 10; Larry Rohter, "Mexicans Protest Delay in Results of the Elections," *The New York Times*, July 11, 1988, p. A1; Alan Riding, " 'Alchemy' Taints Voting in Mexico's Countryside," *The New York Times*, July 14, 1988, p. A1; or Larry Rohter, "Mexican Opposition Parties Move to Overturn Vote Tally," *The New York Times*, August 15, 1988, p. A 5.
3. Robert Long, "Preface," in Robert E. Long, ed., *Mexico* (New York: H. W. Wilson, 1986), p. 5.
4. Jorge Castañeda, "Mexico at the Brink," *Foreign Affairs* 64 (1985–1986), p. 287.
5. A good historical overview can be found in Kenneth Johnson, *Mexican Democracy: A Critical View* (New York: Praeger, 1984). Chapter 2 is titled "The Aztec Legacy and Independence," and Chapter 3 is titled "Emerging Nationhood and the Great Revolution." A different—class-oriented—approach is offered by James D. Cockcroft, *Mexico: Class Formation, Capital Accumulation, and the State* (New York: Monthly Review Press, 1983). A very good general history is that of Michael Meyer and William Sherman, *The Course of Mexican History* (New York: Oxford University Press, 1987).
6. A good discussion of the revolution can be found in Judith Adler Hellman, *Mexico in Crisis* (New York: Holmes and Meier, 1983), pp. 3–31.
7. Robert E. Scott, "Mexico: The Established Revolution," in Lucian W. Pye and Sidney Verba, eds., *Political Culture and Political Development* (Princeton, N.J.: Princeton University Press, 1965), p. 332. A very good description of the modern period can be found in Juan Felipe Leal, "The Mexican State, 1915–1973: A Historical Interpretation," in Nora Hamilton and Timothy F. Harding, eds., *Modern Mexico: State, Economy, and Social Conflict* (Beverly Hills, Calif.: Sage Publications, 1986), pp. 21–42.
8. Edward J. Williams, "The Evolution of the Mexican Military and Its Implications for Civil-Military Relations," in Roderic Camp, *Mexico's Political Stability: The Next Five Years* (Boulder, Col.: Westview Press, 1986), p. 143. For more on this subject, see David Ronfeldt, ed., *The Modern Mexican Military: A Reassessment* (La Jolla: Center for U.S.-Mexican Studies, University of California, San Diego, 1984).
9. Roderic Camp, *The Making of a Government: Political Leaders in Modern Mexico* (Tucson: University of Arizona Press, 1984), p. 1.
10. Daniel C. Levy, "The Political Consequences of Changing Socialization Patterns," in Camp, *Mexico's Political Stability*, p. 19.
11. Ibid., p. 21.
12. Ibid., p. 25.
13. Camp, *The Making of a Government*, pp. 39–40. Camp discusses a wide range of variables significant in the process of political socialization in Mexico, including the role of parents, friends, and events as socializers, the social influence of the school environment, the impact of books and teachers, and the value systems of contemporary Mexican leaders.
14. Much of the discussion in the few paragraphs that follow is derived from much more extensive discussion in Leal, "The Mexican State," pp. 29–32.
15. John Bailey, "The Impact of Major Groups on Policy-Making Trends in

Government-Business Relations in Mexico," in Camp, *Mexico's Political Stability*, p. 125.

16. Leal, "The Mexican State," p. 30.
17. John Bailey, *Governing Mexico: The Statecraft of Crisis Management* (New York: St. Martin's Press, 1988), p. 139.
18. Padgett, *The Mexican Political System*, p. 204.
19. William Glade, "Distributional and Sectoral Problems in the New Economic Policy," in Camp, *Mexico's Political Stability*, p. 95.
20. Bailey, "Impact of Major Groups," p. 126.
21. Johnson, *Mexican Democracy*, p. 116.
22. The constitution requires that the individual chosen must be male.
23. Bailey, *Governing Mexico*, p. 32. Emphasis his.
24. Susan Eckstein, *The Impact of Revolution: A Comparative Analysis of Mexico and Bolivia* (Beverly Hills, Calif.: Sage Publications, 1976), p. 25.
25. Padgett, *The Mexican Political System*, p. 199.
26. Again, in addition to sources cited in note 2, examples of these articles covering the presidential and congressional elections would include Alan Riding, "When the Bubble Burst for the Mexican Rulers," *The New York Times*, July 9, 1988, p. 5; Larry Rohter, "Electoral Panel Prolongs Delay in Mexico Tally," *The New York Times*, July 9, 1988, p. A1; Larry Rohter, "Still Setback Seen for Ruling Party in Mexican Voting," *The New York Times*, July 8, 1988, p. A1.
27. Padgett, *The Mexican Political System*, pp. 188–189.
28. Johnson, *Mexican Democracy*, pp. 123–124.
29. Frank Brandenburg, *The Making of Modern Mexico* (Englewood Cliffs, N.J.: Prentice Hall, 1964), pp. 145-150.
30. Padgett, *The Mexican Political System*, p. 200.
31. Merilee Serrill Grindle, *Bureaucrats, Politicians, and Peasants in Mexico* (Berkeley: University of California Press, 1977), p. 7.
32. Hellman, *Mexico in Crisis*, p. 127.
33. Under the system enacted in 1963, deputies were chosen by a combination of winner-take-all and proportional representation. "Under this system, opposition parties were granted five seats in the Chamber of Deputies if they received at least 2.5 percent of the national vote and up to fifteen additional (twenty in all) deputies, one for each additional 0.5 percent of the national vote. In 1973 the threshhold for representation in the Chamber was lowered from 2.5 to 1.5 percent and the maximum number of seats available to an opposition party under this 'party deputy' system was increased to twenty-five. This greatly improved the opposition's opportunities to win seats in the Chamber but also decreased the PRI's need to allow the opposition to win some district elections as a means of indicating the competitiveness of the political and electoral systems." Joseph Klesner, "Changing Patterns of Electoral Participation and Official Party Support in Mexico," in Judith Gentleman, ed., *Mexican Politics in Transition*, (Boulder, Col.: Westview Press, 1987), p. 99.
34. Roderic Camp, "Potential Strengths of the Political Opposition and What It Means to the PRI," in Camp, *Mexico's Political Stability*, p. 187.
35. Johnson, *Mexican Democracy*, p. 12.
36. Bailey, *Governing Mexico*, p. 62.
37. Discussion of this can be found in some detail in Bailey, *Governing Mexico*, pp. 83-88.
38. Grindle, *Bureaucrats, Politicians, and Peasants in Mexico*, p. 3.
39. Juan José Hinojosa, "El Estado: Empresario por distraccion," *Excelsior*

(Mexico City), December 4, 1974, p. 6, as cited in Grindle, *Bureaucrats, Politicians, and Peasants*, p. 4.

40. Bailey, *Governing Mexico*, p. 61.
41. Daniel Levy and Gabriel Székely, *Mexico: Paradoxes of Stability and Change* (Boulder, Col.: Westview Press, 1983), p. 56.
42. In the Chamber of Deputies elected July 7, 1985, the distribution of seats was as follows:

Institutional Revolutionary Party	289	
National Action Party	9	32
Authentic Party of the Mexican Revolution	2	7
Mexican Democratic Party		12
Unified Socialist Party of Mexico		12
Workers' Socialist Party		12
Popular Socialist Party		11
Revolutionary Workers' Party		6
Mexican Workers' Party	___	_6
Total	300	98

Source: Arthur S. Banks, ed., *Political Handbook of the World* (Binghamton, N.Y.: CSA Publications, 1988), p. 388.

43. A very good description of the 1968 student movement can be found in chap. 6, "The Student Movement of 1968: A Case Study," in Hellman, *Mexico in Crisis*, pp. 173–186.
44. See Evelyn P. Stevens, " 'The Opposition' in Mexico: Always a Bridesmaid, Never Yet the Bride," in Gentleman, *Mexican Politics in Transition*, pp. 217-226.
45. Wayne A. Cornelius, "Political Liberalization in an Authoritarian Regime: Mexico, 1976–1985," in Gentleman, *Mexican Politics in Transition*, pp. 32–36. See also John Bailey, "Can the PRI Be Reformed? Decentralized Candidate Selection," in Gentleman, *Mexican Politics in Transition*, pp. 63-92; and Norman E. Cox, "Changes in the Mexican Political System," in George Philip, ed., *Politics in Mexico* (London: Croom Helm, 1985), p. 15–53.
46. When the party was first organized in 1929 its name was the National Revolutionary party; in 1938 it became the Mexican Revolutionary party. In 1946 the name was changed for the third and last, time to the PRI. A good discussion of the development of the PRI can be found in Hellman, *Mexico in Crisis*, pp. 33–57, chap. 2, "A Ruling Party Is Formed."
47. John Bailey, "What Explains the Decline of the PRI and Will It Continue?" in Camp, *Mexico's Political Stability*, p. 159.
48. Ibid., p. 163.
49. Ibid., p. 179 note 1.
50. See Barry Carr, "The PSUM: The Unification Process on the Mexican Left, 1981–1985," in Gentleman, *Mexican Politics in Transition*, pp. 281–304.
51. Klesner, "Changing Patterns," p. 101.
52. See Dale Store, "The PAN, the Private Sector, and the Future of the Mexican Opposition," in Gentleman, *Mexican Politics in Transition*, pp. 261–273.
53. Johnson, *Mexican Democracy*, p. 145.
54. Camp, "Potential Strengths," p. 186.
55. A very good discussion of this liberalization can be found in Cornelius, "Political Liberalization," pp. 15–40. In this chapter Cornelius seeks to understand "the impulse toward liberalization in a 57-year-old hegemonic party regime, in which the ruling Institutional Revolutionary Party (PRI)

has never lost—or been forced to surrender—a single nationally important office." (p. 15)

56. Klesner, "Changing Patterns of Electoral Participation," p. 95.
57. Ibid., p. 98. Much more discussion of the problem of electoral fraud can be found in Silvia Gomez Tagle, "Democracy and Power in Mexico: The Meaning of Conflict in the 1979, 1982, and 1985 Federal Elections," in Gentleman, *Mexican Politics in Transition*, pp. 153–180.
58. Hellman, *Mexico in Crisis*, p. 115.
59. Robert Long, "Urban Migration: The Dilemma of Mexico City," in Robert E. Long, ed., *Mexico* (New York: H. W. Wilson, 1986), p. 98.
60. Otto Friedrich, "A Proud Capital's Distress," in Long, ibid., p. 100.
61. Johnson, *Mexican Democracy*, p. 19.
62. By one estimate in 1980 more than 3 million Mexicans were in the United States illegally. Johnson, *Mexican Democracy*, p. 20. See Johnson's chap. 7, "Mexican Migration to the United States," pp. 209–229.
63. Edward Williams, "The Implications of the Border for Mexican Policy and Mexican-United States Relations," in Camp, *Mexico's Political Stability*, pp. 211–233.
64. Castañeda, "Mexico at the Brink," p. 287. A good analysis of the problem can be found in William Chislett, "The Causes of Mexico's Financial Crisis and the Lessons to Be Learned: Economic Policy, 1970–1983," in Philip, *Politics in Mexico*, pp. 1–14.
65. *The New York Times*, July 8, 1989, p. 15.
66. Jerry R. Ladman, "The Roots of the Crisis," in Jerry R. Ladman, ed., *Mexico: A Country in Crisis* (El Paso: University of Texas Press, 1986), p. 3.
67. A good discussion of policy discussion in Mexico after the fall of the price of oil can be found in Judith Gentleman, "Mexico After the Oil Boom: PRI Management of the Political Impact of National Disillusionment," in Gentleman, *Mexican Politics in Transition*, pp. 41–61.
68. John S. De Mott, "Mexico Tightens Its Belt," in Long, *Mexico*, pp. 42–43. Much of the trouble Mexico had at this time has been attributed, as well, to a great scandal within the PEMEX management. See, for some detailed discussion of "The Great PEMEX Scandal," Johnson, *Mexican Democracy*, pp. 185-196. Discussion of long-term implications of this can be found in Miguel S. Wionczek, "Mexico's External Debt Revisited: The 1985 Re-scheduling Debt Arrangement: Lessons for Latin America," in *The Debt Crisis in Latin America* (Stockholm: Institute of Latin American Studies, 1986), pp. 81–106.
69. And we should note here that the kinds of problems faced by Mexico are characteristic of problems faced by *many* other developing nations and Latin American nations. See, for an example of discussion of this problem, the monograph published by the Institute of Latin American Studies, *The Debt Crisis in Latin America*; or Economic Commission for Latin America and the Caribbean, *External Debt in Latin America: Adjustment Policies and Renegotiation* (Boulder, Col.: Lynne Rienner Publishers, 1985).
70. David Barkin, "Mexico's Albatross: The U.S. Economy," in Hamilton and Harding, *Modern Mexico: State, Economy, and Social Conflict*, p. 107.
71. Johnson, *Mexican Democracy*, p. 9.
72. William P. Glade, "How Will Economic Recovery Be Managed?" in Camp, *Mexico's Political Stability*, p. 48.

Index

Acclamatory elections, 182
Act of Settlement (British) 32, 220
Act of Union with Scotland (British), 220
Administrative sources of law, 159
Administrative structures, Japanese, 337
Advantage groups, pluralism and, 171
African colonies and France, 260
Aggregate level of analysis, 11
Agriculture in third world, 74–75
Akihito (Japanese emperor), 330
Alexander II (tsar of Russia), 358
Algeria, and France, 260
Almond, Gabriel, 196
  analysis of, 17–18
  on political culture, 18–19
Amending constitutions, 35
American legislatures, committees in, 96–97
American presidency and electoral college,
  121
American Revolution (1776), 210
Analysis, levels of, 10–11
Analytic system, 15

Andropov, Yuri, 371, 397–98
Anglo-American law, 154–55
Aquinas, Thomas, on law, 152
Arafat, Yassir, and Palestine Liberation
  Organization, 211–12
Area studies, 5–6
Argentina, as federal state, 38
Aristotle, 1
  classification of constitutions and ideology
    of, 47–48
  as a comparativist, 1
  on political culture, 19
  on political socialization, 193
  view of politics of, 2
Armed forces, Japanese lack of, 329
Armenia, 362
Attitudes, political, 193–201
Australia:
  court structure in, 161–62
  elections in, 181
  as federal state, 38
  selection of upper house in, 102

Austria, executive power in, 264–65
Azerbaijan SSR, 362

Backbencher, defined, 108
Ballot, structure of German, 310–11
Bangladesh, agriculture in, 74–75
Barbados, size of legislature of, 93
Basic Law (West German constitution), 295–96
Bayeux, de Gaulle speech at, 261
Becker, Theodore, on judicial politics, 166
Begin, Menachem (prime minister of Israel), 211
Belgium, coalition governments in, 141
Benin, agriculture in, 74
Bentham, Jeremy, on law, 152
Bentley, Arthur, 171
Bermuda, as microcolony, 56
Bicameral legislatures, 84–89
  British, 235–42
  in federal states, 87
  French, 272–77
  German, 306–10
  Japanese, 339–40
  Mexican, 415–17
  relations between houses of, 89–92
  Soviet, 376–77
Bill, initiation of, 111
Bill of Rights (British), 32, 128, 220
Biological law, 152
Birth control policy in India, 72–73
Blackstone, William, on British Constitution, 221
Blocked vote, French legislature and, 273
Blondel, Jean, on function of legislatures, 84, 104
Bloody Sunday, in Russian Revolution, 360
Blum, Leon (French premier), 257
Bogota, population problems of, 72
Bolivar, Simón, 412
Bolivia:
  coup d'état in, 211
  infant mortality rate of, 57
  military in politics of, 207
Bolshevik movement in Russia, 359
Brazil:
  as federal state, 38
  trouble paying international debts of, 54, 59
Brezhnev, Leonid, 366, 370, 397
  and new Soviet constitution, 372–73
Brichta, Avraham, on private members' bills, 111

Britain: *see* United Kingdon
British North America Act (Canadian Constitution), 219
Bronstein, Leon: *see* Trotsky
Brown, Bernard, 3
Budgetary process in France, 272
Buildings, legislative, 109
Bulganin, Nikolai, 370
Bundesrat, German, 306–7
Bundestag, German, 306
Bureaucracy:
  British, 233–34
  development and, 66–67
  French, 263–64
  German, 297–98
  Japanese, 337
  Mexican, 418–19
  public administration and, 141–44
  Soviet, 392
Burke, Edmund:
  and concept of Loyal Opposition in Britain, 243
  on elections, 184
  on representation, 106
Burnell, Peter, on economic nationalism, 60–61
Byelorussia, 362

Cabinet:
  British, 225–31, 257–58
  development of, 128–30
  French, 257–58
  German, 302–6
  Japanese, 336–37
  Soviet, 381–84
Cadre political parties, defined, 177
Campaigns, election, 183
Canada:
  constitution of, 34, 219
  court structure in, 161
  election results (1988) in, 100
  as federal state, 38, 40
  legislature of, 91, 93
  minority governments in, 133–34, 141
  political recruitment in, 204
  and Quebec, 22
  representation in Parliament of provinces, 87–88
  upper house in, 102
  voting in, 97–98
Candidate-choice elections, 182
Canton (French unit of government), 264

Carter, Jimmy, 123
Center for Democracy and Progress (French political party), 282
Center for Social Democrats (French political party), 282–83
Centralization (of economy) and development, 62–65
Centralized federalism, 39–40
Chamber of Deputies, French, 256, 416–17
Chamberlain, Neville, 257
Chancellor, German, 302–6
Charles I (Britain), 127
Charles II (Britain), 128
Charles X (France), 255
Chernenko, Konstantin, 371, 397
Chief executive:
  British, selection of, 225–26
  compared with head of state, 124–25
  French, 269–72
  German, 302–6
  Japanese, 332–36
  Mexican, 412–15
  selection of parliamentary, 130–38
  Soviet, 381–84
Chile:
  economic nationalism in, 61
  single-product economy of, 59
China:
  political participation in, 186
  revolution (1927–1949) in, 210
  size of legislature of, 93
  as unitary government, 38
Chirac, Jacques, 271
Christian Democratic party (German political party), 316–18
Christian Socialist Union (German political party), 304, 316–18
Cicero on law, 152
Civilian control of military, 207–8
Civil procedure, 161
Civil service:
  British, 233–34
  development and, 66–67
  French, 263–64
  German, 297–98
  Japanese, 337
  Mexican, 418–19
  public administration and, 141–144
  Soviet, 392
Clark, Joe (prime minister of Canada), 133–34
Classical liberalism, 45
Classical conservatism, 46

Clean Government party (Japanese political party), 344
Coalition governments: 134, 138–41
  British, 257–58
  French, Third and Fourth Republics, 257–58
  German, 302–6
  Israeli, 141
  Japanese, 334–36
Code Napoléon (legal code), 154
Cohabitation (French executive structure), 271
Collective good, 172
Colonialism:
  European, and development, 55
  French in Africa, 260
Committee on Comparative Politics, 21
Committees in legislatures, 95–97, 109
Common law legal culture, 154–55
Common Market: *see* European Economic Community
Commons, House of: *see* House of Commons
Commune (French unit of government), 263
Communication function of legislatures, 104
Communist party:
  French, 280
  German, 316
  Mexican, 420
  Soviet, 389–96
Comparative methodology, 4, 6
Comparative politics, defined, 3
Competitive elections, 181
Concentration of wealth, in Marxism, 367
Confederal system, 36–37
Confidence, vote of:
  British, 225
  defined, 130–31
  French, 274
  German, 303–4
  Japanese, 334–36
Congress:
  Communist party in Soviet Union, 393–95
  Mexican, 415–17
  U.S., 16, 122–23
Congress of Peoples' Deputies (Soviet legislature), 365, 377–78
  election to, 387
Congress party (Indian political party), 177
Conservatism, classical, 46
Constituency relations with legislators, 110
Constituent Assembly, French (1945), 259
Constitution, 30–43
  British, 219–23

Constitution (cont.):
  Canadian, 219
  French 259, 261–62
  functions of, 33–36
  German, 295–96
  importance of, 42–43
  Japanese, 327–29
  Mexican, 410–11
  as source of law, 157–58
  Soviet Communist party, 390
  Soviet Union, 4, 364, 371–76
  of United States, 4, 32–36
  unwritten, 31–33
  written, 31–32
Constitutional court:
  British House of Lords as, 237
  French, 277–78
  German, 299–300
  Japanese, 327–29
  Mexican, 410–11
  Soviet, 387–89
  see also Judicial review
Constitutional government, 31
Constitutional monarchy, development of,
    128–30
Constructive vote of confidence, in Germany,
    303–4
Cooperative federalism, in Germany, 297–98
Corporatism, 170–73
  defined, 172
  Mexican, 410–11
Costa Rica, civilian control of government of,
    207
Council of Ministers, in Soviet Union, 381–84
Council of the Republic, French (1946), 259
Coup d'état, 210–11
Courts, 159–62
  functions of, 162–63
  as nonpolitical structures, 150
  politics and, 163–67
Courts, constitutional:
  British, 237
  French, 277
  German, 299–300
  Japanese, 327–29
  Mexican, 410–11
  Soviet, 387–88
Criminal procedure, 161
Criticism and control function of
    legislatures, 103–4
Cross-cultural studies of socialization, 198
Cuba, selection of president in, 125

Culture:
  development and, 52
  legal, 153–56
  political, 18–20
Curia Regis (early English legislature), 126
Curtis, Michael, 44
Custom as source of law, 157
Czechoslovakia, as federal state, 38
Czudnowski, Moshe, 202

Dahl, Robert, 180–81
Dawson, R. MacGregor, on privy council, 129
Debate function of legislatures, 104
Debré, Michel, 262, 276
Debt, international, 58–60, 75–76
Decembrist uprising, in Russian history, 358
Decentralization (of economy) and
    development, 62–65
Decentralized federalism, 39–40
Decline of legislatures, 112
De facto (real) sources of law, 157
de Gaulle, Charles, 258, 260, 262, 266
De jure (legal) sources of law, 157
  and French presidency, 269
Democratic centralism, in Soviet Union, 390
Democratic Union for the Republic (French
    political party), 282
Denmark, infant mortality rate of, 57
Dennis, Jack, 194–200
Department (French unit of government),
    263–64
Dependence, international, 58–60
  theory of development, 69
Deputies, Chamber of, French, 256
D'Estaing, Valéry Giscard, 280
Development, 20–25
  in Mexico, 422–24
  modernization and, 21
  normative implications of, 52
  problems of, 70–77
  theories of, 69–70
  World Bank definition of, 55
Dialectics, in Marxism, 366–67
Díaz, Porfirio, 408
Dictatorship of the proletariat, in Marxism,
    367
Diet (Japanese legislature), 338–43
Diffuse support, 195
Directory, French (1795), 253
Dissolution of legislature, 134

Distribution:
crisis of, in development, 24–25
of economic resources, 56–58
of population, 72
Divine law, 152
Divine right of kings theory (Britain), 127
Dogan, Mattei, 4
Dominant-party elections, 181
Doubling time, world population, 71
Dreyfus affair, French, 257
Duchacek, Ivo:
on constitutions, 42–43
on federalism, 39
Duma (Russian parliament), 360–61
Duverger, Maurice, 177–78
Dzhugashvili, Joseph: *see* Stalin

Easton, David:
definition of politics of, 2
input-output analysis of, 42
systems theory of, 16–17
Ecological fallacy, 11
Ecological level of analysis, 11
Economic development, 20–25
Mexican, 422–24
modernization and, 21
normative implications of, 52
problems of, 70–77
theories of, 69–70
World Bank definition of, 55
Economic nationalism, 60–61
Economic planning, centralization of, 62–65
Economic resources, distribution of, 56–58
Economics, political, 51–77
Economies, single-product, in Third World, 59
Education:
as function of legislatures, 105
in Third World, 74
EEC: *see* European Economic Community
Ehrmann, Henry, 278
Elections, 180–86
American presidential, 121
British, 246–47
competitive, 181
French legislative, 283–89
French presidential, 269, 285–87
functions of, 182–85
German, 310–16
Japanese, 346–51
law of, 182
legislative, 97–102
Mexican, 415–17, 421
and single-member-district voting, 97–100
Soviet, 385–87
see also Voting
Elite, political, 205–7
Emergency powers of French president, 266–67
Emperor, Japanese, 330–32
Empirical approach to politics, 5
Employment in Third World, 75
Engels, Friedrich, 366
England: *see* United Kingdom
Environmental pollution, Mexican, 422
Equatorial Guinea, size of legislature of, 93
Estonia, 362
Ethiopia, crisis of distribution in, 24
Ethnic group limitations on candidacy, 183
Ethnocentrism, in study of political culture, 13–14, 20
Europe: *see* European Economic Community
European colonialism and developing nations, 55
European Economic Community:
as confederation, 37
and France, 260
Executive, political, 118–46
British, 223–33
French, 264–72
German, 300–306
Japanese, 329–38
legislatures and, 112–13
Locke on, 118
Mexican, 412–15
parliamentary model of, 124–25
presidential model of, 120–24
Soviet, 380–84
Experimental method, 6

Factions, pluralism and, 171
Falkland Islands, as microcolony, 56
Falling of Government, 132
Family planning policy in India, 72–73
Federal chancellor, German, 302–6
Federalism:
and bicameral legislatures, 87
and constitutions, 36–41
defined, 36–38
German, 297–300
Mexican, 411–12
Soviet, 361–65

Federalist, on separation of power, 41
Federal president, German, 301–2
Federation of West Indies, as failed
    federation, 40
Fifth Republic, French, 252, 261–62
Fiji, military in politics of, 207, 211
Finland, executive power in, 264–65
Foreign economic relations in Third World,
    75–76
Fourth Republic, French, 258–61
France:
    cabinet in, 257–58
    Constitutional Council of, 277–78
    Constitution of, 261–63
    electoral process in, 278–79, 283–89
    executive in, 264–72
    Fifth Republic, 261–63
    Fourth Republic, 258–60
    Gaullism in, 279–82
    history of, 252–61
    legislature in, 272–77
    minority governments in, 141
    as occupying power in Germany, 294
    political parties in, 282–83
    presidency of, 264–70
    prime minister in, 270–72
    Senate of, 275–76
    separation of power in, 41
    Third Republic, 255–58
    unitary government in, 36, 263–64
    upper house in, 91, 102
Free Democratic party (German political
    party), 304, 316–18
French Council of 500, seating of, 108–9
French Democratic Union (French political
    party), 282
French Revolution, 210, 253
Frontbencher, defined, 108

Gaullism, 279–82
Gender limitations on candidacy, 183
George I (Britain), 226
George VI (Britain), 224
Georgia, Soviet, 362
Germany:
    Bundesrat in, 306–7
    Bundestag in, 306
    cabinet in, 302–6
    chancellor in, 302–6
    as confederal system (1815–1866), 37
    constitution of, 294–96

elections in, 310–21
executive in, 300–306
federalism in, 39, 297–300
legislative process in, 307–10
legislature in, 306–10
political parties in, 310–21
president in, 301–2
upper house in, 88, 92
Germany, West, and NATO, 260
GNP: *see* Gross national product
Gorbachev, Mikhail, 362, 366, 371, 374, 375,
    377, 379, 381, 383, 389, 395, 397, 398,
    399
Government:
    bill, 111
    defined, 130
    falling of, 132
Great Britain: *see* United Kingdom
Great Reform Act, British, 220
Greece, as developing nation, 53
Green party (German political party), 310,
    316–20
Greenstein, Fred, 200
Gromyko, Andrei, 381, 398
Gross national product, defined, 53
Gross domestic product, World Bank figures,
    56
Group theory, and interest groups, 174
Guatemala, military in politics of, 207
Guerrilla warfare, 211–12

Habeas Corpus Act, British, 220
Haines, Charles, on judicial review, 164
Haiti, elections in, 181
Head of state, 124–25
    British, 223–25
    French, 264–70
    German, 301–2
    Israeli, 125
    Japanese, 330–32
    Mexican, 412–15
    Soviet, 380–81
Hegel, Georg W. F., 366
Heseltine, Michael, 233
Hirohito (Japanese emperor), 327, 330–31
Historical materialism, in Marxism, 367
Hitler, Adolf, 257
Hobbes, Thomas:
    on elections, 184
    on law, 152
    on separation of power, 4

House of Commons (U.K.), 238–40
  development of, 126–27
  relationship with Lords, 235–36
House of Councillors (Japan), 339–43, 346–51
House of Lords (U.K.), 126–27, 236–40
  as constitutional court, 237
  relationship with Commons, 235–36
Hume, David, on law, 152
Huntington, Samuel, 23
  on political decay and modernization, 53
Hyman, Herbert, 194
Ibo population in Nigeria, 22
Iceland, executive power in, 264–65
Identity, crisis of, in development, 21–22
Ideology, 43–47
  Soviet, 366–71
Independent Republican party (French
    political party), 282
India:
  bureaucracy in, 66
  crisis of identity in, 22
  and crisis of legitimacy in Punjab, 22
  economic decentralization in, 63–64
  economic nationalism in, 61
  family planning policy in, 72–73
  as federal state, 38
  income distribution in, 57–58
  military in politics of, 207
  selection of president in, 125
  upper house in, 91
Individualistic fallacy, 12
Individual level of analysis, 11
Indochina War, and France, 260
Industrialization, importance of, in
    developing nations, 60, 75
Institutional Revolutionary party (Mexican
    political party), 416, 419–21
Institutions, governmental, study of, 9
Interest groups, 171–76
  defined, 174
  in legislatures, 110
  political parties and, 176
  pressure groups and, 175
International dependence (financial), 58–60
Inter-Parliamentary Union, 86
Iran, crisis of legitimacy in, 22
Ireland:
  executive power in, 264–65
  per capita income in, 54
Iron Law of Wages, in Marxism, 367
Islamic law, 156
Israel:
  coalition governments in, 141

election campaigns in, 183
legal system of, 156
legislature, size of, 93
political recruitment in, 205
proportional representation voting in,
    100–101
selection of president in, 125
Italy:
  coalition governments in, 141
  open elections in, 181
  selection of upper house in, 102
  as unitary system, 36
  upper house in, 91
Ivan the Terrible, in Russian history, 358

Jacquerie, 210
James I (Britain), 127, 157
James II (Britain), 128
Japan:
  administrative structures in, 337
  bicameralism in, 339–40
  cabinet in, 336–37
  coalition governments in, 141, 334–36
  competitive elections in, 181
  Diet of, 338–43
  electoral system in, 346–51
  emperor in, 330–32
  executive structures in, 329–34
  legal culture of, 154
  legislative process in, 340–43
  legislature of, 338–43
  political history of, 326–29
  political parties in, 343–46
  prime minister in, 332–33
  Socialist party in, 344
  as unitary system, 36
  upper house in, 88, 102
  voting in, 102
Jaros, Dean, 198–99
Jennings, Sir Ivor, 226
Joint committees, 96
Jordan, upper house in, 91
Juárez, Benito, 408
Judicial functions, 162–63
Judicial precedent, 155
Judicial review, 151, 163–67
Judiciaries:
  British, 221, 237
  comparative study of, 149–51
  French, 277

Judiciaries (cont):
  German, 299–300
  Japanese, 327–29
  Soviet, 387–88
Jurisdiction of courts, 161
  as source of law, 158
Justice:
  idea of, 151–53
  in Soviet Union, 387–88
Justinian, law code of, 154

Kaifu, Toshiki (Japanese prime minister), 351
Kazakh SSR, 362
Kenya:
  economic decentralization in, 64
  elections in, 181–82
Kerensky, Alexander, 361
KGB, in Soviet Union, 392
Khrushchev, Nikita, 366, 369–71, 397
Kirgiz SSR, 362
Kohl, Helmut, 304, 318
Komeito (Japanese political party), 344
Komsomol (Communist party organization in Soviet Union), 391
Kosygin, Aleksei, 370

Labour party (British political party), growth of, 177, 246
Länder (German states), 297–300
Lasswell, Harold, definition of politics of, 2
Latin America:
  economic decentralization in, 64–65
  military in politics of, 207–9
  Third World nations of, 55
Latvia, 362
Law, 151–53
  sources of, 156–59
  in Soviet Union, 387–88
Lawmaking function of legislatures, 104
Leadership in Soviet Union, 397–99
Lebanon, crisis of identity in, 22
Legal culture, 153–56
Legal structures, 159–62
Legal systems, non-Western, 156
Legislators:
  constituencies and, 110
  interest groups and, 110
  recruitment of, 110

  selection of, 97–102
  socialization of, 110
Legislatures, 109–10
  bicameral, 84–92
  British, 236–42
  buildings housing, 109
  committees in, 95–97, 109
  decline of, 112
  development of, 65–66
  dissolution of, 134
  and executives, 112–13
  federalism and, 87
  French, 272–77
  functions of, 103–6
  German, 306–10
  Japanese, 340–43
  Mexican, 415–17
  parties in, 94–95, 109
  party discipline in, 94–95
  process in, 110–12
  reasons for studying, 83–84
  reform in, 113
  representation in, 106–7
  roles in, 107–10
  seating in, 108–9
  size of, in Britain, Canada, China, and Equatorial Guinea, 93
  as source of law, 158
  Soviet, 376–78
  staff of, 109
  unicameral, 84–89
  women in, 106–7
Legislative Studies Quarterly (journal), 83
Legislative supremacy, defined, 132
Legitimacy, crisis of, in development, 22–23
Legitimation function of legislatures, 104
Leiserson, Michael, 335
Lenin, Vladimir, 358–59. 360, 361, 366, 368
Levels of analysis, 10–12
Liberal Democratic party (Japanese political party), 334, 343
Liberalism, classical, 45–46
Liberal party (British political party), 245–46
Liberia, upper house in, 91
Lijphart, Arend, on comparative politics, 5
Limited government, 31
Linkage mechanisms:
  interest groups as, 174
  political parties as, 179–80
Literacy requirement for voting, 183–84
Lithuania, 362
Local government:
  British, 234–35

French, 263–64
German, 297–98
Japanese, 337
Locke, John:
  on elections, 184
  on executive branch, 118
  on judiciaries, 149–50
  on law, 151–52
  on legislatures, 82
  on separation of power, 41
Long Parliament (Britain), 127
Lords, House of: *see* House of Lords
Louis XVIII (France), 255
Louisiana, legal code of, 154
Louis Napoleon (France), 255
Louis Philippe (France), 255
Lowi, Theodore, on decline of legislatures,
  158–59
Loyal Opposition, development of concept of
  in Britain, 243

MacArthur, Douglas, 327–28
MacArthur Constitution, Japanese, 327–29,
  330, 343
Machiavelli, on political culture, 19
MacMahon, Patrice de (French president),
  256
Macridis, Roy, 3
Madison, James, and *Federalist* Number 10,
  171
Magna Carta, 32, 126, 220
Major, John, 226, 233
Malaysia:
  economic decentralization in, 64
  as failed federation, 40
Malenkov, Georgi, 370
Malthus, Thomas, on population, 71
Marbury v. Madison (1803), 164
Martinique, as microcolony, 56
Marx, Karl, 366–69
  on justice, 387–88
  on law, 152
  and socialist law, 155
Marxism:
  as an ideology, 45
  in Russia, 358
Marxism-Leninism, 366–71
Mary, queen of England, 128
Mass political parties, defined, 177
Meiji dynasty, in Japan, 326–27
  constitution of, 336
Menshevik movement in Russia, 359

Methodology, comparative, 4
Mexico:
  border with United States, 10
  bureaucracy in, 418–19
  civilian control of government in, 207–8
  communist party in, 420
  Congress of, 415–17
  constitution of, 410–11
  Democratic party in, 420
  economic development of, 422–24
  elections in, 181, 421
  and federalism, 411–12
  and Mexico City's population problems, 72
  political heritage of, 406–8
  political parties in, 419–21
  presidency of, 412–15
  and problems of institutionalization,
    424–25
  single-member-district voting in, 97–98
  single-product economy of, 59
  stability in, 408–9
  upper house in, 91
Migration, Mexican, 422
Milbrath, Lester, 202
Military in politics, 207–9, 211
  in Japan, 329
Mill, John Stuart, on elections, 184
Minority governments, 133, 141
Misery of the masses, in Marxism, 367
Mitterrand, François, 271, 281–82
Modernization, 21
  as an analytic concept, 52
Moldavia, 362
Monarchy:
  British, 223–25
  changing role of, 125–28
  constitutional, development of, 128–30
Montesquieu, 19, 41
Moral law, 152, 156
Morocco and France, 260
Mulroney, Brian (Canadian prime minister),
  91
Multiple executive, parliamentary model of,
  124–25
Multiple-member district voting, 102
  in Japan, 348–51
Munich Agreement of 1938, 257

Nakasone, Yasuhiro (Japanese prime
  minister), 350
Napoleonic Empire, French, 253–55
Narodnik movement in Russia, 358

Nation:
  defined, 10
  importance of, 20–21
National Action party (Mexican political
    party), 419–21
National Assembly, French, 259, 271–77
  elections to, 283–85
National Democratic Front (Mexican
    political party), 416, 420
National Democratic party (German political
    party), 316
Nationalism, economic, 60–61
NATO: *see* North Atlantic Treaty
    Organization
Natural law, 152
Nazi-Soviet Nonaggression Pact of 1939, 257
Neocorporatism, defined, 172
Nicaragua, crisis of legitimacy in, 22
Nicholas II (Russia), 360–61
Nigeria:
  coup d'état in, 211
  crisis of identity in, 22
  as federal state, 38
  military in politics of, 207
  single-product economy of, 59
Nixon, Richard, and Democratic Congress,
    123
No-confidence, vote of, 130–32
Non-Western legal systems, 156
Normative approach to politics, 5
North Atlantic Treaty Organization, France
    and, 260
Norway:
  as bicameral state, only Scandinavian, 85
  upper house in, 91, 102
  women in parliament of, 107
Nuclear family in developing nations, 56

Occupying powers in Germany, 294
OECD: *see* Organization for Economic
    Cooperation and Development
OECS: *see* Organization of Eastern
    Caribbean States
Office space for legislatures, 109
Official Secrets Act, British, 233
Ohira, Masayoshi (Japanese prime
    minister), 350
Old Regime, France, 253
Olson, David, on legislative process, 110
Olson, Mancur, 171–72
Ontario, representation in parliament of,
    87–88

Open elite, 206
Opposition, Loyal, development of concept of
    in U.K., 243
Organization for Economic Cooperation and
    Development, 53
Organization of Eastern Caribbean States,
    18
Orwell, George, on British executive, 223
Owen, David, 245

Pakistan, economic decentralization in, 64
Palestinians, 10
Parastatal corporations (Mexico), 65
Parliament:
  British constitution and, 222
  growth of, in England, 86
  in U.K., 235–42
  see also Legislatures
Parliament Act, British, 221, 236
Parliamentary Council, German, 300
Parliamentary executive, model of, 124–25
  selection of, 130–38
Participation, political, 186–87
  crisis of, in Philippines, 24
  development and, 24
Parties, political: *see* Political parties
Parti Québecois, 22
Party discipline in legislatures, 94–95
  in Britain, 94–95
PEMEX: *see* Petroleos Mexicanos
Penetration, crisis of, in development, 23
Permanent committees in legislatures, 96
Pétain, Henri (French president), 258
Petititon of Right, British, 220
Petroleos Mexicanos (Mexican state
    petroleum company), 65
Philippines:
  crisis of legitimacy in, 22
  crisis of participation in, 24
  economic decentralization in, 64
  elections in, 181
  military in politics of, 207
Physical law, 152
Plato, 1
  on political culture, 18–19
  on political socialization, 193
Plebiscite, French process, 255
Plekhanov, George, 358
Pluralism, 170–73
Poland, narrow elections in, 181
Politburo, of Communist party, 395–96
Political behavior, study of, 9

Political culture, 18–20
  and political socialization, 196
Political development, 20–25
  Mexican, 422–24
Political elite, 205–7
Political ethnocentrism, 13–14
Political Order in Changing Societies
    (Huntington), 23
Political parties:
  British, 242–48
  characteristics of, 175
  development and, 67–68
  French, 278–79, 282–83
  German, 316–21
  interest groups and, 176
  Japanese, 346
  legislatures and, 94–95
  linkage mechanisms and, 179–80
  Mexican, 419–21
  organization of, 179
  sources of, 176–77
  Soviet, 390–91
Political recruitment, 201–5
Political system, 14–18
Political violence, 209–12
Politics, defined, 2
Pompidou, Georges, 269, 280
Population problem:
  in developing world, 71–74
  in India, 72–73
Portugal, as developing nation, 53
Positive law, 152
Positive vote of confidence, in Germany,
    303–4
Power:
  defined, 2
  separation of, 41
Precedent, judicial, 155
Prefectures (Japanese voting units), 346
Premier, French, 270
Presidency:
  American, roles of, 118–19
  French, 261–70, 285–87
  German, 301–2
  Israeli, 125
  Mexican, 410–15
  parliamentary systems and, 124–25
  Soviet, 380–81
Presidential elections, French, 285–87
Presidential executive, model of, 120–24
Presidium of Supreme Soviet, 380–81, 399
Pressure groups and interest groups, 175
Prime minister:

  British, 227–31
  French, 270–72
  development of power of, 128–30
  Japanese, 332–33
  selection of, 130–38
  Soviet, 381–84
Private bills, in British Parliament, 241
Private members:
  bills of, 111
  in French legislature, 273
Privatization in Britain, 232
Privy Council:
  British, 225
  evolution of, 128–30
Procedure, legal, 161
Proportional representation voting, 100–102
  in France, 260, 283
  in Germany, 313–16
  in Israel, 100–101
Przeworski, Adam, 8
Public administration and bureaucracy,
    141–44
Public bills in British Parliament, 241
Public policy, study of, 9
Punjab, crisis of legitimacy in, 22

Qatar, wealth of, 54–55
Quality of life in Third World, 74
QUANGO, in British government, 235
Quebec, 10
  bicameral legislature and, 86–87
  crisis of identity in, 22
  crisis of legitimacy in, 22
  economic nationalism in, 61
  legal code of, 154

Race limitations on candidacy, 183
Radicalism, as an ideology, 45–46
Reactionary ideology, 46–47
Reagan, Ronald, and Democratic Congress,
    123
Recruitment, political, 105, 201–5
  of legislators, 110
Referendum, French, 268
Reform of legislatures, 113
Registration, as voting requirement,
    183–84
Religious sources of law, 156
Representation:
  legislatures and, 104–7
  in Canadian Parliament, 87–88

Republican party (French political party), 282
Residency requirement:
  for candidacy, 183
  for voting, 183–84
Responsible government, defined, 144
Revolution, 210–11
  American, 210
  Chinese, 210
  French, 253
  Russian, 210, 359–61
Rhodesia and Nyasaland, as failed federation, 40
Right, Petition of, British, 220
Riker, William, on federalism, 39–40
Role, political, defined, 196
  legislative, 107–10
Romano-Germanic legal culture, 154
Rossiter, Clinton, on the American presidency, 118–19
Rostow, Walt, on development, 52
Rousseau, Jean-Jacques:
  on elections, 184
  on law, 152
  on political culture, 19
  on political socialization, 193
Russia: *see* Soviet Union
Russian Revolution (1917–1921), 210
Russian Social Democratic party, 359
Ryzhkov, Nikolai (prime minister of Soviet Union), 382–83

St. Vincent:
  single-product economy of, 59
  size of legislature in, 93
Salinas, Carlos de Gortari, 407
Schmidt, Helmut, 304, 318
Scientific law, 152
Seating in legislature, 108–9
Second Republic, French, 255
Secretariat, of Communist party, 395–96
Secrets Act, British, 223
Senate:
  French, 256, 275–77
  Mexican, 415–16
Separation of powers, 41
Shapiro, Martin, 160
Short Parliament (Britain), 127
Sierra Leone, infant mortality rate of, 57
Simon, Jules (French premier), 256
Single-member-district voting, 97–100
  in France, 283

Single-product economies in Third World, 59
Sizes of legislatures, 93–94
Skinner, B.F., on political socialization, 193
Social Democratic party (British political party), 245
Social Democratic party (German political party), 304, 316–19
Socialist law, 155
Socialist party, Japan, 344
Socialization, political, 193–201
  content of, 196–97
  defined, 194
  function of legislatures in, 105, 110
  Mexican, 409
Sources of law, 156–59
South Africa, income distribution in, 58
Soviets (legislatures), 376–77
  Congress of People's Deputies, 377–78
Soviet Union:
  cabinet in, 381–84
  Communist party in, 389–97
  constitution of, 32–36, 371–76
  Council of Ministers in, 381–84
  courts in, 387–89
  elections in, 182, 385–87
  ideology in, 366–70
  justice in, 387–89
  leadership in, 397–99
  legal system of, 155–56
  politburo in, 395–97
  political heritage of, 357–61
  president in, 380–81
  presidium in, 380–81
  secretariat in, 395–97
  selection of upper house in, 102
  succession in, 397–99
  Supreme Soviet in, 378–80
Spain, military in politics of, 207
Sri Lanka:
  crisis of identity in, 22
  military in politics of, 207
Staff and services in legislature, 109
Stalin, Joseph, 358, 361, 363, 366, 368–69
Stalinism, 369–70
Standing committees in legislatures, 96
Stare decisis (judicial precedent), 155
State:
  defined, 10
  importance of, 20–21
Statistical method, 6
Statute of Westminster, British, 221
Steel, David, 245
Structural-functional analysis, 17–18

Subsystems, 15
Succession in Soviet Union, 397–99
Supersystems, 16
Supremacy, legislative, 132
Supreme Soviet, 374, 378–80
Swaziland, unicameral legislature in, 87
Sweden, women in parliament of, 107
Switzerland:
  as confederal system (1815–1874), 37
  as federal state, 38–39
  per capita income in, 54
  upper house in, 91
System, political, 14–18
Systems theory of David Easton, 16–17

Tajik SSR, 362
Takeshita, Noboru (Japanese prime
  minister), 350–51
Tamil population in Sri Lanka, 22
Tanaka, Kakuei (Japanese prime minister),
  350
Tanzania:
  income distribution in, 57–58
  narrow elections in, 181
  poverty of, 57
Terrorism, 211–12
Teune, Henry, 8
Thailand, economic decentralization in, 64
Thatcher, Margaret, 225–26
  and Thatcherism, 231–33
Theories of development, 69–70
Third World:
  characteristics of, 54–55
  compared with developing nations, 54
Third Republic, French, 255–58
Tocqueville, Alexis de, on political culture, 19
Tokugawa shogunate, Japan, 326–27
Trade:
  surplus, defined, 59
  in Third World, 75–76
Tradition as source of law, 157
Trotsky, Leon, 358, 360, 361, 368–69
Truman, David, 171
Tunisia, and France, 260
Turkey:
  as developing nation, 53
  upper house in, 91
Turkmen SSR, 362
Two-party system, U.K. as, 243–44

Uganda, selection of president, 125

Ukrainian SSR, 362
Unicameral legislatures, 84–89
Unified Socialist party of Mexico (Mexican
  political party), 420
Union of Republicans for Progress (French
  political party), 282
Union of Soviet Socialist Republics: *see*
  Soviet Union
Unitary system, 36
  Britain as, 222
  France as, 263–64
United Arab Emirates, wealth of, 57
United Arab Republic, as failed federation,
  40
United Kingdom:
  cabinet in, 226–31, 258
  chief executive, selection of, 225–26
  civil service in, 233–34
  constitution of, 32, 219–23
  elections in, 181
  evolution of parliamentary government in,
    127–30
  executive in, 223–31
  House of Commons in, 238–40
  House of Lords in, 236–38
  legislation in, 240–42
  local government in, 234–35
  minority governments in, 141
  monarchy in, 124–28, 223–25
  as occupying power in Germany, 294
  Parliament of, 94–95, 97–98, 105,
    235–42
  party discipline in Parliament of, 94–95
  political parties in, 242–48
  prime minister in, 226–31
  single-member-district voting in, 97–98
  size of legislature in, 93
  Thatcherism in, 231–33
  as unitary system, 36, 222
  upper house in, 88, 102
  voting in, 242–48
United States:
  as confederal system (1781–1787), 37
  constitution of, 4
  court structure in, 160–61
  electoral law in, 183
  as federal state, 38
  House of Representatives, functions of, in,
    105
  legal culture in, 154
  as occupying power in Germany, 294
  party discipline in legislature of, 95
  political recruitment in, 204

United States (cont.):
  political violence in, 210
  presidency of, and electoral college, 121
  selection of upper house in, 102
  separation of power in, 41
  single-member-district voting in, 97–98
  size of legislature in, 93
  Supreme Court of, and judicial review, 166
  upper house in, 91–92
Uno, Soucuke (Japanese prime minister), 351
Unwritten constitutions, 31–33
Upper house of legislature, 87–92
  functions of, 88
  power of, 89–92
  selection of, 102
Ustinov, Marshal, 398
USSR: *see* Soviet Union
Uzbek SSR, 362

Venezuela, as federal state, 38
Verba, Sidney, 196
Vichy, France, 258
Vietnam, war in, and France, 260
Violence, political, 209–12
Vote of confidence:
  constructive, in Germany, 303–4
  defined, 130–31
Voting:
  behavior, 186–87
  in multiple-member districts, 102
  proportional-representation, 100–102
  requirements, 183–84
  in single-member district, 97–100
  see also Elections

Walpole, Sir Robert (first British prime
  minister), 126, 227
Weber, Max, on public administration, 142
Weiss, Sheva, on private member's bills, 111
Western bias of research, 52
West Indies, as failed federation, 40
Westminster, Statute of, British, 221
Westminster model of government (Britain),
  222
William, Duke of Normandy, and English
  throne, 126
William, Prince of Orange (Britain), 128
William and Mary, and British executive, 224
Women in legislatures, 106–7
World Bank definition of developing states,
  55, 56
Writ of dissolution, 135
Written constitutions, 31–33

Yeltsin, Boris, 362
Yugoslavia:
  as federal state, 38
  upper house in, 91

Zimbabwe, participation in, 24
Zionism, 10